MW01027617

AHS
GREAT
PLANT
GUIDE

DK PUBLISHING, INC.

A DK PUBLISHING BOOK
www.dk.com

PROJECT EDITOR Simon Maughan
EDITOR Tracie Lee
ART EDITOR Ursula Dawson
MANAGING EDITOR Louise Abbott
MANAGING ART EDITOR Lee Griffiths
DTP DESIGN Sonia Charbonnier
PRODUCTION Ruth Charlton
PICTURE RESEARCH Samantha Ruston

First American Edition, 1999
4 6 8 10 9 7 5

Published in the United States by
DK Publishing, Inc.
95 Madison Avenue
New York, New York 10016

Library of Congress Cataloging-in-Publication Data
AHS great plant guide. — 1st American ed.
p.   cm.
Includes index.
ISBN 0-7894-4120-9 (alk. paper)
1. Plants, Ornamental. 2. Plants, Ornamental — Pictorial works.
3. Landscape gardening. I. DK Publishing, Inc.
SB407.A375   1999   635.9 — dc21   98-41283   CIP

Color reproduction by GRB Editrice, Italy.
Printed and bound in Italy by Lego.

CONTENTS

INTRODUCTION

GARDENERS TODAY have plenty of choice when buying plants. Not only are plant breeders constantly producing new and exciting cultivars, but plants are now more widely available in garden centers and nurseries as well as in do-it-yourself superstores. In less traditional plant-buying situations, information and advice may not be readily available or reliable. It is perhaps no wonder, then, that gardeners sometimes find choosing the right plant a bewildering business.

The *AHS Great Plant Guide* was conceived to help gardeners select outstanding and reliable plants for their garden, whatever their level of expertise and experience, and whatever the site. Because all of the plants in this book are suitable for some region of North America, however small or specialized, any gardener, even a novice, can choose plants from here with confidence.

However, these recommendations refer only to the plants themselves, and not to those who offer them. It is impossible to guarantee the quality

Ever-widening plant choice
Exotic flowers, such as this blue poppy (Meconopsis grandis)*, may tempt a gardener, but check the conditions they require before buying.*

of plants offered for sale by any nursery, garden center, or store, and here gardeners must exercise a degree of common sense and good judgment in order to ensure that the individual plants they select and take home will thrive. The following pages include guidance on recognizing healthy, well-grown plants and bulbs, and they show how to choose them wisely and get them off to a good start.

CHOOSING FOR YOUR GARDEN

Selecting plants appropriate to your site and soil is essential, and each plant in the *A–Z of Plants* has its preferences indicated. Well-prepared soil, fertilizing, mulching, and, in dry conditions, watering in the early stages are also important for the well-being of most plants (although in the *Planting Guide* you will find plants to grow in poor soil or dry sites). Entries in the *A–Z* include basic care for the plant concerned, along with specific hints and tips on topics such as pruning and siting, and on winter protection where hardiness is borderline. By following this advice, the plants you choose using the *AHS Great Plant Guide* should get off to a great start and continue to perform well.

USING THE GUIDE

THE *AHS GREAT PLANT GUIDE* is
designed to help you choose plants
in two different ways.

THE A–Z OF PLANTS

Here, over 1,000 plants have full
entries and are illustrated with
photographs. This is the section to
consult to find details about a plant,
whether you are reading its name on
a label or have noted it down from a
magazine article or a television or
radio broadcast. It will tell you what
type of plant it is, how it grows,
what its ornamental features are,
where it grows and looks best, and
how to care for it. For quick
reference, symbols (right) summarize
its main requirements.

THE PLANTING GUIDE

This section provides "shopping lists"
of plants for every purpose –whether
practical, such as a group of plants
for a damp, shady site, or for themed
plantings, such as a selection of
plants to attract birds into your
garden. Page references are given
to plants with entries and portraits
elsewhere. Hundreds of plants not
pictured are also recommended.

Plant sirens (facing page)
*Garden centers and nurseries often
feature new plants to tempt gardeners.*

SYMBOLS USED IN THE GUIDE

SOIL MOISTURE PREFERENCES/TOLERANCES
◊ Well-drained soil
◖ Moist soil
● Wet soil

SUN/SHADE PREFERENCES/TOLERANCES
☼ Full sun
◑ Partial shade: either dappled shade
   or shade for part of the day
● Full shade
*NB Where two symbols appear from the
same category, the plant is suitable for
a range of conditions.*

USDA HARDINESS ZONE RANGES
These are given (as Z 6-9, for example)
for all plants in this book, except
tender plants, for which the minimum
temperature is given, and annuals
(including some perennials commonly
grown as annuals). Many subtropical
plants that tolerate temperatures
slightly below freezing are indicated as
being hardy in Zones 10-11.

AHS HEAT ZONES
The 12 zones of the AHS Heat-Zone
map are based on the average number
of days each year a given region
experiences "heat days" – those days
with temperatures over 86°F (30°C).
Zones are given similarly to hardiness,
except that the hottest zone is given
first, for example H 9-7.
*All ranges given in this book are
intended as approximate guides and
should not be considered definitive.*

THE PLANTS IN THE GUIDE

THE RANGE OF PLANTS – well over 2,000 – featured in the *AHS Great Plant Guide* has been carefully chosen to provide the best selection from among all the different types of plant and for many of the situations for which plants may be required. Many of the plants should be readily available from local sources throughout North America, although gardeners in places not served by large nurseries and garden centers will need to do some research to track down many of these plants. Be aware that many of these plants are not be carried by local suppliers; however, they should be available somewhere from among the many hundreds of mail-order nurseries throughout North America.

WHAT IS A GREAT PLANT?

Calling a plant "great" is, admittedly, the result of a combination of subjective and objective appraisals of a plant, whether on the part of an individual or a committee of experts. It must be remembered that a plant that performs exceedingly well as a great garden plant in one part of North America may be a miserable failure in the rest of the continent, or it may be a noxious weed. Similarly, any "great" plant put into a garden situation not to its liking will fail, if not immediately, then eventually. The perception of an individual plant, genus, or even entire group of plants as "great" can also come and go upon the whims of current gardening trends and fads.

Camellia x williamsii **'Brigadoon'**
Choice forms of the familiar and the unusual are in this book.

Hydrangea macrophylla **'Altona'**
The best selections of many garden stalwarts are recommended.

Geranium **'Kashmir White'**
Plants that are versatile and easily grown are noteworthy for sheer garden value.

Generally, though, a great garden plant that withstands the test of time will meet the following criteria:

• It is excellent for ornamental use, either outdoors (in the open ground or in a container) or under cover

• It is of good constitution, being neither frail and weak nor overly vigorous to the point of being invasive or weedy

• It is available in the horticultural trade, whether locally or through mail order

• It is not particularly susceptible to any pest or disease

• It does not require any highly specialized care other than providing the appropriate conditions for the type of plant or individual plant concerned (for example, acidic soil)

• It should not be subject to an unreasonable degree of reversion in its vegetative or floral characteristics.

To explain this last point simply: many plants with unusual characteristics differing from the species, such as double flowers or variegated leaves, have often been propagated from a single plant or part of a plant – a natural mutation or "sport" – that has appeared spontaneously. Plants bred from sports – especially when raised from seed – are liable to have only the normal leaf color or flower form. It can take several generations of careful and controlled propagation for the special feature to be stable enough for plants to be recognized and registered with a distinct cultivar name (which is usually chosen by the breeder) and then offered for sale. Many never retain the special feature when grown from seed and therefore can be reproduced only by vegetative methods such as cuttings or grafting.

Prunus laurocerasus
This evergreen is handsome year-round, both as a free-standing shrub and as a hedge.

Anemone blanda 'White Splendour'
Floriferous cultivars for every site and season are included in this book.

Acer negundo 'Flamingo'
Plants that are grown for their variegated foliage should not be prone to excessive reversion.

NONPICTURED PLANTS

The Planting Guide section at the back of the book presents (in list form) hundreds of trees, shrubs, climbers, perennials, bulbs, and other plants that could not be pictured and that are suitable for a specific site or garden situation. These lists do not pretend to be exhaustive, but they do present a representative cross-section of plants to consider. The lists also contain plants that are pictured; these are cross-referenced to the appropriate pages.

In some categories of plants, notably annuals (particularly those for summer bedding, such as impatiens, petunias, and salvias) and in some perennial genera, new cultivars appear so rapidly, often superseding others offered for sale, that producers, retailers, and gardeners alike are hard pressed to keep up with developments. In order to give a wider choice in these somewhat underrepresented categories, the *AHS Great Plant Guide* includes, in *The Planting Guide*, selected cultivars that have proved their reliability over the years.

Putting plants to the test
Trials at public gardens and at display gardens at seed companies help select the best forms for gardeners.

FINDING PLANTS BY NAME

The botanical, or so-called "Latin," names for plants are used throughout the Guide, simply because these are the names that gardeners will find on plant tags and in publications. These names are also international, transcending any language barriers or regional variation.

To the uninitiated, plant nomenclature may seem confusing, and sometimes plant names appear to be very similar. It is important to recognize that plant nomenclature is by no means static: plant names, whether scientific or vernacular, are subject to constant revision. Sometimes this is in response to scholarly research, whereby a genus may be split up and given several new names (for example, the genus *Chrysanthemum* is now several new genera); other times it is a marketing technique to create new interest for an already established plant. Some plants have synonyms – older or alternative names – by which they may sometimes be referred to: the *AHS Great Plant Guide* gives synonyms for a number of plants. A brief guide to plant nomenclature can be found on pages 24–25. Many common names for plants or plant types that feature in the *Guide* are also given, both in the *A–Z of Plants* and in the Index.

SHOPPING FOR GOOD PLANTS

THE FIRST STEP in ensuring that your garden will be full of healthy plants is to choose and buy carefully.

WHERE TO BUY

Plants can be found for sale in such a variety of situations today that there are few hard and fast rules. Generally, buy plants only where you feel sure that the plants offered are actually what they say they are, that they have been well grown, and they are not going to bring any pests and diseases into your garden.

PLANTS BY MAIL

Buying plants by mail order is one of the easiest (and most addictive!) ways of obtaining particular plants that you are eager to acquire. It gives you a huge choice, far greater than in most garden centers, and also gives you access to specialty nurseries that concentrate on certain plant groups or genera and which may not be open to visitors. Armed with a buyer's guide to nurseries, you can track down almost any specimen from the comfort of your own home, and provided that someone will be at home on the day it arrives, it should be delivered in perfect health. Mail-order nurseries are usually happy to replace any plant damaged in transit. Often, the plants will arrive with their roots surrounded with soil mix or peat (otherwise bare-root). They are best planted out soon after receipt.

WHEN TO BUY

Trees, shrubs, and roses that are available as bare-root specimens are usually deciduous. Woody plants with roots balled and burlapped may be deciduous or evergreen. Many are available only in the dormant season; they are ideally purchased in late autumn or early spring and should be planted as soon as possible.

Container-grown plants are now extremely popular and are offered for sale throughout the planting season. However, the traditional planting times of spring and autumn, when conditions are not too extreme, are definitely the best. Plants should not be put into near-freezing or baked, dry soil; instead, keep them in their containers until conditions are more favorable.

In colder climates, reliably hardy plants can be planted in autumn. Spring is the time to put in plants of borderline hardiness, and to buy bedding plants. Beware of buying them too early, however tempting they look after the dark, bare days of winter. Bedding sold in early and midspring is intended to be bought by people with greenhouses and cold frames, who can grow the plants on under cover until all danger of frost has passed. If you plant out bedding too early in the season, you risk losing it to late frost.

YOUR SHOPPING LIST

Whether you are stocking a new garden from scratch, replacing a casualty, or simply wanting to add extra touches with some plants for a shady corner or for a half barrel,

Well-grown plants for sale
Healthy, clearly labeled plants in neat, well-kept surroundings are a good indication of excellent nursery care.

informed choice is the key to buying the right plants and to getting the very best and healthiest specimens.

There are many factors to consider about your garden (see pages 16–17) and, equally, buying tips that will help you make the best choice from the selection of plants offered (see pages 18–19). Many gardeners prefer to set out with specific plants in mind. However, no one could deny that impulse buys are one of gardening's great pleasures – and with the *AHS Great Plant Guide* to hand, you will be able to obtain just the right plants for your garden and avoid expensive mistakes.

CHOOSING THE RIGHT PLANTS

ALTHOUGH THERE ARE ways to get around many of plants' climatic and soil requirements, you will avoid extra work and expense by choosing plants well suited to the conditions your garden offers.

HARDINESS

Most of us garden in areas that experience periods of frost and cold (not to mention snow) in winter.

Choose plants that are generally known to be adapted your area by checking the hardiness – and heat – zone ranges as given in this book. Providing good growing conditions throughout the season helps promote survival, including appropriate winter and summer mulches such as pine boughs and light straw. Optimism is no substitute for action if plants are to survive in a particular region,

Extending the range
Container growing may be the answer for gardeners who covet plants with special soil needs, such as acid-loving azaleas, that their open ground cannot meet.

yard, or microclimate, such as a low, poorly drained spot, an unusually hot and dry corner, or an exposed north-facing hillside.

SUN AND SHADE

It is well worth observing your garden to see how much sun areas receive at different times of the day and year. For good growth and the best display of features such as colored foliage, always match plants' sun and shade requirements.

YOUR SOIL

Most plants tolerate soil that falls short of perfect, and many survive in conditions that are very far from ideal. It is always preferable – and far more labor-saving – to choose plants that suit your soil, rather than manipulate your soil to suit plants, by adding, for example, peat or lime. The effect never lasts and is now also considered environmentally inadvisable – local insects, birds, and other fauna may be unable or unwilling to feed on plants to which they are unaccustomed. It is, however, important to add nutrients to the soil, and two aims can be achieved together if you add these not as powder or granules but as a mulch that will also improve soil texture, such as compost or manure.

Determining your soil acidity (or its reverse, alkalinity), measured by units known as pH values, is important. Most plants tolerate a broad range of pH values around neutral, but some groups have specifically evolved to be suited by soil that is either definitely acidic or definitely alkaline. There is no point to ignoring these soil preferences and trying to grow, for example, azaleas in an alkaline soil; they will not thrive. Choose plants that will enjoy your soil or, if you really covet some specialized plant groups, grow them in containers in a soil mix that meets their needs.

DRAINAGE

The expression "well-drained yet moisture-retentive" is one of the most widely used yet seemingly baffling expressions in gardening. However, it is not such a contradiction in terms as it seems. What it applies to is a soil that in composition is not dominated by gravel or grains of sand, which cannot hold water, nor clay, which binds up and retains water in a solid, gluey mass. It is the presence of well-decomposed organic material that enables soil to hold moisture *and* air simultaneously, so that both are readily available to plants. Incorporating well-decomposed organic matter (see page 21) is the most useful way to improve soil texture, either for an entire area or

CHOOSING A HEALTHY PLANT

TRY TO RESIST buying plants that are in poor condition, even if it is the sole example offered of a plant you really want. Nursing a pathetic specimen could take a whole growing season, during which time the plant will scarcely reward you, and with container-grown plants now so widely available it is likely that, later in the season, you will find a healthier specimn that you can plant right away. In practice, however, there are few gardeners that have never taken pity on a neglected or undernourished plant – but you must always harden your heart to those showing signs of pest infestation or disease. You risk importing problems that could spread to other plants.

WHAT TO BUY

Plants offered for sale should be clearly labeled, healthy, undamaged, and free from pests and diseases. Inspect the plant thoroughly for signs of neglect. With balled-and-burlapped plants, check that the root ball is firm and evenly moist, with the netting or burlap intact. Containerized plants should always have been raised in containers. Do not buy plants that appear to have been hastily uprooted from a nursery bed or field and potted up. There should be no sign of roots at the surface.

Look under the pot for pro-truding roots, a sign that the plant is potbound (has been in its container for too long). Always lift the pot to make sure roots have not penetrated the standing area, another sign of a potbound specimen. Crowded roots do not penetrate the surrounding soil readily after planting, and the plant will not establish well.

HEALTHY GROWTH

LEAVES ARE GLOSSY AND HEALTHY

EARLY PRUNING HAS PRODUCED AN ATTRACTIVE SHAPE

ROOTS ARE WELL-GROWN BUT NOT CROWDED

Good specimen
This well-grown skimmia has a substantial root ball that is in good proportion to the bushy top growth.

Healthy bulb
A sound neck, tunic (the papery outer covering), and basal plate (where the roots grow) all recommend this bulb to the gardener.

SOUND, FIRM
BASAL PLATE

Poor specimen
The badly chopped neck, ragged tunic, discolored flesh, and wounded basal plate indicate poor harvesting and storage: the bulb will not do well.

INFECTION MAY ENTER
VIA WOUND

Strong top growth is another key factor. Avoid plants with pale or yellowing foliage, damaged shoot tips, or etiolated growth (soft, pale, overextended, and weak-looking shoots). Look at the soil surface: it should not be covered in weeds, mosses, or liverworts.

With herbaceous plants, small healthy specimens are cheaper than large ones and will soon grow once planted. Groups of three or four plants often look better than single specimens. With all types of herbaceous plants, including young annuals and bedding, pick out the stockiest, bushiest specimens, with (if appropriate) plenty of flower buds, rather than open flowers.

PLANT SHAPE AND FORM

When buying trees and shrubs, which make the longest-lasting contributions to your garden, consider their shape as well as their good health. Choose plants with a well-balanced branch framework and with top growth that is in proportion to the rootball or pot. A stocky, multistemmed plant usually makes the best well-rounded shrub, while young trees with a single trunk should have just that – and a good, straight, sound one, too – right from the start. A one-sided shrub may of course be acceptable for wall-training, but it will put on more growth from the base, and thus cover space better, if its shoot tips are pruned after planting.

BUYING BULBS

Buy bulbs (see above) as if they were onions you were intending to cook with and eat – reject any that are soft, discolored, diseased, or damaged. While it is not ideal, there is no harm in buying bulbs that have begun to sprout a little, as long as the bulbs are planted soon after.

PREPARING THE SOIL

WHILE THE BEST plants for your garden are those suited to the growing conditions available, most soils can be improved to extend the range of plants that can be grown.

IDENTIFYING YOUR SOIL TYPE

Investigating your soil to discover just what its qualities are is one of the most useful things you can do to ensure thriving plants and successful gardening. Generally, the soil will be either sandy or have a clay texture, or somewhere between the two. If your soil has a light, loose texture and drains rapidly, it is probably sandy. Sandy soil has a rough, gritty feel when rubbed and makes a characteristic rasping, scraping sound against the blade of a spade. Although easy to dig, it is low in fertility. Clay soil is heavy, sticky, cold, easy to mold when wet, and can become waterlogged. It is difficult to work but is often very fertile. A good mix of the two – a "medium loam" – is ideal.

To further establish which plants will be best suited by the soil in your garden, you can determine its pH value (to what degree it is acidic or alkaline) and the levels of various nutrients it contains using very simple testing kits that are available at many garden centers.

CLEARING WEEDS

In a new garden, or if you are planting in a previously uncultivated area, your first task will be to clear away any debris and weeds. Pre-planting clearance of all weeds is essential, since they will compete with your plants for light, moisture, and nutrients. Where the ground is infested with perennial weeds, an alternative to laborious hand-clearing is to spray it during the season before planting with a systemic herbicide that will kill the roots. This is most effective when the weeds are growing strongly, usually in early summer. Although this may mean delaying planting, patience at this stage will be amply rewarded later. Repeated applications may be needed.

Isolated perennial weeds can be forked out carefully, removing all root fragments. Annual weeds may be sprayed or hoed off immediately before planting.

WORKING THE SOIL

Digging or forking over the soil helps break down compacted areas and increase aeration, which encourages good plant growth. The deeper you dig the better, but never bring poor-quality subsoil up to the surface: plants need all the nourishment that the darker, more

Digging with ease
The correct tools and technique make digging more comfortable, and safer for your back. Test the weight and height of a spade before buying, and always keep your back straight when using it.

Forking over
Drive the fork into the ground, then lift and turn the fork over to break up and aerate soil. Spread a layer of organic matter over the soil first so that it is incorporated into the soil as you work.

nutritious topsoil can give them. If you need to dig deeply, remove the topsoil, fork over the subsoil, then replace the topsoil.

Dig heavy clay soils in late autumn. The weathering effects of frost and cold over the winter will help improve the soil's texture by breaking it down into smaller pieces. Avoid digging when the soil is wet; this will damage the soil structure. It will save work if you incorporate soil amendmentss as you go.

ADDING SOIL AMENDMENTS

Digging and forking will improve soil texture to some extent, but to really bring a soil to life, the addition of a

soil amendment is invaluable. The drainage, aeration, fertility, and moisture-holding properties of most soil types can be improved simply by adding well-rotted organic matter. This is best done in the season before planting to allow the soil to settle. Well-rotted manure, compost, and leafmold enhance the moisture retention of a sandy soil and improve nutrient levels. Applied regularly, they improve the structure of clay soil. Clay soils can be further opened up by the addition of coarse sand to a depth of at least 12in (30cm). Organic mulches of bark, cocoa shells, or wood chips are also eventually broken down into the soil.

PLANTING OUT

WHATEVER YOU ARE planting, make sure that you give your plants a really promising start. Careful planting saves both time and money, and well-chosen plants positioned in optimum conditions will perform well and should resist attack from pests and diseases.

PREPLANTING PLANNING

Before planting, check the potential heights and spreads of plants to ensure that you leave the correct distances between them. When designing plant groups, consider different plants' season of interest, including their appearance in winter.

WHEN TO PLANT

The best seasons for planting are autumn and spring. Autumn planting allows plants to establish quickly before the onset of winter, since the soil is still warm and moist enough to permit root growth. Spring planting is better in cold areas for plants that are not reliably hardy or dislike wet winter conditions.

Perennials can be planted at any time of the year, except during extreme conditions. They should grow rapidly and usually perform well within their first year. To reduce stress on a perennial when planting during dry or hot weather, prune off

Basic planting
Soak plants well in a bucket of water. Position the plant so that the root ball surface is flush with soil level, then fill around the sides.

Settling the soil
Backfill the hole, gently firming the soil to ensure good contact with the roots. Water in well, then add a layer of mulch over the root area.

its flowers and the largest leaves before planting. In full, hot sun, shade the plant for a few days.

PLANTING TECHNIQUES

For container-grown or balled-and-burlapped plants, dig a hole about twice the size of the rootball. If necessary, water the hole in advance to ensure that the surrounding soil is thoroughly moist. Carefully remove the plant from its pot and gently tease out the roots with your fingers. Check that the plant is at the correct depth, then backfill the hole with a mix of compost, fertilizer, and soil. Firm the soil, then water thoroughly to settle it around the roots. Apply a mulch around, but not touching, the plant base to aid moisture retention and suppress weeds.

For bare-root plants, the planting technique is essentially the same, but it is vital that the roots never dry out before replanting. Dig holes in advance, and if there is any delay in planting, heel the plants in or store in moist sand or compost until conditions are more suitable. Bare-root plants need a planting hole wide enough to accommodate their roots when fully spread. The hole must be at least deep enough to ensure the final soil level will be the same as it was in the pot or nursery. After planting, tread the soil gently to firm.

WALL SHRUBS AND CLIMBERS

Always erect supports before planting. Plant wall shrubs and climbers at least 10in (25cm) from walls and fences so that the roots are not in a rain shadow, and lean the plant slightly inward toward the wall. Fan out the main shoots and attach them firmly to their support. Shrubs and nonclinging climbers will need further tying in as they grow; the shoots of twining climbers may also need gentle guidance.

ANNUALS AND BEDDING

In order to ensure that these plants look their best for the entire time they are in flower, it is essential that they are well planted. A moist soil and regular deadheading are keys to success. Bedding plants need regular feeding throughout the growing season, especially in containers, but many annuals flower best in soil that is not overly fertile. Many annuals are available as seedling "plugs," which should be grown on under cover. When planted, the well-developed root system suffers little damage, ensuring rapid growth.

PLANTING BULBS

In general, bulbs should be planted between three and five times their own depth. Plant small bulbs quite shallowly; those of bigger plants such as large tulips more deeply.

UNDERSTANDING PLANT NAMES

THROUGHOUT THE *AHS Great Plant Guide*, all plants are listed by their current botanical names. The basic unit of plant classification is the species, with a two-part name correctly given in italic text: the first part is the genus, and the second part is the species name or "epithet."

GENUS

A group of one or more species that share a wide range of characteristics, such as *Chrysanthemum* or *Rosa*, is known as a genus. A genus name is much like a family name, because it is shared by a group of individuals that are all closely related. Hybrid genera (crosses between plants from two genera, such as × *Halimiocistus*), are denoted by a multiplication sign before the genus name.

SPECIES

A group of plants capable of breeding together to produce similar offspring are known as a species. In a two-part botanical name, the species epithet distinguishes a species from other plants in the same genus, rather like a given name. A species epithet usually refers to a particular feature of that species, such as *tricolor* (of three colors), or it may refer to the person who first discovered the plant.

SUBSPECIES, VARIETY, AND FORMA

Naturally occurring variants of a species – subspecies, variety, or forma – are given an additional name in italics, prefixed by "subsp.," "var.," or "f.". All of these are

Species
Malus floribunda *is of the same genus as apples (*Malus*); its species name means "mass of flowers."*

Variety
Dictamnus albus *var.* purpureus *has purplish flowers instead of the white of the species.*

Hybrid
The multiplication sign after the genus name in Osmanthus × burkwoodii *denotes its hybrid status.*

concerned with minor subdivisions of a species, differing slightly in their botanical structure or appearance.

HYBRIDS

If different species within the same genus are cultivated together, they may cross-breed, giving rise to hybrids sharing attributes of both parents. This process is exploited by gardeners who wish to combine the valued characteristics of two distinct plants. The new hybrid is then increased by propagation. An example is *Camellia* x *williamsii*, which has the parents *C. japonica* and *C. saluensis*.

CULTIVARS

Variations of a species that are selected or artificially raised are given a vernacular name. This appears in single quotation marks after the species name. Some cultivars are also registered with trademark names, often used commercially instead of the valid cultivar name. If the parentage is obscure or complex, the cultivar name may directly follow the generic name – *Iris* 'Skating Party'. In a few cases, particularly roses, the plant is known by a popular selling name, which is not the correct cultivar name; here, the popular name comes before the cultivar name, as in *Rosa* BONICA 'Meidomonac'.

GROUPS AND SERIES

Several very similar cultivars may, for convenience, be classified in named Groups or Series that denote their similarities. Sometimes, they can be a deliberate mixture of cultivars of the same overall character but with flowers in different colors.

Cultivar
The species parentage of plants like Osteospermum *'Buttermilk' is complex and therefore not given.*

Cultivar of species
Ophiopogon planiscapus *'Nigrescens' is an unusual form cultivated for its black leaves.*

Seed series
Antirrhinum *Sonnet Series is a mixture of brightly colored cultivars for summer bedding.*

THE
A–Z OF
PLANTS

ATTRACTIVE AND RELIABLE plants for every
garden, and for every part of the garden,
can be found in this section. However
much the ornamental features and
season(s) of interest of a given plant might
appeal to you, always check its hardiness,
eventual size, and site and soil
requirements before you buy.

ABELIA 'EDWARD GOUCHER'

This semi-evergreen shrub with arching branches bears glossy, dark green leaves that are bronze when young. Trumpet-shaped, lilac-pink flowers appear from summer to autumn. Like most abelias, it is suitable for a sunny border.

CULTIVATION *Grow in well-drained, fertile soil, in sun with shelter from cold winds. Remove dead or damaged growth in spring, cutting some of the older stems back to the ground after flowering to promote new growth.*

☼ ◊ Z 7-9 H 9-1   ‡5ft (1.5m) ↔6ft (2m)

ABELIA FLORIBUNDA

An evergreen shrub with arching shoots, from which tubular, bright pink-red flowers hang in profuse clusters in early summer. The leaves are oval and glossy dark green. Ideal for a sunny border in warmer areas.

CULTIVATION *Grow in well-drained, fertile soil, in full sun with shelter from cold, drying winds. Prune older growth back after flowering, removing any dead or damaged growth in spring.*

☼ ◊ Z 8-11 H 12-8   ‡10ft (3m) ↔12ft (4m)

ABELIA × *GRANDIFLORA*

A rounded, semi-evergreen shrub
bearing arching branches. Cultivated
for its attractive, glossy dark green
leaves and profusion of fragrant,
pink-tinged white flowers that are
borne from mid-summer to autumn.
Suitable for a sunny border.

CULTIVATION *Grow in well-drained,
fertile soil, in full sun with shelter from
cold, drying winds. Prune back older
growth back after flowering, and
remove damaged growth in spring.*

☼ ◊ Z 6-9 H 9-1   ‡10ft (3m) ↔12ft (4m)

ABUTILON 'KENTISH BELLE'

A semi-evergreen shrub bearing
dark purple-brown shoots and
slender, arching branches. The large,
bell-shaped flowers, which hang
from the branches during summer
and autumn, are apricot-yellow and
red. The leaves are shallowly lobed
and dark green. Where marginally
hardy, provide shelter and support
by training against a warm wall.

CULTIVATION *Grow in well-drained,
fertile soil, in sun. Prune annually in
late winter to preserve a well-spaced,
healthy framework.*

☼ ◊ Z 8-10 H 12-1   ‡↔ to 8ft (2.5m)

ABUTILON MEGAPOTAMICUM

The trailing abutilon is a semi-evergreen shrub bearing pendulous, bell-shaped, red and yellow flowers from summer to autumn. The oval leaves are bright green and heart-shaped at the base. In colder climates, train against a warm wall or grow in a conservatory.

CULTIVATION *Best in well-drained, moderately fertile soil, in full sun. Remove any wayward shoots during late winter or early spring.*

☼ ◊ Z 8-10 H 12-1　　　↔ 6ft (2m)

ABUTILON VITIFOLIUM 'VERONICA TENNANT'

A fast-growing, upright, deciduous shrub that may attain the stature of a small, bushy tree. Masses of large, bowl-shaped mauve flowers, which hang from the stout, gray-felted shoots, are borne in early summer. The softly gray-hairy leaves are sharply toothed.

CULTIVATION *Grow in well-drained, moderately fertile soil, in full sun. Prune young plants after flowering to encourage a good shape; do not prune established plants.*

☼ ◊ Z 8-9 H 12-1　　↕15ft (5m) ↔8ft (2.5m)

ACAENA MICROPHYLLA

This summer-flowering, mat-forming perennial bears heads of small, dull red flowers with spiny bracts that develop into decorative burrs. The finely divided, mid-green leaves are bronze-tinged when young and evergreen through most winters. Good for a rock garden, trough, or raised bed.

CULTIVATION *Grow in well-drained soil, in full sun or partial shade. Pull out rooted stems around the main plant to restrict spread.*

☼ ☽ ◊ Z 6-8 H 8-6 ‡ 2in (5cm) ↔ 6in (15cm)

ACANTHUS SPINOSUS

Bear's breeches is a striking, architectural perennial bearing long, arching, dark green leaves that have deeply cut and spiny edges. From late spring to mid-summer, pure white, two-lipped flowers with purple bracts are borne on tall, sturdy stems; they are good for cutting and drying. Grow in a spacious border.

CULTIVATION *Best in deep, well-drained, fertile soil, in full sun or partial shade. Provide plenty of space to display its architectural merits.*

☼ ☽ ◊ Z 5-9 H 9-5 ‡ 5ft (1.5m) ↔ 24in (60cm)

ACER GRISEUM

The paperbark maple is a slow-growing, spreading, deciduous tree valued for its peeling orange-brown bark. The dark green leaves, divided into three leaflets, turn orange to red and scarlet in autumn. Tiny yellow flowers are carried in hanging clusters during early or mid-spring, followed by brown, winged fruits.

CULTIVATION *Grow in moist but well-drained, fertile soil, in sun or partial shade. In summer only, remove shoots that obscure the bark on the trunk and lower parts of the main branches.*

☼◑ ◊ Z 4-8 H 10-3　　↕↔ 30ft (10m)

ACER GROSSERI
VAR. *HERSII*

This variety of snakebark maple with boldly green- and white-streaked bark is a spreading to upright, deciduous tree. The three-lobed, triangular, bright green leaves turn orange or yellow in autumn. Hanging clusters of tiny, pale yellow flowers appear in spring, followed by pink-brown, winged fruits.

CULTIVATION *Grow in moist but well-drained, fertile soil, in full sun or partial shade. Shelter from cold winds. Remove shoots that obscure the bark on the trunk and main branches in winter.*

☼◑ ◊ Z 5-7 H 8-5　　↕↔ 50ft (15m)

ACER JAPONICUM 'ACONITIFOLIUM'

A deciduous, bushy tree or large shrub bearing deeply lobed, mid-green leaves that turn brilliant orange and red in autumn. It is very free-flowering, producing upright clusters of conspicuous, reddish purple flowers in mid-spring, followed by brown, winged fruits.

CULTIVATION *Grow in moist but well-drained, fertile soil, in partial shade. Where marginally hardy, mulch around the base in autumn. Remove badly placed shoots in winter only.*

☼ ◊ Z 5-7 H 8-3   ‡15ft (5m) ↔ 20ft (6m)

ACER NEGUNDO 'FLAMINGO'

A round-headed, deciduous tree carrying leaves that are divided into several pink-margined, oval leaflets that turn white in summer. With regular hard pruning, it can be grown as part of a shrub border; this also produces larger leaves with an intensified color. Flowers are tiny and inconspicuous.

CULTIVATION *Grow in any moist but well-drained, fertile soil, in full sun or partial shade. For larger leaves and a shrubby habit, cut back to a framework every 1 or 2 years in winter. Remove any branches with all-green leaves.*

☼◐ ◊ Z 5-8 H 8-3 ‡50ft (15m) ↔50ft (10m)

JAPANESE MAPLES (*ACER PALMATUM*)

Cultivars of *Acer palmatum*, the Japanese maple, are mostly small, round-headed, deciduous shrubs, although some, such as 'Sango-kaku', will grow into small trees. They are valued for their delicate and colorful foliage, which often gives a beautiful display in autumn. The leaves of 'Butterfly', for example, are variegated gray-green, white, and pink, and those of 'Osakazuki' turn a brilliant red before they fall. In mid-spring, hanging clusters of small, reddish purple flowers are produced, followed by winged fruits later in the season. Japanese maples are excellent for gardens of any size.

CULTIVATION *Grow in moist but well-drained, fertile soil, in sun or partial shade. Restrict pruning and training to young plants only; remove badly placed or crossing shoots in winter to develop a well-spaced network of branches. Keep pruning to a minimum on established plants.*

☼ ◐ ◊ Z 5-8 H 8-2

1 ↕↔ 15ft (5m)

2 ↕ 10ft (3m) ↔ 5ft (1.5m)

3 ↕ 6ft (2m) ↔ 10ft (3m)

4 ↕↔ 20ft (6m)

5 ↕ 20ft (6m) ↔ 15ft (5m)

1 *A. palmatum* 'Bloodgood' **2** *A. palmatum* 'Butterfly' **3** *A. palmatum* 'Garnet'
4 *A. palmatum* 'Osakazuki' **5** *A. palmatum* 'Sango-kaku'

ACER PSEUDOPLATANUS 'BRILLIANTISSIMUM'

This small, slow-growing cultivar
of sycamore maple is a spreading,
deciduous tree with a dense head.
It bears colorful, five-lobed leaves
that turn from salmon-pink to yellow
then dark green as they mature.
Hanging clusters of tiny, yellow-
green flowers appear in spring,
followed by winged fruit. An
attractive maple for smaller gardens.

CULTIVATION *Grow in any soil, in sun
or partial shade. Tolerates exposed sites.
Prune in summer to develop well-spaced
branches and a clear trunk.*

☼ ◗ ◊ Z 4-7 H 7-1 ‡20ft (6m) ↔25ft (8m)

ACHILLEA 'MOONSHINE'

A clump-forming, evergreen
perennial with narrow, feathery,
gray-green leaves. Light yellow
flowerheads with slightly darker
centers appear from early summer to
early autumn in flattish clusters; they
dry well for arrangements. Excellent
for mixed borders and for informal,
wild, or cottage-style plantings.

CULTIVATION *Grow in well-drained soil,
in an open, sunny site. Divide every 2
or 3 years in spring to maintain vigor.
Rarely needs staking.*

☼ ◊ Z 4-8 H 9-2 ‡↔ 24in (60cm)

ACONITUM 'BRESSINGHAM SPIRE'

A compact perennial producing very upright spikes of hooded, deep violet flowers from mid-summer to early autumn. The leaves are deeply divided and glossy dark green. Ideal for a woodland garden or borders in partial or dappled shade. All parts of this plant are poisonous.

CULTIVATION *Best in cool, moist, fertile soil, in partial shade, but will tolerate most soils and full sun. The tallest stems may need staking.*

☼☀ ◗ Z 3-7 H 8-3 ‡36–39in (90–100cm) ↔12in (30cm)

ACONITUM 'SPARK'S VARIETY'

This upright perennial is taller than 'Bressingham Spire' (above), bearing spikes of hooded, deep violet flowers that are clustered together on branched stems; these are borne in mid- and late summer. The rich green leaves are deeply divided. Like all monkshoods, it is ideal for woodland gardens or shaded sites. All parts of the plant are poisonous.

CULTIVATION *Grow in cool, moist soil, in partial or deep shade. Taller stems may need staking. Divide and replant every third year in autumn or late winter to maintain vigor.*

☼☀ ◗ Z 3-7 H 8-3 ‡5ft (1.5m) ↔ 18in (45cm)

ACTINIDIA KOLOMIKTA

A vigorous, deciduous climber with large, deep green leaves that are purple-tinged when young and develop vivid splashes of white and pink as they mature. Small, fragrant white flowers appear in early summer. Female plants produce small, egg-shaped, yellow-green fruits, but only if a male plant is grown nearby. Train against a wall or into a tree.

CULTIVATION *Best in well-drained, fertile soil. For best fruiting, grow in full sun with protection from strong winds. Tie in new shoots as they develop, and remove badly placed shoots in summer.*

☼ ◊ Z 5-8 H 12-1   ‡ 15ft (5m)

ADIANTUM PEDATUM

A deciduous maidenhair fern bearing long, mid-green fronds up to 3ft (1m) tall. These have glossy dark brown or black stalks that emerge from creeping rhizomes. Grow in a shady border or light woodland.

CULTIVATION *Best in cool, moist soil, in deep or partial shade. Remove old or damaged fronds in early spring. Divide and replant rhizomes every few years.*

☼◐ ◊ Z 3-8 H 8-1   ↔ 12–16in (30–40cm)

AESCULUS PARVIFLORA

A large, thicket-forming, deciduous shrub, closely related to the horse chestnut, that bears large-lobed, dark green leaves. The foliage is bronze when young, turning yellow in autumn. Upright white flowerheads, up to 12in (30cm) tall, appear in mid-summer, followed by smooth-skinned fruits.

CULTIVATION *Grow in moist but well-drained, fertile soil, in sun or partial shade; it will not grow in wet ground. If necessary, restrict spread by pruning stems to the ground after leaf fall.*

☼ ◑ ◊◊ Z 5-9 H 8-4 ↕10ft (3m) ↔15ft (5m)

AETHIONEMA 'WARLEY ROSE'

A short-lived, evergreen or semi-evergreen, compact shrub bearing clusters of bright pink, cross-shaped flowers in late spring and early summer. The small, narrow leaves are blue-gray. Stone cresses are ideal for a rock garden or on a wall.

CULTIVATION *Best in well-drained, fertile, alkaline soil, but tolerates poor, acid soils. Choose a site in full sun.*

☼ ◊ Z 7-9 H 9-7 ↕↔ 6–8in (15–20cm)

AGAPANTHUS CAMPANULATUS
SUBSP. PATENS

A vigorous, clump-forming perennial bearing round heads of bell-shaped, light blue flowers. These appear on strong, upright stems during late summer and early autumn. The narrow, strap-shaped, grayish green leaves are deciduous. Useful in borders or large containers as a late-flowering perennial.

CULTIVATION *Grow in moist but well-drained, fertile soil or soil mix, in full sun. Water freely when in growth, and sparingly in winter.*

☼ ◗ Z 7-10 H 12-8 ‡18in (45cm) ↔12in (30cm)

AGAPANTHUS CAULESCENS

A clump-forming perennial with leeklike stems bearing large, rounded, open flowerheads of bell-shaped, violet-blue flowers. These appear from mid-summer to early autumn above the strap-shaped, mid-green, deciduous leaves. Very useful as a late-flowering perennial, it can also be container-grown in climates with cold winters.

CULTIVATION *Grow in moist but well-drained, fertile soil, in full sun. In cold areas, during winter.*

☼ ◗ Z 9-10 H 12-1 ‡4ft (1.2m) ↔24in (60cm)

AGAVE VICTORIAE-REGINAE

A frost-tender, succulent perennial bearing basal rosettes of triangular, dark green leaves with white marks. The central leaves curve inward, each tipped with a brown spine. Upright spikes of creamy white flowers appear in summer. A good specimen plant: in frost-prone areas, grow in containers for summer display, taking it under cover for winter shelter.

CULTIVATION *Best in sharply drained, moderately fertile, slightly acid soil, or standard cactus soil mix. Site in full sun. Minimum temperature 35°F (2°C).*

☼ ◊ H 12-5   ↔ to 20in (50cm)

AJUGA REPTANS 'ATROPURPUREA'

An excellent evergreen perennial for groundcover, spreading freely over the soil surface by means of rooting stems. Dark blue flowers are borne in whorls along the upright stems during late spring and early summer. The glossy leaves are deep bronze-purple. Invaluable for border edging under shrubs and robust perennials.

CULTIVATION *Best in moist but well-drained, fertile soil, but tolerates most soils. Site in sun or partial shade.*

☼☼ ◊◊ Z 3-9 H 8-2 ‡6in (15cm) ↔3ft (1m)

AJUGA REPTANS 'BURGUNDY GLOW'

A low-growing, evergreen ground-cover perennial with partly hairy stems carrying attractive, silvery green leaves that are suffused deep wine-red. Dark blue flowers are borne in tall, spikelike whorls in late spring and early summer.

CULTIVATION *Best in any moist, fertile soil in partial shade, but will tolerate poor soils, even in full shade.*

☼☀ ◊ Z 3-9 H 8-2 ‡6in (15cm) ↔3ft (1m)

ALCHEMILLA MOLLIS

Lady's mantle is a drought-tolerant, clump-forming, tallish groundcover perennial that produces sprays of tiny, bright greenish yellow flowers from early summer to early autumn. The pale green leaves are rounded with crinkled edges. It looks good in a wildflower or large rock garden. Flowers are ideal for cutting and dry well for winter arrangements.

CULTIVATION *Grow in any moist but well-drained, organic soil, in an open, sunny site. Deadhead soon after flowering: it self-seeds very freely.*

☼ ◊◊ Z 4-7 H 7-1 ‡24in (60cm) ↔30in (75cm)

ORNAMENTAL ONIONS (*ALLIUM*)

Onions grown for garden display are bulbous perennials from the genus *Allium* : their attractive flowerheads make a valuable contribution to mixed or herbaceous borders. The tiny summer flowers are usually massed into dense, rounded or hemispherical heads – like those of *A. giganteum* – or they may hang loosely, like the deep pink heads of *A. cernuum*. When crushed, the strap-shaped, spreading leaves release a pungent aroma; they are often withered by flowering time. The seedheads of the taller alliums tend to dry well and last well into autumn. Some, such as *A. moly*, self-seed and naturalize easily.

CULTIVATION *Grow in fertile, well-drained soil, in full sun, to simulate their dry native habitats. Plant bulbs 2–4in (5–10cm) deep in autumn; divide and replant clumps of older plants at the same time.*

☼ ◊ Zones vary H 9-5

1 ‡12–24in (30–60cm) ↔ 7in (18cm)
2 ‡5–6ft (1.5–2m) ↔ 6in (15cm)
3 ‡4–10in (10–25cm) ↔ 4in (10cm)
4 ‡6–10in (15–25cm) ↔ 2in (5cm)
5 ‡12–24in (30–60cm) ↔ 2in (5cm)

1 *A. cristophii* (syn. *A. albopilosum*) Z 5-8 **2** *A. giganteum* Z 6-10 **3** *A. karataviense* Z 5-9
4 *A. moly* Z 3-9 **5** *A. cernuum* Z 4-10

ALSTROEMERIA
LIGTU HYBRIDS

These summer-flowering, tuberous
perennials produce heads of widely
flared flowers that are considerably
varied in color from white to
shades of pink, yellow, or orange,
often spotted or streaked with
contrasting colors. The mid-green
leaves are narrow and twisted. Ideal
for a sunny, mixed or herbaceous
border, the cut flowers are good for
indoor arrangements.

CULTIVATION *Grow in moist but well-
drained, fertile soil, in full sun. Mulch
thickly for winter where marginally hardy.
Leave undisturbed to form clumps.*

☼ ◊ Z 7-10 H 12-7 ‡20in (50cm) ↔30in (75cm)

AMELANCHIER ×
GRANDIFLORA 'BALLERINA'

A spreading, deciduous tree grown
for its profusion of white spring
flowers and colorful autumn foliage.
When young, the glossy leaves are
tinted bronze, becoming mid-green
in summer, then red and purple in
autumn. The sweet, juicy fruits are
red at first, ripening to purplish
black in summer. They can be eaten
if cooked and are attractive to birds.

CULTIVATION *Grow in moist but well-
drained, fertile, neutral to acid soil, in
full sun or partial shade. Allow shape
to develop naturally; only minimal
pruning is necessary.*

☼◑ ◊◓ Z 5-8 H 8-3 ‡20ft (6m) ↔25ft (8m)

AMELANCHIER LAMARCKII

A many-stemmed, upright, deciduous shrub bearing leaves that are bronze when young, maturing to dark green in summer, then brilliant red and orange in autumn. Hanging clusters of white flowers are produced in spring. The purple-black fruits that follow are edible when cooked, and they are attractive to birds. Similar to *A. canadensis*.

CULTIVATION *Grow in moist but well-drained, organic, neutral to acid soil, in sun or partial shade. Develops its shape naturally with only minimal pruning (in winter, if necessary).*

☼◑ ◊◊ Z 5-8 H 9-3 ↕30ft (10m) ↔40ft (12m)

ANAPHALIS TRIPLINERVIS 'SOMMERSCHNEE'

A clump-forming perennial bearing pale gray-green, white-woolly leaves. The tiny yellow flowerheads, surrounded by brilliant white bracts, appear during mid- and late summer in dense clusters; they are excellent for cutting and drying. Provides good foliage contrast in borders that are too moist for the majority of other gray-leaved plants.

CULTIVATION *Grow in any reasonably well-drained, moderately fertile soil that does not dry out in summer. Choose a position in full sun or partial shade.*

☼◑ ◊ Z 3-8 H 8-3 ↕32–36in (80–90cm) ↔18–24in (45–60cm)

ANCHUSA AZUREA 'LODDON ROYALIST'

An upright, clump-forming perennial that is much valued in herbaceous borders for its spikes of intensely dark blue flowers. These are borne on branching stems in early summer, above the lance-shaped and hairy, mid-green leaves, which are arranged at the base of the stems.

CULTIVATION *Grow in deep, moist but well-drained, fertile soil, in sun. Often short-lived, but easily propagated by root cuttings. If growth is vigorous, staking may be necessary.*

☼ ◊ Z 3-8 H 8-1 ‡36in (90cm) ↔24in (60cm)

ANDROSACE CARNEA SUBSP. *LAGGERI*

An evergreen, cushion-forming perennial that produces small clusters of tiny, cup-shaped, deep pink flowers with yellow eyes in late spring. The pointed, mid-green leaves are arranged in small, tight rosettes. Rock jasmines grow wild in alpine turf and rock crevices, making them ideal for rock gardens, raised beds, or troughs.

CULTIVATION *Grow in moist but sharply drained, gritty soil, in full sun. Provide a top-dressing of grit or gravel to keep the stems and leaves dry.*

☼ ◊ Z 4-7 H 7-1 ‡2in (5cm) ↔6in (15cm)

ANDROSACE LANUGINOSA

A mat-forming, evergreen perennial producing compact heads of flat, small pink flowers with dark pink or greenish yellow eyes, in mid- and late summer. The deep gray-green leaves are borne on trailing, reddish green stems that are covered in silky hairs. Thrives in scree gardens, raised beds, or troughs.

CULTIVATION *Grow in gritty, moist but well-drained soil. Choose a site in full sun. In areas with wet winters, provide shelter under a pane of glass.*

☼ ◊ Z 5-7 H 7-3   ‡to 4in (10cm)
↔to 12in (30cm)

ANEMONE BLANDA 'WHITE SPLENDOUR'

A spreading, spring-flowering perennial that quickly forms clumps of stems growing from knobby tubers. The solitary, upright, flattish white flowers, with pink-tinged undersides, are borne above broadly oval, dark green leaves that are divided into delicately lobed leaflets. Excellent for naturalizing in sunny or shaded sites with good drainage.

CULTIVATION *Grow in well-drained soil that is rich in organic matter. Choose a position in full sun or partial shade.*

☼☼ ◊ Z 4-8 H 9-3   ‡↔ 6in (15cm)

ANEMONE HUPEHENSIS 'HADSPEN ABUNDANCE'

An upright, woody-based, late-flowering border perennial that spreads by shoots growing from the roots. Heads of reddish pink flowers, with petal margins that gradually fade to white, are borne on the ends of branched stems during mid- and late summer. The deeply divided, long-stalked, dark green leaves are oval and sharply toothed.

CULTIVATION *Grow in moist, fertile, organic soil, in sun or partial shade. Provide a mulch in cold areas.*

☼ ◐ ◊◑ Z 4-8 H 9-3 ↕24–36in (60–90cm) ↔16in (40cm)

ANEMONE X *HYBRIDA* 'HONORINE JOBERT'

This upright, woody-based perennial with branched, wiry stems is an invaluable, long-flowering choice for a late summer border. From late summer to mid-autumn, single, slightly cupped, pure white flowers, with pink-tinged undersides and golden-yellow stamens, are borne above the deeply divided, mid-green leaves. Can be rather invasive.

CULTIVATION *Grow in moist but well-drained, moderately fertile, organic soil, in sun or partial shade.*

☼ ◐ ◊◑ Z 4-8 H 9-3 ↕4–5ft (1.2–1.5m) ↔indefinite

ANEMONE NEMOROSA 'ROBINSONIANA'

A vigorous, carpeting perennial that produces a profusion of large, star-shaped, pale lavender-blue flowers. These are borne on maroon stems from spring to early summer, above the deeply divided, mid-green leaves, which die down in mid-summer. Like all wood anemones, it is excellent for underplanting in a shrub border or woodland garden; it naturalizes with ease.

CULTIVATION *Grow in loose, moist but well-drained soil that is rich in organic matter, in light dappled shade.*

☀ ◊ Z 4-8 H 8-1   ↕3–6in (8–15cm)
↔12in (30cm) or more

ANEMONE RANUNCULOIDES

This spring-flowering, spreading perennial is excellent for naturalizing in damp woodland gardens. The large, solitary, buttercup-like yellow flowers are borne above the "ruffs" of short-stalked, rounded, deeply lobed, fresh green leaves.

CULTIVATION *Grow in moist but well-drained, organic soil, in semi-shade or dappled sunlight. Tolerates drier conditions when dormant in summer.*

☀ ◊◊ Z 4-8 H 8-1   ↕2–4in (5–10cm)
↔to 18in (45cm)

ANTENNARIA MICROPHYLLA

A mat-forming, semi-evergreen perennial carrying densely white-hairy, spoon-shaped, gray-green leaves. In late spring and early summer, heads of small, fluffy, rose-pink flowers are borne on short stems. Use in a rock garden, as a low groundcover at the front of a border, or in crevices in walls or paving. The flowerheads dry well for decoration.

CULTIVATION *Best in well-drained soil that is no more than moderately fertile. Choose a position in full sun.*

 Z 5-9 H 9-1 ‡2in (5cm) ↔ to 18in (45cm)

ANTHEMIS PUNCTATA SUBSP. *CUPANIANA*

A mat-forming, evergreen perennial that produces a flush of small but long-lasting, daisylike flowerheads in early summer, and a few blooms later on. The white flowers with yellow centers are borne singly on short stems amid dense, finely cut, silvery gray foliage that turns dull gray-green in winter. Excellent for border edges.

CULTIVATION *Grow in well-drained soil, in a sheltered, sunny position. Cut back after flowering to maintain vigor.*

 Z 6-9 H 7-1 ‡12in (30cm) ↔18in (45cm)

ANTIRRHINUM
SONNET SERIES

Snapdragons are short-lived
perennials best grown as annuals.
The Sonnet Series produces upright
spikes of fragrant, two-lipped flowers
in a broad range of colors, from
white, yellow, and bronze to purple,
pink, and red, from early summer
into autumn. Planted in groups, the
deep green leaves on woody-based
stems are barely visible. Excellent
for cut flowers or summer bedding.

CULTIVATION *Grow in sharply drained,
fertile soil, in full sun. Deadhead flower
spikes to prolong flowering.*

☼ ◊ Z 5-9 H 12-1 ‡12–24in (30–60cm)
↔12in (30cm)

AQUILEGIA VULGARIS
'NIVEA'

An upright, vigorous, clump-forming
perennial bearing leafy clusters of
nodding, short-spurred, pure white
flowers in late spring and early
summer. Each greyish-green leaf is
deeply divided into lobed leaflets.
Attractive in light woodland or in a
herbaceous border. Sometimes sold
as 'Munstead's White'.

CULTIVATION *Best in moist but well-
drained, fertile soil. Choose a position
in full sun or partial shade.*

☼◑ ◊ Z 3-8 H 8-1 ‡36in (90cm) ↔18in (45cm)

AQUILEGIA VULGARIS 'NORA BARLOW'

This upright, vigorous perennial is much valued for its leafy clusters of funnel-shaped, double pompon flowers. These are pink and white with pale green petal tips and appear from late spring to early summer. The grayish green leaves are deeply divided into narrow lobes. Good in herbaceous borders and cottage garden-style plantings.

CULTIVATION *Grow in moist but well-drained, fertile soil. Position in an open, sunny site.*

☼ ◊ Z 3-8 H 7-1 ‡36in (90cm) ↔18in (45cm)

ARABIS PROCURRENS 'VARIEGATA'

A mat-forming, evergreen or semi-evergreen perennial bearing loose clusters of cross-shaped white flowers on tall, slender stems during late spring. The narrow, mid-green leaves, arranged into flattened rosettes, have creamy white margins and are sometimes pink-tinged. Useful in a rock garden.

CULTIVATION *Grow in any well-drained soil, in full sun. Remove completely any stems with plain green leaves.*

☼ ◊ Z 5-8 H 8-1 ‡2–3in (5–8cm) ↔12–16in (30–40cm)

ARBUTUS UNEDO

The strawberry tree is a spreading,
evergreen tree with attractive, rough,
shredding, red-brown bark. Hanging
clusters of small, urn-shaped white
flowers, which are sometimes pink-
tinged, open during autumn as the
previous season's strawberry-like
red fruits ripen. The glossy deep
green leaves are shallowly toothed.
Excellent for a large shrub border,
with shelter from wind.

CULTIVATION *Best in well-drained,
fertile, organic, acid soil. Tolerates
slightly alkaline conditions. Choose a
sheltered site in sun. Prune low branches
in spring, but keep to a minimum.*

☼ ◊ Z 7-9 H 9-4   ↕↔ 25ft (8m)

ARENARIA MONTANA

This sandwort is a low-growing,
spreading, vigorous, evergreen
perennial freely bearing shallowly
cup-shaped white flowers in early
summer. The small, narrowly lance-
shaped, grayish green leaves on
wiry stems form loose mats. Easily
grown in wall or paving crevices, or
in a rock garden.

CULTIVATION *Grow in sandy, moist but
sharply drained, poor soil, in full sun.
Must have adequate moisture.*

☼ ◊ Z 3-5 H 5-1   ↕ ¾–2in (2–5cm)
                          ↔ 12in (30cm)

ARGYRANTHEMUM
'JAMAICA PRIMROSE'

A bushy, evergreen perennial that bears daisylike, primrose-yellow flowerheads with darker yellow centers. These appear throughout summer above the fernlike, grayish green leaves. Where not hardy, grow as summer bedding or plant in containers that can be moved under cover for the winter.

CULTIVATION *Grow in well-drained, fairly fertile soil or soil mix, in a warm, sunny site. Apply a deep, dry mulch to outdoor plants. Pinch out the growing tips to encourage bushiness. Minimum temperature 35°F (2°C).*

☼ ◊ H 12-1   ‡3½ft (1.1m) ↔3ft (1m)

ARGYRANTHEMUM
'VANCOUVER'

This compact, summer-flowering, evergreen subshrub is valued for its double, daisylike pink flowerheads with rose-pink centers and fernlike, gray-green leaves. Use in a mixed or herbaceous border; where not hardy, grow as summer bedding or in containers that can be sheltered in frost-free conditions over winter.

CULTIVATION *Grow in well-drained, fairly fertile soil, in sun. Apply a deep, dry mulch to outdoor plants. Pinch out growing tips to encourage bushiness. Minimum temperature 35°F (2°C).*

☼ ◊ H 12-1   ‡36in (90cm) ↔32in (80cm)

ARMERIA JUNIPERIFOLIA

This tiny, hummock-forming, evergreen subshrub bears small, purplish pink to white flowers that are carried in short-stemmed, spherical clusters during late spring. The small, linear, gray-green leaves are hairy and spine-tipped and are arranged in loose rosettes. Native to mountain pastures and rock crevices, it is ideal for a rock garden or trough. Also known as *A. caespitosa*.

CULTIVATION *Grow in well-drained, poor to moderately fertile soil, in an open position in full sun.*

☼ ◊ Z 5-7 H 8-4   ↕2–3in (5–8cm)
                    ↔to 6in (15cm)

ARMERIA JUNIPERIFOLIA 'BEVAN'S VARIETY'

A compact, cushion-forming, evergreen subshrub that bears small, deep rose-pink flowers. These are carried in short-stemmed, rounded clusters during late spring over the loose rosettes of small and narrow, pointed, gray-green leaves. Good in a rock garden or trough, or position at the front of a border.

CULTIVATION *Grow in well-drained, poor to moderately fertile soil. Choose an open site in full sun.*

☼ ◊ Z 5-7 H 8-4   ↕2in (5cm) ↔6in (15cm)

ARTEMISIA ABSINTHIUM
'LAMBROOK SILVER'

A clump-forming, woody-based, evergreen perennial cultivated for its mass of ferny, aromatic, silvery gray foliage. The grayish yellow flower-heads in late summer are of little ornamental value. Suitable for a rock garden or border, but shelter is needed if grown in an exposed site.

CULTIVATION *Grow in well-drained, fertile soil, in full sun. Short-lived on poorly drained soils. Cut to the base in autumn to maintain a compact habit.*

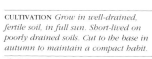

☼ ◊ Z 4-8 H 12-8 ‡30in (75cm) ↔24in (60cm)

ARTEMISIA LUDOVICIANA
'SILVER QUEEN'

An upright, bushy, clump-forming, semi-evergreen perennial bearing narrow, downy leaves that are sometimes jaggedly toothed; silvery white when young, they become greener with age. Slender, white-woolly plumes of brownish yellow flowerheads are borne from mid-summer to autumn. Indispensable in a silver-themed border.

CULTIVATION *Grow in well-drained soil, in an open, sunny site. Cut back in spring for best foliage effect.*

☼ ◊ Z 4-9 H 12-8   ‡30in (75cm)
↔24in (60cm) or more

ARTEMISIA 'POWIS CASTLE'

A vigorous, shrubby, woody-based perennial forming a dense, billowing clump of finely cut, aromatic, silver-gray leaves. Sprays of insignificant, yellow-tinged silver flowerheads are borne in late summer. Excellent in a rock garden or border.

CULTIVATION *Grow in well-drained, fertile soil, in full sun. Will die back in heavy, poorly drained soils and may be short-lived. Cut to the base in autumn to maintain a compact habit.*

☼ ◊ Z 7-9 H 12-8 ‡24in (60cm) ↔36in (90cm)

ASPARAGUS DENSIFLORUS 'MYERSII'

The asparagus fern is an arching and trailing, evergreen perennial forming spires of narrow, feathery, leaflike, light green stems. In warm climates, it bears clusters of small, pink-tinged white flowers in summer, followed by bright red berries. In cold areas, it must be grown under cover and makes an impressive conservatory specimen or a much smaller house- or hanging basket plant.

CULTIVATION *Grow in moist but well-drained, fertile soil, in partial shade. Minimum temperature 45°F (7°C).*

☼ ◊ H 12-1   ‡24–36in (60–90cm)
                    ↔3–4ft (1–1.2m)

ASPLENIUM SCOLOPENDRIUM

The hart's tongue fern is an upright
and evergreen perennial bearing
irregular crowns of shuttlecock-like,
tongue-shaped, leathery, bright green
fronds, to 16in (40cm) long. They
are heart-shaped at the bases and
often have wavy margins. On the
undersides of mature fronds, rust-
colored spore cases are arranged
in a herringbone pattern. Good in
alkaline soils.

CULTIVATION *Grow in moist but well-
drained, organic, preferably alkaline
soil with added grit, in partial shade.*

☀ ◐◊ Z 6-8 H 8-5 ‡18–28in (45–70cm)
↔24in (60cm)

ASTER ALPINUS

This spreading, clump-forming
perennial is grown for its mass of
daisylike, purplish blue or pinkish
purple flowerheads with deep
yellow centers. These are borne
on upright stems in early and mid-
summer above short-stalked, narrow,
mid-green leaves. A low-growing
aster, it is suitable for the front of a
border or in a rock garden. Several
outstanding cultivars are available.

CULTIVATION *Grow in well-drained,
moderately fertile soil, in sun. Mulch
annually after cutting back in autumn.*

☀ ◊ Z 5-7 H 9-1 ‡10in (25cm) ↔18in (45cm)

ASTER AMELLUS 'KING GEORGE'

A clump-forming, bushy perennial bearing loose clusters of large, daisy-like, violet-blue flowerheads with yellow centers that open from late summer to autumn. The rough, mid-green leaves are hairy and lance-shaped. An invaluable late-flowering border plant.

CULTIVATION *Grow in open, well-drained, moderately fertile soil, in full sun. Thrives in alkaline conditions.*

☼ ◊ Z 5-8 H 9-1   ↕↔ 18in (45cm)

ASTER 'ANDENKEN AN ALMA PÖTSCHKE'

This vigorous, upright, clump-forming perennial carries sprays of large, daisylike, bright salmon-pink flowerheads with yellow centers. These open from late summer to mid-autumn on stiff, almost woody stems above the rough, lance-shaped, stem-clasping, mid-green leaves. Good for cutting or in late-flowering displays.

CULTIVATION *Grow in moist but well-drained, fertile, well-cultivated soil, in sun or semi-shade. Divide and replant every third year to maintain vigor and flower quality. May need staking.*

☼◐ ◊ Z 4-8 H 8-1 ↕ 4ft (1.2m) ↔ 24in (60cm)

ASTER × *FRIKARTII*
'MÖNCH'

This upright, bushy perennial provides a continuous show of long-lasting, daisylike, clear lavender-blue flowerheads with orange centers during late summer and early autumn. The dark green leaves are rough-textured and oblong. A useful plant for adding vivid blue to a late summer or autumn display.

CULTIVATION *Best in well-drained, moderately fertile soil. Position in an open, sunny site. Mulch annually after cutting back in late autumn.*

☼ ◊ Z 5-8 H 9-1   ‡28in (70cm)
                              ↔14–16in (35–40cm)

ASTER LATERIFOLIUS
'HORIZONTALIS'

A clump-forming, freely branching perennial bearing clusters of daisy-like, sometimes pink-tinged white flowerheads with darker pink centers from mid-summer to mid-autumn. The slender, hairy stems bear small, lance-shaped, mid-green leaves. An invaluable late-flowerer for a mixed border.

CULTIVATION *Grow in moist but well-drained, moderately fertile soil, in partial shade. Keep moist in summer.*

☼ ◊ Z 4-8 H 9-1 ‡24in (60cm) ↔12in (30cm)

ASTER 'LITTLE CARLOW'

A clump-forming, upright perennial that produces large clusters of daisy-like, violet-blue flowers with yellow centers in early and mid-autumn. The dark green leaves are oval to heart-shaped and toothed. Valuable for autumn displays; the flowers are excellent for cutting and drying.

CULTIVATION *Best in moist, moderately fertile soil, in partial shade, but tolerates well-drained soil, in full sun. Mulch annually after cutting back in late autumn. May need staking.*

☼ ◔ ◊◊ Z 5-8 H 9-1 ‡36in (90cm)
↔18in (45cm)

ASTILBE × *ARENDSII* 'FANAL'

A leafy, clump-forming perennial grown for its long-lasting, tapering, feathery heads of tiny, dark crimson flowers in early summer; they later turn brown, keeping their shape well into winter. The dark green leaves, which are borne on strong stems, are divided into several leaflets. Grow in a damp border or woodland garden, or use for waterside plantings.

CULTIVATION *Grow in moist, fertile, preferably organic soil. Choose a position in full sun or partial shade.*

☼ ◔ ◊ Z 4-9 H 8-2 ‡24in (60cm) ↔18in (45cm)

ASTILBE × *CRISPA* 'PERKEO'

A summer-flowering, clump-forming perennial, low-growing compared with other astilbes, that bears small, upright plumes of tiny, star-shaped, deep pink flowers. The stiff, finely cut, crinkled, dark green leaves are bronze-tinted when young. Suitable for a border or rock garden; the flower color is best in light shade.

CULTIVATION *Grow in reasonably moist, fertile soil that is rich in organic matter. Choose a position in partial shade.*

☼ ◑ ◊ Z 4-8 H 8-2 ‡8in (20cm) ↔6in (15cm)

ASTILBE 'SPRITE'

A summer-flowering, leafy, clump-forming dwarf perennial that is suitable for waterside plantings. The feathery, tapering plumes of tiny, star-shaped, shell-pink flowers arch elegantly over a mass of broad, mid-green leaves composed of many narrow leaflets.

CULTIVATION *Grow in reliably moist, fertile soil that is rich in organic matter. Choose a site in partial shade.*

☼ ◑ ◊ Z 4-8 H 8-2 ‡20in (50cm) ↔to 3ft (1m)

ASTILBE 'STRAUSSENFEDER'

A vigorous, clump-forming perennial that bears loose, arching sprays of rich coral-pink flowers in late summer and early autumn; the flowerheads turn brown when dry and persist into winter. The dark green leaves, divided into oval leaflets, are bronze-tinted when young. Ideal for damp borders, bog gardens, or waterside plantings. Sometimes called 'Ostrich Plume'.

CULTIVATION *Grow in moist, fertile, rich soil, in sun or partial shade. Requires ample moisture in the growing season. Apply an annual mulch in spring of organic matter to hold water in the soil.*

☼☀ ◑ ◊ Z 4-9 H 8-2 ‡36in (90cm) ↔24in (60cm)

ASTRANTIA MAXIMA

Sometimes known as Hattie's pincushion, this mat-forming perennial produces domed, rose-pink flowerheads with star-shaped collars of papery, greenish pink bracts on tall stems during summer and autumn. The mid-green leaves are divided into three toothed lobes. Flowers are good for cutting and drying and for use in cottage-style arrangements.

CULTIVATION *Grow in any moist, fertile, preferably organic soil, in sun or semi-shade. Tolerates drier conditions.*

☼☀ ◊◊ Z 5-8 H 7-1 ‡24in (60cm) ↔12in (30cm)

ASTRANTIA MAJOR 'SUNNINGDALE VARIEGATED'

A clump-forming perennial bearing attractive, deeply lobed, basal leaves that have unevenly variegated, creamy-yellow margins. From early summer, domes of tiny, green or pink, often deep purple-red flowers with star-shaped collars of pale-pink bracts are carried on wiry stems. Thrives in a moist border, woodland garden, or on a stream bank.

CULTIVATION *Grow in any moist but well-drained, fertile soil. Needs sun to obtain the best leaf coloring.*

☼ ◊ Z 4-7 H 7-1   ‡12–36in (30–90cm)
↔18in (45cm)

ATHYRIUM FILIX-FEMINA

The lady fern has much divided, light green, deciduous fronds that are borne like upright shuttlecocks, about 3ft (1m) long, arching outward with age. Frond dissection is very varied, and the stalks are sometimes red-brown. Useful for shaded sites, such as a woodland garden.

CULTIVATION *Grow in moist, fertile, neutral to acid soil enriched with leaf mold or compost. Choose a shaded, sheltered site.*

◑ ◊ Z 4-9 H 8-1   ‡to 4ft (1.2m)
↔24–36in (60–90cm)

AUCUBA JAPONICA 'CROTONIFOLIA' (FEMALE)

This variegated form of spotted laurel is a rounded, evergreen shrub with large, glossy, dark green leaves boldly speckled with golden-yellow. Upright clusters of small purplish flowers are borne in mid-spring, followed by red berries in autumn. Ideal for dense, semi-formal hedging.

CULTIVATION *Grow in any but water-logged soil, in full sun for best foliage color, or in shade. Plant with male cultivars to ensure good fruiting. Tolerates light pruning at any time; cut back in spring to promote bushiness.*

☼ ☀ ◌◗ Z 6-10 H 12-6   ↕↔ 10ft (3m)

AURINIA SAXATILIS

An evergreen perennial that forms dense clusters of bright yellow flowers (in late spring) that give rise to its common name, basket of gold. The oval, hairy, gray-green leaves are arranged in clumps. Ideal for rock gardens, walls, and banks. Also sold as *Alyssum saxatilis*.

CULTIVATION *Grow in moderately fertile soil that is reliably well-drained, in a sunny site. Cut back after flowering to maintain compactness.*

☼ ◌ Z 4-8 H 9-2 ↕8in (20cm) ↔12in (30cm)

BALLOTA PSEUDODICTAMNUS

An evergreen subshrub that forms mounds of rounded, yellow-gray-green leaves on upright, white-woolly stems. Whorls of small, white or pinkish white flowers, each enclosed by a pale green funnel, are produced in late spring and early summer.

CULTIVATION *Grow in poor, very well-drained soil, in full sun with protection from excessive winter moisture. Cut back in spring to keep plants compact.*

☼ ◊ Z 7-9 H 9-7 ‡18in (45cm) ↔24in (60cm)

BAPTISIA AUSTRALIS

Blue false indigo is a gently spreading, upright perennial with a long season of interest. The bright blue-green leaves on gray-green stems are divided into three oval leaflets. Spikes of indigo-blue flowers, often flecked white or cream, open throughout early summer. The dark gray seed pods can be used for winter decoration.

CULTIVATION *Grow in deep, moist but well-drained, fertile, preferably neutral to acid soil, in full sun. Once planted, it is best left undisturbed.*

☼ ◊ Z 3-9 H 9-2 ‡5ft (1.5m) ↔24in (60cm)

FLOWERING BEGONIAS

Usually grown outdoors as annuals, these bold-flowered begonias are very variable in size and shape, offering a range of uses to the gardener: for specific information on growth habit, check the label or ask advice when buying. Upright or compact begonias, such as 'Pin Up' and 'Irene Nuss', are ideal for summer bedding; for containers and hanging baskets, there are pendulous or trailing varieties such as 'Illumination Orange'. Begonias can also be grown as houseplants. The flowers also come in a wide variety of sizes and colors; they are either single or double and appear in loose clusters throughout the summer months.

CULTIVATION *Grow in fertile, organic, neutral to acid soil or soil mix with good drainage. Flowers are best in partial shade; they suffer in direct sun. When in growth, feed with a balanced fertilizer. All grow best at temperatures above 15°C (59°F).*

☼ ◊ H 7-1

3 ‡30in (75cm) ↔ 24in (60cm)

1 ‡8–12in (20–30cm) ↔ 12in (30cm)

2 ‡24in (60cm) ↔ 12in (30cm)

4 ‡10in (25cm) ↔ 8in (20cm)

1 *B.* Cocktail Series **2** *B.* 'Illumination Orange' **3** *B.* 'Irene Nuss'
4 *B.* 'Pin Up'

BEGONIAS WITH DECORATIVE FOLIAGE

These perennial begonias are grown primarily for their large, usually asymmetrical, ornamental leaves that are available in a variety of colors. For example, there are lively leaves of 'Merry Christmas' outlined with emerald green, or there is the more subtle, dark green, metallic foliage of *B. metallica*. Some leaves are valued for their unusual patterns; *B. masoniana* is appropriately known as the iron-cross begonia. Under the right conditions, 'Thurstonii' may reach shrublike proportions, but most,

such as 'Munchkin', are more compact. Grow as house plants, in a conservatory, or as summer bedding.

CULTIVATION *Grow in fertile, well-drained, neutral to acid soil or soil mix, in bright light. Promote compact, leafy growth by pinching out shoot tips during the growing season. When in growth, feed regularly with a high-nitrogen fertilizer. Minimum temperature 59°F (15°C).*

☀ ◊ H 8-1

2 ‡ 10in (25cm) ↔ 12in (30cm)

3 ‡ 36in (90cm) ↔ 24in (60cm)

1 ‡ 20in (50cm) ↔ 18in (45cm)

4 ‡ 8in (20cm) ↔ 10in (25cm)

5 ‡ 6ft (2m) ↔ 18in (45cm)

---

1 *B. masoniana* **2** *B.* 'Merry Christmas' **3** *B. metallica* **4** *B.* 'Munchkin' **5** *B.* 'Thurstonii'

BELLIS PERENNIS 'POMPONETTE'

This double-flowered form of the English daisy is usually grown as a biennial for spring bedding. Pink, red, or white flowerheads with quill-shaped petals appear from late winter to spring, above the dense clumps of spoon-shaped, bright green leaves.

CULTIVATION *Grow in well-drained, moderately fertile soil, in full sun or partial shade. Deadhead to prolong flowering and to prevent self-seeding.*

☼ ☽ ◊ Z 4-8 H 8-1   ‡↔ 4–8in (10–20cm)

BERBERIS DARWINII

The Darwin barberry is a vigorous, arching, evergreen shrub that carries masses of small, deep golden-orange flowers on spiny stems from mid-to late spring; these are followed by blue berries in autumn. The leaves are glossy dark green and spiny. Use as a vandal-resistant or barrier hedge.

CULTIVATION *Grow in any but water-logged soil, in full sun or partial shade with shelter from drying winds. Trim after flowering, if necessary.*

☼ ☽ ◊◊ Z 7-9 H 9-4   ‡10ft (3m) or more
↔10ft (3m)

BERBERIS × *OTTAWENSIS*
'SUPERBA'

This spiny, rounded, deciduous, spring-flowering shrub bears clusters of small, pale yellow, red-tinged flowers that are followed by red berries in autumn. The red-purple leaves turn crimson before they fall. Effective as a specimen shrub or in a mixed border.

CULTIVATION *Grow in almost any well-drained soil, preferably in full sun. Thin out dense growth in late winter.*

☼ ◊◊ Z 5-9 H 8-3 ↔ 8ft (2.5m)

BERBERIS × *STENOPHYLLA*
'CORALLINA COMPACTA'

A small, evergreen shrub bearing spine-tipped, deep green leaves on arching, spiny stems. Large numbers of tiny, light orange flowers appear in mid-spring, followed by small, blue-black berries. Can be grown as an informal hedge.

CULTIVATION *Best in fertile, organic soil that is reliably drained, in full sun. Cut back hard after flowering.*

☼ ◊ Z 6-9 H 9-6 ↔ to 12in (30cm)

BERBERIS THUNBERGII 'BAGATELLE'

A very compact, spiny, spring-flowering, deciduous shrub that bears deep red-purple leaves, which turn orange and red in autumn. The pale yellow flowers are followed by glossy red fruits. Can be grown in a rock garden.

CULTIVATION *Grow in well-drained soil, in full sun for best flower and foliage color. Thin out dense, overcrowded growth in late winter.*

☼ ◊ Z 5-8 H 8-3 ‡12in (30cm) ↔16in (40cm)

BERBERIS THUNBERGII 'ROSE GLOW'

A compact, spiny, deciduous shrub with reddish purple leaves that gradually become flecked with white as the season progresses. Tiny, pale yellow flowers appear in mid-spring, followed by small red berries. Good as a barrier hedge.

CULTIVATION *Grow in any but water-logged soil, in full sun or partial shade. Cut out any dead wood in summer.*

☼◐ ◊◊ Z 5-8 H 8-3 ‡6ft (2m) or more ↔ 6ft (2m)

BERBERIS VERRUCULOSA

A slow-growing, compact, spring-flowering barberry that makes a fine evergreen specimen shrub. The cup-shaped, golden-yellow flowers are carried amid the spine-tipped, glossy dark green leaves on spiny, arching stems. Oval to pear-shaped black berries develop in autumn.

CULTIVATION *Best in well-drained, organic, fertile soil, in full sun. Keep pruning to a minimum.*

☼ ◊ Z 6-9 H 9-4   ↕↔ 5ft (1.5m)

BERBERIS WILSONIAE

A very spiny, semi-evergreen, arching shrub forming dense mounds of gray-green foliage that turns red and orange in autumn. Clusters of pale yellow flowers in summer are followed by coral-pink to pinkish red berries. Makes a good barrier hedge. Avoid seed-grown plants: they may be inferior hybrids.

CULTIVATION *Grow in any well-drained soil, in sun or partial shade. Flowering and fruiting are best in full sun. Thin out dense growth in late winter.*

☼◑ ◊ Z 6-9 H 9-4   ↕ 3ft (1m) ↔ 6ft (2m)

BERGENIA PURPURASCENS 'BALLAWLEY'

This clump-forming, evergreen perennial, one of the first to flower in spring, bears bright crimson flowers that are carried on sturdy red stems. The leathery, oval leaves turn bronze-red in winter. Good for a woodland garden, or plant in groups to edge a mixed border.

CULTIVATION *Grow in any well-drained soil, in full sun or light shade. Shelter from cold winds. Mulch in autumn.*

☼ ◑ ◊◊ Z 3-8 H 9-2   ↕ to 24in (60cm)
↔ 24in (60cm)

BERGENIA 'SILBERLICHT'

An early-flowering, clump-forming, evergreen perennial bearing dense clusters of cup-shaped white flowers, often flushed pink, in spring. The mid-green leaves are round and leathery with toothed margins. Good underplanting for shrubs, which will provide it some winter shelter.

CULTIVATION *Grow in any well-drained soil, in full sun or partial shade. Shelter from cold winds to avoid foliage scorch. Provide a mulch in autumn.*

☼ ◑ ◊◊ Z 3-8 H 9-2   ↕ 12in (30cm)
↔ 20in (50cm)

BETULA NIGRA

The river birch is a tall, conical to spreading, deciduous tree with glossy, mid- to dark green, diamond-shaped leaves. It has shaggy, red-brown bark that peels in layers on young trees; on older specimens, the bark becomes blackish or gray-white and develops cracks. Yellow-brown male catkins are conspicuous in spring. Makes a fine specimen tree, but only for a large garden.

CULTIVATION *Grow in moist but well-drained, moderately fertile soil, in full sun. Remove any damaged, diseased, or dead wood in late autumn.*

☼ ◊ Z 4-9 H 7-2 ‡60ft (18m) ↔40ft (12m)

BETULA PENDULA 'YOUNGII'

Young's weeping birch is a dome-shaped, deciduous tree, often growing wider than it is tall, with an elegant, weeping habit. The yellow-brown male catkins appear in early spring before the triangular, glossy, green leaves; the foliage turns golden-yellow in autumn. An attractive tree for a small garden.

CULTIVATION *Grow in any moist but well-drained soil, in an open, sunny site. Keep pruning to a minimum; remove any shoots growing on the clear trunk in late autumn.*

☼ ◊ Z 2-7 H 7-1 ‡25ft (8m) ↔ 30ft (10m)

BETULA UTILIS VAR. *JACQUEMONTII*

The West Himalayan birch is an open, broadly conical, deciduous tree with smooth, peeling white bark. Catkins are a feature in early spring, and the dark green leaves turn rich golden-yellow in autumn. Plant in groups or on its own, particularly where winter sun will light up the bark.

CULTIVATION *Grow in any moist but well-drained soil, in sun. Remove any damaged or dead wood from young trees in late autumn; once established, keep pruning to a minimum.*

☼ ◊ Z 5-7 H 9-3 ‡50ft (15m) ↔23ft (7.5m)

BIDENS FERULIFOLIA

This clump-forming, spreading, short-lived perennial is often grown as an annual. A profusion of star-shaped, bright golden-yellow flowers are borne over a long period from mid-spring until the first frosts. The leaves are fresh green and finely divided. Ideal for trailing over the edges of hanging baskets and other containers.

CULTIVATION *Grow in moist but well-drained, fairly fertile soil or soil mix, in sun. Short-lived, but easily propagated by stem cuttings in autumn.*

☼ ◊◊ Z 8-10 H 12-8 ‡to 12in (30cm)
↔indefinite

BRACHYGLOTTIS
'SUNSHINE'

A bushy, mound-forming, evergreen shrub bearing oval leaves that are silvery gray when young, becoming dark green with white-felted undersides as they develop. Daisylike yellow flowers appear from early to mid-summer. Some gardeners prefer it as a foliage plant, pinching or snipping off the flower buds before they open. Thrives in coastal sites.

CULTIVATION *Grow in any well-drained soil, in a sunny, sheltered site. Trim back after flowering. Responds well to hard pruning in spring.*

☼ ◊ Z 9-10 H 10-8   ‡3–5ft (1–1.5m)
↔6ft (2m) or more

BRACTEANTHA
BRIGHT BIKINI SERIES

These strawflowers are upright annuals producing papery, double flowers in red, pink, orange, yellow, and white from late spring to autumn. The leaves are mid-green and lance-shaped. Use to edge a border, or grow in a windowbox; flowers are long-lasting and cut and dry well. Formerly *Helichrysum*.

CULTIVATION *Grow in moist but well-drained, moderately fertile soil. Choose a position in full sun.*

☼ ◊ Z 10-11 H 12-3 ‡12in (30cm) ↔12in (30cm)

BRUNNERA MACROPHYLLA 'HADSPEN CREAM'

This clump-forming perennial with attractive foliage is ideal as a groundcover in borders and among deciduous trees. In mid- and late spring, upright clusters of small, bright blue flowers appear above heart-shaped leaves with irregular, creamy white margins.

CULTIVATION *Grow in moist but well-drained, organic soil. Choose a position that is cool and lightly shaded.*

☀ ◊◊ Z 3-7 H 9-3 ‡18in (45cm) ↔24in (60cm)

BUDDLEJA ALTERNIFOLIA

A dense, deciduous shrub with slender, arching branches. Fragrant, lilac-purple flowers are produced in neat clusters during early summer among the narrow, gray-green leaves. Makes a good wall shrub, or it can be trained with a single, clear trunk as a striking specimen. Attractive to beneficial insects.

CULTIVATION *Best in alkaline soil but can be grown in any soil that is well-drained, in full sun. Cut stems back to strong buds after flowering; responds well to hard pruning in spring.*

☀ ◊ Z 6-9 H 10-4 ‡↔12ft (4m)

BUDDLEJA DAVIDII

All cultivars of *B. davidii* (butterfly bush) are fast-growing, deciduous shrubs with a wide range of flower colors. As the popular name suggests, the flowers attract butterflies and other beneficial garden insects in profusion. The long, arching shoots carry lance-shaped, mid- to gray-green leaves, up to 10in (25cm) long. Conical clusters of bright, fragrant flowers, usually about 12in (30cm) long, are borne at the end of arching stems from summer to autumn; those of 'Royal Red' are the largest, up to 20in (50cm) long. These shrubs respond well to hard pruning in spring, which keeps them a compact size for a small garden.

CULTIVATION *Grow in well-drained, fertile soil, in sun. Restrict size and encourage better flowers by pruning back hard to a low framework each spring. To prevent self-seeding, cut spent flowerheads back to a pair of leaves or sideshoots; this often results in a second bloom flush.*

☼ ◊ Z 6-9 H 10-4

1 ‡10ft (3m) ↔ 15ft (5m) 2 ‡10ft (3m) ↔ 15ft (5m) 3 ‡10ft (3m) ↔ 15ft (5m)

1 *B. davidii* 'Empire Blue' 2 *B. davidii* 'Royal Red' 3 *B. davidii* 'White Profusion'

BUDDLEJA GLOBOSA

The orange ball tree is a deciduous or semi-evergreen shrub bearing (unusual for a buddleja) round clusters of tiny, orange-yellow flowers that appear in early summer. The lance-shaped leaves are dark green with woolly under-sides. A large shrub, it is prone to becoming bare at the base and does not respond well to pruning, so grow toward the back of a mixed border.

CULTIVATION *Best on well-drained, alkaline soil, in a sunny position with shelter from cold winds. Pruning should be kept to a minimum or the next year's flowers will be lost.*

☀ ◊ Z 7-9 H 9-6   ↕↔ 15ft (5m)

BUDDLEJA 'LOCHINCH'

A compact, deciduous shrub, very similar to a *Buddleja davidii* (see p. 77), bearing long spikes of lilac-blue flowers from late summer to autumn. The leaves are downy and gray-green when young, becoming smooth and developing white-felted undersides as they mature. Very attractive to butterflies.

CULTIVATION *Grow in any well-drained, moderately fertile soil, in sun. Cut back all stems close to the base each year as the buds begin to swell in spring.*

☀ ◊ Z 6-9 H 9-6   ↕ 8ft (2.5m) ↔ 10ft (3m)

BUXUS SEMPERVIRENS 'ELEGANTISSIMA'

This variegated form of common boxwood is a rounded, dense, evergreen shrub bearing small and narrow, glossy bright green leaves edged with white. The flowers are of little significance. Responding well to trimming, it is very good as an edging plant or for use as a low hedge. It is also effective when planted together with green-leaved boxwood in a knot garden.

CULTIVATION *Grow in any well-drained soil, in sun or light shade. Trim in spring and summer; overgrown shrubs respond well to hard pruning in late spring.*

☼☀ ◊ Z 6-8 H 10-4   ‡↔5ft (1.5m)

BUXUS SEMPERVIRENS 'SUFFRUTICOSA'

A very dense, slow-growing boxwood producing small, evergreen, glossy bright green leaves. Widely used as an edging plant or for clipping into precise shapes. Inconspicuous flowers are borne during late spring or early summer. Excellent as a hedge.

CULTIVATION *Grow in any well-drained, fertile soil, in sun or semi-shade. The combination of dry soil and full sun can cause scorching. Trim hedges in summer; overgrown specimens can be hard-pruned in late spring.*

☼☀ ◊ Z 6-8 H 9-4   ‡3ft (1m) ↔5ft (1.5m)

CALENDULA 'FIESTA GITANA'

This dwarf pot marigold is a bushy, fast-growing annual that produces masses of usually double flower-heads in pastel orange or yellow, including bicolors, from summer to autumn in cooler climates. The leaves are hairy and aromatic. Excellent for cutting, bedding, and containers.

CULTIVATION *Grow in well-drained, poor to moderately fertile soil, in full sun or partial shade. Deadhead regularly to prolong flowering.*

☀️◐ ◊ annual H 6-1 ‡to 12in (30cm) ↔12–18in (30–45cm)

CALLICARPA BODINIERI VAR. *GIRALDII* 'PROFUSION'

An upright, deciduous shrub grown mainly for its long-lasting autumn display of shiny, beadlike, deep violet berries. The large, pale green, tapering leaves are bronze when they emerge in spring. Pale pink flowers appear in summer. Brings a long season of interest to a shrub border; for maximum impact, plant in groups.

CULTIVATION *Grow in any well-drained, fertile soil, in full sun or dappled shade. Cut back about 1 in 5 stems to the base each year in early spring.*

☀️◐ ◊ Z 6-8 H 8-6 ‡10ft (3m) ↔ 8ft (2.5m)

CALLISTEMON CITRINUS 'SPLENDENS'

This attractive cultivar of the crimson bottlebrush is an evergreen shrub usually with arching branches. Dense spikes of brilliant red flowers appear in spring and summer, amid gray-green, lemon-scented leaves, which are bronze-red when young. Grow at the base of a wall to give some protection from winter cold.

CULTIVATION *Best in well-drained, fertile, neutral to acid soil, in full sun. Pinch out tips young of young plants to promote bushiness. Tolerates hard pruning in spring.*

☼ ◊ Z 10-11 H 10-8   ↕6–25ft (2–8m)
                           ↔5–20ft (1.5–6m)

CALLISTEPHUS MILADY SUPER MIXED

This sturdy, partially wilt-resistant mixture of variably colored, fast-growing annuals is ideal for use in bedding and containers. The double, rounded flowerheads, borne from late summer to autumn, are pink, red, scarlet, blue, or white. The leaves are mid-green and toothed.

CULTIVATION *Grow in moist but well-drained, fertile, neutral to alkaline soil, in a sheltered, sunny site. Deadheading may result in a few later flowers.*

☼ ◊◊ annual H 12-1   ↕to 12in (30cm)
                           ↔10in (25cm)

CALLUNA VULGARIS

Cultivars of *C. vulgaris* are upright to spreading, fine-leaved heathers. They make excellent evergreen groundcover plants if weeds are suppressed before planting. Dense spikes of bell-shaped flowers appear from mid-summer to late autumn, in shades of red, purple, pink, or white; 'Kinlochruel' is quite distinctive with its double white flowers in long clusters. Seasonal interest is extended into winter by cultivars with colored foliage, such as 'Robert Chapman' and 'Beoley Gold'. Heathers are very attractive to bees and other beneficial insects and make good companions for dwarf conifers.

CULTIVATION *Best in well-drained, organic, acid soil, in an open, sunny site, to recreate their native moorland habitats. Trim off flowered shoots in early spring with shears, and remove overlong shoots wherever possible, cutting back to their point of origin below the flower cluster.*

☼ ◊ Z 5-7 H 7-5

3 ‡ 10in (25cm) ↔ 16in (40cm)

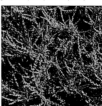

1 ‡ 10in (25cm) ↔ 14in (35cm)   **2** ‡ 14in (35cm) ↔ to 30in (75cm)   **4** ‡ 10in (25cm) ↔ 26in (65cm)

1 *C. vulgaris* 'Darkness' **2** *C. vulgaris* 'Beoley Gold' **3** *C. vulgaris* 'Kinlochruel'
4 *C. vulgaris* 'Robert Chapman'

CALTHA PALUSTRIS

The marsh marigold is a clump-
forming, aquatic perennial that
thrives in a bog garden or at the
margins of a stream or pond. Cup-
shaped, waxy, bright golden-yellow
flowers appear on tall stems in
spring above the kidney-shaped,
glossy green leaves.

CULTIVATION *Best in boggy, rich soil,
in an open, sunny site. Tolerates root
restriction in aquatic containers in
water no deeper than 9in (23cm), but
prefers shallower conditions.*

☼ ◐ Z 3-7 H 7-1   ↕4–16in (10–40cm)
↔18in (45cm)

CAMELLIA 'INSPIRATION'

A dense, upright, evergreen shrub or
small tree bearing masses of saucer-
shaped, semidouble, deep pink
flowers from mid-winter to late
spring. The dark green leaves are
oval and leathery. Good for the back
of a border or as a specimen shrub.

CULTIVATION *Best in moist but well-
drained, fertile, neutral to acid soil, in
partial shade with shelter from cold,
drying winds. Mulch around the base
with shredded bark. After flowering,
prune back young plants to encourage
a bushy habit and a balanced shape.*

☼ ◐◐ Z 7-8 H 12-8   ↕12ft (4m) ↔6ft (2m)

CAMELLIA JAPONICA 'ADOLPHE AUDUSSON'

A fast-growing, open, evergreen shrub or small tree that produces large, saucer-shaped, semidouble, rich dark red flowers with yellow stamens in early and mid-spring. The leaves are oval and glossy dark green. Makes an elegant shrub for a woodland garden.

CULTIVATION *Grow in moist but well-drained, organic, neutral to acid soil. Choose a site in partial shade with shelter from cold winds. Maintain a mulch of leafmold or shredded bark around the base. Needs little pruning.*

☼ ◐◊ Z 7-9 H 10-8 ‡15ft (5m) ↔10ft (3m)

CAMELLIA JAPONICA 'ALEXANDER HUNTER'

This vigorous, upright, evergreen shrub or small tree bears oval, dark green leaves. In early and mid-spring, flattish, single, deep crimson flowers open to reveal bosses of yellow stamens. Excellent as a specimen shrub.

CULTIVATION *Needs moisture-retentive, fertile, neutral to acid soil, in partial shade. Provide shelter from cold, drying winds. Maintain a mulch of shredded bark around the base. Moderate pruning of young plants will help create a balanced shape.*

☼ ◐◊ Z 7-9 H 10-8 ‡15 ft (5m) ↔10ft (3m)

CAMELLIA JAPONICA 'ELEGANS'

A slow-growing, evergreen shrub or
small tree with spreading branches
carrying glossy dark green leaves.
Large, deep rose-pink flowers are
borne freely in early to mid-spring.
Although it needs no pruning, the
flowering stems can be cut for
indoor arrangements.

CULTIVATION *Grow in reliably moist,
fertile, neutral to acid soil, in partial
shade with shelter from cold winds.
Maintain a mulch of leafmold or
shredded bark around the base of the
plant. Little pruning is necessary.*

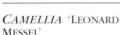 ☼ ◊◊ Z 7-9 H 10-8 ‡15 ft (5m) ↔10ft (3m)

CAMELLIA 'LEONARD MESSEL'

This spreading, evergreen shrub
with oval, leathery, dark green
leaves is one of the hardier
camellias. It produces an abundance
of large, flattish to cup-shaped, semi-
double, clear pink flowers from
early to late spring. Handsome in
a shrub border.

CULTIVATION *Best in moist but well-
drained, fertile, neutral to acid soil.
Position in semi-shade with shelter from
cold, drying winds. Maintain a mulch
of shredded bark or leafmold around
the base. Pruning is not necessary.*

 ☼ ◊◊ Z 7-9 H 10-8 ‡12ft (4m) ↔10ft (3m)

CAMELLIA × WILLIAMSII

Cultivars of *C. × williamsii* are strong-growing, evergreen shrubs much valued for their bright, lustrous foliage and the unsurpassed elegance of their roselike flowers that range from pure white to crimson. Most flower in mid- and late spring, although 'Anticipation' and 'Mary Christian' begin to flower in late winter. The flowers are susceptible to damage in hard frosts. They make handsome specimens for a conservatory or shrub border, and they can be trained against a wall as an informal mass or as a more open and formal espalier. Avoid sites exposed to morning sun.

CULTIVATION *Best in moist but well-drained, acid to neutral soil, in partial shade. Shelter from frost and cold winds, and mulch with shredded bark. Prune young plants after flowering to promote bushiness; wall-trained shrubs should be allowed to develop a strong central stem.*

☼ ◐ ◊◊ Z 7-9 H 10-8

1 ‡12ft (4m) ↔ 6ft (2m)

2 ‡10ft (3m) ↔ 8ft (2.5m)

3 ‡15ft (5m) ↔ 8ft (2.5m)

1 *C. × williamsii* 'Anticipation' **2** *C. × williamsii* 'Brigadoon' **3** *C. × williamsii* 'Donation'

4 ↕↔ 12ft (4m)

5 ↕ 12ft (4m) ↔ 8ft (2.5m)

6 ↕ 12ft (4m) ↔ 8ft (2.5m)

7 ↕ 12ft (4m) ↔ 8ft (2.5m)

8 ↕ 12ft (4m) ↔ 8ft (2.5m)

9 ↕↔ 10ft (3m)

4 *C.* x *williamsii* 'George Blandford'   **5** *C.* x *williamsii* 'Joan Trehane'
6 *C.* x *williamsii* 'J.C. Williams'   **7** *C.* x *williamsii* 'Mary Christian'   **8** *C.* x *williamsii* 'Saint Ewe'
9 *C.* x *williamsii* 'Water Lily'

CAMPANULA COCHLEARIIFOLIA

Fairies' thimbles is a low-growing, rosette-forming perennial bearing, in mid-summer, abundant clusters of open, bell-shaped, mauve-blue or white flowers. The bright green leaves are heart-shaped. It spreads freely by means of creeping stems and so can be invasive. Particularly effective if allowed to colonize areas of gravel, paving crevices, or the tops of dry walls.

CULTIVATION *Prefers moist but well-drained soil, in sun or partial shade. To restrict spread, pull up unwanted plants.*

☼ ◐ ◊ Z 5-7 H 7-4   ‡to 3in (8cm)
↔to 20in (50cm) or more

CAMPANULA GLOMERATA 'SUPERBA'

A fast-growing, clump-forming perennial carrying dense heads of large, bell-shaped, purple-violet flowers in summer. The lance-shaped to oval, mid-green leaves are arranged in rosettes at the base of the plant and along the stems. Excellent in herbaceous borders or informal, cottage-style gardens.

CULTIVATION *Best in moist but well-drained, neutral to alkaline soil, in sun or semi-shade. Cut back after flowering to encourage a second flush of flowers.*

☼ ◐ ◊◊ Z 3-8 H 8-1   ‡30in (75cm)
↔3ft (1m) or more

CAMPANULA LACTIFLORA 'LODDON ANNA'

An upright, branching perennial producing sprays of large, nodding, broadly bell-shaped, soft lilac-pink flowers in mid-summer. The oval, mid-green leaves are arranged in rosettes at the base of the plant and scattered along the stems. Makes an excellent border perennial but may need staking in an exposed site.

CULTIVATION *Best in moist but well-drained, fertile soil, in full sun or partial shade. Deadhead to encourage a second, although less profuse, flush of flowers.*

☼◑ ◊◊ Z 5-7 H 7-4 ↕4–5ft (1.2–1.5m)
↔24in (60cm)

CAMPANULA PORTENSCHLAGIANA

The Dalmatian bellflower is a robust, mound-forming, evergreen perennial that produces long, bell-shaped, deep purple flowers from mid- to late summer. The leaves are toothed and mid-green. Good in a rock garden or on a sunny bank, but it may become invasive.

CULTIVATION *Best in moist but well-drained soil, in sun or partial shade. Very vigorous, so plant away from smaller, less robust plants.*

☼◑ ◊ Z 4-7 H 7-1 ↕to 6in (15cm)
↔20in (50cm) or more

CAMPSIS X *TAGLIABUANA* 'MADAME GALEN'

A woody-stemmed climber that clings with aerial roots, suitable for training against a wall, fence, or pillar or up into a tree. From late summer to autumn, clusters of trumpet-shaped, orange-red flowers are borne among the narrowly oval, toothed leaflets.

CULTIVATION *Prefers moist but well-drained, fertile soil, in a sunny, sheltered site. Tie in new growth until the allotted space is covered by a strong framework. Prune back hard each winter to promote bushiness.*

☼ ◐◖ Z 5-9 H 9-5   ‡30ft (10m) or more

CARDIOCRINUM GIGANTEUM

The giant lily is a spectacular, summer-flowering, bulbous perennial with trumpet-shaped white flowers that are flushed with maroon-purple at the throats. The stems are stout and the leaves broadly oval and glossy green. It needs careful siting and can take up to seven years to flower. Grow in woodland or in a sheltered border in shade.

CULTIVATION *Best in deep, moist but well-drained, reliably cool, organic soil, in semi-shade. Intolerant of hot or dry conditions. Slugs can be a problem.*

☼ ◖ Z 7-9 H 9-7   ‡5–12ft (1.5–4m)
↔18in (45cm)

CAREX ELATA 'AUREA'

Bowles' golden sedge is a colorful, tussock-forming, deciduous perennial for a moist border, bog garden, or the margins of a pond or stream. The bright leaves are narrow and golden-yellow. In spring and early summer, small spikes of relatively inconspicuous, dark brown flowers are carried above the leaves. Often sold as *C.* 'Bowles' Golden'.

CULTIVATION *Grow in moist or wet, reasonably fertile soil. Position in full sun or partial shade.*

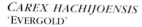 ☼◐ ◊♦ Z 5-9 H 9-3 ↕to 28in (70cm)
↔18in (45cm)

CAREX HACHIJOENSIS 'EVERGOLD'

A popular, evergreen, variegated sedge, bright and densely tufted with narrow, dark green, yellow-striped leaves. Spikes of tiny, dark brown flowers are borne in mid- and late spring. Tolerates better drainage than many sedges and is suitable for a mixed border.

CULTIVATION *Needs moist but well drained, fertile soil, in sun or partial shade. Remove dead leaves in summer.*

☼◐ ◊◊ Z 6-9 H 9-4 ↕12in (30cm)
↔14in (35cm)

CARPENTERIA CALIFORNICA

The California native is a summer-flowering, evergreen shrub bearing large, fragrant white flowers with showy yellow stamens. The glossy, dark green leaves are narrowly oval. It is suitable for wall training, which overcomes its sometimes sprawling habit and provides some protection where it is marginally hardy.

CULTIVATION *Grow in well-drained soil, in full sun with shelter from cold winds. In spring, remove branches that have become exhausted by flowering, cutting them back to their bases.*

☼ ◊ Z 8-9 H 12-8   ‡6ft (2m) ↔6ft (2m)

CARYOPTERIS × CLANDONENSIS 'HEAVENLY BLUE'

A compact, upright, deciduous shrub grown for its clusters of intensely dark blue flowers that appear in late summer and early autumn. The irregularly toothed leaves are gray-green above and silver-hairy beneath.

CULTIVATION *Grow in well-drained, moderately fertile, light soil, in full sun. Prune all stems back to low buds in late spring. A woody framework will soon develop, which should not be cut into.*

☼ ◊ Z 6-9 H 9-4   ‡↔3ft (1m)

CASSIOPE 'EDINBURGH'

A heatherlike, upright, evergreen shrub producing nodding, bell-shaped flowers in spring; these are white, with small, greenish brown outer petals. The scalelike, dark green leaves closely overlap along the stems. Good for a rock garden (but not among limestone).

CULTIVATION *Grow in reliably moist, organic, acid soil, in partial shade. Trim after flowering.*

☼ ◐ ◊ Z 2-6 H 6-1   ↕↔ to 10in (25cm)

CEANOTHUS ARBOREUS 'TREWITHEN BLUE'

A vigorous, spreading, evergreen shrub valued for its profusion of fragrant, mid-blue flowers in spring and early summer. The leaves are dark green and rounded. Suitable for growing against a wall or in a large, sheltered border.

CULTIVATION *Grow in well-drained, fertile soil, in full sun with shelter from cold, drying winds. Tip-prune young plants in spring. Once established, prune only to shape, after flowering.*

☼ ◊ Z 9-10 H 10-8   ↕20ft (6m) ↔25ft (8m)

CEANOTHUS 'AUTUMNAL BLUE'

A vigorous, evergreen shrub that produces a profusion of tiny but vivid, rich sky blue flowers from late summer to autumn. The leaves are broadly oval and glossy dark green. One of the hardiest of the evergreen ceanothus, it is suitable in an open border as well as for informal training on walls; especially where marginally hardy.

CULTIVATION *Grow in well-drained, moderately fertile soil, in full sun with shelter from cold winds. Tip-prune young plants in spring, and trim established plants after flowering.*

☼ ◊ Z 9 -10 H 10-8   ↔ 10ft (3m)

CEANOTHUS 'BLUE MOUND'

This mound-forming, late spring-flowering ceanothus is an evergreen shrub carrying masses of rich, dark blue flowers. The leaves are finely toothed and glossy dark green. Ideal for groundcover, for cascading over banks or low walls, or in a large, sunny rock garden.

CULTIVATION *Grow in well-drained, fertile soil, in full sun. Tip-prune young plants and trim established ones after flowering, in mid-summer.*

☼ ◊ Z 9-10 H 10-8   ↕ 5ft (1.5m) ↔ 6ft (2m)

CEANOTHUS × DELILEANUS 'GLOIRE DE VERSAILLES'

This deciduous ceanothus is a fast-growing shrub that flowers from mid-summer to early autumn. Large spikes of tiny, pale blue flowers are borne amid the broadly oval, finely toothed, mid-green leaves. Ideal for a mixed border; it benefits from harder annual pruning than the evergreen ceanothus.

CULTIVATION *Grow in well-drained, fairly fertile, light soil, in sun. In spring, shorten the previous year's stems by half or more, or cut right back to a low framework.*

☼ ◊ Z 7-10 H 10-8   ↕↔ 5ft (1.5m)

CEANOTHUS THYRSIFLORUS VAR. REPENS

This low and spreading ceanothus is a mound-forming, evergreen shrub, bearing rounded clusters of tiny blue flowers in late spring and early summer. The leaves are dark green and glossy. A good shrub to clothe a sunny or slightly shaded bank, but needs the protection of a warm, sunny site in marginal areas.

CULTIVATION *Best in light, well-drained, fertile soil, in sun or light shade. Trim back after flowering to keep compact.*

☼◑ ◊ Z 8-10 H 10-8 ↕3ft (1m) ↔8ft (2.5m)

CERATOSTIGMA PLUMBAGINOIDES

A spreading, woody-based, sub-shrubby perennial bearing clusters of brilliant blue flowers in late summer. The oval, bright green leaves, carried on upright, slender red stems, become red-tinted in autumn. Good for a rock garden and as a groundcover.

CULTIVATION *Grow in light, moist but well-drained, moderately fertile soil. Choose a sheltered site in full sun. Cut back stems to about 1in (2.5cm) from the ground in early spring.*

☀ ◊ Z 6-9 H 9-6   ‡to 18in (45cm)
                          ↔to 12in (30cm) or more

CERATOSTIGMA WILLMOTTIANUM

The Chinese plumbago is an open and spreading, deciduous shrub carrying pale to mid-blue flowers during late summer and autumn. The roughly diamond-shaped, mid-green leaves turn red in autumn. Dies back to the ground in cold winters. Suitable for a sheltered mixed border.

CULTIVATION *Grow in any fertile soil, including dry soil, in full sun. In mid-spring, cut out all dead wood and shorten the remaining stems to a low woody framework.*

☀ ◊ Z 6-9 H 9-6   ‡3ft (1m) ↔5ft (1.5m)

CERCIS SILIQUASTRUM

The Judas tree is a handsome, broadly spreading, deciduous tree that gradually develops a rounded crown. Clusters of pealike, bright pink flowers appear on the previous year's wood in mid-spring, either before or with the heart-shaped leaves. The foliage is bronze when young, maturing to dark blue-green, then to yellow in autumn.

CULTIVATION *Grow in deep, reliably well-drained, fertile soil, in full sun or light dappled shade. Prune young trees to shape in early summer, removing any winter-damaged growth.*

☼ ◐ ◊ Z 6-9 H 9-6   ‡↔ 30ft (10m)

CHAENOMELES SPECIOSA 'MOERLOOSEI'

A fast-growing and wide-spreading, deciduous shrub bearing large white flowers, flushed dark pink, in early spring. Tangled, spiny branches carry oval, glossy dark green leaves. The flowers are followed in autumn by apple-shaped, aromatic, yellow-green fruits. Use as a free-standing shrub or train against a wall.

CULTIVATION *Grow in well-drained, moderately fertile soil, in full sun for best flowering, or light shade. If wall-trained, shorten sideshoots to 2 or 3 leaves in late spring. Free-standing shrubs require little pruning.*

☼ ◐ ◊ Z 5-8 H 8-5 ‡8ft (2.5m) ↔15ft (5m)

CHAENOMELES × SUPERBA 'CRIMSON AND GOLD'

This spreading, deciduous shrub bears masses of dark red flowers with conspicuous golden-yellow anthers from spring until summer. The dark green leaves appear on the spiny branches just after the first flowers; these are followed by yellow-green fruits. Useful as a groundcover or low hedging.

CULTIVATION *Grow in well-drained, fertile soil, in sun. Trim lightly after flowering; shorten sideshoots to 2 or 3 leaves if grown against a wall.*

☼ ◊ Z 5-8 H 9-4   ↕3ft (1m) ↔6ft (2m)

CHAENOMELES × SUPERBA 'PINK LADY'

A rounded, deciduous shrub with spiny, spreading branches that bear cup-shaped, dark pink flowers from early spring. The glossy, dark green leaves appear after the first bloom of flowers; aromatic, yellow-green fruits follow in autumn.

CULTIVATION *Grow in any but water-logged soil, in full sun or partial shade. Trim back after flowering, as necessary. If grown against a wall, shorten side-shoots to 2 or 3 leaves, in summer.*

☼ ◊◊ Z 5-8 H 9-4   ↕5ft (1.5m) ↔6ft (2m)

LAWSON CYPRESSES (*CHAMAECYPARIS LAWSONIANA*)

Cultivars of *C. lawsoniana* are very popular, evergreen coniferous trees, available in many different shapes, sizes, and foliage colors. They all have red-brown bark and dense crowns of branches that droop at the tips. The flattened sprays of dense, aromatic foliage, occasionally bearing small, rounded cones, make the larger types of Lawson cypress very suitable for thick hedging; examples include the bright blue-gray 'Pembury Blue' or the golden-yellow 'Lane'. Use compact cultivars in smaller gardens; dwarf types, such as 'Ellwood's Gold', make eye-catching trees for containers, rock gardens, or borders.

CULTIVATION *Grow in moist but well-drained soil, in sun. They tolerate alkaline soil but not exposed sites. Trim regularly from spring to autumn; do not cut into older wood. To train as formal hedges, pruning must begin on young plants.*

☼ ◊ Z 5-9 H 9-4

1 ‡5ft (1.5m) or more ↔ 24in (60cm)　2 ‡to 130ft (40m) ↔ to 15ft (5m)　3 ‡to 50ft (15m) ↔ 6–15ft (2–5m)

1 *C. lawsoniana* 'Ellwood's Gold'　2 *C. lawsoniana* 'Lane'　3 *C. lawsoniana* 'Pembury Blue'

CHAMAECYPARIS NOOTKATENSIS 'PENDULA'

This large and drooping conifer develops an open crown as it matures. Hanging from the arching branches are evergreen sprays of dark green foliage with small, round cones that ripen in spring. Its unusual habit makes it an interesting feature for a large garden.

CULTIVATION *Best in full sun, in moist but well-drained, neutral to slightly acid soil; will also tolerate dry, alkaline soil. Regular pruning is not required.*

☼ ◊◊ Z 4-7 H 7-1   ‡to 100ft (30m)
                      ↔to 25ft (8m)

CHAMAECYPARIS OBTUSA 'NANA GRACILIS'

This dwarf form of Hinoki cypress is an evergreen, coniferous tree with a dense pyramidal habit. The aromatic, rich green foliage is carried in rounded, flattened sprays, bearing small cones that ripen to yellow-brown. Useful in a large rock garden, particularly to give an Oriental style.

CULTIVATION *Grow in moist but well-drained, neutral to slightly acid soil, in full sun. Also tolerates dry, alkaline soil. Regular pruning is not necessary.*

☼ ◊ Z 4-8 H 8-1   ‡10ft (3m) ↔6ft (2m)

CHAMAECYPARIS OBTUSA 'TETRAGONA AUREA'

This cultivar of Hinoki cypress, with golden to bronze-yellow, evergreen foliage, is a conical, coniferous tree. The aromatic foliage, carried in flattened sprays on upward-sweeping stems, is greener in the shade and bears small green cones that ripen to brown. Grow as a specimen tree.

CULTIVATION *Best in moist but well-drained, neutral to slightly acid soil. Tolerates alkaline conditions. For the best foliage color, position in full sun. No regular pruning is required.*

☼ ◊ Z 4-8 H 7-1 ‡30ft (10m) ↔10ft (3m)

CHAMAECYPARIS PISIFERA 'BOULEVARD'

A broad, evergreen conifer that develops into a conical tree with an open crown. The soft, blue-green foliage is borne in flattened sprays with angular green cones that mature to brown. Very neat and compact in habit; an interesting specimen tree for poorly drained, damp soil.

CULTIVATION *Grow in reliably moist, preferably neutral to acid soil, in full sun. No regular pruning is required.*

☼ ◊◖ Z 4-8 H 8-1 ‡30ft (10m) ↔to 15ft (5m)

CHIMONANTHUS PRAECOX 'GRANDIFLORUS'

Wintersweet is a vigorous, upright, deciduous shrub grown for the fragrant flowers borne on its bare branches in winter; on this cultivar they are larger, cup-shaped, and deep yellow with maroon stripes inside. The leaves are mid-green. Suitable for a shrub border or for training against a sunny wall.

CULTIVATION *Grow in well-drained, fertile soil, in a sunny, sheltered site. Best left unpruned when young so that mature flowering wood can develop. Cut back flowered stems of wall-trained plants in spring.*

☼ ◊ Z 7-9 H 9-7   ↕12ft (4m) ↔10ft (3m)

CHIONODOXA LUCILIAE

Glory of the snow is a small, bulbous perennial bearing star-shaped, clear blue flowers with white eyes in early spring. The glossy green leaves are usually curved backward. Grow in a sunny rock garden or naturalize under deciduous trees. Sometimes referred to as *C. gigantea* of gardens.

CULTIVATION *Grow in any well-drained soil, with a position in full sun. Plant bulbs 3in (8cm) deep in autumn.*

☼ ◊ Z 3-9 H 9-1   ↕6in (15cm) ↔1¼in (3cm)

CHOISYA TERNATA

Mexican orange blossom is a fast-growing, rounded, evergreen shrub valued for its attractive foliage and fragrant flowers. The aromatic, dark green leaves are divided into three leaflets, and clusters of star-shaped white flowers appear in spring. An excellent, pollution-tolerant shrub for city gardens.

CULTIVATION *Grow in well-drained, fairly fertile soil, in full sun. Naturally forms a well-shaped bush without pruning. Cutting back flowered shoots encourages a second flush of flowers.*

☼ ◊ Z 8-10 H 10-8   ‡↔ 8ft (2.5m)

CHOISYA TERNATA 'SUNDANCE'

This slower-growing, bright yellow-leaved variety of Mexican orange blossom is a compact, evergreen shrub. The aromatic leaves, divided into three leaflets, are a duller yellow-green if positioned in shade. Flowers are rare. Grow against a warm wall for extra protection where marginally hardy.

CULTIVATION *Best in well-drained, fertile soil, in full sun for the best leaf color. Provide shelter from cold winds. Trim wayward shoots in summer, removing any winter-damaged shoots in spring.*

☼ ◊ Z 8-10 H 10-8   ‡↔ 8ft (2.5m)

FLORISTS' CHRYSANTHEMUMS

The upright and bushy perennials known as florists' chrysanthemums are grown primarily for their bright, showy flowerheads that come in a wide range of shapes and colors; they are traditionally used for exhibition and cutting. The lobed or feathery leaves are aromatic and dark green. Flowers appear in early, mid- or late autumn, according to the cultivar; 'Pennine Flute' starts flowering in late summer. Flowerhead shape is also very variable, in the daisylike heads of 'Pennine Alfie', for example, or the reflexed petals of 'George Griffiths'. Lift in autumn and store overwinter in frost-free conditions. Plant out after the risk of frost.

CULTIVATION *Grow in moist but well-drained, neutral to slightly acid soil that is enriched with well-rotted manure. Choose a sheltered site in sun. Flower stems may require staking. Apply a balanced fertilizer when in growth, until buds begin to show.*

☼ ◊ Z 6-9 H 12-1

1 ↕ 4½–5ft (1.3–1.5m) ↔ 30in (75cm)

2 ↕ 12–24in (30–60cm) ↔ 24in (60cm)

1 *C.* 'George Griffiths' **2** *C.* 'Bronze Fairy'

3 ↕4ft (1.2m) ↔ 30in (75cm)

4 ↕4ft (1.2m) ↔ 30in (75cm)

5 ↕4ft (1.2m) ↔ 30in (75cm)

6 ↕4ft (1.2m) ↔ 24–30in (60–75cm)

7 ↕4ft (1.2m) ↔ 30in (75cm)

8 ↕4ft (1.2m) ↔ 24–30in (60–75cm)

9 ↕4ft (1.2m) ↔ 24–30in (60–75cm)

10 ↕4ft (1.2m) ↔ 24–30in (60–75cm)

3 *C.* 'Madeleine' **4** *C.* 'Pennine Alfie' **5** *C.* 'Pennine Flute' **6** *C.* 'Pennine Oriel' **7** *C.* 'Purple Pennine Wine' **8** *C.* 'Wendy' **9** *C.* 'Salmon Margaret' **10** *C.* 'Yvonne Arnaud'

CIMICIFUGA RACEMOSA

The black snakeroot is a clump-forming perennial that produces long, sometimes curved spikes of unpleasantly scented, tiny white flowers in mid-summer. The dark green leaves are broadly oval to lance-shaped. Suitable for a bog garden, moist border, or in light woodland, away from paths and seating areas.

CULTIVATION *Grow in reliably moist, fertile, preferably organic soil, in partial shade. Provide clumps with support, using ring stakes or similar.*

☼ ◑ ◗ Z 3-8 H 8-1   ‡4–7ft (1.2–2.2m) ↔24in (60cm)

CISTUS × AGUILARII 'MACULATUS'

This fast-growing evergreen shrub bears large, solitary white flowers for a few weeks in early and mid-summer. At the center of each flower is a mass of bright golden yellow stamens surrounded by five crimson blotches. The lance-shaped leaves are sticky, aromatic, and bright green. Excellent on a sunny bank or in containers.

CULTIVATION *Grow in well-drained, poor to moderately fertile soil, in a sunny, sheltered site. If necessary, trim lightly in early spring or after flowering, but do not prune hard.*

☼ ◊ Z 9-10 H 10-8   ‡↔4ft (1.2m)

CISTUS × *HYBRIDUS*

A dense, spreading shrub producing
white flowers with yellow blotches
at the centers. These are borne singly
or in clusters of two or three during
late spring and early summer. The
aromatic leaves are wrinkled, oval,
and dark green. Suitable for a shrub
border or rock garden; it benefits
from the protection of a wall where
marginally hardy. Sometimes known
as *C.* × *corbariensis*.

CULTIVATION *Grow in well-drained,
poor to moderately fertile soil, in a
sheltered site in full sun. Tolerates
alkaline soil. If necessary, trim lightly
after flowering, but do not prune hard.*

☼ ◊ Z 8-10 H 8-1 ‡3ft (1m) ↔5ft (1.5m)

CISTUS × *PURPUREUS*

This summer-flowering, rounded,
evergreen shrub bears few-flowered
clusters of dark pink flowers with
maroon blotches at the base of each
petal. The dark green leaves are
borne on upright, sticky, red-flushed
shoots. Good in a large rock garden,
on a sunny bank, or in a container.

CULTIVATION *Grow in well-drained,
poor to moderately fertile soil. Choose a
sheltered site in full sun. Tolerates
alkaline soil. Can be trimmed lightly
after flowering, but avoid hard pruning.*

☼ ◊ Z 9-10 H 10-8 ‡↔3ft (1m)

EARLY-FLOWERING CLEMATIS

The early-flowering species clematis are valued for their showy displays during spring and early summer. They are generally deciduous climbers with mid- to dark green, divided leaves. The flowers of the earliest species to bloom are usually bell-shaped; those of the later *C. montana* types are either flat or saucer-shaped. Flowers are often followed by decorative seedheads. Many clematis, especially *C. montana* types, are vigorous and will grow very quickly, making them ideal for covering featureless or unattractive walls. Allowed to grow through deciduous shrubs, they may flower before their host comes into leaf.

CULTIVATION *Grow in well-drained, fertile, organic soil, in full sun or semi-shade. The roots and base of the plant should be shaded. Immediately after flowering, tie in young growth carefully and prune out shoots that exceed the allotted space.*

☼ ◑ ◊ Z 6-9 H 9-6

3 ↕30ft (10m) ↔ 12ft (4m)

1 ↕6–10ft (2–3m) ↔ 5ft (1.5m)   **2** ↕30ft (10m) ↔ 6–10ft (2–3m)   **4** ↕15ft (5m) ↔ 6–10ft (2–3m)

1 *C. macropetala* 'Markham's Pink'   **2** *C. montana* var. *rubens*   **3** *C. montana* f. *grandiflora*
4 *C. montana* 'Tetrarose'

MID-SEASON CLEMATIS

The mid-season, mainly hybrid clematis are twining and deciduous climbers bearing an abundance of stunning flowers throughout the summer months. Their flowers are large, saucer-shaped, and outward-facing with a plentiful choice of shapes and colors. Toward the end of the summer, blooms may darken. The leaves are pale to mid-green and divided into several leaflets. Mid-season clematis look very attractive scrambling through other shrubs, especially if they bloom before or after their host. Top growth may be damaged in severe winters, but plants are usually quick to recover.

CULTIVATION *Grow in well-drained, fertile, organic soil, with the roots in shade and the heads in sun. Pastel flowers may fade in sun; better in semi-shade. Mulch in late winter, avoiding the immediate crown. Cut back older stems to strong buds in late winter, and tie in young growth carefully.*

☼ ◐ ◊ Z 4-9 H 9-3

1 ↕ 8ft (2.5m) ↔ 3ft (1m)   **2** ↕ 10ft (3m) ↔ 3ft (1m)   **3** ↕ 8ft (2.5m) ↔ 3ft (1m)

4 ↕ 6–10ft (2–3m) ↔ 3ft (1m)   **5** ↕ 6–10ft (2–3m) ↔ 3ft (1m)   **6** ↕ 6–10ft (2–3m) ↔ 3ft (1m)

1 *C.* 'Doctor Ruppel' **2** *C.* 'Henryi' **3** *C.* 'Lasurstern' **4** *C.* 'Nelly Moser' **5** *C.* 'The President'
6 *C.* 'Vyvyan Pennel'

LATE-FLOWERING CLEMATIS

Many large-flowered hybrid clematis flower from mid- to late summer, when the season for the *C. viticella* types, characterized usually by smaller but more profuse flowers, also begins. These are followed by other late-flowering species. They may be deciduous or evergreen, with an enormous variety of flower and leaf shapes and colors. Many, like 'Perle d'Azur', are vigorous and will cover large areas of wall or disguise unsightly buildings. Some develop decorative, silvery gray seedheads that last well into winter. With the exception of 'Bill Mackenzie', most look good when trained up into small trees.

CULTIVATION *Grow in organic, fertile soil with good drainage, with the base in shade and the upper part in sun or partial shade. Mulch in late winter, avoiding the immediate crown. Cut back hard each year before growth begins.*

☼ ☼➊ ◊ Z 6-9 H 9-5

1 ↕12ft (4m) ↔ 5ft (1.5m)

2 ↕22ft (7m) ↔ 6–10ft (2–3m)

3 ↕8ft (2.5m) ↔ 5ft (1.5m)

1 *C.* 'Alba Luxurians' **2** *C.* 'Bill Mackenzie' **3** *C.* 'Duchess of Albany'

4 ↕6–10ft (2–3m) ↔ 3ft (1m)

7 ↕10ft (3m) ↔ 5ft (1.5m)

5 ↕10–15ft (3–5m) ↔ 5ft (1.5m) **6** ↕10ft (3m) ↔ 3ft (1m) **8** ↕10ft (3m) ↔ 3ft (1m)

10 ↕10ft (3m) ↔ 3ft (1m)

9 ↕10ft (3m) ↔ 3ft (1m) **11** ↕10ft (3m) ↔ 3ft (1m) **12** ↕20–22ft (6–7m) ↔ 6–10ft (2–3m)

4 *C.* 'Comtesse de Bouchaud' **5** *C.* 'Etoile Violette' **6** *C.* 'Jackmanii' **7** *C.* 'Madame Julia Correvon' **8** *C.* 'Minuet' **9** *C.* 'Perle d'Azur' **10** *C.* 'Venosa Violacea' **11** *C. viticella* 'Purpurea Plena Elegans' **12** *C. rehderiana*

CLIANTHUS PUNICEUS

Lobster claw is an evergreen, woody-stemmed, climbing shrub with scrambling shoots. Drooping clusters of clawlike, brilliant red flowers appear in spring and early summer. The mid-green leaves are divided into many narrowly oblong leaflets. Suitable for wall-training or the walls of a greenhouse where not hardy.

CULTIVATION *Grow in well-drained, fairly fertile soil, in sun with shelter from wind. Pinch-prune young plants to promote bushiness; otherwise, keep pruning to a minimum.*

☀ ◊ Z 7-11 H 12-7 ‡12ft (4m) ↔10ft (3m)

CODONOPSIS CONVOLVULACEA

A slender, herbaceous, summer-flowering climber with twining stems bearing delicate, bell- to saucer-shaped, soft blue-violet flowers. The leaves are lance-shaped to oval and bright green. Allow to scramble through other plants in a herbaceous border or woodland garden.

CULTIVATION *Grow in moist but well-drained, light, fertile soil, ideally in dappled shade. Provide support or grow through neighboring plants. Cut to the base in spring.*

☀ ◊◊ Z 7-9 H 9-7 ‡to 6ft (2m)

COLCHICUM SPECIOSUM 'ALBUM'

This autumn crocus is a cormous perennial producing thick, weather-resistant, goblet-shaped, pure white flowers. The narrowly oval, mid-green leaves appear in spring and die down long before the flowers appear. Grow at the front of a border, at the foot of a bank, or in a rock garden. All parts of the plant are highly toxic if ingested.

CULTIVATION *Grow in moist but well-drained soil, in full sun. Plant bulbs in late summer, 4in (10cm) below the surface of soil that is deep and fertile.*

☼ ◊ Z 4-9 H 9-1 ‡7in (18cm) ↔4in (10cm)

CONVALLARIA MAJALIS

Lily-of-the-valley is a creeping perennial bearing small, very fragrant white flowers that hang from arching stems in late spring. The narrowly oval leaves are mid- to dark green. An excellent ground-cover plant for woodland gardens and other shady areas, spreading rapidly under suitable conditions.

CULTIVATION *Grow in reliably moist, fertile, organic, leafy soil in deep or partial shade. Top-dress with leaf mold in autumn.*

◑●◒ ◊ Z 2-7 H 7-1 ‡9in (23cm) ↔12in (30cm)

CONVOLVULUS CNEORUM

This compact, rounded, evergreen
shrub bears masses of funnel-shaped,
shining white flowers with yellow
centers that open from late spring to
summer. The narrowly lance-shaped
leaves are silvery green. Excellent in
a rock garden or on a sunny bank.
Where not hardy, grow in a
container and move into a cool
greenhouse in winter. Makes an
attractive topiary.

CULTIVATION *Grow in gritty, very well-
drained, poor to moderately fertile soil,
in a sunny, sheltered site. Trim back
after flowering, if necessary.*

☼ ◊ Z 8-10 H 10-8 ‡24in (60cm) ↔36in (90cm)

CONVOLVULUS SABATIUS

A small, trailing perennial bearing
trumpet-shaped, vibrant blue-purple
flowers from summer into early
autumn. The slender stems are
clothed with small, oval, mid-green
leaves. Excellent in crevices between
rocks. Grow as a container plant to
be overwintered inside where not
hardy. Sometimes offered as
C. mauritanicus.

CULTIVATION *Grow in well-drained,
gritty, poor to moderately fertile soil.
Provide a sheltered site in full sun.*

☼ ◊ Z 8-9 H 9-8 ‡6in (15cm) ↔20in (50cm)

CORDYLINE AUSTRALIS 'ALBERTII'

This New Zealand cabbage palm is a palmlike, evergreen tree carrying lance-shaped, matte green leaves with red midribs, cream stripes, and pink margins. Clusters of creamy white flowers appear on mature specimens in summer, followed by white or blue-tinted berries. Unlikely to grow tall in cool climates, where it is best in a container for placing out during the warmer months.

CULTIVATION *Best in well-drained, fertile soil or soil mix, in sun or partial shade. Remove dead leaves and cut out faded flower stems as necessary.*

☼☀ ◊ Z10-11 H 12-1 ‡30ft (10m) ↔12ft (4m)

CORNUS ALBA 'SIBIRICA'

A deciduous shrub that is usually grown for the winter effect of its bright coral-red, bare young stems. Small clusters of creamy white flowers appear in late spring and early summer amid oval, dark green leaves that turn red in autumn. Particularly effective in a waterside planting or any situation where the winter stems show up well.

CULTIVATION *Grow in any moderately fertile soil, in sun. For the best stem effect, cut back hard and feed every spring once established, although this will be at the expense of the flowers.*

☼ ◊◊ Z 2-8 H 8-1 ‡↔ 10ft (3m)

CORNUS ALBA 'SPAETHII'

A vigorous and upright, deciduous shrub bearing bright green, elliptic leaves that are margined with yellow. It is usually grown for the effect of its bright red young shoots in winter. In late spring and early summer, small clusters of creamy white flowers appear amid the foliage. Very effective wherever the stems show up well in winter.

CULTIVATION *Grow in any moderately fertile soil, preferably in full sun. For the best stem effect, but at the expense of flowers, cut back hard and feed each year in spring, once established.*

☼ ◐◑ Z 2-8 H 8-1   ↕↔ 10ft (3m)

CORNUS CANADENSIS

The creeping dogwood is a superb groundcover perennial for under-planting a shrub border or wood-land garden. Flower clusters with prominent white bracts appear above the oval, bright green leaves during late spring and early summer. These are followed by round, bright red berries.

CULTIVATION *Best in moist, acid, leafy soil, in partial shade. Divide plants in spring or autumn to restrict spread or increase plants.*

☼ ◐ Z 2-7 H 7-1   ↕6in (15cm) ↔indefinite

CORNUS KOUSA
VAR. *CHINENSIS*

This broadly conical, deciduous tree with flaky bark is valued for its dark green, oval leaves, which turn an impressive, deep crimson-purple in autumn. The early summer flowers have long white bracts, fading to red-pink. An effective specimen tree, especially in a woodland setting.

CULTIVATION *Best in well-drained, fertile, neutral to acid soil that is rich in organic matter, in full sun or partial shade. Keep pruning to a minimum.*

☼◑ ◊ Z 5-8 H 8-4 ‡22ft (7m) ↔ 15ft (5m)

CORNUS MAS

The cornelian cherry is a vigorous and spreading, deciduous shrub or small tree. Clusters of small yellow flowers provide attractive late winter color on the bare branches. The oval, dark green leaves turn red-purple in autumn, giving a display at the same time as the fruits ripen to red. Particularly fine as a specimen tree for a woodland garden.

CULTIVATION *Tolerates any well-drained soil, in sun or partial shade. Pruning is best kept to a minimum.*

☼◑ ◊ Z 5-8 H 8-4 ↔ 15ft (5m)

CORNUS STOLONIFERA 'FLAVIRAMEA'

This vigorous, deciduous shrub makes a bright display of its bare yellow-green young shoots in winter, before the oval, dark green leaves emerge in spring. Clusters of white flowers appear in late spring and early summer. The leaves redden in autumn. Excellent in a bog garden or in wet soil near water.

CULTIVATION *Grow in reliably moist soil, in full sun. Restrict spread by cutting out 1 in 4 old stems annually. Prune all stems hard and feed each year in early spring for the best display of winter stems.*

☼ ◊ Z 2-8 H 8-1   ‡6ft (2m) ↔12ft (4m)

CORREA BACKHOUSEANA

The Australian fuchsia is a dense, spreading, evergreen shrub with small clusters of tubular, pale red-green or cream flowers during late autumn to late spring. The hairy, rust-red stems are clothed with oval, dark green leaves. Where marginally hardy, grow against a wall or over-winter in frost-free conditions.

CULTIVATION *Grow in well drained, fertile, acid to neutral soil, in full sun. Trim back after flowering, if necessary.*

☼ ◊ Z 9-10 H 10-8   ‡3–6ft (1–2m)
↔5–8ft (1.5–2.5m)

CORTADERIA SELLOANA 'AUREOLINEATA'

This pampas grass, with rich yellow-margined, arching leaves which age to dark golden-yellow, is a clump-forming, evergreen perennial. Feathery plumes of silvery flowers appear on tall stems in late summer. The flowerheads can be dried for decoration. Also known as 'Gold Band'.

CULTIVATION *Grow in well-drained, fertile soil, in full sun. In late winter, cut out all dead foliage and remove the previous year's flower stems: wear gloves to protect hands from the sharp foliage.*

☼ ◊ Z 7-10 H 12-7   ‡to 7ft (2.2m)

↔5ft (1.5m) or more

CORTADERIA SELLOANA 'SUNNINGDALE SILVER'

This sturdy pampas grass is a clump-forming, evergreen, weather-resistant perennial. In late summer, silky plumes of silvery cream flowers are borne on strong, upright stems above the narrow, arching, sharp-edged leaves. Where marginally hardy, protect the crown with a dry, loose winter mulch.

CULTIVATION *Grow in well-drained, fertile, not too heavy soil, in full sun. Remove old flower stems and any dead foliage in late winter: wear gloves to protect hands from the sharp foliage.*

☼ ◊ Z 7-10 H 12-7   ‡10ft (3m) or more
↔to 8ft (2.5m)

CORYDALIS SOLIDA 'GEORGE BAKER'

A low, clump-forming, herbaceous perennial bearing upright spires of deep salmon-rose flowers. These appear in spring above the delicate, finely cut, grayish green leaves. Excellent in a rock garden or in an alpine house.

CULTIVATION *Grow in sharply drained, moderately fertile soil or soil mix. Site in full sun, but tolerates some shade.*

:☼: ◊ Z 5-7 H 7-5   ↕to 10in (25cm)
                                ↔to 8in (20cm)

CORYLOPSIS PAUCIFLORA

This deciduous shrub bears hanging, catkinlike clusters of small, fragrant, pale yellow flowers on its bare branches during early to mid-spring. The oval, bright green leaves are bronze when they first emerge. Often naturally well-shaped, it makes a beautiful shrub for sites in dappled shade. The flowers may be damaged by frost.

CULTIVATION *Grow in moist but well-drained, organic, acid soil, in partial shade with shelter from wind. Allow room for the plant to spread. The natural shape is easily spoiled, so prune only to remove dead wood.*

:☼: ◊◊ Z 6-9 H 9-6   ↕5ft (1.5m) ↔8ft (2.5m)

CORYLUS AVELLANA 'CONTORTA'

The corkscrew hazel is a deciduous shrub bearing strongly twisted shoots that are particularly striking in winter; they can also be useful in flower arrangements. Winter interest is enhanced later in the season with the appearance of pale yellow catkins. The mid-green leaves are almost circular and toothed.

CULTIVATION *Grow in any well-drained, fertile soil, in sun or semi-shade. Once established, the twisted branches tend to become congested and may split, so thin out in late winter.*

☼ ◑ ◊ Z 3-9 H 9-1   ‡↔ 50ft (15m)

CORYLUS MAXIMA 'PURPUREA'

The purple filbert is a vigorous, open, deciduous shrub that, left unpruned, will grow into a small tree. In late winter, purplish catkins appear before the rounded, purple leaves emerge. The edible nuts ripen in autumn. Effective as a specimen tree, in a shrub border, or as part of a woodland planting.

CULTIVATION *Grow in any well-drained, fertile soil, in sun or partial shade. For the best leaf effect, but at the expense of the nuts, cut back hard in early spring.*

☼ ◑ ◊ Z 4-9 H 9-2   ‡ 20ft (6m) ↔ 15ft (5m)

COSMOS BIPINNATUS 'SONATA WHITE'

A branching but compact annual bearing single, saucer-shaped white flowers with yellow centers from summer to autumn at the ends of upright stems. The leaves are bright green and feathery. Excellent for exposed gardens. The flowers are good for cutting.

CULTIVATION *Grow in moist but well-drained, fertile soil, in full sun. Deadhead to prolong flowering.*

☼ ◊◊ annual H 12-1   ↕↔ 12in (30cm)

COTINUS COGGYGRIA 'ROYAL PURPLE'

This deciduous shrub is grown for its rounded, red-purple leaves, which turn a brilliant scarlet in autumn. Smokelike plumes of tiny, pink-purple flowers are produced on older wood. Good in a shrub border or as a specimen tree; where space permits, plant in groups.

CULTIVATION *Grow in moist but well-drained, fairly fertile soil, in full sun or partial shade. For the best foliage effect, cut back hard to a framework of older wood each spring, before growth begins.*

☼:☼ ◊◊ Z 5-8 H 8-3   ↕↔ 15ft (5m)

COTINUS 'GRACE'

A fast-growing, deciduous shrub
or small tree carrying oval, purple
leaves that turn a brilliant, translucent red in late autumn. The
smokelike clusters of tiny, pink-
purple flowers can appear in
abundance. Provides attractive
season-long color when planted
as a specimen or as part of
a shrub border.

CULTIVATION *Grow in moist but well-
drained, reasonably rich soil, in sun or
partial shade. For the best foliage,
prune hard each spring, just before new
growth begins.*

☼◐ ◊◊ Z 5-8 H 8-3 ‡20ft (6m) ↔15ft (5m)

COTONEASTER ATROPURPUREUS 'VARIEGATUS'

This compact, low-growing shrub,
sometimes seen as *C. horizontalis*
'Variegatus', bears fairly inconspicuous
red flowers in summer, followed in
autumn by a bright display of orange-
red fruits. The small, oval, white-
margined, deciduous leaves turn
pink and red before they drop.
Effective as a groundcover, as an
espalier, or in a rock garden.

CULTIVATION *Grow in well-drained,
moderately fertile soil, in full sun.
Tolerates dry soil and partial shade.
Pruning is best kept to a minimum.*

☼◐ ◊ Z 5-7 H 7-5 ‡18in (45cm) ↔36in (90cm)

COTONEASTER CONSPICUUS 'DECORUS'

A dense, mound-forming, evergreen shrub that is grown for its shiny red berries. These ripen in autumn and will often persist until late winter. Small white flowers appear amid the dark green leaves in summer. Good in a shrub border or under a canopy of deciduous trees.

CULTIVATION *Grow in well-drained, moderately fertile soil, ideally in full sun, but tolerates shade. If necessary, trim lightly to shape after flowering.*

☼◑ ◊ Z 6-8 H 8-6   ‡5ft (1.5m)
                          ↔6–8ft (2–2.5m)

COTONEASTER HORIZONTALIS

A deciduous shrub with spreading branches that form a herringbone pattern. The tiny, pinkish white flowers, which appear in summer, are attractive to bees. Bright red berries ripen in autumn, and the glossy, dark green leaves redden before they fall. Good as a ground cover, but most effective when espaliered against a wall.

CULTIVATION *Grow in any but water-logged soil. Site in full sun for the best berries, or semi-shade. Keep pruning to a minimum; if wall-trained, shorten outward-facing shoots in late winter.*

☼◑ ◊◊ Z 5-7 H 7-5 ‡3ft (1m) ↔5ft (1.5m)

COTONEASTER LACTEUS

This dense, evergreen shrub has arching branches that bear clusters of small, cup-shaped, milky white flowers from early to mid-summer. These are followed by brilliant red berries in autumn. The oval leaves are dark green and leathery, with gray-woolly undersides. Ideal for a wildlife garden, since it provides food for bees and birds; also makes a good windbreak or informal hedge.

CULTIVATION *Grow in well-drained, fairly fertile soil, in sun or semi-shade. Trim hedges lightly in summer, if necessary; keep pruning to a minimum.*

☼ ◐ ◊ Z 7-9 H 9-7 ‡↔ 12ft (4m)

COTONEASTER SIMONSII

An upright, deciduous or semi-evergreen shrub with small, cup-shaped white flowers in summer. The bright orange-red berries that follow ripen in autumn and persist well into winter. Autumn color also occurs in the glossy leaves, which redden from dark green. Good for hedging and can also be clipped fairly hard to a semi-formal outline.

CULTIVATION *Grow in any well-drained soil, in full sun or partial shade. Clip hedges to shape in late winter or early spring, or allow to grow naturally.*

☼ ◐ ◊ Z 6-8 H 8-6 ‡10ft (3m) ↔6ft (2m)

COTONEASTER STERNIANUS

This graceful, evergreen or semi-evergreen shrub bears arching branches that produce clusters of pink-tinged white flowers in summer, followed by a profusion of large, orange-red berries in autumn. The gray-green leaves have white under-sides. Good grown as a hedge.

CULTIVATION *Grow in any well-drained soil, in sun or semi-shade. Trim hedges lightly after flowering, if necessary; pruning is best kept to a minimum.*

☼ ◌ ◊ Z 7-9 H 9-7   ‡↔ 10ft (3m)

COTONEASTER X *WATERERI* 'JOHN WATERER'

A fast-growing, evergreen or semi-evergreen shrub or small tree valued for the abundance of red berries that clothe its branches in autumn. In summer, clusters of white flowers are carried among the lance-shaped, dark green leaves. Good on its own or at the back of a shrub border.

CULTIVATION *Grow in any but water-logged soil, in sun or semi-shade. When young, cut out any badly placed shoots to develop a framework of well-spaced branches. Thereafter, keep pruning to an absolute minimum.*

☼ ◌ ◊◊ Z 6-8 H 8-6   ‡↔ 15ft (5m)

CRAMBE CORDIFOLIA

A tall, clump-forming, vigorous
perennial grown for its stature and
its fragrant, airy, billowing sprays of
small white flowers, which are very
attractive to bees. These are borne
on strong stems in summer above
the large, elegant, dark green leaves.
Magnificent in a mixed border, but
allow plenty of space.

CULTIVATION *Grow in any well-drained,
preferably deep, fertile soil, in full sun
or partial shade. Provide shelter from
strong winds.*

☼◐ ◊ Z 6-9 H 9-6 ↕ 8ft (2.5m) ↔5ft (1.5m)

CRATAEGUS LAEVIGATA
'PAUL'S SCARLET'

This rounded, thorny, deciduous
tree is valued for its long season
of interest. Abundant clusters of
double, dark pink flowers appear
from late spring to summer, followed
in autumn by small red fruits. The
leaves, divided into three or five
lobes, are a glossy mid-green. A
particularly useful specimen tree for
a urban, coastal, or exposed garden.

CULTIVATION *Grow in any but water-
logged soil, in full sun or partial shade.
Pruning is best kept to a minimum.*

☼◐ ◊◊ Z 5-8 H 8-5 ↔ 25ft (8m)

CRATAEGUS × *LAVALLEI* 'CARRIEREI'

This vigorous hawthorn is a broadly spreading, semi-evergreen tree with thorny shoots and leathery green leaves that turn red in late autumn and winter. Flattened clusters of white flowers appear in early summer, followed in autumn by round red fruits that persist into winter. Tolerates pollution, so is good for urban sites. Often listed simply as *C.* × *lavallei*.

CULTIVATION *Grow in any but water-logged soil, in full sun or partial shade. Pruning is best kept to a minimum.*

☼ ◑ ◊◊ Z 5-7 H 7-4 ‡22ft (7m) ↔30ft (10m)

CRINODENDRON HOOKERIANUM

The lantern tree is an upright, evergreen shrub, sometimes a small tree, so called because of its large, scarlet to carmine-red flowers that hang from the upright shoots during late spring and early summer. The leaves are narrow and glossy dark green. It dislikes alkaline soils.

CULTIVATION *Grow in moist but well-drained, fertile, organic, acid soil, in partial shade with protection from cold winds. Tolerates a sunny site if the roots are kept cool and shaded. Trim lightly after flowering, if necessary.*

☼ ◊ Z 9-10 H 10-8 ‡20ft (6m) ↔15ft (5m)

CRINUM × *POWELLII* 'ALBUM'

A sturdy, bulbous perennial bearing clusters of up to ten large, fragrant, widely flared, pure white flowers on upright stems in late summer and autumn. The basally arranged, strap-shaped leaves, to 5ft (1.5m) long, are mid-green and arch over. Where marginally hardy, choose a sheltered site and protect the dormant bulb over winter with a deep, dry mulch.

CULTIVATION *Grow in deep, moist but well-drained, fertile soil that is rich in organic matter, in full sun with shelter from cold and wind.*

☼ ◊ Z 7-10 H 12-8 ‡5ft (1.5m) ↔12in (30cm)

CROCOSMIA × *CROCOSMIIFLORA* 'SOLFATERRE'

This clump-forming perennial produces spikes of funnel-shaped, apricot-yellow flowers on arching stems in mid-summer. The bronze-green, deciduous leaves are strap-shaped, emerging from swollen corms at the base of the stems. Excellent in a border; the flowers are good for cutting.

CULTIVATION *Grow in moist but well-drained, fertile, organic soil, in full sun. Provide a dry mulch over winter.*

☼ ◊ Z 6-9 H 9-6 ‡24–28in (60–70cm) ↔3in (8cm)

CROCOSMIA 'LUCIFER'

A robust, clump-forming perennial with swollen corms at the base of the stems. These give rise to pleated, bright green leaves and, in summer, arching spikes of upward-facing red flowers. Particularly effective at the edge of a shrub border or by a pool.

CULTIVATION *Grow in moist but well-drained, moderately fertile, organic soil. Site in full sun or dappled shade.*

☀☼ ◐◑ Z 6-9 H 9-6   ↕3–4ft (1–1.2m)
                       ↔3in (8cm)

CROCOSMIA MASONIORUM

A robust, late-summer-flowering perennial bearing bright vermilion, upward-facing flowers. These are carried above the dark green foliage on arching stems. The flowers and foliage emerge from a swollen, bulb-like corm. Thrives in coastal gardens. Where marginally hardy, grow in the shelter of a wall.

CULTIVATION *Best in moist but well-drained, fairly fertile, organic soil, in full sun or partial shade. In colder areas, provide a dry winter mulch.*

☀☼ ◐ Z 7-9 H 9-7   ↕4ft (1.2m) ↔3in (8cm)

SPRING-FLOWERING CROCUS

Spring-flowering crocus are indispensable dwarf perennials because they bring a welcome splash of early spring color into the garden. Some cultivars of *C. sieberi*, such as 'Tricolor' or 'Hubert Edelstein', bloom even earlier, in late winter. The goblet-shaped flowers emerge from swollen, underground corms at the same time as or just before the narrow, almost upright foliage. The leaves are mid-green with silver-green central stripes and grow markedly as the blooms fade. Very effective in drifts at the front of a mixed or herbaceous border or in massed plantings in rock gardens or raised beds.

CULTIVATION *Grow in gritty, well-drained, poor to moderately fertile soil, in full sun. Water freely during the growing season, and apply a low-nitrogen fertilizer each month. C. corsicus must be kept completely dry over summer. Can be naturalized under the right growing conditions.*

☼ ◊ Z 3-8 H 8-1 (corsicus Z 6-9 H 9-6)

1 ‡3–4in (8–10cm) ↔ 1½in (4cm)

2 ‡3in (7cm) ↔ 2in (5cm)

3 ‡2–3in (5–8cm) ↔ 1in (2.5cm)

4 ‡2–3in (5–8cm) ↔ 1in (2.5cm)

5 ‡2–3in (5–8cm) ↔ 1in (2.5cm)

1 *C. corsicus* **2** *C. chrysanthus* 'E.A. Bowles' **3** *C. sieberi* 'Albus'
4 *C. sieberi* 'Tricolor'

AUTUMN-FLOWERING CROCUS

These crocus are made invaluable for their late-flowering, goblet-shaped flowers with showy insides. They are dwarf perennials with underground corms that give rise to the foliage and autumn flowers. The leaves are narrow and mid-green with silver-green central stripes, appearing at the same time or just after the flowers. All types are easy to grow in the right conditions and look appealing when planted in groups in a rock garden. Rapid-spreading crocus, such as *C. ochroleucus*, are useful for naturalizing in grass or under deciduous shrubs. *C. banaticus* is effective planted in drifts at the front of a border, but do not allow it to become swamped by larger plants.

CULTIVATION *Grow in gritty, well-drained, poor to moderately fertile soil, in full sun. Reduce watering during the summer for all types except* C. banaticus, *which prefers damper soil and will tolerate partial shade.*

☼ ◊ Z 3-8 H 8-1(ochroleucus Z 5-8 H 8-4)

1 ↕ 4in (10cm) ↔ 2in (5cm)

2 ↕ 4in (10cm) ↔ 2in (5cm)

3 ↕ 2½–3in (6–8cm) ↔ 2in (5cm)

4 ↕ 3in (8cm) ↔ 1in (2.5cm)

5 ↕ 2in (5cm) ↔ 1in (2.5cm)

6 ↕ 4–5in (10–12cm) ↔ 1½in (4cm)

1 *C. banaticus* **2** *C. goulimyi* **3** *C. kotschyanus* **4** *C. medius* **5** *C. ochroleucus*
6 *C. pulchellus*

CRYPTOMERIA JAPONICA 'ELEGANS COMPACTA'

This small, slow-growing conifer looks good in a heather bed or rock garden with other dwarf conifers. It has feathery sprays of slender, soft green leaves, which turn a rich bronze-purple in winter. Mature trees usually have a neat cone shape.

CULTIVATION *Grow in any well-drained soil, in full sun or partial shade. Needs no formal pruning, but to renovate trees, cut back to within about 28in (70cm) of ground level, in spring.*

☼ ◑ ◊ Z 6-9 H 9-6   ↕6–12ft (2–4m)
↔6ft (2m)

CUPHEA IGNEA

The cigar flower is a spreading, evergreen shrub or subshrub grown as an annual in cold climates. It bears small, slender, dark orange-red flowers over a long period from spring to autumn amid the lance-shaped, dark green leaves. In frost-free areas it is good in a shrub border; otherwise, treat as a bedding plant or grow in a greenhouse.

CULTIVATION *Grow in well-drained, moderately fertile soil or soil mix, in full sun or partial shade. Pinch-prune young plants to encourage bushiness.*

☼ ◑ ◊ Z 10-11 H 12-1   ↕12–30in (30–75cm)
↔12–36in (30–90cm)

CYCLAMEN COUM
PEWTER GROUP

This winter- to spring-flowering,
tuberous perennial is excellent for
naturalizing beneath trees or shrubs.
The compact flowers have upswept
petals that vary from white to shades
of pink and carmine-red. These
emerge from swollen, underground
tubers at the same time as the
rounded, silver-green leaves. Provide
a deep, dry mulch in colder areas.

CULTIVATION *Grow in gritty, well-
drained, fertile soil that dries out in
summer, in sun or light shade. Mulch
annually when the leaves wither.*

☼☀ ◊ Z 5-9 H 9-4   ‡2–3in (5–8cm)
↔4in (10cm)

CYCLAMEN
HEDERIFOLIUM

An autumn-flowering, tuberous
perennial bearing shuttlecock-like
flowers that are pale to deep pink
and flushed deep maroon at the
mouths. The ivylike leaves, mottled
with green and silver, appear after
the flowers from a swollen, underground tuber. It self-seeds freely,
forming extensive colonies under
trees and shrubs, especially where
protected from summer rainfall.

CULTIVATION *Grow in well-drained,
fertile soil, in sun or partial shade.
Mulch each year after the leaves wither.*

☼☀ ◊ Z 8-9 H 9-7   ‡4–5in (10–13cm)
↔6in (15cm)

CYNARA CARDUNCULUS

The cardoon is a clump-forming, statuesque, late-summer-flowering perennial that looks very striking in a border. The large, thistlelike purple flowerheads, which are very attractive to bees, are carried above the deeply divided, silvery leaves on stout, gray-woolly stems. The flowerheads dry well for indoor display and are very attractive to bees; when blanched, the leaf stalks can be eaten.

CULTIVATION *Grow in any well-drained, fertile soil, in full sun with shelter from cold winds. For the best foliage effect, remove the flower stems as they emerge.*

☀ ◊ Z 7-9 H 9-7 ‡5ft (1.5m) ↔4ft (1.2m)

CYTISUS BATTANDIERI

Pineapple broom develops a loose and open-branched habit. It is a semi-evergreen shrub bearing dense clusters of pineapple-scented, bright yellow flowers from early to midsummer. The silvery gray leaves, divided into three leaflets, make an attractive backdrop to herbaceous and mixed plantings. Best grown against a wall in marginal areas.

CULTIVATION *Grow in any well-drained, not too rich soil, in full sun. Very little pruning is necessary, but old wood can be cut out after flowering to be replaced with strong, young growth. Resents transplanting.*

☀ ◊ Z 7-9 H 9-7 ↕↔ 15ft (5m)

CYTISUS × *BEANII*

This low-growing and semi-trailing, deciduous, spring-flowering shrub carries an abundance of pealike, rich yellow flowers on arching stems. The leaves are small and dark green. It is a colorful bush for a rock garden or raised bed and is also effective if allowed to cascade over a wall.

CULTIVATION *Grow in well-drained, poor to moderately fertile soil, in full sun. Trim lightly after flowering, but avoid cutting into old wood.*

☼ ◊ Z 7-8 H 8-7   ‡24in (60cm) ↔3ft (1m)

CYTISUS × *PRAECOX* 'ALLGOLD'

This compact, deciduous shrub is smothered by a mass of pealike, dark yellow flowers from mid- to late spring. The tiny, gray-green leaves are carried on arching stems. Suitable for a sunny shrub border or very large rock garden.

CULTIVATION *Grow in well-drained, acid to neutral soil, in sun. Pinch out the growing tips to encourage bushiness, then cut back new growth by up to two-thirds after flowering; avoid cutting into old wood. Replace old, leggy specimens.*

☼ ◊ Z 6-9 H 9-6   ‡4ft (1.2m) ↔5ft (1.5m)

DABOECIA CANTABRICA 'BICOLOR'

This straggling, heatherlike shrub bears slender spikes of urn-shaped flowers over a long period from spring to autumn. They are white, pink, or beet red, sometimes striped with two colors. The leaves are small and dark green. Good for filling space in a heather bed or among other acid-loving plants.

CULTIVATION *Best in sandy, well-drained, acid soil, in full sun; tolerates neutral soil and some shade. Clip lightly in early spring to remove spent flowers, but do not cut into old wood.*

☼ ◐ ◊ Z 6-8 H 8-6 ‡18in (45cm) ↔24in (60cm)

DABOECIA CANTABRICA 'WILLIAM BUCHANAN'

This vigorous, compact, heatherlike shrub bears slender spikes of bell-shaped, purple-crimson flowers from late spring to mid-autumn. The narrow leaves are dark green above with silver-gray undersides. Good with other acid-loving plants or among conifers in a rock garden.

CULTIVATION *Grow in well-drained, sandy, acid to neutral soil, preferably in sun, but tolerates light shade. Trim in early to mid-spring to remove old flowers, but do not cut into old wood.*

☼ ◊ Z 6-8 H 8-6 ‡18in (45cm) ↔24in (60cm)

DAHLIAS

Dahlias are showy, deciduous perennials, grown as annuals in many areas, with swollen underground tubers that should be stored in frost-free conditions where not hardy. They are valued for their massive variety of brightly colored flowers, which bloom from mid-summer to autumn, when many other plants are past their best. The leaves are mid- to dark green and divided. Very effective in massed plantings, wherever space allows; in smaller gardens, choose among the dwarf types to fill gaps in borders or to grow in containers. The flowers are ideal for cutting.

CULTIVATION *Best in well-drained soil, in sun. Where not hardy, lift tubers and store in barely moist peat or perlite over winter. Plant out after the last frost. Feed with high-nitrogen fertilizer every week in early summer. Taller varieties need staking. Deadhead to prolong flowering.*

☼ ◊ Z 8-11 H 12-1

1 ‡3½ft (1.1m) ↔ 18in (45cm)

2 ‡3½ft (1.1m) ↔ 24in (60cm)

3 ‡24in (60cm) ↔ 18in (45cm)

4 ‡4ft (1.2m) ↔ 24in (60cm)

5 ‡3½ft (1.1m) ↔ 24in (60cm)

1 *D.* 'Bishop of Llandaff' 2 *D.* 'Clair de Lune' 3 *D.* 'Fascination' (dwarf)
4 *D.* 'Hamari Accord' 5 *D.* 'Conway'

6 ‡4ft (1.2m) ↔ 24in (60cm) 7 ‡3½ft (1.1m) ↔ 24in (60cm) 8 ‡1.2m (4ft) ↔ 60cm (24in)

9 ‡3ft (1m) ↔ 18in (45cm) 10 ↔ 18–20in (45–50cm)

11 ‡3½ft (1.1m) ↔ 24in (60cm) 12 ‡3½ft (1.1m) ↔ 24in (60cm)

13 ‡24in (60cm) ↔ 18in (45cm) 14 ‡4ft (1.2m) ↔ 24in (60cm) 15 ‡4ft (1.2m) ↔ 24in (60cm)

6 *D.* 'Hamari Gold' 7 *D.* 'Hillcrest Royal' 8 *D.* 'Kathryn's Cupid' 9 *D.* 'Rokesley Mini'
10 *D.* 'Sunny Yellow' (dwarf) 11 *D.* 'So Dainty' 12 *D.* 'Wootton Cupid'
13 *D.* 'Yellow Hammer' (dwarf) 14 *D.* 'Zorro' 15 *D.* 'Wootton Impact'

DAPHNE BHOLUA
'GURKHA'

An upright, deciduous shrub bearing clusters of strongly fragrant, tubular, white and purplish pink flowers on its bare stems in late winter. They open from deep pink-purple buds and are followed by round, black-purple fruits. The lance-shaped leaves are leathery and dark green. A fine plant for a winter garden. All parts are highly toxic if ingested.

CULTIVATION *Grow in well-drained but moist soil, in sun or semi-shade. Mulch to keep the roots cool. Best left unpruned.*

☼ ◑ ◊ Z 8-9 H 7-3   ‡6–12ft (2–4m)
                                ↔5ft (1.5m)

DAPHNE PETRAEA
'GRANDIFLORA'

A very compact, slow-growing, evergreen shrub bearing clusters of fragrant, deep rose-pink flowers in late spring. The spoon-shaped leaves are leathery and glossy dark green. Ideal for a rock garden. All parts of the plant are highly toxic.

CULTIVATION *Grow in reasonably moist but well-drained, fairly fertile soil that is rich in humus, in sun or semi-shade. Regular pruning is not necessary.*

☼ ◑ ◊ Z 5-7 H 7-3   ‡4in (10cm)
                                ↔10in (25cm)

DAPHNE TANGUTICA RETUSA GROUP

These dwarf, evergreen shrubs, sometimes listed simply as *D. retusa*, are valued for their clusters of very fragrant, white to purple-red flowers that are borne during late spring and early summer. The lance-shaped leaves are glossy and dark green. Useful in a variety of sites, such as a large rock garden, shrub border, or mixed planting. All parts are toxic.

CULTIVATION *Grow in well-drained, moderately fertile, organic soil that does not dry out, in full sun or dappled shade. Pruning is rarely necessary.*

☼☀ ◊ Z 7-9 H 9-7 ↔ 30in (75cm)

DARMERA PELTATA

A handsome, spreading perennial, sometimes included in the genus *Peltiphyllum*, that forms an imposing, umbrella-like clump with large, round, mid-green leaves, to 24in (60cm) across, that turn red in autumn. The foliage appears after the compact clusters of star-shaped, white to bright pink, spring flowers. Ideal for a bog garden or by the edge of a pond or stream.

CULTIVATION *Grow in reliably moist, moderately fertile soil, in sun or partial shade; tolerates drier soil in shade.*

☼☀ ◊ Z 5-9 H 9-4 ‡4ft (1.2m) ↔3ft (1m)

DELPHINIUMS

Delphiniums are clump-forming perennials cultivated for their towering spikes of exquisite, shallowly cup-shaped, spurred, single or double flowers. These appear in early to mid-summer and are available in a range of colors from creamy whites through lilac-pinks and clear sky blues to deep indigo blue. The toothed and lobed, mid-green leaves are arranged around the base of the stems. Grow tall delphiniums in a mixed border or island bed with shelter to prevent them from being blown over in strong winds; shorter ones are nice in a rock garden. The flowers are good for cutting.

CULTIVATION *Grow in well-drained, fertile soil, in full sun. For quality blooms, feed weekly with a balanced fertilizer in spring, and thin out the young shoots when they reach 3in (7cm) tall. Most cultivars need staking. Remove spent flower spikes. Cut back all growth in autumn.*

☼ ◊ Z 3-7 H 6-1

1 ‡5½ft (1.7m) ↕24–36in (60–90cm) **2** ‡6ft (2m) ↔24–36in (60–90cm) **3** ‡6ft (2m) ↔30in (75cm)

1 *D.* 'Emily Hawkins' **2** *D.* 'Gillian Dallas' **3** *D.* 'Mighty Atom'

5 ‡to 5ft (1.5m) ↔ 30in (75cm)

4 ‡6ft (2m) ↔ 24–36in (60–90cm)

6 ‡5ft (1.5m) ↔ 24–36in (60–90cm)

4 *D.* 'Bruce'   **5** *D.* 'Sandpiper'   **6** *D.* 'Sungleam'

DEUTZIA ×
ELEGANTISSIMA
'ROSEALIND'

This compact, rounded, deciduous shrub bears profuse clusters of small, deep carmine-pink flowers. These are carried from late spring to early summer amid the oval, dull green leaves. Very suitable for a mixed border.

CULTIVATION *Grow in any well-drained, fertile soil that does not dry out, in full sun or partial shade. Tip-prune when young to encourage bushiness; after flowering, thin out by cutting some older stems back to the ground.*

☼ ◐ ◊ Z 6-8 H 8-6 ‡4ft (1.2m) ↔5ft (1.5m)

DEUTZIA × HYBRIDA
'MONT ROSE'

A dense, upright shrub, very similar to *D.* × *elegantissima* 'Rosealind' (above), but with smaller flower clusters. These consist of small, star-shaped, light pink or pinkish purple flowers, borne in early summer amid the narrow, dark green, deciduous leaves. Good as a specimen shrub or in a mixed border.

CULTIVATION *Grow in any fertile, well-drained but not too dry soil. Best in sun, but tolerates light shade. Tip-prune on planting; in subsequent years, prune young shoots below the flowered wood.*

☼ ◐ ◊ Z 6-8 H 8-6 ‡↔4ft (1.2m)

SUMMER-FLOWERING PINKS (*DIANTHUS*)

Summer-flowering pinks belong, like carnations, to the genus *Dianthus* and are widely grown for their charming, often clove-scented flowers and narrow, blue-gray leaves. They flower profusely over long periods; when cut, the stiff-stemmed blooms last exceptionally well. Thousands of cultivars are available, which are usually in shades of pink, white, carmine, salmon, or mauve with double or single flowers; they may be plain (self), marked with a contrasting color, or laced around the margins. Most make excellent border plants; tiny alpine pinks such as 'La Bourboule' and 'Joan's Blood' are well suited to a rock garden.

CULTIVATION *Best in well-drained, neutral to alkaline soil, in an open, sunny site. Alpine pinks need very sharp drainage. Feed with a balanced fertilizer in spring. Deadhead all types to to prolong flowering and to maintain a compact habit.*

☼ ◊ Zones vary H 8-1

1 ‡3in (8cm) ↔ to 4in (10cm)

2 ‡10–18in (25–45cm) ↔ 16in (40cm)

3 ‡10–18in (25–45cm) ↔ 16in (40cm)

4 ‡10–18in (25–45cm) ↔ 16in (40cm)

5 ‡3–4in (8–10cm) ↔ 8in (20cm)

6 ‡10–18in (25–45cm) ↔ 16in (40cm)

1 *D. alpinus* 'Joan's Blood' (Z 3-8) **2** *D.* 'Doris' (Z 5-10) **3** *D.* 'Gran's Favourite' (Z 5-10) **4** *D.* 'Haytor White' (Z 5-10) **5** *D.* 'La Bourboule' (Z 3-8) **6** *D.* 'Monica Wyatt' (Z 5-10)

DIASCIA BARBERAE 'BLACKTHORN APRICOT'

A mat-forming perennial bearing loose spikes of apricot flowers. These are produced over a long period from summer to autumn above the narrowly heart-shaped, mid-green leaves. Good in a rock garden, at the front of a mixed border, or on a sunny bank.

CULTIVATION *Grow in moist but well-drained, fertile soil, in full sun. In areas where marginally hardy, mulch heavily or overwinter young plants under glass.*

☼ ◊ Z 8-9 H 9-8   ‡10in (5cm)
      ↔to 20in (50cm)

DIASCIA RIGESCENS

This trailing perennial is valued for its tall spires of salmon-pink flowers. These appear above the mid-green, heart-shaped leaves during summer. Excellent in a rock garden or raised bed, or at the front of a border. Where marginally hardy, grow at the base of a sunny wall.

CULTIVATION *Grow in moist but well-drained, fertile soil that is rich in organic matter. Site in full sun. Overwinter young plants under glass.*

☼ ◊ Z 7-9 H 9-7 ‡12in (30cm) ↔20in (50cm)

DICENTRA SPECTABILIS

Bleeding heart is an elegant, old-fashioned perennial. In spring it bears rows of hanging, red-pink and white, heart-shaped flowers on arching stems. The leaves are deeply cut and mid-green. A beautiful plant for a shady border or woodland garden. Dies to the ground in summer; cover the spot with annuals.

CULTIVATION *Grow in reliably moist, fertile, organic, neutral or slightly alkaline soil. Prefers a site in partial shade, but tolerates full sun.*

☼ ◐ ◊ Z 3-9 H 9-1 ‡4ft (1.2m) ↔18in (45cm)

DICENTRA SPECTABILIS 'ALBA'

This white-flowered form of bleeding heart is otherwise very similar to the species (above), so to avoid possible confusion, purchase plants during the flowering period. The leaves are deeply cut and light green, and the heart-shaped flowers are borne along arching stems in spring.

CULTIVATION *Grow in reliably moist but well-drained soil that is enriched with well-rotted organic matter. Prefers partial shade, but tolerates full sun.*

☼ ◐ ◊ Z 3-9 H 9-1 ‡4ft (1.2m) ↔18in (45cm)

DICENTRA 'STUART BOOTHMAN'

A spreading perennial that bears heart-shaped pink flowers along the tips of arching stems during late spring and summer. The very finely cut foliage is fernlike and gray-green. Very attractive for a shady border or woodland planting.

CULTIVATION *Best in moist but well drained, organic, neutral to slightly alkaline soil, in partial shade. Divide and replant clumps in early spring.*

☼ ◐ ◊◊ Z 3-9 H 9-1 ‡12in (30cm) ↔16in (40cm)

DICTAMNUS ALBUS

Burning bush is a tall, woody-based perennial that looks good in both mixed and herbaceous borders. Dense spikes of star-shaped, fragrant white flowers appear above the lemon-scented, light green foliage in late spring. The aromatic oils produced by the flowers and ripening seedpods can be ignited in hot, still weather, hence the common name.

CULTIVATION *Grow in well-drained, fertile soil, in sun or partial shade. Does not respond well to root disturbance, so avoid transplanting older plants.*

☼ ☼ ◊ Z 3-8 H 8-1 ‡16–36in (40–90cm) ↔24in (60cm)

DICTAMNUS ALBUS VAR. PURPUREUS

This purple-flowered perennial is otherwise identical to the species (see facing page, below). Upright spikes of flowers are borne in early summer, above the highly aromatic, light green leaves. Striking in a mixed or herbaceous border.

CULTIVATION *Grow in any dry, well-drained, moderately fertile soil, in full sun or partial shade.*

☼ ◐ ◇ Z 3-8 H 8-1 ‡16–36in (40–90cm) ↔24in (60cm)

DIGITALIS GRANDIFLORA

The yellow foxglove is a short-lived, evergreen perennial producing upright spikes of tubular, pale yellow flowers from early to mid-summer. The leaves are oval and mid-green. Smaller and more subtle than many cultivated foxgloves, it looks attractive in woodland gardens or "natural" plantings.

CULTIVATION *Grow in moist but well-drained soil that is not allowed to dry out. Site in partial shade. Self-seeds freely, so deadhead after flowering to prevent unwanted seedlings.*

◐ ◇◇ Z 3-8 H 8-1 ‡3ft (1m) ↔ 18in (45cm)

DIGITALIS × *MERTONENSIS*

An evergreen, clump-forming, short-lived perennial grown for its spires of flared, strawberry-pink flowers that are borne from late spring to early summer. The leaves are dark green and lance-shaped. A beautiful plant for mixed or herbaceous borders or woodland plantings.

CULTIVATION *Best in moist but well-drained soil, in partial shade, but tolerates full sun and dry soil.*

☼☀ ◊◊ Z 3-8 H 8-1   ‡to 36in (90cm)
↔12in (30cm)

DIGITALIS PURPUREA F. *ALBIFLORA*

This ghostly form of the common foxglove is a tall biennial producing robust, stately spires of tubular, pure white flowers during summer. The coarse, lance-shaped leaves are bright green. A lovely addition to a woodland garden or mixed border. May be sold as *D. purpurea* 'Alba'.

CULTIVATION *Grow in moist but well-drained soil, in partial shade, but also tolerates dry soil in full sun.*

☼☀ ◊◊ Z 4-8 H 8-1   ‡3–6ft (1–2m)
↔to 24in (60cm)

DODECATHEON MEADIA F. ALBUM

This herbaceous perennial is valued for its open clusters of creamy white flowers with strongly reflexed petals. These are borne on arching stems during mid- to late spring, above the rosettes of oval, pale green, toothed leaves. Pretty in a woodland or shady rock garden; flowering is followed by a period of dormancy.

CULTIVATION *Grow in moist, organic soil, in partial shade. May be prone to slug and snail damage in spring.*

☀ ◐ ◊ Z 4-8 H 8-1 ‡16in (40cm) ↔10in (25cm)

DRYOPTERIS FILIX-MAS

The male fern is a deciduous foliage perennial forming large clumps of lance-shaped, mid-green fronds that emerge from a stout, scaly crown in spring. Ideal for a shady border or corner, by the side of a stream or pool, or in woodland.

CULTIVATION *Grow in reliably moist, organic soil. Site in partial shade with shelter from cold, drying winds.*

◐ ◊ Z 4-8 H 8-1 ↕↔ 3ft (1m)

DRYOPTERIS WALLICHIANA

Wallich's wood fern is a deciduous foliage perennial with a strongly upright, shuttlecock-like habit. The fronds are yellow-green when they emerge in spring, becoming dark green in summer. A fine architectural specimen for a moist, shady site.

CULTIVATION *Best in damp soil that is rich in organic matter. Choose a sheltered position in partial shade.*

☀ ◊ Z 10-11 H 12-10 ‡6ft (1–2m) ↔30in (75cm)

ECCREMOCARPUS SCABER

The Chilean glory flower is a fast-growing, scrambling climber with clusters of brilliant orange-red, tubular flowers in summer. The leaves are divided and mid-green. Grow as a short-lived perennial to clothe an arch or pergola, or up into a large shrub. Where not hardy, use as a trailing annual.

CULTIVATION *Grow in free-draining, fertile soil, in a sheltered, sunny site. Cut back to within 12–24in (30–60cm) of the base in spring.*

☀ ◊ Z 10-11 H 12-10 ‡6in (15cm) ↔8in (20cm)

ECHEVERIA AGAVOIDES

A lovely, star-shaped, succulent perennial forming rosettes of chunky, sharply pointed, pale green leaves. Clusters of yellow-tipped red flowers appear above the foliage in spring and early summer. Usually grown in a conservatory or as a houseplant in cold areas, but where hardy, it will form clumps in a succulent border.

CULTIVATION *Grow in well-drained, fairly fertile soil, or cactus soil mix, in sun. Keep barely moist in winter; increase watering in spring. Minimum temperature 45°F (7°C).*

☼ ◊ H 12-1   ‡6in (15cm)
           ↔12in (30cm) or more

ECHINOPS RITRO

This species of globe thistle is a compact perennial forming clumps of eye-catching, globelike flower-heads. These are metallic blue at first, turning a brighter blue as the flowers open. The leathery green leaves have white-downy under-sides. Excellent for a wild garden. The flowers dry well if cut before they are fully open.

CULTIVATION *Grow in well-drained, poor to moderately fertile soil. Site in full sun, but tolerates partial shade. Deadhead to prevent self-seeding.*

☼◑ ◊ Z 3-9 H 9-1 ‡24in (60cm) ↔18in (45cm)

ELAEAGNUS × EBBINGEI 'GILT EDGE'

A large, dense, evergreen shrub grown for its oval, dark green leaves, which are edged with rich golden-yellow. Inconspicuous yet highly scented, creamy white flowers are produced in autumn. Makes an excellent, fast-growing, well-shaped specimen shrub; can also be planted as an informal hedge.

CULTIVATION *Grow in well-drained, fertile soil, in full sun. Dislikes very alkaline soil. Trim to shape in late spring; completely remove any shoots with plain green leaves as soon as seen.*

☼ ◊ Z 7-10 H 12-7 ↔ 12ft (4m)

ELAEAGNUS PUNGENS 'MACULATA'

This large, evergreen foliage shrub bears oval, dark green leaves that are generously splashed in the center with dark yellow. Small but very fragrant flowers are produced in mid-autumn, followed by red fruits. Tolerates coastal conditions.

CULTIVATION *Best in well-drained, fairly fertile soil, in sun. Dislikes very alkaline soil. Trim lightly in spring, as needed. Remove completely any shoots with plain green leaves as soon as seen.*

☼ ◊ Z 7-9 H 9-7 ‡12ft (4m) ↔15ft (5m)

ELAEAGNUS 'QUICKSILVER'

A fast-growing shrub with an open
habit bearing small yellow flowers
in summer that are followed by
yellow fruits. The silvery, deciduous
leaves are lance-shaped and are
carried on silvery shoots. Makes an
excellent specimen shrub, or can
be planted to great effect with other
silver-leaved plants. May be offered
as *E. angustifolia* var. *caspica*.

CULTIVATION *Grow in any but alkaline
soil that is fertile and well-drained, in
full sun. Tolerates dry soil and coastal
winds. Keep pruning to a minimum.*

☼ ◊ Z 3-8 H 8-1   ↔ 12ft (4m)

ENKIANTHUS CAMPANULATUS

A spreading, deciduous shrub grown
for its dense, hanging clusters of
bell-shaped, creamy yellow flowers
in late spring. The dull green leaves
make a showy autumn display when
they change to orange-red. Good in
an open site in a woodland garden;
can become treelike with age.

CULTIVATION *Grow in reliably moist but
well-drained, organic, acid soil. Best in
full sun, but tolerates some shade. Keep
pruning to a minimum.*

☼ ◐ ◊◊ Z 5-8 H 8-4   ↔ 12–15ft (4–5m)

EPIMEDIUM × PERRALCHICUM

A robust, clump-forming, evergreen perennial that produces spikes of delicate, bright yellow flowers above the glossy dark green foliage in mid-spring. The leaves are tinged bronze when young. Very useful as a groundcover under trees or shrubs.

CULTIVATION *Grow in moist but well-drained, moderately fertile soil that is enriched with organic matter, in partial shade. Provide shelter from wind.*

☼ ◔◑ Z 5-9 H 9-2 ‡16in (40cm) ↔24in (60cm)

EPIMEDIUM × RUBRUM

A compact perennial bearing loose clusters of pretty crimson flowers with yellow spurs in spring. The divided leaves are tinted bronze-red when young, aging to mid-green, then reddening in autumn. Clump together to form drifts in a damp, shady border or woodland garden.

CULTIVATION *Grow in moist but well-drained, moderately fertile, organic soil, in partial shade. Cut back old, worn foliage in late winter so that the flowers can be seen in spring.*

☼ ◔◑ Z 4-8 H 8-1 ‡↔ 12in (30cm)

EPIMEDIUM × YOUNGIANUM 'NIVEUM'

A clump-forming perennial that bears dainty clusters of small white flowers in late spring. The bright green foliage is bronze-tinted when young and, despite being deciduous, persists well into winter. Makes a good groundcover in damp, shady borders and woodland areas.

CULTIVATION *Grow in moist but well-drained, fertile, organic soil, in partial shade. In late winter, cut back old, worn foliage so that the new flowers can be seen in spring.*

☼ ◐ ◊◊ Z 5-9 H 9-5 ↕8–12in (20–30cm) ↔12in (30cm)

ERANTHIS HYEMALIS

Winter aconite is one of the earliest spring-flowering bulbs, bearing buttercup-like, bright yellow flowers. They sit on a ruff of light green leaves, covering the ground from late winter until early spring. Ideal for naturalizing beneath deciduous trees and large shrubs.

CULTIVATION *Grow in moist but well-drained, fertile soil that does not dry out in summer. Best in dappled shade.*

☼ ◊◊ Z 4-9 H 9-1 ↕3in (5–8cm) ↔2in (5cm)

ERICA ARBOREA VAR. ALPINA

This tree heath is an upright shrub, much larger than other heathers, densely clothed with clusters of small, honey-scented white flowers from late winter to late spring. The evergreen leaves are needlelike and dark green. A fine centerpiece for a heather garden.

CULTIVATION *Grow in well-drained, ideally sandy, acid soil, in an open, sunny site. Tolerates alkaline conditions. Cut back young plants in early spring by about two-thirds to promote bushy growth; in later years, pruning is unnecessary. Tolerates hard renovation pruning.*

☀ ◊ Z 9-10 H 10-9   ‡6ft (2m) ↔34in (85cm)

ERICA × VEITCHII 'EXETER'

An upright, open, evergreen shrub that bears masses of highly scented, tubular to bell-shaped white flowers from mid-winter to spring. The needlelike leaves are bright green. Good in a large rock garden with conifers or as a focal point among low-growing heathers.

CULTIVATION *Grow in sandy soil that is well-drained, in sun. Best in acid soil, but tolerates slightly alkaline conditions. When young, cut back by two-thirds in spring to encourage a good shape; reduce pruning as the plant gets older.*

☀ ◊ Z 8-9 H 9-8   ‡6ft (2m) ↔26in (65cm)

EARLY-FLOWERING HEATHS (*ERICA*)

The low-growing, early flowering heaths are evergreen shrubs valued for their urn-shaped flowers in winter and spring. The flowers come in white and a wide range of pinks, bringing invaluable early interest during the winter months. This effect can be underlined by choosing cultivars with colorful foliage; *E. erigena* 'Golden Lady', for example, has bright golden-yellow leaves, and *E. carnea* 'Foxhollow' carries yellow, bronze-tipped foliage that turns a deep orange in cold weather. Excellent as a groundcover, either in groups of the same cultivar or with other heathers and dwarf conifers.

CULTIVATION *Grow in open, well-drained, preferably acid soil, but tolerate alkaline conditions. Choose a site in full sun. Cut back flowered stems in spring to remove most of the previous year's growth; remove any winter-killed growth in spring.*

☼ ◊ Z 5-7 H 7-5

1 ‡6in (15cm) ↔ 10in (25cm) 2 ‡6in (15cm) ↔ 16in (40cm) 3 ‡6in (15cm) ↔ 18in (45cm)

4 ‡6in (15cm) ↔ 14in (35cm) 5 ‡12in (30cm) ↔ 24in (60cm) 6 ‡12in (30cm) ↔ 16in (40cm)

1 *E. carnea* 'Ann Sparkes' 2 *E. carnea* 'Foxhollow' 3 *E. carnea* 'Springwood White'
4 *E. carnea* 'Vivellii' 5 *E. x darleyensis* 'Jenny Porter' 6 *E. erigena* 'Golden Lady'

LATE-FLOWERING HEATHS (*ERICA*)

Mostly low and spreading in form, the summer-flowering heaths are all evergreen shrubs. They look good on their own or mixed with other heathers and dwarf conifers. Flowers are borne over a very long period; *E.* x *stuartii* 'Irish Lemon' starts in late spring, and cultivars of *E. ciliaris* and *E. vagans* bloom well into autumn. Their season of interest can be further extended by choosing types with colorful foliage; the young shoots of *E. williamsii* 'P.D. Williams' are tipped with yellow in spring, and the golden foliage of *E. cinerea* 'Windlebrooke' turns a deep red in winter.

CULTIVATION *Grow in well-drained, acid soil, although* E. vagans *and* E. williamsii *tolerate alkaline conditions. Choose an open site in full sun. Prune lightly in early spring, cutting back to strong shoots below the flower clusters.*

☼ ◊ ciliaris Z 8-9; cinerea Z 6-8; vagans Z 7-9; all others Z 5-7; H 5-8

1 ↕9in (22cm) ↔ 14in (35cm)

4 ↕25cm (10in) ↔ 50cm (20in)

2 ↕to 16in (40cm) ↔ 18in (45cm)

3 ↕8in (20cm) ↔ 20in (50cm)

5 ↕6in (15cm) ↔ 18in (45cm)

1 *E. ciliaris* 'Corfe Castle' **2** *E. ciliaris* 'David McClintock' **3** *E. cinerea* 'Eden Valley'
4 *E. cinerea* 'C.D. Eason' **5** *E. cinerea* 'Windlebrooke'

6 ↕10in (25cm) ↔ 18in (45cm)

7 ↕10in (25cm) ↔ 20in (50cm)

8 ↕8in (20cm) ↔ 12in (30cm)

9 ↕12in (30cm) ↔ 20in (50cm)

10 ↕10in (25cm) ↔ 20in (50cm)

11 ↕12in (30cm) ↔ 18in (45cm)

12 ↕6in (15cm) ↔ 12in (30cm)

13 ↕8in (20cm) ↔ to 34in (85cm)

14 ↕12in (30cm) ↔ 18in (45cm)

6 *E. cinerea* 'Fiddler's Gold' 7 *E.* x *stuartii* 'Irish Lemon' 8 *E. tetralix* 'Alba Mollis'
9 *E. vagans* 'Birch Glow' 10 *E. vagans* 'Lyonesse' 11 *E. vagans* 'Mrs. D.F. Maxwell'
12 *E. vagans* 'Valerie Proudley' 13 *E. watsonii* 'Dawn' 14 *E.* x *williamsii* 'P.D. Williams'

ERIGERON KARVINSKIANUS

This carpeting, evergreen perennial with gray-green foliage produces an abundance of yellow-centered, daisylike flowerheads in summer. The outer petals are initially white, maturing to pink and purple. Ideal for wall crevices or cracks in paving. Sometimes sold as *E. mucronatus*.

CULTIVATION *Grow in well-drained, fertile soil. Choose a site in full sun, ideally with some shade at mid-day.*

☼ ◊ Z 5-7 H 7-4   ‡6–12in (15–30cm)
↔3ft (1m) or more

ERINUS ALPINUS

The fairy foxglove is a tiny, short-lived, evergreen perennial producing short spikes of pink, purple, or white daisylike flowers in late spring and summer. The lance- to wedge-shaped leaves are soft, sticky, and mid-green. Ideal for a rock garden or in crevices in walls.

CULTIVATION *Grow in light, moderately fertile soil that is well drained. Tolerates semi-shade but is best in full sun.*

☼ ◑ ◊ Z 4-7 H 7-1 ‡3in (8cm) ↔4in (10cm)

ERYNGIUM ALPINUM

This spiky, upright, thistlelike perennial bears cone-shaped, purple-blue flowerheads in summer; these are surrounded by prominent, feathery bracts. The deeply toothed, mid-green leaves are arranged around the base of the stems. An excellent textural plant for a sunny garden. The flowerheads can be cut, and they dry well for arrangements.

CULTIVATION *Grow in free-draining but not too dry, poor to moderately fertile soil, in full sun. Choose a site not prone to excessive winter moisture.*

☼ ◊ Z 5-8 H 8-4 ‡28in (70cm) ↔18in (45cm)

ERYNGIUM ×
OLIVERIANUM

An upright, herbaceous perennial, taller than *E. alpinum* (above), bearing cone-shaped, bright silver-blue flowerheads with a flat ring of silvery, daggerlike bracts around the base. These are produced from mid-summer to early autumn, above the spiny-toothed, dark green leaves. An essential architectural addition to a dry, sunny border with a theme of silver- or gray-leaved plants.

CULTIVATION *Grow in free-draining, fairly fertile soil, in full sun. Choose a site not excessively wet in winter.*

☼ ◊ Z 5-8 H 8-4 ‡36in (90cm) ↔18in (45cm)

ERYNGIUM ×
TRIPARTITUM

This delicate but spiky, upright
perennial bears conelike heads of
tiny, metallic blue flowers in late
summer and autumn. The flowerheads
sit on a ring of pointed bracts and
are carried above rosettes of gray-
green foliage on the tips of wiry,
blue-tinted stems. The flowers dry
well if cut before fully open.

CULTIVATION *Grow in free-draining,*
moderately fertile soil. Choose a position
not prone to excessive winter moisture,
in full sun. Trim lightly after flowering
to prevent legginess.

☼ ◊ Z 5-8 H 8-5   ‡24–36in (60–90cm)
↔ 20in (50cm)

ERYSIMUM 'BOWLES'
MAUVE'

This vigorous, shrubby wallflower
is one of the longest-flowering of
all perennials. It forms a rounded,
evergreen bush of narrow, gray-green
leaves and produces dense spikes of
small, four-petaled, rich mauve
flowers from spring to autumn. An
excellent border plant that benefits
from the shelter of a wall where it is
marginally hardy.

CULTIVATION *Grow in any well-drained,*
preferably alkaline soil, in full sun.
Trim lightly after flowering to keep
compact. Often short-lived, but easily
propagated by cuttings in summer.

☼ ◊ Z 7-10 H 12-6 ‡30in (75cm) ↔24in (60cm)

ERYSIMUM CHEIRI
'HARPUR CREWE'

A short-lived, upright and bushy, evergreen perennial that brings long-lasting spring color to the front of a warm, sunny border or raised bed. Spikes of sweetly scented, bright yellow flowers are borne from late winter to early summer above the narrow, gray-green leaves. May be sold as *Cheiranthus* 'Harpur Crewe'.

CULTIVATION *Grow in well-drained, poor to moderately fertile, preferably alkaline soil, in full sun. Trim lightly after flowering to prevent legginess. Usually dies after just a few years, but easily propagated by cuttings in summer.*

☼ ◊ Z 5-8 H 7-1 ‡12in (30cm) ↔24in (60cm)

ERYSIMUM 'WENLOCK BEAUTY'

A bushy, evergreen perennial that produces clusters of bluish pink and salmon, bronze-shaded flowers from early to late spring. The lance-shaped leaves are softly hairy and mid-green. Good for early-season color in a sunny rock garden or dry wall; where marginally hardy, choose a warm, sheltered spot.

CULTIVATION *Grow in poor or fairly fertile, ideally alkaline soil that has good drainage, in full sun. Trim lightly after flowering to keep compact.*

☼ ◊ Z 5-8 H 8-5 ↔ 18in (45cm)

ERYTHRONIUM 'PAGODA'

This very vigorous, clump-forming, bulbous perennial looks good planted in groups under deciduous trees and shrubs. Clusters of pale sulfur-yellow flowers droop from slender stems in spring, above the large, oval, bronze-mottled, glossy dark green leaves.

CULTIVATION *Grow in moist but well-drained, organic soil. Choose a position in partial shade.*

☼ ◐ ◊◊ Z 4-9 H 9-1 ‡6–14in (15–35cm)
↔4in (10cm)

ESCALLONIA 'APPLE BLOSSOM'

A compact, evergreen shrub carrying dense, glossy dark green foliage. From early to mid-summer, it bears a profusion of small, pink-flushed white flowers. Besides its value in a shrub border, it can also be grown as a hedge, barrier, or windbreak. Particularly useful in coastal areas, provided that the prevailing winds are not unusually cold.

CULTIVATION *Grow in any well-drained, fertile soil, in full sun. In colder areas, shelter from wind. Cut out old or damaged growth after flowering.*

☼ ◊ Z 8-9 H 9-8 ‡↔ 8ft (2.5m)

ESCALLONIA 'IVEYI'

A vigorous, upright, evergreen shrub bearing large clusters of fragrant, pure white flowers from mid- to late summer. The rounded leaves are glossy dark green. Grow in a shrub border or use as a hedge; the foliage often takes on bronze tints in cold weather.

CULTIVATION *Grow in any fertile soil with good drainage, in full sun with shelter from cold, drying winds. Remove damaged growth in autumn, or in spring if flowering finishes late.*

☼ ◊ Z 8-9 H 9-8   ↕↔ 10ft (3m)

ESCALLONIA 'LANGLEYENSIS'

This graceful, semi-evergreen shrub produces abundant clusters of small, rose-pink flowers. These are borne from early to mid-summer above the oval, glossy bright green leaves. Thrives in coastal gardens as an informal hedge or in a shrub or mixed border.

CULTIVATION *Best in well-drained, fertile soil, in a sunny site. Protect from cold, drying winds in marginal areas. Cut out dead or damaged growth after flowering; old plants can be renovated by hard pruning in spring.*

☼ ◊ Z 8-9 H 9-8   ↕ 6ft (2m) ↔ 10ft (3m)

ESCHSCHOLZIA CAESPITOSA

A tufted annual bearing a profusion of scented, bright yellow flowers in summer. The blue-green leaves are finely divided and almost thread-like. Suitable for a sunny border, rock garden, or gravel patch. The flowers close up in dull weather.

CULTIVATION *Grow in well-drained, poor soil. Choose a site in full sun. For early flowers the following year, sow seed directly outdoors in autumn.*

☼ ◊ annual H 9-2   ‡↔ to 6in (15cm)

ESCHSCHOLZIA CALIFORNICA

The California poppy is a mat-forming annual with cup-shaped flowers borne on slender stems throughout summer. These are produced in a variety of colors including white, red, pink, or yellow, but most are usually orange. The leaves are finely cut and grayish green. Grow in a sunny border or rock garden.

CULTIVATION *Best in light, poor soil with good drainage, in full sun. For early flowers the following year, sow seed directly outdoors in autumn.*

☼ ◊ annual H 9-2   ‡12in (3cm) ↔6in (15cm)

EUCALYPTUS GUNNII

The cider gum is a vigorous, evergreen tree useful as a fast-growing feature in a new garden. The new yellow- to grayish green bark is revealed in late summer as the old, whitish-green layer is shed. Young plants have rounded, gray-blue leaves; on adult growth they are lance-shaped. Protect where marginally hardy with a thick, dry mulch, especially when young.

CULTIVATION *Grow in well-drained, fertile soil, in sun. To keep compact and for the best display of young foliage, cut back hard each spring.*

☼ ◊ Z 8-10 H 10-8   ‡30–80ft (10–25m)
↔20–50ft (6–15m)

EUCALYPTUS PAUCIFLORA SUBSP. *NIPHOPHILA*

The snow gum is a handsome, silvery, evergreen tree with open, spreading branches and attractively peeling, white and gray bark. Young leaves are oval and dull blue-green; on mature stems they are lance-shaped and deep blue-green. The flowers are less significant.

CULTIVATION *Grow in well-drained, fertile soil, in full sun. For the best display of young foliage, cut back hard each year in spring.*

☼ ◊ Z 8-10 H 12-9   ‡↔ to 20ft (6m)

EUCRYPHIA × NYMANSENSIS 'NYMANSAY'

A column-shaped, evergreen tree that bears clusters of large, fragrant, glistening white flowers with yellow stamens. These are borne in late summer to early autumn amid the oval, glossy dark green leaves. Makes a magnificent flowering specimen tree; best in mild and damp climates.

CULTIVATION *Grow in well-drained, reliably moist soil, preferably in full sun with shade at the roots, but will tolerate semi-shade. Shelter from cold winds. Remove damaged growth in spring.*

☼ ◊◊ Z 8-9 H 9-8 ‡50ft (15m) ↔15ft (5m)

EUONYMUS ALATUS

The burning bush is a dense, deciduous shrub with winged stems, much valued for its spectacular autumn display: small purple and red fruits split to reveal orange seeds as the oval, deep green foliage turns to scarlet. The flowers are much less significant. Excellent as a hedge or in a shrub border or light woodland; may become invasive. The fruits are poisonous.

CULTIVATION *Grow in any well-drained, fertile soil. Tolerates light shade, but fruiting and autumn color are best in full sun.*

☼☼ ◊ Z 4-9 H 9-1 ‡6ft (2m) ↔10ft (3m)

EUONYMUS EUROPAEUS 'RED CASCADE'

A treelike, deciduous shrub that produces colorful autumn foliage. Inconspicuous flowers in early summer are followed by rosy-red fruits that split to reveal orange seeds. The oval, mid-green leaves turn scarlet-red at the end of the growing season. The fruits are toxic.

CULTIVATION *Grows in any fertile soil with good drainage, but thrives on chalky soil. Tolerates light shade, but fruiting and autumn color are best in full sun. Two or more specimens are required to guarantee a good crop of fruits. Very little pruning is necessary.*

☼☀ ◊ Z 4-7 H 7-1 ‡10ft (3m) ↔8ft (2.5m)

EUONYMUS FORTUNEI 'EMERALD 'N' GOLD'

A small and scrambling, evergreen shrub that will climb if supported. The bright green, oval leaves have broad, bright golden-yellow margins and take on a pink tinge in cold weather. The spring flowers are insignificant. Use to fill gaps in a shrub border, or train on a wall.

CULTIVATION *Grow in any but water-logged soil. The leaves color best in full sun, but tolerate light shade. Trim in mid-spring. Trained up a wall, it may reach a height of up to 15ft (5m).*

☼☀ ◊◊ Z 5-9 H 9-3 ‡24in (60cm) or more ↔36in (90cm)

EUONYMUS FORTUNEI 'SILVER QUEEN'

A compact, upright or scrambling, evergreen shrub that looks most effective when grown as a climber against a wall or up into a tree. The dark green leaves have broad white edges that become pink-tinged in prolonged cold. The greenish white flowers in spring are insignificant.

CULTIVATION *Grow in any but water-logged soil, in sun or light shade. Leaf color is best in full sun. Trim shrubs in mid-spring. Allowed to climb, it can grow up to 20ft (6m) tall.*

☼ ◑ ◊◊ Z 5-9 H 9-5 ‡8ft (2.5m) ↔5ft (1.5m)

EUPHORBIA AMYGDALOIDES VAR. ROBBIAE

Mrs. Robb's bonnet, also known simply as *E. robbiae*, is a spreading, evergreen perennial bearing open heads of yellowish green flowers in spring. The long, dark green leaves are arranged in rosettes at the base of the stems. Particularly useful in shady areas. Can be invasive.

CULTIVATION *Grow in well-drained but moist soil, in full sun or partial shade. Tolerates poor, dry soil. Dig up invasive roots to contain spread. The milky sap can irritate skin.*

☼ ◑ ◊◊ Z 6-9 H 9-6 ‡30-32in (75-80cm) ↔12in (30cm)

EUPHORBIA CHARACIAS

A shrubby, evergreen perennial that forms clumps of narrow, dark blue-green leaves. Large, rounded heads of dark-eyed, pale yellowish green flowers are carried at the tips of the upright stems in spring and early summer. A dramatic structural plant, bringing long-lasting color to a spacious Mediterranean-style garden.

CULTIVATION *Grow in well-drained, light soil, in full sun with shelter from cold winds. Cut the flowered stems back to the base in autumn; wear gloves, since the milky sap can irritate skin.*

☼ ◊ Z 7-10 H 12-7 ↔ 4ft (1.2m)

EUPHORBIA CHARACIAS SUBSP. *WULFENII* 'JOHN TOMLINSON'

This billowing, shrubby perennial bears larger flowerheads than the species (above). The flowers are bright yellow-green, without dark eyes, and are borne in rounded heads above the narrow, gray-green leaves. Where marginally hardy it is best grown at the base of a sunny wall.

CULTIVATION *Grow in light soil that has good drainage, in full sun. Shelter from cold winds. Cut the flowered stems back to the base in autumn; wear gloves, since the milky sap can irritate skin.*

☼ ◊ Z 7-10 H 12-7 ↔ 4ft (1.2m)

EUPHORBIA × *MARTINII*

This upright, clump-forming, evergreen subshrub bears spikes of yellow-green flowers with very distinctive, dark red nectar glands. These are carried on red-tinged shoots from spring to mid-summer above lance-shaped, mid-green leaves that are often tinged purple when young. A choice plant with an architectural look for a hot, dry site.

CULTIVATION *Grow in well-drained soil, in a sheltered, sunny site. Deadhead after flowering, wearing gloves to protect hands from the milky sap, which may irritate skin.*

☼ ◊ Z 7-10 H 12-7   ↕↔3ft (1m)

EUPHORBIA MYRSINITES

A small, evergreen perennial bearing sprawling stems that are densely clothed with a spiral arrangement of fleshy, elliptic, blue-green leaves. Clusters of yellow-green flowers brighten the tips of the stems in spring. Excellent in a dry, sunny rock garden or trailing over the edge of a raised bed.

CULTIVATION *Grow in well-drained, light soil, in full sun. Deadhead after flowering; it self-seeds freely. Wear gloves to avoid contact with the milky sap, which is a potential skin irritant.*

☼ ◊ Z 5-8 H 8-5   ↕4in (10cm)
       ↔to 12in (30cm)

EUPHORBIA POLYCHROMA

This evergreen perennial forms a neat, rounded clump of softly hairy, mid-green foliage. It is covered with clusters of brilliant greenish yellow flowers over long periods in spring. Excellent with spring bulbs, in a border, or in light woodland. Tolerates a wide range of soil types. Also known as *E. epithymoides*.

CULTIVATION *Grow in either well-drained, light soil, in full sun, or moist, organic soil, in light dappled shade. Deadhead after flowering. The milky sap can irritate skin.*

☀ ☀ ◊◊ Z 4-9 H 9-4   ‡16in (40cm) ↔24in (60cm)

EUPHORBIA SCHILLINGII

This vigorous, clump-forming perennial that, unlike many euphorbias, dies back in winter. It bears clusters of long-lasting, yellowish green flowers from mid-summer to mid-autumn. The lance-shaped leaves are dark green and have pale green or white central veins. Ideal for lighting up a wood-land planting or shady wild garden.

CULTIVATION *Grow in reliably moist, organic soil, in light dappled shade. Deadhead after flowering. The milky sap can irritate skin.*

◖ ◊ Z 7-9 H 9-7   ‡3ft (1m) ↔12in (30cm)

EXOCHORDA X MACRANTHA 'THE BRIDE'

A dense, spreading, deciduous shrub grown for its gently arching habit and abundant clusters of fragrant, pure white flowers. These are borne in late spring and early summer amid the oval, fresh green leaves. An elegant foil to other plants in a mixed border.

CULTIVATION *Grow in any well-drained soil, in full sun or light dappled shade. Does not like shallow, alkaline soil. Very little pruning is necessary.*

☼ ☀ ◊ Z 5-9 H 9-5   ‡6ft (2m) ↔10ft (3m)

FALLOPIA BALDSCHUANICA

Russian vine, sometimes still included in *Polygonum*, is an extremely vigorous, woody-stemmed, deciduous climber that bears hanging clusters of tiny, pink-tinted white flowers during summer and autumn. The leaves are oval and mid-green. Use to cover unsightly buildings or in a wild garden where there is plenty of space. In other situations, it can be difficult to control.

CULTIVATION *Grow in any well-drained, poor to moderately fertile soil, in sun or partial shade. Flowering is best in sun. Cut back as necessary in early spring.*

☼ ☀ ◊ Z 5-9 H 9-5   ‡40ft (12m)

FARGESIA NITIDA

Fountain bamboo is a slow-growing
perennial that forms a dense clump
of upright, dark purple-green canes.
In the second year after planting,
cascades of narrow, dark green
leaves are produced from the top of
the clump. A handsome plant for a
wild garden; to restrict spread, grow
in a large container. May be sold as
Sinarundinaria nitida.

CULTIVATION *Grow in reliably moist,
fertile soil, in light dappled shade.
Shelter from cold, drying winds.*

☼ ◑ Z 7-10 H 10-7   ↕ to 15ft (5m)
↔ 15ft (1.5m) or more

× *FATSHEDERA LIZEI*

The tree ivy is a mound-forming,
evergreen shrub cultivated for its
large, handsome, glossy dark green,
ivylike leaves. Small white flowers
appear in autumn. Excellent in
shady areas; where marginally
hardy, grow in a sunny, sheltered
site. Given support, it can be trained
against a wall; it also makes a fine
house- or conservatory plant.

CULTIVATION *Best in moist but well-
drained, fertile soil, in sun or partial
shade. No regular pruning is required.
Tie in to grow against a support.*

☼☀ ◐◑ Z 8-10 H 12-7   ↕ 4–6ft (1.2–2m)
↔ 10ft (3m)

FATSIA JAPONICA

The Japanese aralia is a spreading, evergreen shrub grown for its large, palm-shaped, glossy green leaves. Broad, upright clusters of rounded, creamy white flowerheads appear in autumn. An excellent architectural plant for a shady border. Tolerates atmospheric pollution and thrives in sheltered city gardens.

CULTIVATION *Grow in any well-drained soil, in sun or shade. Provide shelter from cold winds and cold snaps, especially when young. Little pruning is necessary, except to cut out wayward shoots and damaged growth in spring.*

☼ ☀ ◊ Z 8-10 H 12-8 ‡↔ 5–12ft (1.5–4m)

FELICIA AMELLOIDES 'SANTA ANITA'

This blue daisy, with white-marked, bright green foliage, is a rounded, evergreen subshrub. The large, daisylike flowers, with blue petals and bright yellow centers, appear in succession over a long period from late spring to autumn. Good in a sunny rock garden or in hanging baskets or other containers. Best treated as an annual in most regions.

CULTIVATION *Grow in well-drained, fairly fertile soil, in sun. Pinch-prune to encourage bushiness, and deadhead to prolong flowering.*

☼ ◊ Z 11 H 12-1 ‡↔ 12–24in (30–60cm)

FESTUCA GLAUCA 'BLAUFUCHS'

This blue fescue is a densely tufted, evergreen, perennial grass. It is excellent in a border or rock garden as a foil to other plants. Spikes of not particularly striking, violet-flushed, blue-green flowers are borne in early summer above the foliage. The narrow, bright blue leaves are its chief attraction.

CULTIVATION *Grow in dry, well-drained, poor to moderately fertile soil, in sun. For the best foliage color, divide and replant clumps every 2 or 3 years.*

☼ ◊ Z 4-8 H 8-1 ↕12in (30cm) ↔10in (25cm)

FILIPENDULA PURPUREA

An upright, clump-forming perennial that looks good planted in groups to form drifts of elegant, dark green foliage. Feathery clusters of red-purple flowers are carried above the leaves on purple-tinged stems in summer. Suitable for a waterside planting or bog garden; it can also be naturalized in damp woodland.

CULTIVATION *Grow in reliably moist, moderately fertile, organic soil, in partial shade. Can be planted in full sun where the soil does not dry out.*

☼◑ ◊◊ Z 4-9 H 9-1 ↕4ft (1.2m) ↔24in (60cm)

FILIPENDULA RUBRA 'VENUSTA'

A vigorous, upright perennial that produces feathery plumes of tiny, soft pink flowers on tall, branching stems in mid-summer. The large, dark green leaves are jaggedly cut into several lobes. Excellent in a bog garden, in moist soil by the side of water, or in a damp wild garden.

CULTIVATION *Grow in reliably moist, moderately fertile soil, in partial shade. Thrives in wet or boggy soil, where it will tolerate full sun.*

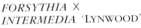

☀ ◐ ◖◗ Z 3-9 H 9-1 ‡6–8ft (2–2.5m)
↔4ft (1.2m)

FORSYTHIA × *INTERMEDIA* 'LYNWOOD'

A vigorous, deciduous shrub with upright stems that arch slightly at the tips. Its golden-yellow flowers appear in profusion on bare branches in early spring. Mid-green, oval leaves emerge after flowering. A reliable shrub for a mixed border or as an informal hedge: particularly effective with spring bulbs. The flowering stems are good for cutting

CULTIVATION *Grow in well-drained, fertile soil, in full sun. Tolerates partial shade, although flowering will be less profuse. On established plants, cut out some old stems after flowering.*

☀ ◐ ◖ Z 6-9 H 9-6 ‡↔ 10ft (3m

FORSYTHIA SUSPENSA

A deciduous shrub, the weeping
forsythia is less bushy than *F. x
intermedia* (see facing page, below),
with more strongly arched stems. It
is valued for the nodding, bright
yellow flowers that open on its bare
branches from early to mid-spring.
The leaves are oval and mid-green.
Good as a specimen, as an informal
hedge, or in a shrub border.

CULTIVATION *Best in well-drained,
fertile soil, ideally in full sun; flowering
is less spectacular in shade. Cut out
some of the older stems on established
plants after flowering.*

☀️◑ ◊ Z 6-8 H 8-6   ↕↔ 10ft (3m)

FOTHERGILLA MAJOR

This slow-growing, upright shrub
bears spikes of bottlebrush-like,
fragrant white flowers in late spring.
It is also valued for its blaze of
autumn foliage. The deciduous
leaves are glossy dark green in
summer, then turn orange, yellow,
and red before they fall. An
attractive addition to a shrub
border or in light woodland.

CULTIVATION *Best in moist but well-
drained, acid soil that is rich in
organic matter. Choose a position in
full sun for the best flowers and autumn
color. Requires very little pruning.*

☀️◑ ◊◑ Z 5-8 H 8-5   ↕ 8ft (2.5m) ↔ 6ft (2m)

FREMONTODENDRON 'CALIFORNIA GLORY'

A vigorous, upright, semi-evergreen shrub producing large, cup-shaped, golden-yellow flowers from late spring to mid-autumn. The rounded leaves are lobed and dark green. Excellent for wall-training: where marginally hardy, grow against a wall that receives plenty of sun.

CULTIVATION *Best in well-drained, poor to moderately fertile, neutral to alkaline soil, in sun. Shelter from cold winds. Best with no pruning, but wall-trained plants should be trimmed in spring.*

☼ ◊ Z 8-10 H 12-8 ‡20ft (6m) ↔12ft (4m)

FRITILLARIA ACMOPETALA

This bulbous perennial is grown for its drooping, bell-shaped, pale green flowers that are stained red-brown on the insides. They appear singly or in clusters of two or three in late spring, at the same time as the narrow, blue-green leaves. Suitable for a rock garden or sunny border.

CULTIVATION *Grow in fertile soil that has good drainage, in full sun. Divide and replant bulbs in late summer.*

☼ ◊ Z 6-8 H 8-6 ‡to 16in (40cm) ↔2–3in (5–8cm)

FRITILLARIA MELEAGRIS

The checkered lily is a bulbous
perennial that naturalizes well in
grass where summers are cool and
damp. The drooping, bell-shaped
flowers are pink, pinkish purple,
or white, and they are strongly
checkered. They are carried singly
or in pairs during spring. The
narrow leaves are gray-green.

CULTIVATION *Grow in any moist but
well-drained soil that is rich in organic
matter, in full sun or light shade. Divide
and replant bulbs in late summer.*

☼☀ ◊◊ Z 3-8 H 8-1   ‡to 12in (30cm)
↔2–3in (5–8cm)

FRITILLARIA PALLIDIFLORA

In late spring, this robust, bulbous
perennial bears bell-shaped, foul-
smelling flowers above the gray-
green, lance-shaped leaves. They
are creamy yellow with green bases,
checkered brown-red inside. Good
in a rock garden or border in
areas with cool, damp summers.
Naturalizes easily in damp meadows.

CULTIVATION *Grow in moist but well-
drained, moderately fertile soil, in sun
or partial shade. Divide and replant
bulbs in late summer.*

☼☀ ◊◊ Z 5-8 H 8-1   ‡to 16in (40cm)
↔2–3in (5–8cm)

HARDY FUCHSIAS

The hardy fuchsias are wonderfully versatile shrubs: as well as being useful in mixed borders and as flowering hedges, they can be trained as espaliers or fans against walls or grown as free-standing standards or pillars. Hanging flowers, varying in form from single to double, appear throughout summer and into autumn. Where marginally hardy, these fuchsias will lose some or all of their top growth during winter. They are fast to recover, however, and most will retain their leaves if overwintered in a cool greenhouse or if temperatures stay above 39°F (4°C).

CULTIVATION *Grow in well-drained but moist, fertile soil. Choose a position in sun or semi-shade with shelter from cold winds. Provide a deep winter mulch. Pinch-prune young plants to encourage a bushy habit. In early spring, remove cold-damaged growth back to plump, healthy-looking buds.*

☼ ◑ ◊◐ Z 7-9 H 12-1

1 ‡↔ 30–36in (75–90cm)

2 ‡6–12in (15–30cm) ↔ 18in (45cm)

3 ‡↔ 3–3½ft (1–1.1m)

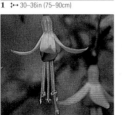

4 ‡6–10ft (2–3m) ↔ 3–6ft (1–2m)

5 ‡↔ 6–12in (15–30cm)

6 ‡ to 10ft (3m) ↔ 6–10ft (2–3m)

1 *F.* 'Genii' **2** *F.* 'Lady Thumb' **3** *F.* 'Mrs. Popple' **4** *F.* 'Riccartonii'
5 *F.* 'Tom Thumb' **6** *F. magellanica* 'Versicolor'

TENDER FUCHSIAS

The tender fuchsias are flowering shrubs that require at least some winter protection in most climates. The compensation for this extra care is an increased range of beautiful summer flowers for the garden; from the massed petals of 'Swingtime' to the elongated tubes of 'Thalia'. All types can be grown outdoors and make superb specimen plants when grown in containers, either pinch-pruned into dense bushes or trained as columns or standards. Where not hardy, shelter in a greenhouse or cool conservatory during the winter months; 'Thalia' is the most tender and needs a minimum temperature of 50°F (10°C).

CULTIVATION *Grow in moist but well-drained, fertile soil or soil mix, in sun or partial shade. Pinch-prune young plants to promote bushiness, and trim after flowering to remove spent blooms. Prune back to an established framework in early spring.*

☼ ◐ ◊◊ Z 8-10 H 12-1

1 ‡↔ 18–30in (45–75cm)
2 ‡↔ 12–24in (30–60cm)
3 ‡6–18in (15–45cm) ↔ 18in (45cm)
4 ‡ to 24in (60cm) ↔ 30in (75cm)
5 ‡↔ 18–36in (45–90cm)

1 *F.* 'Celia Smedley' **2** *F.* 'Annabel' **3** *F.* 'Nellie Nuttall'
4 *F.* 'Swingtime' **5** *F.* 'Thalia'

TRAILING FUCHSIAS

Fuchsia cultivars with a trailing or spreading habit are the perfect plants to have trailing over the edge of a tall container, windowbox, or hanging basket, where their pendulous flowers will be shown to great effect. They bloom continuously throughout summer and into early autumn and can be left in place undisturbed right up until the end of the season. After this, they are best discarded and new plants bought the following year. An alternative, longer-lived option is to train trailing fuchsias into attractive weeping standards, but they must be overwintered indoors in most areas.

CULTIVATION *Grow in fertile, moist but well- drained soil or soil mix, in full sun or partial shade. Shelter from cold, drying winds. Little pruning is necessary, except to remove wayward growth. Regularly pinch out the tips of young plants to encourage bushiness and a well-balanced shape.*

☼ ◑ ◊◊◗ Z 8-10

1 ‡6–12in (15–30cm) ↔ 18in (45cm)

2 ‡6–12in (15–30cm) ↔ 18in (45cm)

3 ‡18in (45cm) ↔ 24in (60cm)

4 ‡to 24in (60cm) ↔ 30in (75cm)

1 *F.* 'La Campanella' **2** *F.* 'Golden Marinka' **3** *F.* 'Jack Shahan' **4** *F.* 'Lena'

GAILLARDIA 'DAZZLER'

A bushy, short-lived perennial that
bears large, daisylike flowers over a
long period in summer. These have
yellow-tipped, bright orange petals
surrounding an orange-red center.
The leaves are soft, lance-shaped,
and mid-green. Effective in a sunny
mixed or herbaceous border; the
flowers are good for cutting. May
not survive winter in wet soils.

CULTIVATION *Grow in well-drained, not
too fertile soil, in full sun. May need
staking. Often short-lived, but can be
reinvigorated by division in spring.*

☼ ◊ Z 3-8   ‡24–34in (60–85cm)
                   ↔ 18in (45cm)

GALANTHUS ELWESII

This robust snowdrop is a bulbous
perennial that produces slender,
honey-scented, pure white flowers
in late winter, above the bluish
green foliage. The inner petals have
green markings. Good for borders
and rock gardens; naturalizes easily
in light woodland.

CULTIVATION *Grow in moist but well-
drained, organic soil that does not dry
out in summer. Choose a position in
partial shade.*

☼ ◊◊ Z 3-9   ‡4–6in (10–15cm)
                   ↔ 3in (8cm)

GALANTHUS 'MAGNET'

This tall snowdrop is a vigorous bulbous perennial bearing drooping, pear-shaped, pure white flowers during late winter and early spring; the inner petals have a deep green, V-shaped mark at the tips. The strap-shaped, gray-green leaves are arranged around the base of the plant. Good for naturalizing in grass or in a woodland garden.

CULTIVATION *Grow in moist but well-drained, fertile soil that does not dry out in summer. Choose a position in partial shade.*

☼ ◊◊ Z 4-9 H 9-1   ‡8in (20cm) ↔3in (8cm)

GALANTHUS NIVALIS 'FLORE PLENO'

This double-flowered form of the common snowdrop is a robust, bulbous perennial. Drooping, pear-shaped, pure white flowers appear from late winter to early spring, with green markings on the tips of the inner petals. The narrow leaves are gray-green. Good for naturalizing under deciduous trees or shrubs.

CULTIVATION *Grow in reliably moist but well-drained, fertile soil, in light shade. Divide and replant every few years after flowering to maintain vigor.*

☼ ◊◊ Z 3-9 H 9-1   ‡↔ 4in (10cm)

GALANTHUS 'S. ARNOTT'

This honey-scented snowdrop, which has even larger flowers than 'Magnet' (facing page, above), is a fast-growing, bulbous perennial. Nodding, pear-shaped, pure white flowers appear in late winter to early spring and have a green, V-shaped mark at the tip of each inner petal. The narrow leaves are gray-green. Grow in a rock garden.

CULTIVATION *Grow in moist but well-drained, fertile soil, in dappled shade. Keep reliably moist in summer. Divide and replant clumps after flowering.*

☼ ◑ ◊◊ Z 4-9 H 9-1   ‡8in (20cm) ↔3in (8cm)

GARRYA ELLIPTICA 'JAMES ROOF'

This silk-tassel bush is an upright, evergreen shrub, becoming treelike with age. It is grown for its long, silver-gray catkins that dangle from the branches in winter and early spring. The leaves are dark sea-green and have wavy margins. Excellent in a shrub border, against a shady wall, or as hedging; tolerates coastal conditions.

CULTIVATION *Grow in well-drained, moderately fertile soil, in full sun or partial shade. Tolerates poor, dry soil. Trim after flowering, as necessary.*

☼ ◑ ◊ Z 8-10 H 10-8   ‡↔ 12ft (4m)

GAULTHERIA MUCRONATA 'MULBERRY WINE' (FEMALE)

This evergreen, spreading shrub, sometimes included in *Pernettya*, is much valued for its autumn display of large, rounded, magenta to purple berries that show off well against the toothed, glossy dark green leaves. Small white flowers are borne throughout summer.

CULTIVATION *Grow in reliably moist, peaty, acid to neutral soil, in partial shade or full sun. Plant close to male varieties to ensure a reliable crop of berries. Chop away spreading roots with a spade to restrict the overall size.*

☼ ◑ ◗ Z 8-9 H 9-8   ↔ 4ft (1.2m)

GAULTHERIA MUCRONATA 'WINTERTIME' (FEMALE)

An evergreen, spreading shrub, sometimes included in the genus *Pernettya*, bearing large, showy white berries that persist well into winter. Small white flowers are borne from late spring into early summer. The glossy dark green leaves are elliptic to oblong and toothed.

CULTIVATION *Grow in reliably moist, acid to neutral, peaty soil. Best in light shade, but tolerates sun. Plant close to male varieties to ensure a good crop of berries. Dig out spreading roots as necessary to restrict the overall size.*

☼ ◑ ◗ Z 8-9 H 9-8   ↔ 4ft (1.2m)

GAZANIA
CHANSONETTE SERIES

These vigorous, spreading, summer-flowering perennials are usually grown as annuals for their colorful, daisylike flowers. They come in vivid shades of pink, red, yellow, bronze, or orange and are often zoned in contrasting colors. The spoon-shaped leaves are dark green with white-silky undersides. Good for containers or summer bedding; they tolerate coastal conditions.

CULTIVATION *Grow in well-drained, sandy soil, in full sun. Deadhead regularly to prolong flowering.*

☼ ◊ Z 8-10 H 12-8 ‡8in (20cm) ↔10in (25cm)

GENISTA AETNENSIS

The Mount Etna broom is an upright, almost leafless, deciduous shrub that is excellent on its own or at the back of a border in hot, dry situations. Masses of fragrant, pea-like, golden-yellow flowers cover the weeping, mid-green stems during mid-summer.

CULTIVATION *Grow in well-drained, light, poor to moderately fertile soil, in full sun. Keep pruning to a minimum; old, straggly plants are best replaced.*

☼ ◊ Z 9-10 H 12-9 ‡↔ 25ft (8m)

GENISTA LYDIA

This low, deciduous shrub forms a mound of arching, prickle-tipped branches that are covered with yellow, pealike flowers in early summer. The small, narrow leaves are blue-green. Ideal for hot, dry sites such as a rock garden or raised bed.

CULTIVATION *Grow in well-drained, light, poor to moderately fertile soil, in full sun. Keep pruning to a minimum; old, straggly plants are best replaced.*

☼ ◊ Z 6-9 H 9-6   ‡24in (60cm) ↔3ft (1m)

GENTIANA ACAULIS

The trumpet gentian is a mat-forming, evergreen perennial that bears large, trumpet-shaped, vivid deep blue flowers in spring. The leaves are oval and glossy dark green. Good in a rock garden, raised bed, or trough; thrives in areas with cool, damp summers.

CULTIVATION *Grow in reliably moist but well-drained, organic soil, in full sun or partial shade. Protect from hot sun in areas with warm, dry summers.*

☼ ◑ ◊◊ Z 5-8 H 8-5   ‡3in (8cm) ↔to 12in (30cm)

GENTIANA ASCLEPIADEA

The willow gentian is an arching, clump-forming perennial producing trumpet-shaped, dark blue flowers in late summer and autumn; these are often spotted or striped with purple on the insides. The leaves are lance-shaped and fresh green. Suitable for a border or large rock garden.

CULTIVATION *Grow in moist, fertile, organic soil. Best in light shade, but tolerates sun if the soil is reliably moist.*

☼ ◐ ◊ Z 6-9 H 9-6   ‡24–36in (60–90cm)
                          ↔18in (45cm)

GENTIANA SEPTEMFIDA

This late summer-flowering gentian is a spreading to upright, clump-forming herbaceous perennial. Clusters of narrowly bell-shaped, bright blue flowers with white throats are borne amid the oval, mid-green leaves. Good for a rock garden or raised bed; thrives in areas with cool, damp summers.

CULTIVATION *Grow in moist but well-drained, organic soil, in full sun or partial shade. Protect from hot sun in areas with warm, dry summers.*

☼☼ ◊◊ Z 6-8 H 8-6   ‡to 6–8in (15–20cm)
                          ↔to 12in (30cm)

SMALL GERANIUMS

The relatively low-growing members of the genus *Geranium* are versatile plants, useful not only at the front of borders but also in rock gardens or as groundcover. These semi-evergreen to evergreen perennials are long-lived and undemanding, tolerating a wide range of sites and soil types. The lobed and toothed leaves are often variegated or aromatic. In summer, they bear typically saucer-shaped flowers ranging in color from white through soft blues (such as 'Johnson's Blue') to the intense magenta-pink of *G. cinereum* var. *caulescens*, often with contrasting veins, eyes, or other markings.

CULTIVATION *Grow in sharply drained, organic soil, in full sun. Feed with a balanced fertilizer every month during the growing season, but water sparingly in winter. Remove withered flower stems and old leaves to encourage fresh growth.*

☼ ◊ Z 4-8 H 9-1

1 ↕ to 18in (45cm) ↔ 3ft (1m) or more

2 ↕ to 6in (15cm) ↔ to 12in (30cm)

1 *G.* 'Ann Folkard'   **2** *G. cinereum* 'Ballerina'

3 ‡ to 6in (15cm) ↔ to 12in (30cm)

4 ‡ to 18in (45cm) ↔ indefinite

5 ‡ to 6in (15cm) ↔ 20in (50cm)

6 ‡ 12in (30cm) ↔ 24in (60cm)

7 ‡ to 18in (45cm) ↔ 30in (75cm)

8 ‡ to 12in (30cm) ↔ to 3ft (1m)

9 ‡ 12in (30cm) ↔ 4ft (1.2m)

3 *G. cinereum* var. *subcaulescens* **4** *G. clarkei* 'Kashmir White' **5** *G. dalmaticum* Z
6 *G. himalayense* 'Gravetye' **7** *G.* 'Johnson's Blue' **8** *G.* × *riversleaianum* 'Russell Prichard'
9 *G. wallichianum* 'Buxton's Variety'

LARGE GERANIUMS

The taller, clump-forming types of perennial geranium – not to be confused with the genus *Pelargonium* (see pages 319–321) – make effective, long-lived border plants or filler among shrubs, requiring a minimum of attention. They are especially suited to cottage garden plantings and between roses. Their lobed, evergreen leaves may be colored or aromatic and give a long season of interest. Throughout summer, this is heightened by an abundance of saucer-shaped flowers in white and shades of blue, pink, and purple. Markings on flowers vary, from the dramatic, contrasting dark eyes of *G. psilostemon* to the delicate venation of *G. sanguineum* var. *striatum*.

CULTIVATION *Best in well-drained, fairly fertile soil, in full sun or partial shade, but tolerant of any soil that is not waterlogged. Remove old leaves and withered flower stems to encourage new growth.*

☼ ☀ ◊◊ Z 4-8 H 8-1

1 ↕18in (45cm) ↔ 24in (60cm)

2 ↔24in (60cm)

3 ↕20in (50cm) ↔ 24in (60cm)

1 *G. endressii* **2** *G.* × *magnificum* **3** *G. macrorrhizum* 'Ingwersen's Variety'

4 ‡24–36in (60–90cm) ↔ 24in (60cm)

5 ‡24–48in (60–120cm) ↔ 24in (60cm)

6 ‡↔ 12in (30cm)

8 ‡24in (60cm) ↔ 36in (90cm)

7 ‡4in (10cm) ↔ 12in (30cm)

9 ‡24in (60cm) ↔ 36in (90cm)

4 *G. pratense* 'Mrs. Kendall Clark' **5** *G. psilostemon* (syn. *G. armenum*) **6** *G. renardii*
7 *G. sanguineum* var. *striatum* **8** *G. sylvaticum* 'Mayflower' **9** *G.* x *oxonianum* 'Wargrave Pink'

GEUM 'LADY STRATHEDEN'

This is a clump-forming perennial bearing double, bright yellow flowers on arching stems over a long period in summer. The mid-green leaves are large and lobed. An easy, long-flowering plant for brightening up a mixed or herbaceous border.

CULTIVATION *Grow in moist but well-drained, fertile soil, in full sun. Avoid sites that become waterlogged in winter.*

☼ ◊◖ Z 5-9 H 9-5 ‡16–24in (40–60cm)
↔24in (60cm)

GEUM MONTANUM

A small, clump-forming perennial grown for its solitary, cup-shaped, deep golden-yellow flowers. These are produced in spring and early summer above large, lobed, dark green leaves. Excellent for a rock garden, raised bed, or trough.

CULTIVATION *Grow in well-drained, preferably gritty, fertile soil, in full sun. Will not tolerate waterlogging in winter.*

☼ ◊ Z 4-8 H 8-3 ‡6in (15cm) ↔12in (30cm)

GILLENIA TRIFOLIATA

Sometimes offered as *Porteranthus*, this is an upright, graceful perennial that forms clumps of olive green leaves that turn red in autumn. Delicate white flowers with slender petals are borne on wiry red stems in summer. Effective in a shady border or light woodland; the cut flowers last well.

CULTIVATION *Grow in moist but well drained, fertile soil. Best in partial shade, but tolerates some sun if shaded during the hottest part of the day.*

☀ ◐ ◊◊ Z 5-9 H 9-5 ‡3ft (1m) ↔24in (60cm)

GLADIOLUS CALLIANTHUS

An upright, cormous perennial that bears strongly scented white flowers with purple-red throats. These hang from elegant stems during summer above fans of narrow, mid-green leaves. Ideal for mixed borders; the flowers are suitable for cutting. Also offered as *Acidanthera*.

CULTIVATION *Grow in fertile soil, in full sun. Plant on a layer of sand to improve drainage. Where not hardy, lift the corms when the leaves turn yellow-brown, snap off the leaves, and store the corms in frost-free conditions.*

☀ ◊ Z 8-10 H 12-1 ‡28–39in (70–100cm) ↔2in (5cm)

GLADIOLUS COMMUNIS SUBSP. *BYZANTINUS*

In late spring, this upright, cormous perennial produces a blaze of magenta flowers with purple-marked lips. These are arranged in spikes above fans of narrow, mid-green leaves. An elegant subject for a mixed or herbaceous border; the flowers are good for cutting.

CULTIVATION *Grow in fertile soil, in full sun. Plant corms on a bed of sharp sand to improve drainage. Where marginally hardy, grow at the base of a wall for extra protection in winter.*

☼ ◊ Z 8-10 H 12-1   ‡3ft (1m) ↔3in (8cm)

GLEDITSIA TRIACANTHOS 'SUNBURST'

This fast-growing honeylocust is a broadly conical, deciduous tree valued for its beautiful foliage and light canopy. The finely divided leaves are bright gold-yellow when they emerge in spring, maturing to dark green, then yellowing again before they fall. A useful, pollution-tolerant tree for a small garden.

CULTIVATION *Grow in any well-drained, fertile soil, in full sun. Prune only to remove dead, damaged or diseased wood, from late summer to mid-winter.*

☼ ◊ Z 3-7 H 7-1   ‡40ft (12m) ↔30ft (10m)

GOMPHRENA HAAGEANA 'STRAWBERRY FAYRE'

An upright, bushy annual bearing brilliant red flowerheads throughout summer to early autumn. These are carried on upright stems above narrow, mid-green leaves that are covered with white hairs when young. Good for summer bedding; the flowers can also be cut, and they dry well for winter decoration.

CULTIVATION *Grow in any moderately fertile soil with good drainage. Choose a position in full sun.*

☀ ◊ annual H 12-1   ‡30–32in (75–80cm)
↔to 12in (30cm)

GUNNERA MANICATA

A massive, clump-forming perennial that produces the largest leaves of any garden plant, to 6ft (2m) long. These are rounded, lobed, sharply toothed, and dull green, with stout, prickly stalks. Tall spikes of tiny, greenish red flowers appear in summer. An imposing plant by water or in a bog garden.

CULTIVATION *Best in permanently moist, fertile soil, in full sun or partial shade. Shelter from cold winds. Protect the crown by folding the dead leaves over it before winter.*

☀◑ ◐ Z 7-10 H 12-7   ‡8ft (2.5m)
↔10–12ft (3–4m)

GYMNOCALYCIUM ANDREAE

This prickly cactus forms clusters of spherical, dark blue-green or black-green stems with warty ribs and pale yellow-white spines. Bright yellow flowers are borne in early summer. Ideal for a cactus garden; must be grown in a warm conservatory or heated greenhouse in cold climates.

CULTIVATION *Best in sharply drained, poor soil, or standard cactus soil mix, in sun. Keep dry in winter. Minimum temperature range 35–50°F (2–10°C).*

☼ ◊ H 12-10 ‡to 2½in (6cm) ↔to 6in (15cm)

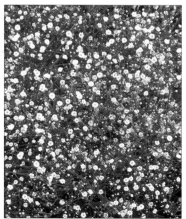

GYPSOPHILA PANICULATA 'BRISTOL FAIRY'

This herbaceous perennial forms a mound of slightly fleshy, lance-shaped, blue-green leaves on very slender, wiry stems. The profusion of tiny, double white flowers in summer forms a cloudlike display. Very effective cascading over a low wall or as a foil to more upright, sharply defined flowers.

CULTIVATION *Grow in well-drained, deep, moderately fertile, preferably alkaline soil, in full sun. Resents being disturbed after planting.*

☼ ◊ Z 4-9 H 9-4 ↔ to 4ft (1.2m)

GYPSOPHILA 'ROSENSCHLEIER'

A mound-forming perennial, also sold as 'Rosy Veil' or 'Veil of Roses', carrying trailing stems which look good cascading over a low wall. In summer, tiny, double white flowers that age to pale pink are carried in airy sprays, forming a dense cloud of blooms. The slightly fleshy leaves are lance-shaped and blue-green. The flowers dry well for decoration.

CULTIVATION *Grow in well-drained, deep, moderately fertile, preferably alkaline soil. Choose a position in full sun. Resents root disturbance.*

☼ ◊ Z 4-9 H 9-3   ‡50cm (20in) ↔1m (3ft)

HAKONECHLOA MACRA 'AUREOLA'

This colorful grass is a deciduous perennial forming a clump of narrow, arching, bright yellow leaves with cream and green stripes. They flush red in autumn and persist well into winter. Reddish brown flower spikes appear in late summer. A versatile plant that can be used in a border, rock garden, or containers.

CULTIVATION *Grow in moist but well-drained, fertile, organic soil. Leaf color is best in partial shade, but it tolerates full sun.*

☼ ◑ ◊◊ Z 5-9 H 9-5   ‡14in (35cm) ↔16in (40cm)

x *HALIMIOCISTUS SAHUCII*

A compact shrub that forms mounds of linear, dark green leaves with downy undersides. Masses of saucer-shaped white flowers are produced throughout summer. Good in a border, at the base of a wall, or in a rock garden.

CULTIVATION *Best in freely draining, poor to moderately fertile, light, gritty soil, in a sunny site. Shelter from excessive winter moisture.*

☼ ◊ Z 8-9 H 9-8 ‡18in (45cm) ↔36in (90cm)

x *HALIMIOCISTUS WINTONENSIS* 'MERRIST WOOD CREAM'

A spreading, evergreen shrub bearing creamy yellow flowers with red bands and yellow centers in late spring and early summer. The lance-shaped leaves are gray-green. Good at the front of a mixed border or at the foot of a wall. Also good in a raised bed or rock garden.

CULTIVATION *Grow in freely draining, poor to moderately fertile soil, in full sun. Choose a position protected from excessive winter wet.*

☼ ◊ Z 7-9 H 9-7 ‡24in (60cm) ↔36in (90cm)

HALIMIUM 'SUSAN'

A small, spreading, evergreen shrub valued for its single or semi-double summer flowers; these are bright yellow with deep purple markings. The leaves are oval and grey-green. Good for rock gardens in warm, coastal areas. Provide shelter at the foot of a wall in climates that have cold winters. Flowering is best during long, hot summers.

CULTIVATION *Grow in freely draining, fairly fertile, light, sandy soil, in full sun. Provide shelter from cold winds. Trim lightly in spring, as necessary.*

 ☼ ◊ Z 9-10 H 12-9 ‡18in (45cm) ↔24in (60cm)

HAMAMELIS × INTERMEDIA 'ARNOLD PROMISE'

This witch hazel is a large, spreading, deciduous shrub grown for the clusters of yellow flowers that appear on its bare branches in mid-to late winter. The flowers are very fragrant and have crimped petals. The broadly oval, mid-green leaves turn an attractive yellow in autumn. A fine specimen for a small garden.

CULTIVATION *Grow in well-drained, fertile, peaty soil, in sun or semi-shade. Provide shelter from cold winter winds. Pruning is best kept to a minimum.*

☼◑ ◊ Z 5-9 H 9-5 ‡↔ 12ft (4m)

HAMAMELIS × *INTERMEDIA* 'PALLIDA'

This witch hazel is an open shrub with spreading branches and dark green, deciduous foliage. Valued for the spidery, sulfur-yellow flowers with an enchanting fragrance, which adorn its bare branches from mid- to late winter. The leaves turn yellow in autumn. Good on its own or planted in groups in a larger garden.

CULTIVATION *Grow in well-drained, fertile, peaty soil, in sun or semi-shade. Provide shelter from cold winter winds. Pruning is best kept to a minimum.*

☀:◐ ◊ Z 5-9 H 9-5   ‡↔ 12ft (4m)

HEBE CUPRESSOIDES 'BOUGHTON DOME'

This dwarf, evergreen shrub is grown for its neat shape and dense foliage that forms a pale green dome. Flowers are infrequent. The congested, slender, grayish green branches carry scalelike, pale green leaves. Excellent in a rock garden; gives a topiary effect without any clipping. Thrives in coastal gardens.

CULTIVATION *Grow in moist but well-drained, poor to moderately fertile soil, in full sun or partial shade. No regular pruning is necessary.*

☀:◐ ◊ ◊◊ Z 8-9 H 9-8   ‡12in (30cm)
↔24in (60cm)

HEBE × *FRANCISCANA* 'VARIEGATA'

A dense, rounded, evergreen shrub bearing colorful, oval leaves; these are mid-green with creamy white margins. Purple flowers that contrast well with the foliage are carried in dense spikes during summer and autumn. A fine, pollution-tolerant plant for a mixed border or rock garden. Where marginally hardy, shelter at the foot of a wall.

CULTIVATION *Grow in moist but well-drained, poor to moderately fertile soil, in sun or light shade. Shelter from cold, drying winds. No pruning is necessary.*

☼☀ ◊◊ Z 9-10 H 10-9 ‡↔ 48in (120cm)

HEBE 'GREAT ORME'

An open, rounded, evergreen shrub that carries slender spikes of small, deep pink flowers which fade to white. These are borne from mid-summer to mid-autumn amid the lance-shaped, glossy dark green leaves. Good in a mixed or shrub border; shelter at the base of a warm wall in cold climates.

CULTIVATION *Grow in moist but well-drained, poor to moderately fertile soil, in sun or light shade. Shelter from cold winds. Pruning is unnecessary, but leggy plants can be cut back in spring.*

☼☀ ◊◊ Z 9-10 H 10-9 ‡↔ 4ft (1.2m)

HEBE PINGUIFOLIA 'PAGEI'

A low-growing, evergreen shrub bearing purple stems with four ranks of leathery, oval, blue-green leaves. Abundant clusters of white flowers appear at the tips of the shoots in late spring and early summer. Plant in groups as groundcover or in a rock garden.

CULTIVATION *Grow in moist but well-drained, poor to moderately fertile soil, in sun or partial shade. Best with some shelter from cold, drying winds. Trim to neaten in early spring, if necessary.*

☼ ◑ ◊◊ Z 8-10 H 10-8 ↕12in (30cm) ↔36in (90cm)

HEBE RAKAIENSIS

A rounded, evergreen shrub bearing spikes of white flowers from early to mid-summer. The leaves are elliptic and glossy bright green. Ideal either as a small, spreading specimen shrub or as a focal point in a large rock garden.

CULTIVATION *Grow in moist but well-drained, poor to moderately fertile soil, in sun or partial shade. Best with some shelter from cold, drying winds. Trim to shape in early spring, if necessary.*

☼ ◑ ◊◊ Z 8-10 H 10-8 ↕3ft (1m) ↔4ft (1.2m)

HEDERA COLCHICA 'DENTATA'

This Persian ivy is a very vigorous, evergreen, self-clinging climber carrying large, heart-shaped, drooping, glossy green leaves. The stems and leaf stalks are flushed purple. A handsome plant for covering an unattractive wall in shade; also effective as groundcover.

CULTIVATION *Best in moist but well-drained, fertile, ideally alkaline soil, in partial to deep shade. Prune at any time of the year to restrict size .*

☼◐ ◊◊ Z 5-10 H 12-5 ↕30ft (10m)

HEDERA COLCHICA 'SULPHUR HEART'

This colored-leaf Persian ivy is a very vigorous, self-clinging evergreen climber that can also be grown as a groundcover. The large, heart-shaped leaves are dark green suffused with creamy yellow; as they mature, the color becomes more even. Will quickly cover a wall in shade.

CULTIVATION *Grow in moist but well-drained, fertile, preferably alkaline soil. Tolerates partial shade, but leaf color is more intense in sun. Prune at any time of the year to restrict size.*

☼◐ ◊◊ Z 5-10 H 12-5 ↕15ft (5m)

ENGLISH IVIES (*HEDERA*)

Hedera helix, the English ivy, is an evergreen, woody-stemmed, self-clinging climber and the parent of an enormous selection of cultivars. Leaf forms vary from heart-shaped to deeply lobed, ranging in color from the bright gold 'Buttercup' to the deep purple 'Atropurpurea'. They make excellent groundcover, tolerating even dry shade and quickly covering featureless walls. They can damage paintwork or invade gutters if not kept in check. Variegated cultivars are especially useful for enlivening dark corners and shaded walls. Small ivies make good houseplants and can be trained over topiary frames.

CULTIVATION *Best in moist but well-drained, organic, alkaline soil. Choose a position in full sun or shade; ivies with variegated leaves may lose their color in shade. Trim as necessary to keep under control. 'Goldchild' and 'Little Diamond' are less cold-tolerant.*

☼ ◐ ◊◊ Z 5-10 H 12-5

1 ‡25ft (8m)   2 ‡6ft (2m)   3 ‡6ft (2m)

4 ‡3ft (1m)   5 ‡3ft (1m)   6 ‡12in (30cm)

1 *H. helix* 'Atropurpurea'   2 *H. helix* 'Buttercup'   3 *H. helix* 'Glacier'
4 *H. helix* 'Goldchild'   5 *H. helix* 'Ivalace'   6 *H. helix* 'Little Diamond'

HEDERA HIBERNICA

Irish ivy is a vigorous, evergreen,
self-clinging climber valued for its
broadly oval, dark green leaves that
have gray-green veins and five
triangular lobes. Useful for a wall
or against a large tree, or as fast-
growing groundcover under trees
or shrubs.

CULTIVATION *Best in moist but well-
drained, fertile, ideally alkaline soil, in
partial to full shade. Prune at any time
of the year to restrict spread.*

☼ ◑ ● ◊ ◖ Z 6-10 H 12-6　　‡to 30ft (10m)

HELIANTHEMUM '*FIRE DRAGON*'

This rock rose, also called 'Mrs.
Clay', is a small, spreading, evergreen
shrub bearing a profusion of saucer-
shaped, bright orange-red flowers.
These open in succession during late
spring and summer amid the oblong,
gray-green leaves. Ideal for a rock
garden or raised bed or as groundcover in groups on a sunny bank.

CULTIVATION *Grow in well-drained,
slightly alkaline soil, in full sun. Trim
after flowering to keep compact. Often
short-lived, but easily propagated by
softwood cuttings taken in late spring.*

☼ ◊ Z 6-8 H 8-6　　‡8–12in (20–30cm)
　　　　↔12in (30cm) or more

HELIANTHEMUM 'HENFIELD BRILLIANT'

This rock rose is a small, spreading, evergreen shrub bearing saucer-shaped, brick-red flowers in late spring and summer. The leaves are narrow and gray-green. Effective in groups on a sunny bank; also good in a rock garden or raised bed or at the front of a border.

CULTIVATION *Grow in moderately fertile, well-drained, neutral to alkaline soil, in sun. Trim after flowering to keep bushy. Often short-lived, but easily propagated by softwood cuttings in late spring.*

☼ ◊ Z 6-8 H 8-6   ↕8–12in (20–30cm)
↔12in (30cm) or more

HELIANTHEMUM 'RHODANTHE CARNEUM'

This long-flowering rock rose, also sold as 'Wisley Pink', is a low and spreading, evergreen shrub. Pale pink, saucer-shaped flowers with yellow-flushed centers appear from late spring to summer amid narrow, gray-green leaves. Good in a rock garden, raised bed, or mixed border.

CULTIVATION *Best in well-drained, moderately fertile, neutral to alkaline soil, in full sun. Trim after flowering to encourage further blooms.*

☼ ◊ Z 6-8 H 8-6   ↕to 12in (30cm)
↔to 18in (45cm) or more

HELIANTHEMUM 'WISLEY PRIMROSE'

This primrose-yellow-flowered rock rose is a fast-growing, spreading, evergreen shrub. It bears a profusion of saucer-shaped flowers with golden centers over long periods in late spring and summer. The leaves are narrowly oblong and gray-green. Group together in a rock garden, raised bed, or sunny bank.

CULTIVATION *Grow in well-drained, moderately fertile, preferably neutral to alkaline soil, in full sun. Trim after flowering to encourage further blooms.*

☼ ◊ Z 6-8 H 8-6 ↕ to 12in (30cm)
↔ to 18in (45cm) or more

HELIANTHUS 'LODDON GOLD'

This double-flowered sunflower is a tall, spreading perennial with coarse, oval, mid-green leaves that are arranged along the upright stems. Grown for its large, bright yellow flowers, which open during late summer and last into early autumn. Use to extend the season of interest in herbaceous and mixed borders.

CULTIVATION *Grow in moist to well-drained, moderately fertile, organic soil. Choose a sheltered site in full sun. Flowers best in areas with long, hot summers. Stake flower stems.*

☼ ◊◊ Z 5-9 H 9-5 ↕ 5ft (1.5m) ↔ 36in (90cm)

HELIANTHUS 'MONARCH'

This semi-double sunflower is a tall, spreading perennial with sturdy, upright stems bearing oval and toothed, mid-green leaves. Large, starlike, bright golden-yellow flowers with yellow-brown centers are produced from late summer to autumn. A statuesque plant for late-summer interest in a herbaceous or mixed border.

CULTIVATION *Grow in any well-drained, moderately fertile soil. Choose a sunny, sheltered site. The stems need support.*

☼ ◊ Z 5-9 H 9-5   ↕6ft (2m) ↔4ft (1.2m)

HELICHRYSUM PETIOLARE

The licorice plant is a silvery, mound-forming, evergreen shrub with trailing stems. Its small leaves are densely felted and silver-gray. The inconspicuous summer flowers are often pinched off, since they spoil the foliage effect. Where not hardy, grow as an annual in a hanging basket or other container; in warm areas it is useful as a groundcover.

CULTIVATION *Grow in any well-drained soil, in full sun. Pinch young stems to promote bushiness. May be trained into standards and other formal shapes.*

☼ ◊ Z 10-11 H 12-1   ↕20in (50cm) or more ↔6ft (2m)

HELICHRYSUM PETIOLARE 'VARIEGATUM'

This variegated licorice plant is a trailing, evergreen shrub grown for its densely felted, silver-gray and cream leaves. Small, creamy yellow flowers appear in summer but are of little ornamental interest and may be removed. Excellent in hanging baskets or other containers; in cold areas, grow as an annual or over-winter in frost-free conditions.

CULTIVATION *Grow in any well-drained soil, in full sun. Trim regularly and pinch off unwanted flowers as they form. Useful for training into formal shapes.*

 Z 10-11 H 12-1 ‡20in (50cm) or more ↔6ft (2m)

HELICHRYSUM SPLENDIDUM

A compact, white-woolly, evergreen perennial bearing linear, aromatic, silver-gray foliage. Small, bright yellow flowerheads open at the tips of the upright stems from mid-summer to autumn and last into winter. Suitable for a mixed border or rock garden; the flowers can be dried for winter decoration.

CULTIVATION *Grow in well-drained, poor to moderately fertile, neutral to alkaline soil, in full sun. Remove dead or damaged growth in spring, cutting back leggy shoots into old wood.*

☀ ◊ Z 9-11 H 12-1 ‡↔4ft (1.2m)

HELIOTROPIUM 'PRINCESS MARINA'

A compact, evergreen shrub that is usually grown as an annual or as a conservatory plant in cold climates. Much valued for its fragrant heads of deep violet-blue flowers that appear in summer above the oblong, wrinkled, mid- to dark green, often purple-tinged leaves. Good at the front of a border, in containers, or as summer bedding.

CULTIVATION *Grow in any moist but well-drained, fertile soil or mix, in sun. Propagate superior forms by cuttings.*

☼ ◊◊ Z 11 H 12-1   ‡↔ to 12in (30cm)

HELLEBORUS ARGUTIFOLIUS

The large Corsican hellebore, sometimes known as *H. corsicus*, is an early-flowering, clump-forming, evergreen perennial bearing large clusters of nodding, pale green flowers. These appear in winter and early spring above the handsome dark green leaves, which are divided into three sharply toothed leaflets. Excellent for early interest in a woodland garden or mixed border.

CULTIVATION *Grow in moist, fertile, preferably neutral to alkaline soil, in full sun or partial shade. Often short-lived, but self-seeds readily.*

☼☼ ◊ Z 6-9 H 9-6   ‡4ft (1.2m) ↔36in (90cm)

HELLEBORUS FOETIDUS

The stinking hellebore is an upright, evergreen perennial forming clumps of dark green, divided leaves that smell unpleasant when crushed. In winter and early spring, clusters of small, nodding, cup-shaped flowers appear above the foliage; their green petals are edged with red. A striking specimen for late winter interest.

CULTIVATION *Grow in moist, fertile, neutral to alkaline soil. Choose a position in sun or partial shade.*

☼ ◑ ◊ Z 6-9 H 9-6   ‡to 32in (80cm)
↔18in (45cm)

HELLEBORUS NIGER

A clump-forming, usually evergreen perennial valued for its nodding clusters of cup-shaped white flowers in winter and early spring. The dark green leaves are divided into several leaflets. Effective with snowdrops beneath early-flowering shrubs, but can be difficult to naturalize.

CULTIVATION *Grow in deep, fertile, neutral to alkaline soil that is reliably moist. Site in dappled shade with shelter from cold, drying winds.*

☼ ◑ ◊ Z 4-8 H 8-1   ‡12in (30cm) ↔18in (45cm)

DAYLILIES (*HEMEROCALLIS*)

Daylilies are clump-forming, herbaceous perennials, so-called because each of their showy flowers lasts for only one day; in nocturnal daylilies, such as 'Green Flutter', the flowers open in late afternoon and last through the night. The blooms are abundant and rapidly replaced, some starting in late spring, while other cultivars flower into autumn. Flower shapes vary from circular to spider-shaped, in a wide range of colors and patterns. The leaves are straplike and sometimes evergreen.

Daylilies make a dramatic contribution to a mixed or herbaceous border; dwarf types, such as 'Stella de Oro', are useful for small gardens or in containers.

CULTIVATION *Grow in well-drained but moist, fertile soil, in sun or semi-shade. Mulch in spring, and feed with a balanced fertilizer monthly until buds form. Divide and replant every few years, in spring or autumn.*

☼ ◐ ◊◊ Z 3-10 H 12-1

1 ‡28in (70cm) ↔ 16in (40cm)

2 ‡36in (90cm) ↔ 18in (45cm)

3 ‡20in (50cm) ↔ 3ft (1m)

4 ↔ 3ft (1m)

5 ‡24in (60cm) ↔ 3ft (1m)

6 ‡12in (30cm) ↔ 18in (45cm)

1 *H.* 'Corky' **2** *H.* 'Golden Chimes' **3** *H.* 'Green Flutter' **4** *H. lilioasphodelus* **5** *H.* 'Nova'
6 *H.* 'Stella de Oro'

HEPATICA NOBILIS

A small, slow-growing, anemone-like,
semi-evergreen perennial bearing
saucer-shaped, purple, white, or
pink flowers. These appear in early
spring, usually before the foliage has
emerged. The mid-green, sometimes
mottled leaves are leathery and
divided into three lobes. Good for
a shady rock garden.

CULTIVATION *Grow in moist but well-
drained, fertile, neutral to alkaline soil,
in partial shade. Provide a mulch of
leaf mold in autumn or spring.*

☼ ◐ ◊◊ Z 5-8 H 8-4 ↕4in (10cm) ↔6in (15cm)

HEUCHERA MICRANTHA VAR. DIVERSIFOLIA 'PALACE PURPLE'

A clump-forming perennial valued
for its glistening, dark purple-red,
almost metallic foliage, which is
topped by airy sprays of white
flowers in summer. The leaves have
five pointed lobes. Plant in groups
as a groundcover for a shady site
(but it can be slow to spread).

CULTIVATION *Grow in moist but well-
drained, fertile soil, in sun or partial
shade. Tolerates full shade where the
ground is reliably moist. Lift and divide
clumps every few years, after flowering.*

☼◑◐ ◊◊ Z 4-8 H 8-1 ↕↔ 24in (60cm)

HEUCHERA
'RED SPANGLES'

This clump-forming, evergreen perennial is valued for its sprays of small, bell-shaped, crimson-scarlet flowers. These are borne in early summer, with a repeat bloom in late summer, on dark red stems above the lobed, heart-shaped, purplish green leaves. Effective as a ground-cover when grouped together.

CULTIVATION *Grow in moist but well-drained, fertile soil, in sun or partial shade. Tolerates full shade where the ground is reliably moist. Lift and divide clumps every three years, after flowering.*

☼ ◐ ◊◊ Z 3-8 H 8-1   ↕20in (50cm)
                              ↔10in (25cm)

HIBISCUS SYRIACUS
'OISEAU BLEU'

Also known as 'Blue Bird', this vigorous, upright, deciduous shrub bears large, mallowlike, lilac-blue flowers with red centers. These are borne from mid- to late summer amid deep green leaves. Ideal for a mixed or shrub border.

CULTIVATION *Grow in moist but well-drained, fertile, neutral to slightly alkaline soil, in full sun. Prune young plants hard in late spring to encourage branching at the base; keep pruning to a minimum once established.*

☼ ◊◊ Z 5-9 H 9-1   ↕10ft (3m) ↔6ft (2m)

HIBISCUS SYRIACUS
'WOODBRIDGE'

A fast-growing, upright, deciduous shrub producing large, deep rose-pink flowers with maroon blotches around the centers. These are borne from late summer to mid-autumn amid the lobed, dark green leaves. Valuable for its late and long season of interest.

CULTIVATION *Grow in moist but well-drained, fertile, slightly alkaline soil, in full sun. Prune young plants hard to encourage branching; keep pruning to a minimum once established.*

☼ ◊◊ Z 5-9 H 9-1   ‡10ft (3m) ↔6ft (2m)

HIPPOPHAE
RHAMNOIDES

Sea buckthorn is a spiny, deciduous shrub with attractive fruits and foliage. Small yellow flowers in spring are followed by orange berries on female plants; they persist well into winter. The silvery gray leaves are narrow and clawlike. Good for hedging, especially in coastal areas.

CULTIVATION *Best in sandy, moist but well-drained soil, in full sun. For fruiting, plants of both sexes must grow together. Little pruning is required; trim hedges in late summer, as necessary.*

☼ ◊◊ Z 3-8 H 8-1   ‡↔ 20ft (6m)

HOSTAS

Hostas are evergreen perennials grown principally for their dense mounds of large, overlapping, lance- to heart-shaped leaves. A wide choice of foliage color is available, from the cloudy blue-green of 'Halcyon' to the bright yellow-green 'Golden Tiara'. Many have leaves marked with yellow or white; *H. fortunei* var. *albopicta* has bold, central splashes of creamy yellow. Upright clusters of funnel-shaped flowers, varying from white through lavender-blue to purple, are borne on tall stems in summer. Hostas are effective at the front of a mixed border, in containers, or as groundcover under deciduous trees.

CULTIVATION *Grow in well-drained but reliably moist, fertile soil, in full sun or partial shade. Yellow-leaved hostas color best in full sun with shade at midday. Mulch in spring to conserve moisture throughout the summer.*

☼☀◑ ◐ Z 3-8 H 8-1

1 ↕ 20in (50cm) ↔ 3ft (1m)

2 ↕ 22in (55cm) ↔ 3ft (1m)

3 ↕ 22in (55cm) ↔ 3ft (1m)

4 ↕ 22in (55cm) ↔ 3ft (1m)

5 ↕ 24in (60cm) ↔ 3ft (1m)

6 ↕ 12in (30cm) ↔ 20in (50cm)

1 *H.* 'Crispula' **2** *H.* 'Fortunei Albopicta' **3** *H.* 'Fortunei Aureomarginata' **4** *H.* 'Francee'
5 *H.* 'Frances Williams' **6** *H.* 'Golden Tiara'

7 ↕14–16in (35–40cm) ↔ 28in (70cm)

8 ↕3ft (1m) ↔ 30in (75cm)

9 ↕24in (60cm) ↔ 4ft (1.2m)

10 ↕18in (45cm) ↔ 30in (75cm)

11 ↕3ft (1m) ↔ 4ft (1.2m)

12 ↕20in (50cm) ↔ 3ft (1m)

13 ↕2in.(5cm) ↔ 10in (25cm)

14 ↕30in (75cm) ↔ 3ft (1m)

7 *H.* 'Halcyon' **8** *H.* 'Honeybells' **9** *H.* 'Royal Standard' **10** *H.* 'Shade Fanfare'
11 *H. sieboldiana* var. *elegans* **12** *H. ventricosa* **13** *H. venusta* **14** *H.* 'Wide Brim'

HUMULUS LUPULUS
'AUREUS'

Golden hops is a twining, perennial climber grown for its attractively lobed, bright golden-yellow foliage. Hanging clusters of papery, cone-like, greenish yellow flowers appear in autumn. Train over a fence or trellis or up into a small tree. The flowers dry well for garlands and swags.

CULTIVATION *Grow in moist but well drained, moderately fertile, organic soil. Tolerates partial shade, but leaf color is best in full sun. Give the twining stems support. Cut back any dead growth to ground level in early spring.*

☼◑ ◊◊ Z 4-8 H 8-3　　　‡20ft (6m

HYACINTHUS ORIENTALIS
'BLUE JACKET'

This hyacinth is a bulbous perennial bearing dense, upright spikes of fragrant, bell-shaped blue flowers with purple veins. These appear in early spring above the lance-shaped, bright green leaves. Good for spring bedding; bulbs can be planted in pots during autumn and kept cold and moist durng winter for an indoor display of early flowers.

CULTIVATION *Grow in any well-drained moderately fertile soil or soil mix, in sun or partial shade. Protect container-grown bulbs from excess winter moisture*

☼◑ ◊ Z 5-9 H 9-5　　‡8–12in (20–30cm
　　　　　　　↔3in (8cm

HYACINTHUS ORIENTALIS 'CITY OF HAARLEM'

This primrose-yellow hyacinth is a spring-flowering, bulbous perennial bearing upright spikes of fragrant, bell-shaped flowers. The lance-shaped leaves are bright green and emerge from the base of the plant. Good for spring bedding or in containers; bulbs can be planted in autumn for early flowers indoors (see 'Blue Jacket').

CULTIVATION *Grow in well-drained, fairly fertile soil or soil mix, in sun or partial shade. Protect container-grown plants from excessive winter moisture.*

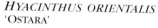

☼ ◐ ◊ Z 5-9 H 9-5   ↕8–12in (20–30cm)
↔3in (8cm)

HYACINTHUS ORIENTALIS 'OSTARA'

This violet-blue hyacinth is a bulbous perennial grown as spring bedding for its dense, upright spikes of bell-shaped, fragrant flowers with dark stripes. The bright green, lance-shaped leaves emerge from the base of the plant. Bulbs can be planted indoors during autumn for winter flowers (see 'Blue Jacket').

CULTIVATION *Best in well-drained, moderately fertile soil or soil mix, in sun or partial shade. Protect pot-grown plants from excessive winter moisture.*

☼ ◐ ◊ Z 5-9 H 9-5   ↕8–12in (20–30cm)
↔3in (8cm)

HYACINTHUS ORIENTALIS 'PINK PEARL'

This deep pink hyacinth, bearing dense, upright spikes of fragrant, bell-shaped flowers with paler edges, is a spring-flowering, bulbous perennial. The leaves are narrow and bright green. Excellent in a mixed or herbaceous border; bulbs can be planted in pots during autumn for an indoor display of early flowers (see 'Blue Jacket').

CULTIVATION *Grow in any well-drained, moderately fertile soil or soil mix, in sun or partial shade. Protect pot-grown bulbs from excess winter moisture.*

☼ ◐ ◊ Z 5-9 H 9-5 ‡8–12in (20–30cm) ↔3in (8cm)

HYDRANGEA ANOMALA SUBSP. *PETIOLARIS*

The climbing hydrangea, often sold simply as *H. petiolaris*, is a woody-stemmed, deciduous, self-clinging climber usually grown on shady walls for its large, lacecaplike heads of creamy white, summer flowers. The mid-green leaves are oval and coarsely toothed. Often slow to establish, but normally long-lived.

CULTIVATION *Grow in any reliably moist, fertile soil in sun or deep shade. Little pruning is required, but as the allotted space is filled, cut back overlong shoots after flowering.*

☼ ◐ ◊ Z 4-9 H 9-1 ‡50ft (15m)

HYDRANGEA ARBORESCENS 'ANNABELLE'

An upright, deciduous shrub bearing large, rounded heads of densely packed, creamy white flowers from mid-summer to early autumn. The bright green leaves are broadly oval and pointed. Good on its own or in a shrub border; the flowerheads can be dried for winter decoration.

CULTIVATION *Grow in moist but well-drained, moderately fertile, organic soil, in sun or partial shade. Keep pruning to a minimum, or cut back hard each spring to a low framework.*

☼ ☀ ◑◐ Z 4-9 H 9-3 ‡5ft (1.5m) ↔ 8ft (2.5m)

HYDRANGEA ASPERA VILLOSA GROUP

A group of spreading to upright, deciduous shrubs that can become treelike with age. In late summer, they produce flattened, lacecaplike heads of small blue-purple or rich blue flowers, surrounded by larger, lilac-white or rose-lilac flowers. The leaves are lance-shaped and dark green. Excellent in a woodland or wild garden; in colder areas they may benefit from wall training.

CULTIVATION *Grow in moist but well-drained, organic, moderately fertile soil. Site in full sun or semi-shade. Little pruning is necessary.*

☼ ◑◐ Z 6-9 H 9-5 ‡3–12ft (1–4m)

HYDRANGEA MACROPHYLLA

Cultivars of the common hydrangea, *H. macrophylla*, are rounded shrubs with oval, mid- to dark green, deciduous leaves. Their large, showy flowerheads, borne from mid- to late summer, are available in two distinct forms: lacecaps, such as 'Veitchii', have flat flowerheads, and mop-head hydrangeas (Hortensias), such as 'Altona', have round flowerheads. Except in white-flowered cultivars, flower color is influenced by soil pH; generally, acid soils produce blue flowers, and alkaline soils give rise to pink flowers.

All types of hydrangea are useful for a range of garden sites, and the flowerheads dry well for indoor arrangements.

CULTIVATION *Grow in moist but well-drained, fertile soil, in sun or partial shade with shelter from cold winds. Prune hard in spring to enhance flowering, cutting stems back to strong pairs of buds. Flower color can be influenced by manipulating pH.*

☀ ◐ ◊◊ Z 6-9 H 9-2

1 ‡3ft (1m) ↔ 5ft (1.5m) **2** ‡6ft (2m) ↔ 8ft (2.5m) **3** ‡↔ 5ft (1.5m) **4** ‡6ft (2m) ↔ 8ft (2.5m) **5** ‡6ft (2m) ↔ 8ft (2.5m)

1 *H. macrophylla* 'Altona' (Mop-head) **2** *H. macrophylla* 'Blue Wave' (syn. 'Mariesii Perfecta') (Lacecap) **3** *H. macrophylla* 'Lanarth White' (Lacecap) **4** *H. macrophylla* 'Générale Vicomtesse de Vibraye' (Mop-head) **5** *H. macrophylla* 'Veitchii' (Lacecap)

HYDRANGEA PANICULATA

Cultivars of *H. paniculata* are fast-growing, upright, deciduous shrubs, with oval, mid- to dark green leaves. They are cultivated for their large clusters of lacy flowers that usually appear during late summer and early autumn; some cultivars, such as 'Praecox', bloom earlier in the summer. Flowers are mostly creamy white; some forms, such as 'Floribunda', become pink-tinged as they age. These versatile shrubs are suitable for many different garden uses as specimen plants, in groups, or in containers. The flowerheads look very attractive when dried for indoor decoration.

CULTIVATION *Grow in moist but well-drained, fertile soil. Site in sun or partial shade. Pruning is not essential, but flower size is increased if pruned back annually, in early spring, to the lowest pair of healthy buds on a permanent, woody framework.*

☼☀ ◊◊ Z 4-8 H 8-1

1 ↕10–22ft (3–7m) ↔ 8ft (2.5m)

2 ↕10–22ft (3–7m) ↔ 8ft (2.5m)

3 ↕10–22ft (3–7m) ↔ 8ft (2.5m)

1 *H. paniculata* 'Floribunda' **2** *H. paniculata* 'Grandiflora' **3** *H. paniculata* 'Praecox'

HYDRANGEA QUERCIFOLIA

The oakleaf hydrangea is a mound-forming, deciduous shrub bearing conical heads of white flowers that fade to pink, from mid-summer to autumn. The deeply lobed, mid-green leaves turn bronze-purple in autumn, and the peeling bark is attractive in winter. Useful in a range of garden sites.

CULTIVATION *Prefers well-drained but moist, moderately fertile soil, in sun or partial shade. Leaves may become yellow in shallow, chalky soil. Keep pruning to a minimum, in spring.*

☼:◐ ◁ Z 5-9 H 9-2 ↕6ft (2m) ↔8ft (2.5m)

HYDRANGEA SERRATA 'BLUEBIRD'

A compact, upright, long-flowering, deciduous shrub bearing attractive, flattened flowerheads. These are made up of tiny, rich blue flowers surrounded by larger, pale blue flowers from summer to autumn. The narrowly oval, pointed, mid-green leaves turn red in autumn. The flowerheads can be dried for indoor arrangements.

CULTIVATION *Grow in moist but well-drained, moderately fertile, organic soil, in sun or partial shade. Flowers may turn pink in alkaline soils. Cut back weak, thin shoots in mid-spring.*

☼:◐ ◁ Z 6-9 H 10-8 ↕↔4ft (1.2m)

HYDRANGEA SERRATA 'ROSALBA'

An upright, compact, deciduous shrub valued for its flat flowerheads that appear from summer to autumn; these are made up of tiny pink flowers in the center, surrounded by larger white flowers that become red-marked as they age. The leaves are oval, mid-green, and pointed. Ideal as a specimen plant or in a shrub border.

CULTIVATION *Grow in well-drained but moist, moderately fertile, organic soil, in full sun or partial shade. Flowers may turn blue on acid soils. Very little pruning is needed.*

☼◑ ◊ Z 6-9 H 10-8　↔4ft (1.2m)

HYPERICUM 'HIDCOTE'

This dense, evergreen or semi-evergreen shrub produces abundant clusters of large, cupped, golden-yellow flowers that open from mid-summer to early autumn. The leaves are dark green and lance-shaped. Suitable for a shrub border.

CULTIVATION *Grow in well-drained but moist, moderately fertile soil, in sun or partial shade. Cut back annually in spring and deadhead regularly to increase the flowering potential.*

☼◑ ◊◊ Z 6-9 H 9-6　↕4ft (1.2m) ↔5ft (1.5m)

IBERIS SEMPERVIRENS

A spreading, evergreen subshrub bearing dense, rounded heads of small, unevenly shaped white flowers that may be flushed with pink or lilac. These appear in late spring and early summer, covering the spoon-shaped, dark green leaves. Best grown in a rock garden or large wall pocket.

CULTIVATION *Grow in well-drained, poor to moderately fertile, neutral to alkaline soil, in full sun. Trim lightly after flowering for neatness.*

☼ ◊ Z 5-9 H 9-8 ‡ to 12in (30cm)
↔ to 16in (40cm)

ILEX × *ALTACLERENSIS* 'LAWSONIANA' (FEMALE)

This dense and bushy holly forms a compact, evergreen tree or shrub. It bears large, usually spineless, oval, bright green leaves, which are splashed with gold and paler green in the centers. Red-brown berries, ripening to red, develop in autumn.

CULTIVATION *Grow in moist but well-drained soil, in sun for best leaf color. Grow a male holly nearby to ensure a display of berries. Free-standing plants may need some shaping when young. Remove any all-green shoots as seen.*

☼ ◊ Z 7-9 H 9-7 ‡ to 6m (20ft) ↔ 15ft (5m)

ENGLISH HOLLIES (*ILEX AQUIFOLIUM*)

Ilex aquifolium, the English holly, has many different cultivars of upright, evergreen trees or large shrubs, which are usually grown on their own or as spiny hedges. They have purple stems, gray bark, and dense, glossy foliage. Most cultivars have multicolored, spiny leaves, although those of 'J.C. van Tol' are spineless and dark green. 'Ferox Argentea' has extra-spiny leaves. Male and female flowers are borne on separate plants, so female hollies, like 'Madame Briot', must be near males, such as 'Golden Milkboy', if they are to bear a good crop of berries. Tall specimens make effective windbreaks.

CULTIVATION *Grow in moist, well-drained, fertile, organic soil. Choose a site in full sun for good leaf variegation, but tolerates partial shade. Remove any damaged wood and shape young trees in spring; hedges should be trimmed in late summer. Over-enthusiastic pruning will spoil their form.*

☼ ◑ ◊ Z 7-9 H 9-7

1 ‡ to 25ft (8m) ↔ 12ft (4m)

2 ‡ 20ft (6m) ↔ 12ft (4m)

3 ‡ 25ft (8m) ↔ 15ft (5m)

4 ‡ 20ft (6m) ↔ 12ft (4m)

5 ‡ 30ft (10m) ↔ 15ft (5m)

6 ‡ 30ft (10m) ↔ 12ft (4m)

1 *I. aquifolium* 'Ferox Argentea' (male) **2** *I. aquifolium* 'Golden Milkboy' (male)
3 *I. aquifolium* 'Handsworth New Silver' (female) **4** *I. aquifolium* 'J.C. van Tol' (female)
5 *I. aquifolium* 'Madame Briot' (female) **6** *I. aquifolium* 'Silver Queen' (male)

ILEX CRENATA
'CONVEXA' (FEMALE)

This bushy form of Japanese holly is
a dense, evergreen shrub with
purple-green stems and spineless,
oval to elliptic, glossy, mid- to dark
green leaves. It bears an abundance
of small, black berries in autumn.
Lends itself for use in hedging or
as topiary.

CULTIVATION *Needs moist but well-
drained, organic soil, in full sun or
partial shade. Grow near a male holly
for a good crop of berries. Cut out badly
placed growth in early spring, and trim
shaped plants in summer.*

☼◐ ◊ Z 5-7 H 7-4 ‡8ft (2.5m) ↔6ft (2m)

ILEX × *MESERVEAE*
'BLUE PRINCESS' (FEMALE)

This blue holly is a vigorous, dense,
evergreen shrub with oval, softly
spiny, very glossy, greenish blue
leaves. White to pinkish white, late
spring flowers are followed by a
profusion of glossy red berries in
autumn. The dark purplish green
young stems show well when
hedging plants are regularly clipped.
Dislikes coastal conditions.

CULTIVATION *Grow in moist but well-
drained, moderately fertile soil, in full
sun or semi-shade. For berries, a male
holly will need to be nearby. Prune in
late summer to maintain shape.*

☼◐ ◊ Z 5-9 H 9-5 ‡↔10ft (3m)

IMPATIENS
SUPER ELFIN SERIES

These impatiens, grown as annual
bedding plants, have spreading stems
bearing long-lasting summer flowers
with flattened faces and slender
spurs. These bloom in a range of
pastel colors and shades of orange,
red, and violet. The oval leaves are
light green. Excellent summer
bedding or container plants for a
partially shaded site.

CULTIVATION *Grow in well-drained but
moist, organic soil, in partial shade
with shelter from wind. Plant out after
danger of frost has passed.*

☀ ◗ annual H 12-1　　‡ to 24in (60cm)
　　　　　　　　　　↔ to 10in (25cm)

IMPATIENS TEMPO SERIES

These impatiens, in either single
colors or mixed, bear a profusion of
flattened, spurred flowers that range
in color from violet and lavender-
blue to orange, pink, and red; some
have contrasting edges or bicolored
petals. Leaves are light green and
slightly toothed. Grown as an annual
bedding plant, it also provides long-
lasting color in containers and
summer borders.

CULTIVATION *Grow in moist but well-
drained, organic soil, in a sheltered
site. Tolerates shade. Plant out after any
danger of frost has passed.*

☀ ◗ annual H 12-1　　‡ to 9in (23cm)
　　　　　　　　　　↔ to 10in (25cm)

INDIGOFERA HETERANTHA

A medium-sized, spreading shrub grown for its pealike flowers and elegant foliage. The arching stems carry gray-green leaves made up of many oval to oblong leaflets. Dense upright clusters of small, purple-pink flowers appear from early summer to autumn. Train against a wall where marginally hardy.

CULTIVATION *Grow in well-drained but moist, moderately fertile soil, in full sun. Prune in early spring, cutting back to just above ground level.*

☼ ◊ Z 6-9 H 9-6   ‡↔ 6–10ft (2–3

IPHEION UNIFLORUM 'WISLEY BLUE'

A vigorous, clump-forming, mainly spring-flowering, bulbous perennial bearing scented, star-shaped, lilac-blue flowers; each petal has a pale base and a dark midrib. Narrow, straplike, light blue-green leaves are produced in autumn. Useful in a rock garden or for underplanting herbaceous plants.

CULTIVATION *Grow in moist but well-drained, moderately fertile, organic soil, in full sun. Where marginally hardy, provide a winter mulch.*

☼ ◊ Z 6-9 H 9-6   ‡6–8in (15–20

IPOMOEA
'HEAVENLY BLUE'

This summer-flowering, twining,
fast-growing form of morning glory
is grown as a climbing annual. The
large, funnel-shaped flowers, azure-
blue with pure white throats, appear
singly or in clusters of two or three.
The heart-shaped, light to mid-green
leaves have slender tips. Suitable for
a summer border scrambling among
other plants, or on a trellis. Seeds
are highly toxic if ingested.

CULTIVATION *Grow in well-drained,
moderately fertile soil, in sun. Plant out
seedlings after the last frost.*

☼ ◊ annual H 12-1   ‡ to 10–12ft (3–4m)

IPOMOEA INDICA

The blue dawn flower is a vigorous,
evergreen climber, perennial in frost-
free conditions. Abundant, rich
purple-blue, funnel-shaped flowers
that often fade to red are borne in
clusters of three to five from late
spring to autumn. The mid-green
leaves are heart-shaped or three-
lobed. Grow as annuals in a summer
border or on a trellis.
The seeds are toxic.

CULTIVATION *Grow in well-drained,
faily fertile soil. Plant out after all
danger of frost has passed. Minimum
temperature 45°F (7°C).*

☼ ◊ annual H 12-1   ‡ to 20ft (6m)

IRISES FOR MOIST TO WET SOIL

Irises that flourish in reliably moist or wet soils all produce swollen, horizontal creeping stems, known as rhizomes, that lie just below the ground. They have strap-shaped, sometimes curved leaves, that are arranged like fans. Each active rhizome produces several new offsets each year, and this spread can continue indefinitely; in three years a fast-growing iris, such as *I. pseudacorus*, may have a root spread of over 3 ft (90cm). Stems may be branched; during late spring and early summer they bear flowers that are available in a wide range of colors. All are ideal for pond or stream margins and moist borders. Some, such as *I. laevigata*, tolerate shallow water.

CULTIVATION *Grow in deep, damp to wet, acid soil that is enriched with well-rotted organic matter, in full sun or light shade. Best in areas with hot summers. Plant rhizomes in early autumn.*

☼◐ ◊◊ Z 3-9 H 9-1

1 ‡30in (75cm) ↔ to 6ft (1.8m)

2 ‡32in (80cm) ↔ indefinite

3 ‡32in (80cm) ↔ indefinite

4 ‡8–32in (20–80cm) ↔ indefinite

5 ‡3–5ft (0.9–1.5m) ↔ indefinite

1 *I.* × *robusta* 'Gerald Darby' **2** *I. laevigata* **3** *I. laevigata* 'Variegata' **4** *I. versicolor*
5 *I. pseudacorus*

IRIS BUCHARICA

A fast-growing, spring-flowering, bulbous perennial that carries up to six golden-yellow to white flowers on each stem. The glossy, straplike leaves die back after flowering. The most commonly available form of this iris has yellow and white flowers.

CULTIVATION *Grow in rich but well-drained, neutral to slightly alkaline soil, in full sun. Water moderately when in growth; after flowering, maintain a period of dry dormancy.*

☼ ◊ Z 5-9 H 9-5   ‡8–16in (20–40cm)
↔ 5in (12cm)

IRIS CONFUSA

This freely spreading, rhizomatous perennial with bamboolike foliage produces a succession of up to 30 short-lived flowers on each stem during spring. They are white with yellow crests surrounded by purple or yellow spots. The leaves are arranged in fans at the base of the plant. Suitable for a sheltered, mixed or herbaceous border.

CULTIVATION *Grow in moist but well-drained, rich soil, in sun or semi-shade. Water moderately when in growth. Keep neat-looking by removing flowered stems.*

☼◑ ◊ Z 8-10 H 12-8   ‡3ft (1m) or more
↔ indefinite

IRIS DOUGLASIANA

A robust, rhizomatous perennial with branched flower stems that each bear two or three white, cream, blue, lavender-blue, or red-purple flowers in late spring and early summer. The stiff, glossy dark green leaves are often red at the bases. A good display plant for a raised bed or trough.

CULTIVATION *Grow in well-drained, neutral to slightly acid loam. Site in full sun for the best flowers, or light shade. Does not transplant well.*

☼ ◐ ◊ Z 7-9 H 9-7 ‡6–28in (15–70cm)
↔ indefin

IRIS FORRESTII

An elegant, early summer-flowering rhizomatous perennial with slender flower stems that each carry one or two scented, pale yellow flowers with brown markings. The very narrow, glossy leaves are mid-green above and gray-green below. Grow in an open border.

CULTIVATION *Grow in moist but well-drained, neutral to slightly acid loam. Position in full sun or partial shade.*

☼ ◐ ◊◊ Z 6-9 H 9-6 ‡14–16in (35–40cm)
↔ indefi

IRIS GRAMINEA

A deciduous, rhizomatous perennial bearing bright green, straplike leaves. From late spring, rich purple-violet flowers, with fall petals tipped white and violet-veined, are borne either singly or in pairs; they are often hidden among the leaves. The flowers have a fruity fragrance.

CULTIVATION *Grow in moist but well-drained, neutral to slightly acid loam. Choose a site in full sun or semi-shade. Does not respond well to transplanting.*

☀◐ ◊ Z 6-9 H 9-6 ‡8–16in (20–40cm)
↔ indefinite

IRIS 'KATHARINE HODGKIN'

This very vigorous, tiny but robust, deciduous, bulbous perennial bears delicately patterned, pale blue and yellow flowers with darker blue and gold markings, in late winter and early spring. The pale to mid-green leaves grow after the flowers have faded. Excellent in a rock garden or at the front of a border, where it will spread slowly to form a group.

CULTIVATION *Grow in well-drained, neutral to slightly alkaline soil, in an open site in full sun.*

☀ ◊ Z 5-8 H 8-5 ‡12cm (5in) when flowering
↔ 5–8cm (2–3in)

IRIS LACUSTRIS

This dwarf, deciduous, rhizomatous perennial bears small flowers in late spring. These are purple-blue to sky blue with gold crests and a white patch on each of the the fall petals; they arise from basal fans of narrow leaves. Suitable for growing in a rock garden or trough.

CULTIVATION *Grow in reliably moist, lime-free soil that is rich in organic matter, in sun or partial shade. Water moderately when in growth.*

☼ ◑ ◊ Z 4-8 H 8-1 ↕4in (10cm) ↔ indefini

IRIS PALLIDA 'VARIEGATA'

This semi-evergreen, rhizomatous perennial is among the most versatile and attractive variegated iris. The straplike, bright green leaves are clearly striped with golden-yellow. The two to six large scented, soft blue flowers with yellow beards are borne on branched stems in late spring and early summer. Grow in a mixed or herbaceous border.

CULTIVATION *Best in well-drained, fertile, slightly alkaline soil, in sun. Water moderately when in growth.*

☼ ◊ Z 5-9 H 9-5 ↕to 4ft (1.2m) ↔ indefi

IRIS SIBIRICA 'WHITE SWIRL'

An elegant, early summer-flowering, rhizomatous perennial that produces flowers with rounded, flared, pure white petals that are yellow at the bases. The mid-green leaves are narrow and grasslike. Suitable for growing in an open herbaceous or mixed border.

CULTIVATION *Best in moist but well-drained, neutral to slightly acid loam. Position in full sun or partial shade.*

☼ ◑ ◊◊ Z 4-9 H 9-1 ‡3ft (1m) ↔ indefinite

IRIS UNGUICULARIS

A fast-growing, rhizomatous, evergreen perennial, sometimes called *I. stylosa*, with short flower stems bearing large, fragrant blooms from late winter (sometimes sooner) to early spring. The pale lavender to deep violet flower petals have contrasting veins and a band of yellow on each fall petal. The leaves are grasslike and mid-green. Ideal for the base of a sunny wall.

CULTIVATION *Grow in sharply drained, neutral to alkaline soil. Choose a warm, sheltered site in full sun. Does not like to be disturbed. Keep neat by removing dead leaves in late summer and spring.*

☼ ◊ Z 7-9 H 9-7 ‡12in (30cm) ↔ indefinite

IRIS VARIEGATA

This slender and robust, deciduous, rhizomatous perennial bears three to six flowers on each branched stem in spring or early summer. The striking flowers are pale yellow with brown or violet veins on the fall petals; there are other color combinations available. The deep green leaves are strongly ribbed.

CULTIVATION *Grow in well-drained, neutral to alkaline soil, in sun or light shade. Avoid mulching with organic matter, which may encourage rot.*

☼ ◖ ◊ Z 5-9 H 9-5 ‡8–18in (20–45cm) ↔ indefinit

ITEA ILICIFOLIA

An evergreen shrub bearing upright (at first) then spreading, arching shoots. The oval, hollylike leaves are sharply toothed. Tiny, greenish white flowers are borne in long, catkin like clusters from mid-summe to early autumn. Needs a sheltered position wher marginally hardy.

CULTIVATION *Grow in well-drained bu moist, fertile soil, preferably against a sunny wall. Protect with a winter mulch when young where marginal.*

☼ ◊ Z 7-9 H 9-7 ‡10–15ft (3–5m) ↔10ft (3

JASMINUM MESNYI

The primrose jasmine is a scrambling, evergreen shrub with large, usually semi-double, bright yellow flowers. These appear singly or in small clusters during spring and summer, amid the glossy, dark green leaves, which are divided into three oblong to lance-shaped leaflets. Will climb if tied to a support.

CULTIVATION *Grow in any well-drained, fertile soil, in full sun or partial shade. Cut back flowered shoots in summer to encourage strong growth from the base.*

☼ ◑ ◊ Z 8-10 H 12-8　　↕ to 10ft (3m)
　　　　　　　　　　　　↔ 3–6ft (1–2m)

JASMINUM NUDIFLORUM

Winter jasmine is a lax, mound-forming, deciduous shrub with slender, arching stems. Small, tubular yellow flowers are borne singly on the leafless, green shoots in late winter. The dark green leaves, which develop after the flowers, are divided into three leaflets. Tie in a framework of stems against a wall, or let it sprawl unsupported.

CULTIVATION *Grow in well-drained, fertile soil. Tolerates semi-shade, but flowers best in sun. Encourage strong growth by cutting back flowered shoots.*

☼ ◑ ◊ Z 6-9 H 9-6　　↕↔ to 10ft (3m)

JASMINUM OFFICINALE 'ARGENTEOVARIEGATUM'

This variegated form of the common jasmine is a vigorous, deciduous or semi-deciduous, woody climber. The gray-green, cream-edged leaves are made up of five to nine sharply pointed leaflets. Clusters of fragrant white flowers are produced from summer to early autumn. If tied in initially, it will twine over supports, such as a trellis or an arch.

CULTIVATION *Grow in well-drained, fertile soil. Tolerates shade, but flowers best in full sun. Thin out crowded growth after flowering.*

☼ ◐ ◊ Z 9-10 H 12-9   ‡to 40ft (12

JASMINUM POLYANTHUM

A fast-growing, woody-stemmed, twining, evergreen climber that bears abundant clusters of small, strongly fragrant white flowers. These open from pink buds in late spring and early summer, amid the deep green, divided leaves. Allow to climb over a trellis, fence, arch, or large shrub. May also be grown under glass for early spring blooms.

CULTIVATION *Grow in well-drained, moderately fertile soil, or in a hanging basket under glass. Thin out overcrowded growth after flowering.*

☼ ◊ Z 9-10 H 12-9   ‡to 12ft (3

JUNIPERUS COMMUNIS 'COMPRESSA'

This slow-growing, spindle-shaped, dwarf form of the common juniper bears deep to blue-green, aromatic, evergreen foliage. The pointed, scalelike leaves are borne in whorls of three along the stems. Small, oval or spherical fruits remain on the plant for three years, ripening from green through to cloudy blue to black. Suitable for growing in a barrel or other large container.

CULTIVATION *Grow in any well-drained soil, preferably in full sun or light dappled shade. No pruning is needed.*

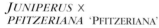

☀◑ ◊ Z 2-6 H 6-1 ‡to 32in (80cm) ↔18in (45cm)

JUNIPERUS X *PFITZERIANA* 'PFITZERIANA'

This spreading, dense, evergreen shrub has ascending branches of gray-green foliage that droop at the tips; it eventually forms a flat-topped, tiered bush. The flattened, scalelike leaves are borne in whorls of three. Spherical fruits are at first dark purple, becoming paler as they age. Looks good as a specimen plant or in a very large rock garden.

CULTIVATION *Grow in any well-drained soil, preferably in full sun or light dappled shade. Can be pruned hard in spring to reduce size if necessary.*

☀◑ ◊ Z 4-9 H 9-1 ‡4ft (1.2m) ↔10ft (3m)

JUNIPERUS PROCUMBENS 'NANA'

A compact, mat-forming conifer
that is excellent as a groundcover
in a wide range of situations. The
needlelike, aromatic, yellow-green
or light green leaves are carried in
groups of three. Bears berrylike,
brown to black, fleshy fruits that
take two or three years to ripen.

CULTIVATION *Grow in any well-drained
soil, including sandy, dry, or alkaline
conditions. Site in full sun or dappled
shade. No pruning is required.*

☼ ◑ ◊ Z 5-9 H 9-5   ‡6–8in (15–20cm)
↔30in (75cm)

JUNIPERUS SQUAMATA 'BLUE STAR'

This conifer is a low-growing, dense,
compact, rounded bush with rust-
colored, flaky bark. The silvery blue
leaves are sharply pointed and
grouped in whorls of three. The ripe
fruits are oval and black. Useful as a
groundcover or in a rock garden.

CULTIVATION *Grow in any well-drained
soil, in full sun or dappled shade. Very
little pruning is required.*

☼ ◑ ◊ Z 5-8 H 8-5   ‡to 16in (40cm)
↔to 3ft (1m)

KALMIA LATIFOLIA

Mountain laurel is a dense, evergreen shrub producing large clusters of flowers from late spring to early summer. These are cup-shaped, pink or occasionally white, and open from distinctively crimped buds. The oval leaves are glossy and dark green. An excellent specimen shrub for woodland gardens, but flowers best in full sun.

CULTIVATION *Grow in moist, organic, acid soil, in sun or partial shade. Mulch each spring with pine needles or leaf mold. Requires very little pruning, although deadheading is worthwhile.*

☼◐ ◊ Z 5-9 H 9-5   ‡↔ 10ft (3m)

KERRIA JAPONICA 'GOLDEN GUINEA'

This vigorous, suckering, deciduous shrub forms clumps of arching, canelike shoots that arise from ground level each year. Large, single yellow flowers are borne in mid-spring along the previous year's growth. The bright green leaves are oval and sharply toothed. Good in an open woodland planting.

CULTIVATION *Grow in well-drained, fertile soil, in full sun or partial shade. Cut flowered canes back to different levels to obtain flowers at different heights. Chop out unwanted canes and suckers with a spade to restrict spread.*

☼◐ ◊ Z 4-9 H 9-1   ‡6ft (2m) ↔8ft (2.5m)

KNIPHOFIA 'LITTLE MAID'

This clump-forming, deciduous perennial has tall heads of tubular flowers that appear from late summer to early autumn. They are pale green in bud, opening to pale buff-yellow, then fading to ivory. The leaves are narrow and grass-like. Good for displays in a mixed or herbaceous border.

CULTIVATION *Grow in well-drained, deep, fertile, organic soil, in full sun. Keep moist when in growth. In their first winter (especially in colder areas), provide a mulch of straw or leaves.*

☼ ◊ Z 6-9 H 9-6 ‡24in (60cm) ↔18in (45c

KNIPHOFIA 'ROYAL STANDARD'

A clump-forming, herbaceous perennial of classic red-hot poker appearance that bears tall, conical flowerheads from mid- to late summer. The bright yellow, tubular flowers open from red buds, startin at the base and moving upward. T arching, grasslike leaves are deciduous, dying back in winter.

CULTIVATION *Grow in deep, moist but well-drained, organic soil, in sun. Water freely when in growth. Provide a mulch in colder areas, especially fo young plants in their first winter.*

☼ ◊◊ Z 6-9 H 9-6 ‡3ft (1m) ↔24in (60

KNIPHOFIA TRIANGULARIS

A clump-forming, deciduous perennial grown for its early to mid-autumn display of long, reddish orange, tubular flowers. These are borne in dense, spikelike heads and become slightly yellow around the mouths. The leaves are narrow, grasslike, and arching. A good specimen for waterside planting.

CULTIVATION *Best in deep, moist but well-drained, organic, fertile soil, in full sun. Water freely when in growth. Mulch in cold areas, especially young plants in their first winter.*

☼ ◐◖ Z 6-9 H 9-1 ‡24–36in (60–90cm)
↔18in (45cm)

KOLKWITZIA AMABILIS 'PINK CLOUD'

The beautybush is a fast-growing, suckering, deciduous shrub with an arching habit. Dense clusters of bell-shaped pink flowers with yellow-flushed throats appear in abundance from late spring to early summer. The leaves are dark green and broadly oval. Excellent for a shrub border or as a specimen plant.

CULTIVATION *Grow in any well-drained, fertile soil, in full sun. Let the arching habit of young plants develop without pruning, then thin out the stems each year after flowering, to maintain vigor.*

☼ ◊ Z 5-9 H 9-5 ‡10ft (3m) ↔12ft (4m)

LABURNUM × WATERERI 'VOSSII'

This spreading, deciduous tree bears long, hanging clusters of golden-yellow, pealike flowers in late spring and early summer. The dark green leaves are made up of three oval leaflets. A fine specimen tree for small gardens; it can also be trained on an arch, pergola, or tunnel frame-work. All parts are toxic if eaten.

CULTIVATION *Grow in well-drained, moderately fertile soil, in full sun. Cut back badly placed growth in early spring. Remove any suckers or buds at the base of the trunk.*

☼ ◊ Z 6-8 H 8-6   ↕↔ 25ft (8m)

LAGURUS OVATUS

Hare's tail is an annual grass that bears fluffy, oval flowerheads in summer. These are pale green, often purple-tinged, and fade to a pale creamy buff. The flat, narrow leaves are pale green. Effective in a border; the flowers can be cut for indoor arrangements; for drying, pick the heads before they are fully mature.

CULTIVATION *Best in light, well-drained, moderately fertile, ideally sandy soil. Choose a position in full sun.*

☼ ◊ annual H 12-1 ↕20in (50cm) ↔12in (30cm)

LAMIUM MACULATUM 'WHITE NANCY'

This colorful deadnettle is a semi-evergreen perennial that spreads to form mats; this makes it effective as a groundcover between shrubs. Spikes of pure white, two-lipped flowers are produced in summer above triangular to oval, silver leaves that are edged with green.

CULTIVATION *Grow in moist but well-drained soil, in partial or deep shade. Can be invasive, so position away from other small plants, and dig up invasive roots or shoots to limit spread.*

☀☀ ◐◊◊ Z 4-8 H 8-1   ‡to 6in (15cm)
          ↔to 3ft (1m) or more

LAPAGERIA ROSEA

The Chilean bellflower is a long-lived, twining, evergreen climber. From summer to late autumn, it produces large, narrowly bell-shaped, waxy red flowers that are borne either singly or in small clusters. The leaves are oval and dark green. Where marginally hardy, it benefits from the protection of a wall.

CULTIVATION *Grow in well-drained, moderately fertile soil, preferably in partial shade. Where marginally hardy, shelter from wind and provide a winter mulch. Keep pruning to a minimum, removing damaged growth in spring.*

☀ ◊ Z 10-11 H 12-10   ‡15ft (5m)

LATHYRUS LATIFOLIUS

The everlasting or perennial pea is a tendril-climbing, herbaceous perennial with winged stems, ideal for growing through shrubs or over a bank. Clusters of pealike, pink-purple flowers appear during summer and early autumn amid the deciduous, blue-green leaves, which are divided into two oblong leaflets. The seeds are not edible.

CULTIVATION *Grow in well-drained, fertile, organic soil, in sun or semi-shade. Cut back to ground level in spring and pinch out shoot tips to encourage bushiness. Resents disturbance.*

☼ ◑ Z 5-9 H 9-3   ↕6ft (2m) or more

LATHYRUS VERNUS

Spring vetchling is a dense, clump-forming, herbaceous perennial with upright stems. Despite its pealike appearance, it does not climb. In spring, clusters of purplish blue flowers appear above the mid- to dark green leaves, which are divided into several pointed leaflets. Suitable for a rock garden or woodland.

CULTIVATION *Grow in well-drained soil, in full sun or partial shade. Tolerates poor soil, but resents disturbance.*

☼ ◑ ◊ Z 5-9 H 9-3   ↕8–18in (20–45cm
↔ 18in (45cm

SWEET PEAS (*LATHYRUS ODORATUS*)

The many cultivars of *Lathyrus odoratus* are annual climbers cultivated for their display of beautiful and fragrant flowers that cut well for indoors and are available in most colors except yellow. The flowers are arranged in clusters on long stems; some consist of one color, while others are bicolored or variably marked. The seeds are not edible. Most look very effective when trained onto a pyramid of stakes or a trellis or when scrambling through shrubs and perennials; a few do not climb.

Sweet peas grow best in areas with cool summers, where they will bloom from spring until late summer.

CULTIVATION *Grow in well-drained, fertile soil; for the best flowers, add well-rotted manure the season before planting. Site in full sun or partial shade. Feed with a balanced fertilizer every two weeks when in growth. Deadhead or cut flowers for the house regularly. Support the climbing stems.*

☼◑ ◊◊ annual H 8-1

‡6–8ft (2–2.5m)

2 ‡6–8ft (2–2.5m)

3 ‡6–8ft (2–2.5m)

L. odoratus. 'Jayne Amanda'   **2** *L. odoratus* 'Noel Sutton'   **3** *L. odoratus* 'White Supreme'

LAURUS NOBILIS

Sweet bay is a conical, evergreen tree grown for its oval, aromatic, leathery, dark green leaves, which are used in cooking. Clusters of small, greenish yellow flowers appear in spring, followed by black berries in autumn. Effective when trimmed into formal shapes.

CULTIVATION *Grow in well-drained but moist, fertile soil, in sun or semi-shade with shelter from cold, drying winds. Grow male and female plants together for a reliable crop of berries. Prune young plants to shape in spring; trim established plants lightly in summer.*

☼☀ ◊ Z 8-10 H 12-7 ‡40ft (12m) ↔30ft (10m)

LAURUS NOBILIS 'AUREA'

The yellow-leaved bay is a conical tree bearing aromatic, evergreen leaves. These are oval and leathery and can be used in cooking. In spring, clusters of small, greenish yellow flowers appear, followed in autumn by black berries on female plants. Good for topiary and in containers, where it makes a much smaller plant.

CULTIVATION *Grow in well-drained but moist, fertile soil. Position in full sun or partial shade with shelter from cold winds. Prune young plants to shape in spring; once established, trim lightly in summer to encourage a dense habit.*

☼☀ ◊ Z 8-10 H 12-7 ‡40ft (12m) ↔30ft (10m)

LAVANDULA ANGUSTIFOLIA 'HIDCOTE'

This compact lavender with thin, silvery gray leaves and dark purple flowers is an evergreen shrub useful for edging. Dense spikes of fragrant, tubular flowers, borne at the ends of long, unbranched stalks, appear during mid- to late summer. Like all lavenders, the flowers dry best if cut before they are fully open.

CULTIVATION *Grow in well-drained, fertile soil, in sun. Cut back flower stems in autumn, and trim the foliage lightly with shears at the same time. In colder areas, leave trimming until spring. Do not cut into old wood.*

☼ ◊ Z 5-8 H 9-3 ‡24in (60cm) ↔30in (75cm)

LAVANDULA ANGUSTIFOLIA 'TWICKEL PURPLE'

This evergreen shrub is a close relative of 'Hidcote' (above) with a more spreading habit, paler flowers, and greener leaves. Dense spikes of fragrant purple flowers are borne in mid-summer above narrowly oblong, gray-green leaves. Good in a shrub border; like all lavenders, the flowers are very attractive to bees.

CULTIVATION *Grow in well-drained, fairly fertile soil, in full sun. Trim in autumn, or delay until spring in colder areas. Do not cut into old wood.*

☼ ◊ Z 5-8 H 9-3 ‡24in (60cm) ↔3ft (1m)

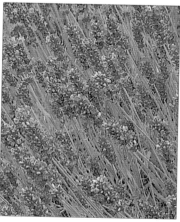

LAVANDULA STOECHAS SUBSP. *PEDUNCULATA*

French lavender is a compact, evergreen shrub that blooms from late spring to summer. Dense spikes of tiny, fragrant, dark purple flowers, each spike topped by distinctive, rose-purple bracts, are carried on long stalks well above the narrow, woolly, silvery gray leaves. Effective in a shrub border or rock garden.

CULTIVATION *Grow in well-drained, fairly fertile soil, in sun. Trim back in spring or, in milder areas, after flowering. Avoid cutting into old wood.*

☼ ◊ Z 8-9 H 12-7   ↔ 24in (60cm)

LAVATERA 'BARNSLEY'

A vigorous, summer-flowering, upright, semi-evergreen subshrub that produces abundant clusters of open, red-eyed white flowers with deeply notched petals. They slowly fade to soft pink. The gray-green leaves have three to five lobes. Best grown in a shrub border; it flowers abundantly on new growth and should be cut back hard each year.

CULTIVATION *Grow in well-drained, moderately fertile soil, in a sunny, sheltered site. Once the plant is growing strongly, prune back hard to the base each year in spring.*

☼ ◊ Z 7-9 H 9-7   ↔ 6ft (2m)

LAVATERA 'ROSEA'

This fast-growing, semi-evergreen, upright subshrub bears an abundance of large, open funnel-shaped, dark-pink flowers. These are clustered on the current season's growth during summer. The leaves have three to five lobes and are downy and pale green. Tolerates coastal conditions, but only in warmer climates.

CULTIVATION *Grow in well-drained, moderately fertile soil. Position in sun with shelter from cold, drying winds. In spring, cut out weak or damaged growth, and prune all other stems to within 12in (30cm) of ground level.*

☼ ◊ Z 8-10 H 12-3   ↔ 6ft (2m)

LEPTOSPERMUM RUPESTRE

This low-growing, evergreen shrub with dense foliage bears star-shaped white flowers from late spring to summer. The small, aromatic leaves are glossy, elliptic, and dark green. Native to coastal areas of Tasmania, it is useful in seaside gardens, provided that the climate is mild. May be sold as *L. humifusum.*

CULTIVATION *Grow in well-drained, fertile soil, in full sun or partial shade. Trim young growth in spring to promote bushiness, but do not cut into old wood.*

☼◑ ◊ Z 9-10 H 12-3   ↕ 1–5ft (0.3–1.5m)
↔ 3–5ft (1–1.5m)

LEPTOSPERMUM SCOPARIUM 'KIWI'

A compact shrub with arching shoots bearing an abundance of small, flat, dark crimson flowers during late spring and early summer. The small, aromatic leaves are flushed with purple when young, maturing to mid- or dark green. Suitable for a large rock garden and attractive in a greenhouse.

CULTIVATION *Grow in well-drained, moderately fertile soil, in full sun or partial shade. To encourage bushiness, trim new growth in spring, but avoid cutting into old wood.*

☼◑ ◊ Z 9-10 H 12-9 ↕↔ 3ft (1m)

LEUCANTHEMUM × *SUPERBUM* 'WIRRAL SUPREME'

A robust, clump-forming, daisy-flowered perennial, sometimes sold as a *Chrysanthemum*, that produces dense, double white flowerheads from early summer to early autumn. These are carried singly at the end of long stems above the lance-shaped, toothed, dark green leaves. Excellent as cut flowers.

CULTIVATION *Grow in moist but well-drained, moderately fertile soil, in full sun or partial shade. May need staking.*

☼◑ ◊◊ Z 5-8 H 8-1 ↕ 36in (90cm)
↔30in (75cm)

LEUCOJUM AESTIVUM 'GRAVETYE GIANT'

This robust cultivar of summer snowflake is a spring-flowering, bulbous perennial with upright, strap-shaped, dark green leaves, to 16in (40cm) tall. The faintly chocolate-scented, drooping, bell-shaped white flowers with green petal-tips are borne in clusters. Good planted near water or for naturalizing in grass.

CULTIVATION *Grow in reliably moist, organic soil, preferably near water. Choose a position in partial shade*

☀ ◐ ◊ Z 4-9 H 9-1   ↕3ft (1m) ↔ 3in (8cm)

LEUCOJUM AUTUMNALE

A slender, late-summer-flowering, bulbous perennial bearing stems of two to four drooping, bell-shaped white flowers, tinged red at the petal bases. Narrow, upright, grasslike leaves appear at the same time as or just after the flowers. Suitable for a rock garden.

CULTIVATION *Grow in any moist but well-drained soil. Choose a position in full sun. Divide and replant bulbs once the leaves have died down.*

☀ ◊◊ Z 5-9 H 9-1   ↕4–6in (10–15cm)
↔2in (5cm)

LEWISIA COTYLEDON

This evergreen perennial produces tight clusters of open funnel-shaped, usually pinkish purple flowers; they may be white, cream, yellow, or apricot. These are borne on long stems from spring to summer. The dark green, fleshy, lance-shaped leaves are arranged in basal rosettes. Suitable for growing in wall crevices.

CULTIVATION *Grow in sharply drained, fairly fertile, organic, neutral to acid soil. Choose a site where plants will be sheltered from excess winter moisture.*

☀ ◊ Z 6-8 H 8-4   ↕6–12in (15–30 cm)
                         ↔8–16in (20–40cm)

LEWISIA TWEEDYI

An evergreen perennial with upright to arching stems that bear one to four open funnel-shaped, white to peach-pink flowers in spring and early summer. Lance-shaped, fleshy, deep green leaves flushed with purple are arranged in rosettes at the base of the plant. Good in a rock garden or in an alpine house.

CULTIVATION *Grow in sharply drained, organic, fairly fertile, neutral to acid soil, in light shade. Protect plants in winter from excessive winter moisture.*

☀ ◊ Z 4-7 H 7-1   ↕8in (20cm) ↔12in (30cm)

LIGULARIA 'GREGYNOG GOLD'

A large, robust, clump-forming perennial that produces pyramidal spikes of daisylike, golden-orange, brown-centered flowers from late summer to early autumn. These are carried on long, upright stems above the large, rounded, toothed, mid-green leaves. Excellent as a water-side plant; it naturalizes readily in moist soils.

CULTIVATION *Grow in reliably moist, deep, moderately fertile soil. Position in full sun with some midday shade, and shelter from strong winds.*

☀☀ ◐ ◊ Z 4-8 H 8-1 ‡to 6ft (2m) ↔3ft (1m)

LIGUSTRUM LUCIDUM

The Chinese privet is a vigorous, conical, evergreen shrub with glossy dark green, oval leaves. Loose clusters of small white flowers are produced in late summer and early autumn, followed by oval, blue-black fruits. Good as hedging, but it also makes a useful, well-shaped plant for a shrub border.

CULTIVATION *Best in well-drained soil, in full sun or partial shade. Cut out any unwanted growth in late winter.*

☀☀ ◊ Z 8-10 H 12-8 ‡↔ 30ft (10m)

LIGUSTRUM LUCIDUM 'EXCELSUM SUPERBUM'

This variegated Chinese privet, with yellow-margined, bright green leaves, is a fast-growing, conical, evergreen shrub. Loose clusters of small, creamy white flowers appear in late summer and early autumn, followed by oval, blue-black fruits.

CULTIVATION *Grow in any well-drained soil, in full sun for the best leaf color. Remove unwanted growth in winter. Remove any shoots that have plain green leaves as soon as seen.*

☼ ◊ Z 8-10 H 12-8   ↕↔ 30ft (10m)

LILIUM CANDIDUM

The Madonna lily is an upright, bulbous perennial bearing up to 20 highly fragrant, trumpet-shaped flowers on each stiff stem in mid-summer. The flowers have pure white petals with tinted yellow bases, and yellow anthers. The lance-shaped, glossy bright green leaves that appear after the flowers often last over winter.

CULTIVATION *Grow in well-drained, neutral to alkaline soil that is rich in well-rotted organic matter. Tolerates drier soil than most lilies. Position in full sun with the base in shade.*

☼ ◊ Z 6-9 H 9-6   ↕ 3–6ft (1–2m)

LILIUM FORMOSANUM
VAR. PRICEI

An elegant, clump-forming perennial bearing very fragrant, slender, trumpet-shaped flowers. These are borne singly or in clusters of up to three during summer. The flowers have curved petal tips, white insides, and strongly purple-flushed outsides. Most of the oblong, dark green leaves grow at the base of the stem. Generally blooms the first year from seed if started early.

CULTIVATION *Grow in moist, neutral to acid, organic soil or compost, in sun with the base in shade. Protect from excessively hot sun.*

☀ ◐ ◊ Z 7–9 H 8–4 ↕2–5ft (0.6–1.5m)

LILIUM HENRYI

A fast-growing, clump-forming bulbous perennial that bears a profusion of slightly scented, turkscap flowers (with backward-bending petals) in late summer. These are deep orange with brown spots and red anthers, carried on purple-marked green stems above lance-shaped leaves. Excellent for a wild garden or woodland planting.

CULTIVATION *Grow in well-drained, neutral to alkaline soil with added leaf mold or well-rotted organic matter. Choose a position in partial shade.*

☀ ◐ ◊ Z 3–8 H 8–1 ↕3–10ft (1–3m)

LILIUM LONGIFLORUM

The Easter lily is a fast-growing perennial carrying short clusters of one to six pure white, strongly fragrant, trumpet-shaped flowers with yellow anthers. They appear during mid-summer above scattered, lance-shaped, deep green leaves. One of the smaller, less hardy lilies, it grows well in containers and under glass.

CULTIVATION *Best in well-drained soil or soil mix with added organic matter, in partial shade. Tolerates alkalinity.*

☼ ◊ Z 7-9 H 9-1 ‡16–39in (40–100cm)

LILIUM MARTAGON
VAR. *ALBUM*

A clump-forming, vigorous perennial bearing up to 50 small, nodding, glossy white, turkscap flowers with strongly curled petals. The leaves are elliptic to lance-shaped, mostly borne in dense whorls. Unlike most lilies, it has an unpleasant smell and is better sited in a border or wild garden, for which it is well suited.

CULTIVATION *Best in almost any well-drained soil, in full sun or partial shade. Water freely when in growth.*

☼ ◊ Z 3-7 H 8-1 ‡3–6 ft (1–2m)

LILIUM MONADELPHUM

This stout, clump-forming perennial, also known as *L. szovitsianum*, bears up to 30 large, fragrant, trumpet-shaped flowers on each stiff stem in early summer. The blooms are pale yellow, flushed brown-purple on the outsides and flecked purple-maroon on the insides. The scattered, bright green leaves are narrowly oval. Good for containers, since it tolerates drier conditions than most lilies.

CULTIVATION *Grow in any well-drained soil, in full sun. Tolerates fairly heavy, alkaline soils.*

☼ ◊ Z 5-8 H 8-5 ↕3–5ft (1–1.5m)

LILIUM PINK PERFECTION GROUP

These sturdy-stemmed lilies bear clusters of large, scented, trumpet-shaped flowers with curled petals in mid-summer. Flower color ranges from deep purplish red to purple-pink, all with bright orange anthers. The mid-green leaves are straplike. Excellent for cutting.

CULTIVATION *Grow in well-drained soil that is enriched with leaf mold or well-rotted organic matter. Choose a position in full sun with the base in shade.*

☼ ◊ Z 4-8 H 8-1 ↕5–6ft (1.5–2m)

LILIUM PYRENAICUM

A relatively short, bulbous lily that produces up to 12 nodding, green-yellow or yellow, purple-flecked flowers per stem, in early to mid-summer. Their petals are strongly curved back. The green stems are sometimes spotted with purple, and the lance-shaped, bright green leaves often have silver edges. Not a good lily for patio planting, since its scent is unpleasant.

CULTIVATION *Grow in well-drained, neutral to alkaline soil with added leaf mold or well-rotted organic matter. Position in full sun or partial shade.*

☼:◑: ◊ Z 4-7 H 7-1 ‡12–39in (30–100cm)

LILIUM REGALE

The regal lily is a robust, bulbous perennial with very fragrant, trumpet-shaped flowers opening during mid-summer. They can be borne in umbels of up to 25 and are white, flushed with purple or purplish brown on the outsides. The narrow leaves are numerous and glossy dark green. A bold statement in a mixed border. Suitable for growing in pots.

CULTIVATION *Grow in well-drained soil enriched with organic matter. Dislikes very alkaline conditions. Position in full sun or partial shade.*

☼:◑: ◊ Z 4-7 H 7-1 ‡2–6ft (0.6m–2m)

LIMNANTHES DOUGLASII

The poached-egg plant is an upright to spreading annual that produces a profusion of white-edged, yellow flowers from summer to autumn. The deeply toothed, glossy, bright yellow-green leaves are carried on slender stems. Good for brightening up a rock garden or path edging, and attractive to hoverflies, which help control aphids.

CULTIVATION *Grow in moist but well-drained, fertile soil, in full sun. Sow seed outdoors during spring or autumn. After flowering, it self-seeds freely.*

☼ ◊ annual H 9-1 ‡↔ to 6in (15cm) or more

LIMONIUM SINUATUM 'FOREVER GOLD'

An upright plant bearing tightly packed clusters of bright yellow flowers from summer to early autumn. The stiff stems have narrow wings. Most of the dark green leaves are arranged in rosettes around the base of the plant. Suitable for a sunny border; the flowers dry well for indoor arrangements. Like other statice, this is usually grown as an annual since it often fails to live through the winter.

CULTIVATION *Grow in well-drained, preferably sandy soil, in full sun. Tolerates dry and stony conditions.*

☼ ◊ Z 8-9 H 12-3 ‡24in (60cm) ↔ 12in (30cm)

LINUM 'GEMMELL'S HYBRID'

A dome-forming, semi-evergreen, perennial flax bearing abundant clusters of yellow, broadly funnel-shaped flowers that open for many weeks throughout summer. The leaves are oval and blue-green. Suitable for a rock garden.

CULTIVATION *Grow in light, moderately fertile, organic soil, with protection from excess winter moisture, in full sun.*

☼ ◊ Z 6-9 H 9-5 ‡6in (15cm) ↔ 8in (20cm)

LIRIODENDRON TULIPIFERA

The stately tulip tree has a broadly columnar habit, spreading with age. The deciduous, squarish, lobed leaves are dark green, turning butter-yellow in autumn. Tulip-shaped, pale green flowers, tinged orange at the base, appear in late spring and are followed by conelike fruits in autumn. An excellent specimen tree for a large garden.

CULTIVATION *Grow in moist but well-drained, moderately fertile, preferably slightly acid soil. Choose a site in full sun or partial shade. Keep pruning of established specimens to a minimum.*

☼◑ ◊ Z 5-9 H 9-1 ‡100ft (30m) ↔ 50ft (15m)

LIRIOPE MUSCARI

This stout, evergreen perennial forms dense clumps of dark green, strap-like leaves. Spikes of small, violet-purple flowers open in autumn amid the foliage and may be followed by black berries. Good in a woodland border, or use as a drought-tolerant groundcover for shady areas.

CULTIVATION *Grow in light, moist but well-drained, moderately fertile soil. Prefers slightly acid conditions and tolerates drought. Position in partial or full shade. Cut back hard in late winter.*

☀◐ ◌◖ Z 6-10 H 8-1   ‡12in (30cm)
                ↔18in (45cm)

LITHODORA DIFFUSA
'HEAVENLY BLUE'

A spreading, evergreen shrub, sometimes sold as *Lithospermum* 'Heavenly Blue', that grows flat along the ground. Deep azure-blue, funnel-shaped flowers are borne in profusion over long periods from late spring into summer. The leaves are elliptic, dark green, and hairy. Good for an open position in a rock garden or raised bed.

CULTIVATION *Grow in well-drained, organic, acid soil, in full sun. Trim lightly after flowering.*

☀ ◌ Z 6-8 H 8-6   ‡6in (15cm)
            ↔24in (60cm) or more

LOBELIA 'CRYSTAL PALACE'

A compact, bushy perennial that is almost always grown as an annual, with vibrant clusters of two-lipped, dark blue flowers during summer to autumn. The tiny leaves are dark green and bronzed. Useful for edging and to spill over the edges of containers.

CULTIVATION *Grow in deep, fertile soil or soil mix that is reliably moist, in full sun or partial shade. Plant out, after the risk of frost has passed, in spring.*

☼ ◐ ◊ annual H 8-1   ‡to 4in (10c ↔4–6in (10–15cr

LOBELIA 'QUEEN VICTORIA

This short-lived, clump-forming perennial bears almost luminous spikes of vivid red, two-lipped flowers from late summer to mid-autumn. Both the leaves and stems are deep purple-red. Effective in a mixed border or waterside planting

CULTIVATION *Grow in deep, reliably moist, fertile soil, in full sun. Short-lived, but it can be easily propagated b division in spring.*

☼ ◊ Z 4-9 H 8-1   ‡3ft (1m) ↔12in (30c

LONICERA × AMERICANA

This vigorous, deciduous, woody-stemmed honeysuckle is a free-flowering, twining or scrambling climber. In summer and early autumn it bears large whorls of tubular, very fragrant, soft flesh-pink flowers, flushed red-purple with yellow insides; red berries follow later in the season. The leaves are oval and dark green. Train onto a wall or up into a small tree.

CULTIVATION *Grow in moist but well-drained, fertile, organic soil, in full sun or partial shade. Once established, cut back shoots by up to one-third after they have flowered.*

☼ ◑ ◊◊ Z 6-9 H 9-6　　‡22ft (7m)

LONICERA NITIDA 'BAGGESEN'S GOLD'

A dense, evergreen shrub bearing tiny, oval, bright yellow leaves on arching stems. Inconspicuous yellow-green flowers are produced in spring, occasionally followed by small, blue-purple berries. Excellent for hedging or topiary in urban gardens, since it is pollution-tolerant.

CULTIVATION *Grow in any well drained soil, in full sun or partial shade. Trim hedges at least 3 times a year, between spring and autumn. Plants that become bare at the base will put out renewed growth if cut back hard.*

☼ ◑ ◊ Z 6-9 H 9-6　　↕↔ 5ft (1.5m)

LONICERA PERICLYMENUM 'GRAHAM THOMAS'

This long-flowering form of common honeysuckle is a woody, deciduous, twining climber bearing abundant, very fragrant, tubular white flowers. These mature to yellow over a long period in summer. The leaves are mid-green and oval in shape.

CULTIVATION *Grow in moist but well-drained, fertile, organic soil. Thrives in full sun, but prefers shade at the base. Once established, cut back shoots by up to one-third after flowering.*

☀ ◊◊ Z 5-9 H 9-5 ↕22ft (7m)

LONICERA PERICLYMENUM 'SEROTINA'

The late Dutch honeysuckle is a fast-growing, deciduous, twining climber with very fragrant, rich red-purple flowers that appear in abundance during mid- and late summer. These may be followed by red berries. The leaves are oval and mid-green. If given plenty of space, it scrambles naturally with little pruning needed.

CULTIVATION *Grow in well-drained but moist, organic, fertile soil, in sun with shade at the base. To keep trained specimens within bounds, prune shoots back by one-third after flowering.*

☀ ◊◊ Z 5-9 H 9-5 ↕22ft (7m)

LONICERA × *PURPUSII* 'WINTER BEAUTY'

This dense, semi-evergreen shrub makes an excellent winter-flowering hedge with an appealing scent. The clusters of small, highly fragrant, creamy white flowers, borne during winter to early spring, are carried on red-purple shoots. The leaves are dark green, and the flowers are occasionally followed by red berries.

CULTIVATION *Grow in any well-drained soil, in full sun for the best flowers, or partial shade. Prune after flowering to remove dead wood or to restrict size.*

☼ ◑ ◊ Z 7-9 H 9-7 ‡6ft (2m) ↔8ft (2.5m)

LONICERA × *TELLMANNIANA*

A twining, deciduous, woody-stemmed climber that bears clusters of coppery-orange, tubular flowers that open from late spring to mid-summer. The deep green, elliptic leaves have blue-white undersides. Train onto a wall or fence, or up into a large shrub.

CULTIVATION *Grow in moist but well-drained, fertile, organic soil. Will tolerate full sun, but it produces better flowers in a more shaded position. After flowering, trim shoots by one-third.*

☼ ◑ ◊◑ Z 7-9 H 9-7 ‡15ft (5m)

LOTUS BERTHELOTII

Known as parrot's beak because of its hooked flowers, this trailing, evergreen subshrub bears narrowly cut silvery leaves on long stems. Striking orange-red to scarlet flowers appear in profusion throughout spring and early summer. It should be planted out in containers during summer and brought under glass for the winter months.

CULTIVATION *Grow in well-drained, moderately fertile soil or soil mix, in full sun. Cut out some older stems after flowering to encourage new growth. Minimum temperature 35°F (2°C).*

☼ ◊ Z 8-9 H 12-9 ‡8in (20cm) ↔indefinite

LUPINUS ARBOREUS

The tree lupine is a fast-growing, sprawling, semi-evergreen shrub grown for its spikes of fragrant, clear yellow flowers that open through the summer. The divided leaves are bright and gray-green. Native to scrub of coastal California, it is tolerant of seaside conditions.

CULTIVATION *Grow in light or sandy, well-drained, fairly fertile, slightly acid soil, in full sun. Cut off seedheads to prevent self-seeding, and trim after flowering to keep compact.*

☼ ◊ Z 8-9 H 9-8 ‡↔6ft (2m)

LYCHNIS CHALCEDONICA

Maltese cross is a clump-forming
perennial that produces slightly
domed, brilliant red flowerheads in
early to mid-summer. These are
borne on upright stems above the
oval, mid-green, basal leaves. The
flowers are small and cross-shaped.
Good for a sunny border or wild
garden, but it needs some support.
It self-seeds freely.

CULTIVATION *Grow in moist but well-
drained, fertile, organic soil, in full sun
or light dappled shade.*

☼ ◐ ◊◊ Z 4–8 H 8–1
‡3–4ft (1–1.2m)
↔12in (30cm)

LYSICHITON
AMERICANUS

Yellow skunk cabbage is a striking,
colorful perennial that flowers
in early spring and is ideal for a
waterside planting. Each dense spike
of tiny, greenish yellow flowers is
hooded by a bright yellow spathe
and has an unpleasant, slightly
musky scent. The large, dark green
leaves, 20–48in (50–120cm) long,
emerge from the base of the plant.

CULTIVATION *Grow in moist, fertile,
organic soil. Position in full sun or
partial shade, allowing plenty of room
for the large leaves to develop.*

☼ ◐ ◊ Z 7–9 H 9–7 ‡3ft (1m) ↔4ft (1.2m)

LYSICHITON CAMTSCHATCENSIS

White skunk cabbage is a bold waterside perennial with a slightly musky scent. In early spring, dense spikes of tiny green flowers emerge, cloaked by pointed white spathes. The large, dark green leaves, up to 3ft (1m) long, grow from the base. Ideal beside a stream or a pool.

CULTIVATION *Grow in moist, waterside conditions, in fertile, organic soil. Position in full sun or partial shade, allowing room for the leaves to develop.*

☼ ◑ ◑ Z 7-9 H 9-7   ↕↔ to 3ft (1m)

LYSIMACHIA CLETHROIDES

This spreading, clump-forming, herbaceous perennial is grown for its tapering spikes of tiny, star-shaped white flowers that droop when in bud, straightening up as the flowers open in mid- to late summer. The narrow leaves are yellow-green when young, maturing to mid-green with pale undersides. Naturalizes to the point of invasiveness in a border or woodland garden.

CULTIVATION *Grow in reliably moist soil that is rich in organic matter, in full sun or partial shade.*

☼ ◑ ◑ Z 4-9 H 9-1   ↕3ft (1m) ↔24in (60cm)

LYSIMACHIA NUMMULARIA 'AUREA'

Golden creeping Jenny is a rampant, sprawling, evergreen perennial that makes an excellent groundcover plant. Its golden-yellow leaves are broadly oval in shape, with heart-shaped bases. The bright yellow, cup-shaped, summer flowers further enhance the foliage color.

CULTIVATION *Grow in reliably moist soil that is enriched with well-rotted organic matter. Site in full sun or partial shade.*

☼ ◑ ◊ Z 4-8 H 8-1 ‡2in (5cm) ↔ indefinite

LYTHRUM SALICARIA 'FEUERKERZE'

This cultivar of purple loosestrife, with more intense rose-red flowers than the species, is a clump-forming, upright perennial. The slender spikes of flowers bloom from mid-summer to early autumn above the lance-shaped, mid-green foliage. Do not plant near wetlands, where *Lythrum* has become ecologically damaging. Sometimes sold as 'Firecandle'.

CULTIVATION *Grow in moist, preferably fertile soil, in full sun. Remove flowered stems to prevent self-seeding.*

☼ ◊ Z 4-9 H 9-1 ‡3ft (1m) ↔ 18in (45cm)

MACLEAYA × *KEWENSIS* 'KELWAY'S CORAL PLUME'

A clump-forming perennial grown for its foliage and large, graceful plumes of tiny, coral-pink to deep-buff flowers. These open from pink buds from early summer, appearing to float above the large, olive-green leaves. Grow among shrubs, or group to form a hazy screen.

CULTIVATION *Best in moist but well-drained, moderately fertile soil, in sun or light shade. Shelter from wind. May be invasive; chop away roots at the margins of the clump to confine.*

☼◐ ◊◊ Z 4-9 H 9-1 ↕7ft (2.2m) ↔3ft (1m) or more

MAGNOLIA GRANDIFLORA 'EXMOUTH'

This cultivar of Southern magnolia is a dense, evergreen tree bearing glossy dark green leaves with russet-haired undersides. *M. grandiflora* is quite distinct from other magnolias, since it blooms sporadically from late summer to autumn, producing flowers that are large, very fragrant, cup-shaped, and creamy white.

CULTIVATION *Best in well-drained but moist, organic, acid soil, in full sun or light shade. Tolerates dry, alkaline conditions. Mulch with leaf mold in spring. Keep pruning to a minimum.*

☼◐ ◊◊ Z 7-9 H 10-7 ↕20-60ft (6-18m) ↔to 50ft (15m)

MAGNOLIA GRANDIFLORA 'GOLIATH'

This Southern magnoliacultivar is slightly less hardy than 'Exmouth' (see previous page, below) but has noticeably larger flowers, to 12in (30cm) across. It is a dense, conical, evergreen tree with slightly twisted, dark green leaves. The cup-shaped, very fragrant, creamy white flowers appear from late summer to autumn.

CULTIVATION *Best in well-drained but moist, organic, acid soil, in full sun or light shade. Tolerates dry, alkaline conditions. Mulch with leaf mold in spring. Keep pruning to a minimum.*

☼ ◑ ◊◊ Z 7-9 H 10-7 ‡20–60ft (6–18m)
↔to 50ft (15m)

MAGNOLIA LILIIFLORA 'NIGRA'

A dense, summer-flowering shrub bearing goblet-shaped, deep purple-red flowers. The deciduous leaves are elliptic and dark green. Plant as a specimen or among other shrubs and trees. Unlike many magnolias, it begins to flower when quite young.

CULTIVATION *Grow in moist but well-drained, rich, acid soil, in sun or semi-shade. Provide a mulch in early spring. Prune young shrubs in mid-summer to encourage a good shape; once mature, very little other pruning is needed.*

☼ ◑ ◊◊ Z 6-9 H 9-1 ‡10ft (3m) ↔8ft (2.5m)

SPRING-FLOWERING MAGNOLIAS

Spring-flowering magnolias are handsome deciduous trees and shrubs valued for their elegant habit and beautiful, often fragrant blooms that emerge just before the leaves. Flowers range from the tough but delicate-looking, star-shaped blooms of *M. stellata* to the exotic, gobletlike blooms of hybrids such as 'Ricki'. Attractive red fruits may form in autumn. The architectural branch framework of the bare branches makes an interesting display for a winter garden. *M.* x *soulangeana* 'Rustica Rubra' can be trained against a wall as an espalier.

CULTIVATION *Best in deep, moist but well-drained, organic, neutral to acid soil. M. wilsonii tolerates alkaline conditions. Choose a position in full sun or partial shade. After formative pruning when young, restrict pruning to the removal of dead or diseased branches after flowering.*

☼◑ ◊◊ Zones vary H 9-5

1 ‡30ft (10m) ↔ 25ft (8m)

2 ‡50ft (15m) ↔ 30ft (10m)

3 ‡↔ 30ft (10m)

4 ‡30ft (10m) ↔ 20ft (6m)

1 *M.* x *loebneri* 'Merrill' (Z 5-9) **2** *M. campbellii* 'Charles Raffill' (Z 7-9) **3** *M. denudata* (Z 6-9)
4 *M.* 'Elizabeth' (Z 6-9)

5 ↕↔ 12ft (4m)

6 ↕ 25ft (8m) ↔ 20ft (6m)

7 ↕ 30ft (10m) ↔ 15ft (5m)

8 ↕↔ 20ft (6m)

9 ↕ 28ft (9m) ↔ 20ft (6m)

10 ↕ 25ft (8m) ↔ 20ft (6m)

11 ↕ 10ft (3m) ↔ 12ft (4m)

5 *M.* 'Ricki' (Z 6-9) **6** *M.* x *loebneri* 'Leonard Messel' (Z 5-9) **7** *M. salicifolia* (Z 6-9)
8 *M.* x *soulangeana* 'Rustica Rubra' (Z 5-9) **9** *M.* x *kewensis* 'Wada's Memory' (Z 6-9)
10 *M. wilsonii* (Z 7-9) **11** *M. stellata* (Z 5-9)

MAHONIA AQUIFOLIUM 'APOLLO'

Oregon grape is a low-growing, evergreen shrub with dark green leaves; these are divided into seven spiny leaflets and turn brownish purple in winter. Dense clusters of deep golden flowers open in spring, followed by small, blue-black fruits. Can be grown as a groundcover.

CULTIVATION *Grow in moist but well-drained, rich, fertile soil, in semi-shade; tolerates sun if the soil remains moist. Every 2 years after flowering, shear groundcover plants close to the ground.*

☼ ◑ ◊◊ Z 6-9 H 9-3 ‡24in (60cm) ↔4ft (1.2m)

MAHONIA JAPONICA

A dense, upright, late winter-flowering, evergreen shrub carrying large, glossy dark green leaves divided into many spiny leaflets. Long, slender spikes of fragrant, soft yellow flowers are borne from late autumn into spring, followed by purple-blue fruits. Good in a shady border or woodland garden.

CULTIVATION *Grow in well-drained but moist, moderately fertile, humus-rich soil. Prefers shade, but will tolerate sun if soil remains moist. Limit pruning to removal of dead wood, after flowering.*

☼ ◑ ◊◊ Z 7-8 H 8-7 ‡6ft (2m) ↔10ft (3m)

MAHONIA × MEDIA 'BUCKLAND'

A vigorous, upright, evergreen shrub bearing dense and sharply spiny, dark green foliage. Small, fragrant, bright yellow flowers are produced in arching spikes from late autumn to early spring. A good vandal-resistant shrub for a boundary or front garden.

CULTIVATION *Best in moist but well-drained, fairly fertile, organic soil. Thrives in semi-shade but will become leggy in deep shade. Little pruning is needed, but over-long stems can be cut back to a low framework after flowering.*

☀ ◌◑ Z 8-9 H 9-8   ‡15ft (5m) ↔12ft (4m)

MAHONIA × MEDIA 'CHARITY'

A fast-growing, evergreen shrub, very similar to 'Buckland' (above), but it has more upright, densely packed flower spikes. The dark green leaves are spiny, making it useful for barrier or vandal-proof planting. Fragrant yellow flowers are borne from late autumn to spring.

CULTIVATION *Grow in moist but well-drained, moderately fertile, rich soil. Prefers partial shade and will become leggy in deep shade. After flowering, bare, leggy stems can be pruned hard to promote strong growth from lower down.*

☀ ◌◑ Z 8-9 H 9-8   ‡15ft (5m) ↔12ft (4m)

MALUS FLORIBUNDA

The Japanese crabapple is a dense, deciduous tree with a long season of interest. Graceful, arching branches, bearing dark green foliage, flower during mid- to late spring to give a glorious display of pale pink blossoms. The flowers are followed by small yellow crabapples; these often persist, providing a valuable source of winter food for garden wildlife.

CULTIVATION *Grow in moist but well-drained, moderately fertile soil, in sun or light shade. Prune to shape in late winter when young; older specimens require little pruning.*

☼ ◑ ◊◊ Z 4-8 H 8-1   ‡↔ 30ft (10

MALUS 'JOHN DOWNIE'

This vigorous, deciduous tree is upright when young, becoming conical with age. Large, cup-shaped white flowers, which open from pa pink buds in late spring, are followe by egg-shaped, orange and red cra apples. The oval leaves are bright green when young, maturing to da green. An ideal small garden tree.

CULTIVATION *Grow in well-drained bu moist, fairly fertile soil. Flowers and fru are best in full sun, but it tolerates sor shade. Remove damaged or crossing shoots when dormant to form a well-spaced crown. Avoid hard pruning of established branches.*

☼ ◑ ◊◊ Z 5-8 H 8-1 ‡30ft (10m) ↔20ft (t

MALUS TSCHONOSKII

This upright, deciduous tree with upswept branches produces pink-flushed white blossoms in late spring, followed in autumn by red-flushed yellow crabapples. The leaves turn from green to a vibrant gold, then red-purple, in autumn. It is taller than many crabapples but is still a beautiful specimen tree that can be accommodated in small gardens.

CULTIVATION *Grow in well-drained, moderately fertile soil. Best in full sun, but tolerates some shade. Forms a good shape with little or no pruning; does not respond well to hard pruning.*

☀ ◊ Z 5-8 H 8-5 ‡40ft (12m) ↔22ft (7m)

MALUS × ZUMI
'GOLDEN HORNET'

A broadly pyramidal, deciduous tree bearing a profusion of large, cup-shaped, pink-flushed white flowers that open from deep pink buds in late spring. Small yellow crabapples follow and persist well into winter. The display of golden fruit is further enhanced when the dark green foliage turns yellow in autumn.

CULTIVATION *Grow in any but water-logged soil, in full sun for best flowers and fruit. To produce a well-spaced crown, remove damaged or crossing shoots on young plants when dormant. Do not prune older specimens.*

☀ ◊◊ Z 5-8 H 8-5 ‡30ft (10m) ↔25ft (8m)

MALVA MOSCHATA F. ALBA

This white- to very light pink-flowered musk mallow is a bushy, upright perennial suitable for wildflower gardens or borders. The very attractive and showy flowers are borne in clusters from early to late summer amid the slightly musk-scented, mid-green foliage.

CULTIVATION *Grow in moist but well-drained, moderately fertile soil, in full sun. Taller plants may need staking. Often short-lived but self-seeds readily.*

☼ ◊ Z 4-8 H 8-1   ‡3ft (1m) ↔24in (60cr

MATTEUCCIA STRUTHIOPTERIS

The ostrich fern forms clumps of upright or gently arching, pale green, deciduous fronds. In summe smaller, dark brown fronds form at the center of each clump and persis until late winter. An excellent foliag perennial for a damp, shady border and woodland or waterside planting

CULTIVATION *Grow in moist but well-drained, organic, neutral to acid soil. Chose a site in light dappled shade.*

☼ ◊◊ Z 3-8 H 8-1   ‡3–5ft (1–1.5r
                     ↔18–30in (45–75cr

MATTHIOLA
CINDERELLA SERIES

This woody-based stock, a short-lived perennial grown as annual, is valued for its dense spikes of sweet-scented, double flowers. These come in a range of colors from white through pink to dark blue-purple and open from late spring to summer above the gray-green foliage. An attractive addition to a summer border; the flowers cut well.

CULTIVATION *Grow in well-drained but moist, fertile, neutral to acid soil, in a sheltered, sunny site. Plant out after the danger of frost has passed.*

☼ ◊ Z 7-8 H 9-1 ‡8–10in (20–25cm) ↔to 10in (25cm)

MECONOPSIS
BETONICIFOLIA

The Tibetan blue poppy is a clump-forming perennial bearing upright stems of large, saucer-shaped flowers that are clear blue or often purple-blue or white. These appear in early summer above the oval and bluish green leaves. Naturalizes well in a woodland garden.

CULTIVATION *Best in moist but well-drained, rich, acid soil. Site in partial shade with shelter from cold winds. May be short-lived, especially in hot or dry conditions. Divide clumps after flowering to maintain vigor.*

☼ ◊◊ Z 7-8 H 8-7 ‡4ft (1.2m) ↔18in (45cm)

MECONOPSIS GRANDIS

The Himalayan blue poppy is an upright, clump-forming perennial, similar to *M. betonicifolia* (see previous page, bottom), but with larger, less clustered, rich blue to purplish red flowers. These are carried above the mid- to dark green foliage in early summer. Appealing when grown in large groups in a woodland setting.

CULTIVATION *Grow in moist, leafy, acid soil. Position in partial shade with shelter from cold, drying winds. Mulch generously and water in dry spells; may fail to flower if soil becomes too dry*

☼ ◊ Z 5-8 H 8-5 ‡4ft (1.2m) ↔24in (60cm)

MELIANTHUS MAJOR

The honey bush is an excellent foliage shrub of upright to spreading habit. From late spring to mid-summer, spikes of blood-red flowers may appear above the gray-green to bright blue-green, divided leaves. In cold areas, treat as a tender perennial, but in milder climates it is ideal for a coastal garden.

CULTIVATION *Grow in moist but well-drained, fertile soil. Choose a sunny site protected from wind and excess winter moisture. Where not hardy, overwinter indoors under glass; where hardy, cut out flowered stems in autumn.*

☼ ◊ Z 8-10 H 12-8 ‡6–10ft (2–3m) ↔3–10ft (1–3m)

MIMULUS AURANTIACUS

This domed or sprawling, evergreen shrub bears open trumpet-shaped, yellow, orange, or dark red flowers from late summer to autumn. The rich green leaves are lance-shaped and toothed. Where not hardy, overwinter in a cool conservatory.

CULTIVATION *Best in well-drained, organic soil or soil mix, in full sun. Often short-lived but easily propagated by cuttings in mid-summer.*

☼ ◊ Z 7-10 H 12-7   ‡↔ 3ft (1m)

MIMULUS CARDINALIS

The scarlet monkey flower is a creeping perennial with tubular, scarlet, sometimes yellow-marked flowers. They appear throughout summer amid the oval, light green leaves, on hairy stems. Good for adding color to a warm border.

CULTIVATION *Grow any well-drained, fertile, organic soil; tolerates quite dry conditions. Position in sun or light dappled shade. May be short-lived but is easily propagated by division in spring.*

☼ ◊ Z 6-9 H 9-6 ‡3ft (1m) ↔24in (60cm)

MOLINIA CAERULEA 'VARIEGATA'

The purple moor grass is a tufted perennial forming clumps of cream-striped, narrow, dark green leaves. Dense, purple flowering spikes are produced over a long period from spring to autumn on tall, ochre-tinted stems. A good structural plant for a border or a woodland garden.

CULTIVATION *Grow in any moist but well-drained, preferably acid to neutral soil, in full sun or partial shade.*

☼☀ ◊ Z 5-9 H 9-5   ‡to 24in (60cm)
↔16in (40cm)

MONARDA 'CAMBRIDGE SCARLET'

This hybrid bee balm is a clump-forming perennial bearing shaggy heads of rich scarlet red, tubular flowers from mid-summer to early autumn. They appear in profusion above the aromatic leaves and are very attractive to bees, hence the common name. A colorful addition to any mixed or herbaceous border.

CULTIVATION *Prefers moist but well-drained, moderately fertile, organic soil, in full sun or light dappled shade. Keep moist in summer, but protect from excessive moisture in winter.*

☼☀ ◊◊ Z 4-9 H 9-1 ‡3ft (1m) ↔18in (45cm)

MONARDA
'CROFTWAY PINK'

A clump-forming, herbaceous perennial that is similar to 'Cambridge Scarlet' (see facing page, bottom) but with pink flowers and smaller, lighter green leaves. Shaggy heads of tubular flowers are carried above the aromatic foliage from mid-summer to early autumn. Good in mixed or herbaceous borders; the flowers are attractive to bees.

CULTIVATION *Grow in well-drained, fairly fertile, organic soil that is reliably moist in summer. Site in full sun or light shade, with protection from excessive winter moisture.*

☼ ☀ ◑ ◊ Z 4-8 H 8-1 ‡3ft (1m) ↔18in (45cm)

MUSCARI ARMENIACUM

A vigorous, bulbous perennial that bears dense spikes of tubular, rich blue flowers in early spring. The mid-green leaves are straplike and begin to emerge in autumn. Plant massed together in borders or allow to spread and naturalize in grass, although it can be invasive.

CULTIVATION *Grow in moist but well-drained, fairly fertile soil, in full sun. Divide clumps of bulbs in summer.*

☼ ◊ Z 4-8 H 8-1 ‡8in (20cm) ↔2in (5cm)

MUSCARI AUCHERI

This bulbous perennial, less invasive than *M. armeniacum* (see previous page, bottom), bears dense spikes of small, bright blue spring flowers. The flower spikes, often topped with paler blue flowers, are carried above the basal clumps of strap-shaped, mid-green leaves. Suitable for a rock garden. Sometimes known as *M. tubergianum*.

CULTIVATION *Grow in moist but well-drained, moderately fertile soil. Choose a position in full sun.*

☼ ◊ Z 6-9 H 9-6 ‡6in (15cm) ↔2in (5cm)

MYRTUS COMMUNIS

The common myrtle is a rounded shrub with dense, evergreen foliage. From mid-summer to early autumn, amid the small, glossy dark green, aromatic leaves, it bears great numbers of fragrant white flowers with prominent tufts of stamens. Purple-black berries appear later in the season. Can be grown as an informal hedge or a specimen shrub. Where marginally hardy, grow against a warm, sunny wall.

CULTIVATION *Best in well-drained but moist, fertile soil, in full sun. Protect from cold, drying winds. Trim in spring; tolerates close clipping.*

☼ ◊ Z 8-9 H 9-8 ‡↔10ft (3m)

MYRTUS COMMUNIS SUBSP. *TARENTINA*

This dense, evergreen shrub is more compact and rounded than the species (see facing page, below), with smaller leaves and pink-tinted cream flowers. These appear during mid-spring to early autumn and are occasionally followed by white berries. Grow in a border or as an informal hedge, or as topiary.

CULTIVATION *Grow in moist but well-drained, moderately fertile soil. Choose a site in full sun with shelter from cold, drying winds. Trim back in spring; tolerates close clipping.*

☀ ◊ Z 8-9 H 9-8 ↕↔5ft (1.5m)

NANDINA DOMESTICA

Heavenly bamboo is an upright, evergreen or semi-evergreen shrub with good spring and autumn color. The divided leaves are red when young, maturing to green, then flush red again in late autumn. Conical clusters of small white flowers with yellow centers appear in mid-summer, followed by long-lasting, bright red fruits excellent for indoor decoration.

CULTIVATION *Grow in moist but well-drained soil, in full sun. Cut back upon planting, then prune in mid-spring to keep the plant neat.*

☀ ◊ Z 6-9 H 9-3 ↕6ft (2m) ↔5ft (1.5m)

SMALL DAFFODILS (*NARCISSUS*)

Small and miniature daffodils make good spring-flowering, bulbous perennials both indoors and outdoors. They are cultivated for their elegant, mostly yellow or white flowers, of which there is great variety in shape. The blooms are carried either singly or in clusters above basal clumps of long, strap-shaped leaves on upright, leafless stems. All small daffodils are suitable for a rock garden, and they can look effective when massed together to form drifts. Because of their manageable size,

these daffodils are useful for indoor displays. Some, such as *N. bulbocodium*, will naturalize in short, thin grass.

CULTIVATION *Best in well-drained, fertile soil that is moist during growth, preferably in sun. Feed with a balanced fertilizer after flowering. Deadhead as flowers fade, and allow the leaves to die down naturally; do not tie them into bunches.*

☼ ◊ Z 3-9 H 9-1

1 ‡14in (35cm) ↔ 3in (8cm)

2 ‡4–6in (10–15cm) ↔ 2–3in (5–8cm)

3 ‡12in (30cm) ↔ 3in (8cm)

4 ‡6–8in (15–20cm) ↔ 2–3in (5–8cm)

5 ‡12in (30cm) ↔ 3in (8cm)

6 ‡12in (30cm) ↔ 3in (8cm)

1 *N.* 'Avalanche' (Z 6-9) **2** *N. bulbocodium* **3** *N.* 'Charity May'
4 *N. cyclamineus* **5** *N.* 'Dove Wings' **6** *N.* 'February Gold'

7 ‡7in (17cm) ↔ 2–3in (5–8cm)

8 ‡8in (20cm) ↔ 3in (8cm)

9 ‡8in (20cm) ↔ 3in (8cm)

10 ‡7in (17cm) ↔ 2–3in (5–8cm)

11 ‡4–6in (10–15cm) ↔ 2–3in (5–8cm)

12 ‡6in (15cm) ↔ 2–3in (5–8cm)

13 ‡4–10in (10–25cm) ↔ 2–3in (5–8cm)

7 *N.* 'Hawera' **8** *N.* 'Jack Snipe' **9** *N.* 'Jetfire' **10** *N.* 'Jumblie'
11 *N. minor* **12** *N.* 'Tête-à-tête' **13** *N. triandrus*

LARGE DAFFODILS (*NARCISSUS*)

Large daffodils are bulbous perennials, easily cultivated for their showy, mostly white, orange, or yellow flowers in spring. These are borne singly or in clusters on upright, leafless stems above long, strap-shaped, mid-green foliage arising from the bulb. A great diversity of elegant flower shapes is available; those illustrated are all excellent for cutting. 'Sweetness' has blooms that last particularly well when cut. Most look very effective flowering in large groups between shrubs or in a border.

Some naturalize easily in grass or under deciduous trees and shrubs in a woodland garden.

CULTIVATION *Best in well-drained, fertile soil, preferably in full sun. Keep soil reliably moist during the growing season and feed with a balanced fertilizer after flowering to ensure good blooms the following year. Deadhead as flowers fade, and allow leaves to die down naturally.*

☼ ◊ Z 3-9 H 9-1

1 ↕18in (45cm) ↔ 6in (15cm)

2 ↕16in (40cm) ↔ 5in (12cm)

3 ↕16in (40cm) ↔ 5in (12cm)

4 ↕16in (40cm) ↔ 6in (15cm)

1 *N.* 'Actaea' **2** *N.* 'Empress of Ireland' **3** *N.* 'Ceylon' **4** *N.* 'Cheerfulness'

5 ‡16in (40cm) ↔ 6in (15cm)

6 ‡18in (45cm) ↔ 6in (15cm)

7 ‡14in (35cm) ↔ 6in (15cm)

8 ‡18in (45cm) ↔ 6in (15cm)

9 ‡16in (40cm) ↔ 6in (15cm)

10 ‡16in (40cm) ↔ 3in (8cm)

11 ‡18in (45cm) ↔ 6in (15cm)

12 ‡18in (45cm) ↔ 6in (15cm)

13 ‡16in (40cm) ↔ 3in (8cm)

14 ‡18in (45cm) ↔ 6in (15cm)

5 *N.* 'Ice Follies' **6** *N.* 'Kingscourt' **7** *N.* 'Merlin' **8** *N.* 'Mount Hood' **9** *N.* 'Passionale'
10 *N.* 'Suzy' **11** *N.* 'Saint Keverne' **12** *N.* 'Tahiti' **13** *N.* 'Sweetness' **14** *N.* 'Yellow Cheerfulness'

NERINE BOWDENII

This bulbous perennial is one of the showiest late-flowering bulbs. In autumn, it bears open sprays of five to ten trumpet-shaped, faintly scented, bright pink flowers with curled, wavy-edged petals. The straplike, fresh green leaves appear after the flowers. It may survive milder-than-normal winters if grown at the base of a sunny wall. The flowers are good for cutting.

CULTIVATION *Grow in well-drained soil, in a sunny, sheltered position. Provide a deep, dry mulch in winter.*

☼ ◊ Z 8-10 H 12-8   ‡18in (45cm)
                          ↔5–6in (12–15cm)

NICOTIANA 'LIME GREEN'

This striking flowering tobacco is an upright, free-flowering, bushy annual, ideal for a summer border. It bears loose clusters of night-scented, yellow-green flowers with long throats and flattened faces from mid- to late summer. The leaves are mid-green and oblong. Plant near patios, where the evening scent can be appreciated.

CULTIVATION *Grow in moist but well-drained, fertile soil. Choose a position in full sun or partial shade.*

☼◑ ◊ ann. H 12-1 ‡24in (60cm) ↔10in (25cm)

NICOTIANA SYLVESTRIS

A vigorous, upright perennial that is grown as an annual in most areas. Throughout summer, open clusters of long-tubed, flat-faced, sweetly scented white flowers are borne above the dark green, sticky leaves. Although plants are tall (and may need staking), try to position where their scent can be appreciated.

CULTIVATION *Grow in any well-drained, moderately fertile soil, in sun or partial shade; the flowers close in full sun. Where marginally hardy it may survive winter if mulched, resprouting from the base in spring.*

☼ ◐ ◊ Z10-11 H 12-1 ‡5ft(1.5m) ↔2ft (60cm)

NIGELLA 'MISS JEKYLL'

During summer, this tall, slender annual bears pretty, sky blue flowers that are surrounded by a feathery ruff of bright green foliage. These are followed later in the season by attractive, inflated seed pods. The blooms last well when cut, and the seed pods can be dried for flower arrangements.

CULTIVATION *Grow in well-drained soil, in full sun. Like all nigellas, it self-seeds freely, although seedlings may differ from the parent.*

☼ ◊ annual H 12-1 ‡to 18in (45cm)
↔to 9in (23cm)

OENOTHERA FRUTICOS. 'FYRVERKERI'

An upright, clump-forming perenr
carrying handsome foliage and
clusters of short-lived, cup-shaped
bright yellow flowers that open in
succession from late spring to late
summer. The lance-shaped leaves
are flushed red-purple when youn
contrasting beautifully with the re
stems. It associates well with bron
or copper-leaved plants. Sometim
sold as 'Fireworks'.

CULTIVATION *Grow in sandy, well-
drained soil that is well fertilized.
Choose a site in full sun.*

☼ ◊ Z 4-8 H 8-1   ‡12–39in (30–10C
↔12in (30

OENOTHERA MACROCARPA

This vigorous perennial has simila
flowers to *O. fruticosa* 'Fyrverkeri'
(above), but its trailing habit make
this plant more suitable for borde
edging. The golden-yellow bloom
appear from late spring to early
autumn among the lance-shaped,
mid-green leaves. Can be used in
a scree bed or rock garden. Also
known as *O. missouriensis*.

CULTIVATION *Grow in well-drained,
poor to moderately fertile soil. Positio
in full sun, in a site that is not prone
to excessive winter moisture.*

☼ ◊ Z 5-8 H 8-3   ‡6in (15cm) ↔20in (5(

OLEARIA MACRODONTA

An summer-flowering, evergreen shrub or small tree that forms an upright, broadly columnar habit. Large clusters of fragrant, daisylike white flowers with reddish brown centers are borne amid the sharply toothed, glossy dark green leaves. A good hedging plant or windbreak in coastal areas with mild climates; in colder regions it is better grown as part of a sheltered shrub border.

CULTIVATION *Grow in well-drained, fertile soil, in full sun with shelter from cold, drying winds. Prune unwanted or cold-damaged growth in spring.*

☼ ◊ Z 9-10 H 12-9 ‡20ft (6m) ↔15ft (5m)

OMPHALODES CAPPADOCICA

This clump-forming, shade-loving, evergreen perennial bears sprays of small, azure blue, forget-me-not-like flowers with white centers. These appear in early spring above the pointed, mid-green leaves. Effective planted in groups throughout a woodland garden.

CULTIVATION *Grow in moist, organic, moderately fertile soil. Choose a site in partial shade.*

☀ ◊ Z 6-8 H 8-6 ‡to 10in (25cm)
↔to 16in (40cm)

OMPHALODES CAPPADOCICA 'CHERRY INGRAM'

This clump-forming, evergreen perennial is very similar to the species (see previous page, bottom) but bears larger, deep blue flowers that have white centers. These appear in early spring above the pointed, finely hairy, mid-green leaves. Good in a woodland garden.

CULTIVATION *Best in reliably moist, moderately fertile, organic soil. Choose a site in partial shade.*

☼ ◐ ◊ Z 6-8 H 8-6 ‡to 10in (25cm) ↔to 16in (40cm)

ONOCLEA SENSIBILIS

The sensitive fern forms a beautifully textured mass of arching finely divided, broadly lance-shaped deciduous fronds. The foliage is pinkish bronze in spring, maturing to pale green. Thrives at the edge of water or in a damp, shady border. The fronds die down at the first frost, hence the common name.

CULTIVATION *Grow in moist, organic, preferably acid soil. Site in partial shade, since fronds will scorch in sun.*

☼ ◐ ◊◊ Z 4-9 H 9-1 ‡24in (60cm) ↔indefin

OPHIOPOGON PLANISCAPUS 'NIGRESCENS'

This evergreen, spreading perennial forms clumps of grasslike, curving, almost black leaves. It looks very unusual and effective when planted in gravel-covered soil. Spikes of small, tubular, white to lilac flowers appear in summer, followed by round, blue-black fruits in autumn.

CULTIVATION *Grow in moist but well-drained, fertile, slightly acid soil that is rich in organic matter, in full sun or partial shade. Top-dress with leaf mold in autumn.*

☼ ◑ ◊ Z 6-10 H 12-6 ‡8in (20cm) ↔12in (30cm)

ORIGANUM LAEVIGATUM

A woody-based, bushy perennial bearing open clusters of small, tubular, purplish pink flowers from late spring to autumn. The oval, dark green leaves are aromatic, powerfully so when crushed. Good in a rock garden or scree bed. The flowers are very attractive to bees.

CULTIVATION *Grow in well-drained, poor to moderately fertile, preferably alkaline soil. Position in full sun. Trim back flowered stems in early spring.*

☼ ◊ Z 7-10 H 12-7 ‡24in (60cm) ↔18in (45cm)

ORIGANUM LAEVIGATUM 'HERRENHAUSEN'

A low-growing perennial that is more hardy than the species (see previous page, bottom), with purple flushed young leaves and denser whorls of pink flowers in summer. The mature foliage is dark green and aromatic. Good in a Mediterranean-style planting or in a rock garden.

CULTIVATION *Grow in very well-drained, poor to fairly fertile, preferabl alkaline soil, in full sun. Trim back flowered stems in early spring.*

☼ ◊ Z 6-10 H 12-7   ‡↔ 18in (45cn

ORIGANUM VULGARE 'AUREUM'

Golden marjoram is a colorful, bushy perennial with tiny, golden-yellow leaves that age to greenish yellow. Short spikes of tiny, pretty pink flowers are occasionally produced in summer. The highly aromatic leaves can be used in cooking. Good as a groundcover on a sunny bank or in a herb garden, although it tends to spread.

CULTIVATION *Grow in well-drained, poor to moderately fertile, alkaline soil. Position in full sun. Trim back after flowering to maintain a compact form.*

☼ ◊ Z 5-9 H 9-5   ‡↔ 12in (30cn

OSMANTHUS x *BURKWOODII*

A dense and rounded, evergreen shrub, sometimes known as x *Osmarea burkwoodii*, carrying oval, slightly toothed, leathery, dark green leaves. Profuse clusters of small, very fragrant white flowers, with long throats and flat faces, are borne in spring. Ideal for a shrub border or as a hedge.

CULTIVATION *Grow in well-drained, fertile soil, in sun or partial shade with shelter from cold, drying winds. Prune to shape after flowering, giving hedges a trim in summer.*

☼ ◐ ◊ Z 7-9 H 9-7   ↕↔ 10ft (3m)

OSMANTHUS DELAVAYI

A rounded, fragrant, evergreen shrub with arching branches bearing small, glossy dark leaves. Profuse clusters of sweetly scented, pure white flowers appear in mid- to late spring. Good for a shrub border or woodland garden, and excellent for hedging. May also be wall-trained.

CULTIVATION *Grow in well-drained, fertile soil, in full sun or partial shade with shelter from cold winds. Tolerates alkaline conditions. Prune to shape after flowering; trim hedges in summer.*

☼ ◐ ◊ Z 7-9 H 9-7   ↕6–20ft (2–6m)
                            ↔12ft (4m) or more

OSMUNDA REGALIS

The royal fern is a stately, clump-forming perennial with bright green, finely divided foliage. Distinctive, rust-colored fronds are produced at the center of each clump in summer. Excellent in a damp border or at the margins of a pond or stream.

CULTIVATION *Grow in very moist, fertile, organic soil, in semi-shade. Tolerates full sun if conditions are reliably damp.*

☼ ◐ ◊◊ Z 4-9 H 9-4 ‡6ft (2m) ↔12ft (4m

OSTEOSPERMUM 'BUTTERMILK'

An upright, evergreen subshrub that is grown as an annual in many areas. The large, daisylike flowers, with dark bluish mauve centers and white-based, yellow-tipped petals, are borne in succession from late spring to autumn. A fine border or patio plant; good in containers.

CULTIVATION *Grow in well-drained, moderately fertile soil, in a sunny, sheltered site. Deadhead regularly to prolong flowering. Where not hardy, plant out after any risk of frost.*

☼ ◊ Z 10-11 H 6-1 ‡↔ 24in (60cm

OSTEOSPERMUM JUCUNDUM

A neat, clump-forming, woody-based perennial bearing large, daisylike, mauve-pink flowers that are flushed bronze-purple on the undersides. The blooms open in succession from late spring until autumn. Ideal for wall crevices or at the front of a border. Also known as *O. barberiae*.

CULTIVATION *Best in light, well-drained, fairly fertile soil. Choose a site in full sun. Deadhead to prolong flowering.*

☼ ◊ Z 9-10 H 6-1   ‡4–20in (10–50cm)
                        ↔20–39in (50–100cm)

OSTEOSPERMUM 'WHIRLIGIG'

A spreading, evergreen, woody-based subshrub that is grown as an annual in many areas. From late spring to autumn, daisylike, dark blue-centered flowers with distinctively spoon-shaped, white petals open above the gray-green, aromatic foliage. The flowers are ideal for cutting.

CULTIVATION *Grow in well-drained, fairly fertile soil, in a sunny, sheltered position. Deadhead to prolong flowering. Where not hardy, plant out after the danger of frost has passed. Minimum temperature 35°F (2°C).*

☼ ◊ H 6-1   ‡↔ 24in (60cm)

OXALIS ADENOPHYLLA

A bulbous perennial forming clump
of pretty, gray-green leaves that are
divided into many heart-shaped
leaflets. In late spring, widely
funnel-shaped, purple-pink flowers
contrast beautifully with the foliage
Native to the Andes, it looks good
a well-drained rock garden, trough,
or raised bed.

CULTIVATION *Grow in any moderately
fertile soil with good drainage. Choose
position in full sun.*

☼ ◊ Z6-8 H 8-6 ‡4in (10cm) ↔6in (15c

PACHYSANDRA
TERMINALIS

This freely spreading, bushy,
evergreen foliage perennial makes
a very useful groundcover plant for
a shrub border or woodland garden
The oval, glossy, dark green leaves
are clustered at the tips of the stem
Spikes of small white flowers are
produced in early summer.

CULTIVATION *Grow in any (but not ver
dry), organic soil. Choose a position in
partial or full shade.*

◐◑ ◊ Z 4-8 H 8-1 ‡8in (20cm) ↔indefin

PAEONIA DELAVAYI

An upright, sparsely branched, deciduous shrub bearing nodding, bowl-shaped, rich dark red flowers in early summer. The dark green leaves are deeply cut into pointed lobes and have blue-green under-sides. A tall tree peony, good in a shrub border.

CULTIVATION *Grow in deep, moist but well-drained, fertile, organic soil. Position in full sun or partial shade with shelter from wind. Occasionally cut an old, leggy stem back to ground level in autumn, but avoid regular or hard pruning.*

☼ ◑ ◊◊ Z 5-8 H 8-1 ‡6ft (2m) ↔4ft (1.2m)

PAEONIA LACTIFLORA 'BOWL OF BEAUTY'

A herbaceous, clump-forming perennial bearing very large, bowl-shaped flowers in early summer. These have carmine-pink, red-tinted petals arranged around a dense cluster of creamy white stamens. The leaves are mid-green and divided into many leaflets. Ideal for a mixed or herbaceous border.

CULTIVATION *Grow in deep, moist but well-drained, fertile, organic soil, in full sun or partial shade. Provide support. Resents being disturbed.*

☼ ◑ ◊◊ Z 3-8 H 8-1 ‡↔39in (100cm)

PAEONIA LACTIFLORA 'DUCHESSE DE NEMOURS'

This clump-forming, free-flowering, herbaceous perennial produces large, fully double flowers that open from green-flushed buds in early summer. They are fragrant and pure white with ruffled, yellow-based inner petals. The leaves are deep green and divided. Ideal for a mixed or herbaceous border.

CULTIVATION *Grow in moist but well-drained, deep, fertile, organic soil, in full sun or semi-shade. Flowers may need support. Does not like to be disturbed once established.*

☼☀ ◊◊ Z 3-8 H 8-1 ↕↔ 28–32in (70–80cm)

PAEONIA LACTIFLORA 'SARAH BERNHARDT'

This herbaceous peony is similar to 'Duchesse de Nemours' (above), but with very large, rose-pink flowers. The blooms appear during late spring or early summer above the clumps of mid-green, deeply divided leaves. A lovely addition to a border.

CULTIVATION *Grow in moist but well-drained, deep, organic, fertile soil. Position in full sun or partial shade and provide support for the flowering stems. Does not respond well to root disturbance.*

☼☀ ◊◊ Z 3-8 H 8-1 ↕↔ to 3ft (1m)

PAEONIA LUTEA
VAR. *LUDLOWII*

This vigorous, deciduous tree peony
has an upright and open form. In
late spring, large, bright yellow,
nodding flowers open amid the
bright green foliage. The leaves are
deeply divided into several pointed
leaflets. Good in a shrub border or
featured as a specimen.

CULTIVATION *Best in deep, well-drained
but moist, fertile, organic soil. Site in
sun or semi-shade with shelter from
wind. Avoid hard pruning, but
occasionally cut old, leggy stems to
ground level in autumn.*

☼☀ ◊◑ Z 5-8 H 8-1   ↔ 5ft (1.5m)

PAEONIA OFFICINALIS
'RUBRA PLENA'

This long-lived, clump-forming,
herbaceous peony makes a fine
early summer-flowering addition to
any border or bed. The large, fully
double, vivid crimson flowers, with
ruffled, satiny petals, contrast well
with the deep green, divided leaves.

CULTIVATION *Grow in well-drained but
moist, deep, fertile, organic soil. Choose
a site in full sun or partial shade.
Support the flowering stems.*

☼☀ ◊◑ Z 3-9 H 8-1   ↔ 30in (75cm)

PAPAVER ORIENTALE
'BEAUTY OF LIVERMERE'

This tall Oriental poppy with crimson-scarlet flowers is an upright, clump-forming perennial. The flowers open during late spring to mid-summer and develop into large seed pods. Each petal has a bold, black mark at the base. The mid-green, divided leaves are borne on upright, bristly stems. Looks spectacular in a border.

CULTIVATION *Grow in well-drained, poor to moderately fertile soil. Choose a position in full sun.*

☼ ◊ Z 4-9 H 9-1   ‡3–4ft (1–1.2m)
↔36in (90cm)

PAPAVER ORIENTALE
'BLACK AND WHITE'

This Oriental poppy, white-flowered with crimson-black markings at the petal bases, is a clump-forming perennial. The flowers are borne above the mid-green foliage at the tips of white-bristly, upright stems during early summer; they are followed by distinctive seed pods. Makes a good border perennial.

CULTIVATION *Best in deep, moderately fertile soil with good drainage. Choose a position in full sun.*

☼ ◊ Z 4-9 H 9-1   ‡18–36in (45–90cm)
↔24–36in (60–90cm)

PAPAVER ORIENTALE
'CEDRIC MORRIS'

This Oriental poppy has very large, soft pink flowers with black-marked bases that are set off well against the gray-hairy foliage. It forms upright clumps that are well-suited to a herbaceous or mixed border. Distinctive seed pods develop after the flowers have faded.

CULTIVATION *Grow in deep, moderately fertile soil with good drainage. Choose a position in full sun.*

☼ ◊ Z 4-9 H 9-1 ↕18–36in (45–90cm)
↔24–36in (60–90cm)

PAPAVER RHOEAS
SHIRLEY MIXED

These field poppies are summer-flowering annuals with single, semi-double or double, bowl-shaped flowers in shades of yellow, orange, pink, and red. These appear on upright stems above the finely divided, bright green leaves. Can be naturalized in a wildflower meadow.

CULTIVATION *Best in well-drained, poor to moderately fertile soil, in full sun.*

☼ ◊ annual H 12-1 ↕3ft (1m) ↔12in (30cm)

PARAHEBE CATARRACTAE

A small evergreen subshrub bearing loose clusters of white summer flowers with purple veins and red eyes. The leaves are dark green and oval, purple-tinged when young. Looks very effective tumbling over walls or rocks.

CULTIVATION *Grow in well-drained, poor to moderately fertile soil, in full sun. Where marginally hardy, provide shelter from cold, drying winds.*

☼ ◊ Z 9-10 H 12-3 ‡↔ 12in (30cm

PARAHEBE PERFOLIATA

Digger's speedwell is a spreading, evergreen perennial bearing short spikes of blue, saucer-shaped flowers in late summer. The blue- or gray-green, overlapping leaves are oval and slightly leathery. Suitable for gaps in walls or in a rock garden.

CULTIVATION *Grow in poor to fairly fertile soil with good drainage, in full sun. Where marginally hardy, provide shelter from cold, drying winds.*

☼ ◊ Z 9-10 H 12-3 ‡24–30in (60–75cm
↔18in (45cm

PARTHENOCISSUS HENRYANA

This attractive vine is a woody, twining, deciduous climber with colorful foliage in autumn. The insignificant summer flowers are usually followed by blue-black berries. The conspicuously white-veined leaves, made up of three to five leaflets, turn bright red late in the season. Train over a wall or a strongly built fence.

CULTIVATION *Grow in well-drained but moist, fertile soil. Tolerates sun, but leaf color is best in deep or partial shade. Young plants may need some support. Prune back unwanted growth in autumn.*

☼ ◐ ◌◊ Z 7-8 H 8-7 ↕30ft (10m)

PARTHENOCISSUS TRICUSPIDATA

Boston ivy is a vigorous, woody, deciduous climber with foliage that turns a beautiful color in autumn. The variably lobed, bright green leaves flush a brilliant red, fading to purple before they fall. Creates an interesting textural effect on drab, featureless walls.

CULTIVATION *Best in moist but well-drained, fertile, organic soil. Position in partial or full shade. Young plants may need some support before they are established. Remove any unwanted growth in autumn.*

☼ ◐ ◌◊ Z 4-8 H 8-1 ↕70ft (20m)

PASSIFLORA CAERULEA

The blue passionflower is a fast-growing, evergreen climber valued for its large, exotic flowers, crowned with prominent blue- and purple-banded filaments. These are borne from summer to autumn amid the dark green, divided leaves. Where marginally hardy, grow in the protection of a warm wall.

CULTIVATION *Best in moist but well-drained, moderately fertile soil, in a sunny, sheltered site. Remove crowded growth in spring, cutting back flowered shoots at the end of the season.*

☼ ◊◐ Z 6-9 H 9-6   ‡30ft (10m) or mor

PASSIFLORA CAERULEA 'CONSTANCE ELLIOTT'

A fast-growing, evergreen climber, resembling the species (above), but with white flowers borne from summer to autumn. The leaves are dark green and deeply divided into three to nine lobes. Good for a pergola or trellis. Benefits from the shelter of a warm wall where marginally hardy.

CULTIVATION *Grow in moist but well-drained, moderately fertile soil. Choose a sheltered site, in full sun. Remove weak growth in spring, cutting back flowered shoots at the end of the season*

☼ ◊◐ Z 6-9 H 9-6   ‡30ft (10m) or mor

FOLIAGE GERANIUMS (*PELARGONIUM*)

*Pelargonium*s, commonly called geraniums, are tender, evergreen perennials. Many are grown specifically for their decorative or scented foliage. Choice of leaf shape varies from smooth to deeply crinkled; most distinctive are the trailing, ivy-leaved geraniums, which make spectacular hanging baskets. The foliage is often patterned with white, cream, or yellow. Scented-leaved geraniums range in fragrance from sweet or spicy to the lemon scent of *P. crispum* 'Variegatum'

or the peppermint-like *P. tomentosum*. Use as edging alongside a path: here they are likely to be brushed against and will release their scent.

CULTIVATION *Grow in well-drained, fertile, neutral to alkaline soil or soil mix, in sun. Pinch regularly. Overwinter in frost-free conditions, cutting back top growth by one-third. Cut back further and repot as growth resumes. Minimum temperature 35°F (2°C).*

☼ ◊ H 12-1

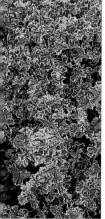

2 ‡12–16in (30–40cm) ↔ 8in (20cm)

3 ‡8–10in (20–25cm) ↔ 8in (20cm)

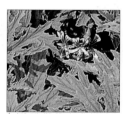

4 ‡12–14in (30–35cm) ↔ 6in (15cm)

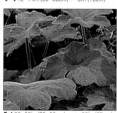

5 ‡30–36in (75–90cm) ↔ to 30in (75cm)

‡14–18in (35–45cm) ↔ 6in (15cm)

P. crispum 'Variegatum' 2 *P.* 'Lady Plymouth' 3 *P.* 'L'Elégante' 4 *P.* 'Mabel Grey'
P. tomentosum

FLOWERING GERANIUMS (*PELARGONIUM*)

Geraniums grown for their bold flowers are tender, evergreen perennials: most cultivars are bushy, but there are also trailing types for windowboxes and hanging baskets. Flower forms vary from the tightly frilled 'Apple Blossom Rosebud' to the delicate, narrow-petaled 'Bird Dancer'; colors range from shades of orange through pink and red to rich purple, and some have colored foliage. A popular choice for bedding plants, flowering from spring into summer, although many will flower throughout the year if kept above 45°F (7°C), making them excellent for a conservatory and as houseplants.

CULTIVATION *Grow in well-drained, fertile, neutral to alkaline soil or soil mix, in sun or partial shade. Deadhead regularly to prolong flowering. Overwinter in frost-free conditions, cutting back by one-third. Repot in late winter as new growth resumes. Minimum temperature 35°F (2°C).*

☼ ◑ ◊ H 12-1

1 ↕10–12in (25–30cm) ↔ to 10in (25cm)

2 ↕to 12in (30cm) ↔ 10in (25cm)

3 ↕12–16in (30–40cm) ↔ 8–10in (20–25cm)

1 *P.* 'Alice Crousse'   **2** *P.* 'Amethyst'   **3** *P.* 'Apple Blossom Rosebud'

5 ‡10–12in (25–30cm) ↔ 6in (15cm)

6 ‡16–18in (40–45cm) ↔ 10in (25cm)

‡6–8in (15–20cm) ↔ 6in (15cm)

7 ‡10–12in (25–30cm) ↔ 5in (12cm)

8 ‡10–12in (25–30cm) ↔ 12in (30cm)

‡16–18in (40–45cm) ↔ 8in (20cm)

10 ‡to 24in (60cm) ↔ to 10in (25cm)

1 ‡12–16in (30–40cm) ↔ 8in (20cm)

12 ‡to 24in (60cm) ↔ 10in (25cm)

13 ‡8in (20cm) ↔ 7in (18cm)

. *P.* 'Bird Dancer' **5** *P.* 'Dolly Varden' **6** *P.* 'Happy Thought' **7** *P.* 'Mr. Henry Cox'
. *P.* Multibloom Series **9** *P.* 'Paton's Unique' **10** *P.* 'The Boar' **11** *P.* 'Tip Top Duet'
2 *P.* 'Voodoo' **13** *P.* Video Series

PENSTEMONS

Penstemons are elegant, semi-evergreen perennials valued for their spires of tubular, foxglovelike flowers in white and shades of pink, red, and purple, held above lance-shaped leaves. Smaller penstemons, such as *P. newberryi*, are at home in a rock garden or as edging plants, while larger cultivars make showy border perennials that flower throughout summer and into autumn. 'Andenken an Friedrich Hahn' and 'Schoenholzeri' are among the hardiest cultivars, although most types benefit from a dry winter mulch where marginally hardy. Penstemons tend to be short-lived and are best replaced as necessary.

CULTIVATION *Grow border plants in well-drained, organic soil, and dwarf cultivars in sharply drained, gritty, poor to moderately fertile soil. Choose a site in full sun or partial shade. Deadhead regularly to prolong the flowering season.*

☼ ◑ ◊ Zones vary H 10-7

1 ‡4ft (1.2m) ↔ 18in (45cm) **2** ‡↔ 18–24in (45–60cm) **3** ‡30in (75cm) ↔ 24in (60cm)

1 *P.* 'Alice Hindley' (Z 7-10) **2** *P.* 'Apple Blossom' (Z 4-10)
3 *P.* 'Andenken an Friedrich Hahn' (syn. *P.* 'Garnet') (Z 7-10)

4 ‡36in (90cm) ↔ 30in (75cm)

5 ‡18–24in (45–60cm) ↔ 12in (30cm)

5 ‡10in (25cm) ↔ 12in (30cm)

7 ‡36in (90cm) ↔ 24in (60cm)

8 ‡24in (60cm) ↔ 18in (45cm)

4 *P.* 'Chester Scarlet' (Z 6-9) **5** *P.* 'Evelyn' (Z 7-10) **6** *P. newberryi* (Z 5-7) **7** *P.* 'Schoenholzeri' syn. *P.* 'Firebird', *P.* 'Ruby') (Z 7-10) **8** *P.* 'White Bedder' (syn. *P.* 'Snowstorm') (Z 6-9)

PERILLA FRUTESCENS VAR. *CRISPA*

An upright, bushy annual grown for its frilly, pointed, deep purple leaves that are flecked with green. Spikes of tiny white flowers appear in summer. The dark foliage makes a good contrasting background to the bright flowers of many summer bedding plants.

CULTIVATION *Grow in moist but well-drained, fertile soil. Position in sun or partial shade. Plant in spring after the danger of frost has passed. Self-seeds.*

☼ ◑ ◊◑ annual H 12-1   ↕to 3ft (1m) ↔to 12in (30cm)

PEROVSKIA 'BLUE SPIRE'

This upright, deciduous subshrub, grown for its foliage and flowers, looks good in a mixed or herbaceous border. Branching, airy spikes of tubular, violet-blue flowers are borne in profusion during late summer and early autumn, above the silvery gray, divided leaves. Tolerates coastal conditions.

CULTIVATION *Best in poor to moderately fertile soil that is well drained. Tolerates alkaline soil. For vigorous, bushy growth, prune back hard each spring to a low framework. Position in full sun.*

☼ ◊ Z 6-9 H 9-4   ↕4ft (1.2m) ↔3ft (1m)

PERSICARIA AFFINIS
'SUPERBA'

A vigorous, evergreen perennial,
formerly in the genus *Polygonum*,
that forms mats of lance-shaped,
deep green leaves that turn rich
brown in autumn. Dense spikes
of long-lasting, pale pink flowers,
which mature to dark pink, are
carried above the foliage from mid-
summer to mid-autumn. Plant in
groups at the front of a border or
use as a groundcover.

CULTIVATION *Grow in any moist soil,
in full sun or partial shade. Dig out
invasive roots in spring or autumn.*

☼◐ ◊ Z 3-8 H 8-1   ↕to 10in (25cm)
                ↔24in (60cm)

PERSICARIA BISTORTA
'SUPERBA'

A fast-growing, semi-evergreen
perennial, formerly in the genus
Polygonum, that makes a good
groundcover. Dense, cylindrical,
soft pink flowerheads are produced
over long periods from early
summer to mid-autumn above
the clumps of mid-green foliage.

CULTIVATION *Best in any well-drained,
reliably moist soil, in full sun or partial
shade. Tolerates dry soil.*

☼◐ ◊◊ Z 4-8 H 8-1   ↕30in (75cm)
                ↔36in (90cm)

PERSICARIA VACCINIIFOLIA

This creeping, evergreen perennial, formerly in the genus *Polygonum*, bears glossy mid-green leaves that flush red in autumn. In late summer and autumn, spikes of deep pink flowers appear on branching, red-tinted stems. Good in a rock garden by water, or at the front of a border. Good as a groundcover.

CULTIVATION *Grow in any moist soil, in full sun or semi-shade. Control spread by digging up invasive roots in spring or autumn.*

☼ ◑ ◊ Z 7-9 H 9-7　　　‡8in (20cm
↔20in (50cm) or more

PETUNIA
CARPET SERIES

These very compact, spreading petunias are usually grown as annuals for their abundant, trumpet-shaped flowers. These open over a long period from late spring to early autumn in shades of pink through strong reds and oranges to yellow and white. The leaves are oval and dark green. Ideal as dense, colorful summer bedding, particularly in poor soil.

CULTIVATION *Grow in well-drained soil, in a sunny, sheltered site. Deadhead to prolong flowering. Plant out after all danger of frost has passed.*

☼ ◊ annual H 12-3 ‡6in (15cm) ↔to 3ft (1m

PETUNIA
MIRAGE SERIES

These dense, spreading annuals
are very similar to the Carpet
Series (facing page, below), but
the trumpet-shaped flowers come
in shades of not only red and pink
but also blues and purples. These
are borne from late spring until early
autumn above the dark green, oval
leaves. Particularly useful as a
bedding plant on poor soils.

CULTIVATION *Grow in any light, well-
drained soil, in full sun with shelter
from wind. Deadhead to prolong
flowering. Plant out after the danger
of frost has passed.*

☀ ◊ annual H 12-3 ‡12in (30cm) ↔3ft (1m)

PHALARIS ARUNDINACEA
'PICTA'

Gardeners' garters is an evergreen,
clump-forming perennial grass with
narrow, white-striped leaves. Tall
plumes of pale green flowers, fading
to buff as they mature, are borne on
upright stems during early to mid-
summer. Good as a groundcover,
but it is normally highly invasive.

CULTIVATION *Grow in any soil, in full
sun or partial shade. Cut down all but
the new young shoots in early summer
to encourage fresh growth. To control
spread, lift and divide regularly.*

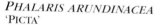

☼ ◐ Z 4-9 H 9-1 ‡to 3ft (1m) ↔indefinite

PHILADELPHUS 'BEAUCLERK'

A slightly arching, deciduous shrub valued for its clusters of fragrant, large white flowers with slightly pink-flushed centers. These are borne in early and mid-summer amid the broadly oval, dark green leaves. Grow in a shrub border on its own, or as a screen.

CULTIVATION *Grow in any well-drained, moderately fertile soil. Tolerates shallow, alkaline soil and light shade, but flowers are best in full sun. Cut back 1 in 4 stems to the ground after flowering to maintain strong growth.*

☀️◐ ◊ Z 5-8 H 8-1   ‡↔ 8ft (2.5m)

PHILADELPHUS 'BELLE ETOILE'

This arching, deciduous shrub is similar to but more compact than 'Beauclerk' (above). An abundance of very fragrant, large white flowers with purple-marked centers appear during late spring to early summer. The leaves are tapered and dark green. Good in a mixed border.

CULTIVATION *Grow in any moderately fertile soil with good drainage. Flowers are best in full sun, but it tolerates partial shade. After flowering, cut 1 in 4 stems back to the ground to maintain strong new growth.*

☀️◐ ◊ Z 5-8 H 8-1   ‡4ft (1.2m) ↔8ft (2.5

PHILADELPHUS CORONARIUS 'VARIEGATUS'

This upright, deciduous shrub has attractive, mid-green leaves that are heavily marked with white around the edges. Short clusters of very fragrant white flowers open in early summer. Use to brighten up the back of a mixed border or woodland garden, or grow as a specimen.

CULTIVATION *Grow in any fairly fertile soil with good drainage, in sun or semi-shade. For the best foliage, grow in light shade and prune in late spring. For the best flowers, grow in sun, cutting a few stems to the ground after flowering.*

☼ ☀ ◊ Z 5-8 H 8-3   ‡8ft (2.5m) ↔6ft (2m)

PHILADELPHUS 'MANTEAU D'HERMINE'

This flowering, deciduous shrub is low and spreading in habit, with long-lasting, double, very fragrant, creamy white flowers. These appear from early to mid-summer amid the pale to mid-green, elliptic leaves. Good in a mixed border.

CULTIVATION *Grow in any well-drained, fairly fertile soil. Tolerates partial shade, but flowers are best in full sun. Cut back 1 in 4 stems to the ground after flowering for strong new growth.*

☼ ☀ ◊ Z 5-8 H 8-3   ‡3ft (1m) ↔5ft (1.5m)

PHLOMIS FRUTICOSA

Jerusalem sage is a mound-forming, spreading, evergreen shrub, carrying sagelike, aromatic, gray-green leaves with woolly undersides. Short spikes of hooded, dark golden-yellow flowers appear from early to mid-summer. Effective when massed in a border.

CULTIVATION *Best in light, well-drained, poor to fairly fertile soil, in sun. Prune out any weak or leggy stems in spring.*

☼ ◊ Z 8-9 H 9-8   ‡3ft (1m) ↔5ft (1.5m)

PHLOMIS RUSSELIANA

An upright, evergreen border perennial, sometimes known as either *P. samia* or *P. viscosa*, bearing pointed, hairy, mid-green leaves. Spherical clusters of hooded, pale yellow flowers appear along the stems from late spring to autumn.

CULTIVATION *Grow in any well-drained, moderately fertile soil, in full sun or light shade. May self-seed.*

☼ ◐ ◊ Z 4-9 H 9-1   ‡3ft (1m) ↔30in (75cm)

PHLOX
'CHATTAHOOCHEE'

A short-lived, semi-evergreen border
perennial bearing many flat-faced,
long-throated, lavender-blue flowers
with red eyes. These are produced
over a long period from summer to
early autumn amid the lance-shaped
leaves, which are carried on purple-
tinted stems.

CULTIVATION *Grow in moist but well-
drained, organic, fertile soil. Chose a
site in partial shade.*

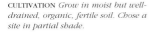 ☀ ◊◊ Z 4-8 H 8-1 ‡6in (15cm) ↔12in (30cm)

PHLOX DOUGLASII
'BOOTHMAN'S VARIETY'

A low and creeping, evergreen
perennial that forms mounds of
narrow, dark green leaves. Dark-
eyed, violet-pink flowers with long
throats and flat faces appear in late
spring or early summer. Good in a
rock garden or wall or as edging
for beds.

CULTIVATION *Grow in well-drained,
fertile soil, in full sun. In areas with low
rainfall, position in dappled shade.*

☀☀ ◊ Z 5-7 H 7-3 ‡8in (20cm) ↔12in (30cm)

PHLOX DOUGLASII 'RED ADMIRAL'

A low-growing, spreading, evergreen perennial that looks good trailing over rocks or spilling over the edge of a border. The mounds of dark green foliage are carpeted with deep crimson, flat-faced flowers during late spring and early summer.

CULTIVATION *Grow in well-drained, fertile soil, in full sun. In areas with low rainfall, position in partial shade.*

☼◑ ◊ Z 5-7 H 7-3 ‡8in (20cm) ↔12in (30cm)

PHLOX 'KELLY'S EYE'

A vigorous, evergreen, mound-forming perennial producing a colorful display of long-throated, flat-faced, pale pink flowers with red-purple centers in late spring and early summer. The leaves are dark green and narrow. Suitable for a rock garden or wall crevices.

CULTIVATION *Grow in fertile soil that has good drainage, in full sun. In low-rainfall areas, site in partial shade.*

☼◑ ◊ Z 4-8 H 8-1 ‡6in (15cm) ↔8in (20cm)

PHLOX PANICULATA

Cultivars of garden phlox, *P. paniculata*, are herbaceous plants bearing dome-shaped or conical clusters of flowers above lance-shaped, toothed, mid-green leaves. Appearing throughout summer and into autumn, the flat-faced, long-throated, delicately fragranced flowers are white, pink, red, purple, or blue, often with contrasting centers; they are long-lasting when cut. Larger flowers can be encouraged by removing the weakest shoots in spring when the growth is still quite small. All types are well-suited to a herbaceous border; some cultivars need staking, but others, such as 'Fujiyama', have particularly sturdy stems.

CULTIVATION *Grow in any reliably moist, fertile soil. Choose a position in full sun or partial shade. Feed with a balanced liquid fertilizer in spring and deadhead regularly to prolong flowering. After flowering, cut back all foliage to ground level.*

☼ ☀ ◑ ◊ Z 4-8 H 8-1

1 ↕ 3ft (1m) ↔ 18in (45cm)

2 ↕ 36in (90cm) ↔ 18in (45cm)

3 ↕ 4ft (1.2m) ↔ 24in (60cm)

4 ↕ 4ft (1.2m) ↔ 24in (60cm)

1 *P. paniculata* 'Mother of Pearl' **2** *P. paniculata* 'Eventide' **3** *P. paniculata* 'Brigadier'
4 *P. paniculata* 'Fujiyama'

PHORMIUM COOKIANUM
SUBSP. HOOKERI 'TRICOLOR'

This striking perennial, very useful as a focal point in a border, forms arching clumps of broad, light green leaves, to 5ft (1.5m) long; they are boldly margined with creamy yellow and red stripes. Tall spikes of tubular yellow-green flowers are borne in summer. Where not hardy, grow in a container during the summer and overwinter under glass.

CULTIVATION *Grow in moist but well-drained soil, in sun. Provide a deep, dry winter mulch where marginal.*

☼ ◊◔ Z 9-10 H 12-1   ‡2–6ft (0.6–2m)
↔1–10ft (0.3–3m)

PHORMIUM TENAX
PURPUREUM GROUP

An evergreen perennial that forms clumps of long, stiff, sword-shaped leaves. These are deep copper to purple-red and are arranged at the base of the plant. Large spikes of dark red, tubular flowers on blue-purple stems appear in summer. Ideal for coastal gardens. As with many phormiums, it can be container-grown.

CULTIVATION *Grow in deep, fertile, organic soil that is reliably moist. Position in full sun with shelter from cold winds. Where marginally hardy, provide a deep, dry mulch in winter.*

☼ ◊ Z 9-10 H 12-1 ‡6–8ft (2–2.5m) ↔3ft (1m)

PHOTINIA × FRASERI 'RED ROBIN'

An upright, compact, evergreen shrub often grown as a formal or semi-formal hedge for its bright red young foliage, the effect of which is prolonged by clipping. The mature leaves are leathery, lance-shaped, and dark green. Clusters of small white flowers appear in mid-spring.

CULTIVATION *Grow in moist but well-drained, fertile soil, in full sun or semi-shade. Clip hedges 2 or 3 times a year to perpetuate the colorful foliage.*

☼ ◐ ◊◊ Z 8-9 H 9-8   ↔ 15ft (5m)

PHYGELIUS AEQUALIS 'YELLOW TRUMPET'

An upright, evergreen shrub forming loose spikes of hanging, tubular, pale cream-yellow flowers during summer. The leaves are oval and pale green. Good for a herbaceous or mixed border; where marginally hardy, grow against a warm wall.

CULTIVATION *Best in moist but well-drained soil, in sun. Provide shelter from wind and cut cold-damaged stems back to the base in spring. Deadhead to prolong flowering. Dig up unwanted shoots to contain spread.*

☼ ◊◊ Z 7-9 H 9-7   ↕↔ 3ft (1m)

PHYGELIUS × RECTUS 'AFRICAN QUEEN'

An upright, evergreen border shrub that bears long spikes of hanging, tubular, pale red flowers with orange to yellow mouths. These appear in summer above the oval, dark green leaves. Best against a warm wall where marginally hardy.

CULTIVATION *Grow in moist but well-drained, fertile soil, in sun with shelter from wind. Cut cold-damaged stems back to the base in spring. Deadhead to prolong flowering.*

☼ ◊◊ Z 8-9 H 9-8 ↕3ft (1m) ↔4ft (1.2m)

PHYLLOSTACHYS NIGRA

Black bamboo is an arching, clump-forming, evergreen grass. The lance-shaped, dark green leaves are produced on slender green canes that turn black in their second or third year. Use as a screen or as a large feature plant.

CULTIVATION *Grow in moist but well-drained soil, in sun or partial shade with shelter from wind. Mulch over winter. Cut out damaged and overcrowded canes in spring or early summer. Confine spread by burying a barrier around the roots.*

☼☀ ◊◊ Z 7-10 H 12-7 ↕10–15ft (3–5m)
↔6–10ft (2–3m)

PHYLLOSTACHYS NIGRA VAR. *HENONIS*

This clump-forming, evergreen bamboo is similar to the black bamboo in habit (see facing page, below), but it has bright green canes that mature to yellow-green in the second or third year. The lance-shaped, dark green leaves are downy and rough when young.

CULTIVATION *Grow in well-drained but moist soil, in sun or semi-shade. Shelter from wind, and mulch over winter. Thin crowded clumps in late spring. Bury a barrier around the roots to confine spread.*

☀◐ ◊◊ Z 7-10 H 12-7   ‡10–15ft (3–5m)
↔6–10ft (2–3m)

PHYSOCARPUS OPULIFOLIUS 'DART'S GOLD'

A rounded and thicket-forming, deciduous shrub valued for its three-lobed leaves, which are a spectacular golden-yellow when young. Dense clusters of small, white or pale pink flowers appear in spring. Lightens up a shrub border.

CULTIVATION *Best in moist but well-drained, acid soil, but tolerates most conditions. Site in sun or partial shade. Cut old stems back to the base after flowering; dig out spreading shoots to confine spread.*

☀◐ ◊◊ Z 3-7 H 7-1   ‡6ft (2m) ↔8ft (2.5m)

PHYSOSTEGIA VIRGINIANA 'VIVID'

An upright, densely clump-forming border perennial bearing spikes of bright purple-pink, hooded flowers. These appear from mid-summer to early autumn above the narrow, mid-green leaves. The flowers are good for cutting and will remain in a new position if they are moved on the stalks, hence the common name of obedient plant.

CULTIVATION *Grow in reliably moist, fertile soil that is rich in organic matter. Position in full sun or partial shade.*

☼ ◑ ◊ Z 4-8 H 8-1   ‡12–24in (30–60cm ↔12in (30cm

PICEA GLAUCA VAR. *ALBERTIANA* 'CONICA'

A conical, slow-growing, evergreen conifer carrying dense, blue-green foliage. The short, slender needles are borne on buff to ash-gray stems. Makes an excellent neat specimen shrub or grouping for a small garden, and it is an excellent subject for growing in containers.

CULTIVATION *Grow in deep, moist but well-drained, preferably neutral to acid soil, in full sun. Prune in winter if necessary, but keep to a minimum.*

☼ ◊◑ Z 3-7 H 6-1   ‡6–20ft (2–6m ↔3–8ft (1–2.5m

PICEA MARIANA 'NANA'

This dwarf, low-growing form of black spruce is a mound-forming conifer with scaly, gray-brown bark. The evergreen, bluish gray needles are short, soft, and slender. Useful in a rock garden or conifer planting or as an unusual edging plant.

CULTIVATION *Best in deep, moist but well-drained, fertile, organic soil, in partial shade. Completely remove any shoots that show vigorous upright growth as soon as they are seen.*

☼ ◑ ◊ Z 3-7 H 6-1　　　↕↔ 20in (50cm)

PICEA PUNGENS 'KOSTER'

This conical evergreen conifer with distinctly horizontal branches becomes more columnar with age, and the young growth is clothed in silvery blue foliage. The long, sharp-pointed needles turn greener as they mature. Cylindrical green cones are borne during the summer, aging to pale brown. Good in larger gardens as a prominent specimen tree.

CULTIVATION *Grow in well-drained, fertile, neutral to acid soil, in full sun. Prune in late autumn or winter if necessary, but keep to a minimum.*

☼ ◊ Z 3-8 H 8-1　　↕ 50ft (15m) ↔ 15ft (5m)

PIERIS 'FOREST FLAME'

An upright, evergreen shrub valued for its slender, glossy, lance-shaped leaves that are bright red when young; they mature through pink and creamy white to dark green. Upright clusters of white flowers enhance the effect in early to mid-spring. Ideal for a shrub border or a peaty, acidic soil; it will not grow well in alkaline soil.

CULTIVATION *Grow in moist but well-drained, fertile, organic, acid soil, in full sun or partial shade. Shelter from cold, drying winds. Trim only lightly after flowering.*

☼◑ ◊◊ Z 6-9 H 9-6 ‡12ft (4m) ↔6ft (2m)

PIERIS FORMOSA VAR. FORRESTII 'WAKEHURST'

This upright, evergreen, acid-soil-loving shrub has brilliant red young foliage that matures to dark green. The large, slightly drooping clusters of small, fragrant white flowers are attractive in late winter and early spring. Grow in a woodland garden or shrub border.

CULTIVATION *Best in well-drained but moist, fertile, organic, acid soil. Site in full sun or partial shade with shelter from wind where marginally hardy. Trim lightly after flowering.*

☼◑ ◊◊ Z 7-9 H 9-7 ‡15ft (5m) ↔12ft (4m)

PIERIS JAPONICA 'BLUSH'

A rounded, evergreen shrub that bears small, pink-flushed white flowers in late winter and early spring. These are carried in long, drooping clusters amid the glossy dark green foliage. A good early-flowering border shrub, although it will not thrive in alkaline soil.

CULTIVATION *Grow in well-drained but moist, fertile, organic, acid soil. Site in full sun or partial shade. Trim lightly after flowering, removing any dead, damaged, or diseased shoots.*

☼ ◐ ◊◑ Z 6-8 H 8-6 ↕12ft (4m) ↔10ft (3m)

PILEOSTEGIA VIBURNOIDES

A slow-growing, woody, evergreen climber that is dusted with feathery clusters of tiny, creamy white flowers in late summer and autumn. The glossy dark green, leathery leaves look very attractive against a large tree trunk or shady wall.

CULTIVATION *Grow in well-drained, fertile soil, in full sun or shade. Shorten stems after flowering as the plant begins to outgrow the allotted space.*

☼ ◐ ◊ Z 7-10 H 12-7 ↕20ft (6m)

PINUS MUGO 'MOPS'

This dwarf pine is an almost spherical conifer with scaly, gray bark and thick, upright branches. The shoots are covered with long, well-spaced, dark to bright green needles. The dark brown, oval cones take a few years to ripen. Effective in a large rock garden or (where space allows) planted in groups.

CULTIVATION *Grow in any well-drained soil, in full sun. Very little pruning is required, since growth is slow.*

☼ ◊ Z 3-7 H 7-1 ‡to 3ft (1m) ↔to 6ft (2m)

PITTOSPORUM TENUIFOLIUM

A columnar, evergreen shrub that is much valued for its glossy green leaves with wavy edges. It is fast growing at first; as it matures, it broadens out into a tree. Tiny, honey scented, purple-black, bell-shaped flowers open from late spring. Makes a very attractive hedge.

CULTIVATION *Grow in well-drained but moist, fertile soil, in full sun or partial shade. Where marginal, shelter from cold winds. Trim to shape in spring; avoid pruning after mid-summer.*

☼ ◐ ◊◊ Z 9-10 H 12-9 ‡12–30ft (4–10m) ↔6–15ft (2–5m)

PITTOSPORUM TENUIFOLIUM
'TOM THUMB'

A compact, rounded, evergreen
foliage shrub that is ideal for a
mixed border designed for year-
round interest. The glossy bronze-
purple leaves are elliptic and wavy-
edged. Tiny, honey-scented, purple
flowers are borne in late spring
and early summer. Shelter against a
warm wall where marginally hardy.

CULTIVATION *Grow in well-drained but
moist, fertile soil, in full sun for best
color. Provide protection where
marginal. Trim to shape in spring;
established plants need little pruning.*

☼ ◐◊◊ Z 9-10 H 12-9 ‡3ft (1m) ↔24in (60cm)

PITTOSPORUM TOBIRA

Japanese mock orange is a rounded,
evergreen shrub or small tree with
leathery, dark green, oval leaves.
Clusters of sweet-scented, creamy
white flowers that age to yellow are
borne in late spring and early
summer; these are followed by
yellow-brown seed capsules. A fine
specimen plant that must be pot-
grown and overwintered under glass
where not hardy.

CULTIVATION *Best in moist but well-
drained, fertile soil or soil mix, in full
sun or partial shade. Prune back (to
restrict growth) in winter or early spring.*

☼ ◐ ◊◊ Z 9-10 H 12-9 ‡6–30ft (2–10m)
↔5–10ft (1.5–3m)

PLATYCODON GRANDIFLORUS

The balloon flower is a clump-forming perennial producing clusters of large, shallowly bell-shaped, purple to violet-blue flowers. These open from balloon-shaped buds in late summer above the bluish green, oval leaves. Suitable for a larger rock garden or herbaceous border.

CULTIVATION *Best in deep, well-drained, loamy, fertile soil that does not dry out, in full sun or partial shade. Flower stems may need staking. Established plants dislike root disturbance.*

☼ ◑ ◊ Z 4-9 H 9-4   ↕ to 24in (60cm)
↔ 12in (30cm)

PLEIOBLASTUS AURICOMUS

This upright bamboo is an evergreen grass grown for its brilliant green, yellow-striped foliage. The bristly-edged, lance-shaped leaves are carried on purple-green canes. Effective in an open glade in a woodland garden. Good in sun, backed by trees or tall shrubs.

CULTIVATION *Grow in moist but well-drained, fertile, organic soil, in full sun for best leaf color. Provide shelter from cold, drying winds. Thin over-crowded clumps in late spring or early summer. Confine spread by burying a barrier around the roots.*

☼ ◐◑ Z 7-11 H 12-7   ↕↔ to 5ft (1.5m)

PLEIOBLASTUS VARIEGATUS

This upright, evergreen bamboo is
much shorter than *P. auricomis* (see
facing page, below), with cream-
and green-striped foliage. The lance-
shaped leaves, borne on hollow,
pale green canes, are covered in fine
white hairs. Use in a sunny border
backed by shrubs; where it has
space to spread; it will swamp less
vigorous neighbors unless confined.

CULTIVATION *Grow in moist but well-
drained, fertile, organic soil, in sun
with shelter from cold winds. Thin out
clumps in late spring. Bury a barrier
around the roots to confine spread.*

☼ ◑◊ Z 7-11 H 12-7 ‡30in (75cm) ↔4ft (1.2m)

PLUMBAGO AURICULATA

Cape leadwort is a scrambling, semi-
evergreen, frost-tender shrub often
trained as a climber. It bears clusters
of long-throated, sky blue flowers
from summer to late autumn amid
the oval leaves. Where not hardy,
plants overwintered under glass can
be moved outside in summer. Often
sold as *P. capensis*.

CULTIVATION *Grow in well-drained,
fertile soil or soil mix, in full sun or
light shade. Pinch out the tips of young
plants to promote bushiness, and tie
climbing stems to a support. Cut back to
a permanent framework in early spring.*

☼☼ ◊ Z 9-10 H 12-1 ‡10–20ft (3–6m)
↔3–10ft (1–3m)

POLEMONIUM 'LAMBROOK MAUVE'

This clump-forming perennial, a garden variety of Jacob's ladder, forms rounded mounds of neat, divided, mid-green leaves. An abundance of funnel-shaped, sky blue flowers cover the foliage from late spring to early summer. Good in a border or in a wild garden.

CULTIVATION *Grow in well-drained but moist, moderately fertile soil, in full sun or partial shade.*

☼ ☽ ◑◑ Z 4-8 H 8-1 ↕↔ to 18in (45cm)

POLYGONATUM × HYBRIDUM

Common Solomon's seal is a perennial for a shady border, bearing hanging clusters of tubular, small white flowers with green mouths along slightly arching stems. These appear in late spring among the elliptic, bright green leaves. Spherical, blue-black fruits develop after the flowers. Suitable for a woodland garden.

CULTIVATION *Grow in moist but well-drained, fertile, organic soil. Position in partial or full shade.*

☼ ● ◑◑ Z 6-9 H 9-6 ↕ to 5ft (1.5m)
↔ 12in (30cm)

POLYSTICHUM ACULEATUM

The prickly shield fern is an elegant, evergreen perennial producing a shuttlecock of finely divided, dark green fronds. An excellent foliage plant for shady areas in a rock garden or well-drained border.

CULTIVATION *Grow in fertile soil that has good drainage, in partial or deep shade. Choose a site sheltered from excessive winter moisture. Remove the previous year's dead fronds before the new growth unfurls in spring.*

☀◑ ◊ Z 3-6 H 6-1 ‡24in (60cm) ↔3ft (1m)

POLYSTICHUM SETIFERUM

The hedge fern is an evergreen perennial, taller than *P. aculeatum* (above), with finely divided, dark green fronds that are soft to the touch. The foliage forms splayed, shuttlecock-like clumps. Good in a shady border or rock garden.

CULTIVATION *Grow in well-drained, fertile soil, in partial or deep shade. Choose a site that is protected from excessive winter moisture. Remove any dead or damaged fronds in spring.*

☀◑ ◊ Z 6-9 H 9-6 ‡4ft (1.2m) ↔3ft (1m)

POTENTILLA FRUTICOSA

Cultivars of *P. fruticosa* are compact and rounded, deciduous shrubs that produce an abundance of flowers over a long period from late spring to mid-autumn. The leaves are dark green and composed of several oblong leaflets. Flowers are saucer-shaped and single rose-like, sometimes borne singly but often in clusters of three. Many cultivars are yellow-flowered, but blooms may also be white, as with 'Abbotswood', or flushed with pink, as in 'Daydawn'. These are undemanding shrubs that make invaluable additions to mixed or shrub borders; they can also be grown as attractive low hedges.

CULTIVATION *Grow in well-drained, poor to moderately fertile soil. Best in full sun, but many tolerate partial shade. Trim lightly after flowering, cutting older wood to the base and removing weak, twiggy growth. Old shrubs sometimes respond well to renovation but may be better replaced.*

☼ ◊ Z 3-7 H 7-1

1 ‡ 30in (75cm) ↔ 4ft (1.2m)

2 ‡ 3ft (1m) ↔ 5ft (1.5m)

3 ‡ 3ft (1m) ↔ 4ft (1.2m)

4 ‡ 3ft (1m) ↔ 5ft (1.5m)

1 *P. fruticosa* 'Abbotswood' **2** *P. fruticosa* 'Elizabeth' **3** *P. fruticosa* 'Daydawn'
4 *P. fruticosa* 'Primrose Beauty'

POTENTILLA 'GIBSON'S SCARLET'

A dense, clump-forming herbaceous perennial grown for its very bright scarlet flowers that are borne in succession throughout summer. The soft green leaves are divided into five leaflets. Good for a rock garden or for bold summer color in a mixed or herbaceous border.

CULTIVATION *Grow in well-drained, poor to moderately fertile soil. Choose a position in full sun.*

☼ ◊ Z 5-8 H 8-5 ‡18in (45cm) ↔24in (60cm)

POTENTILLA MEGALANTHA

A compact, clump-forming perennial bearing a profusion of upright, cup-shaped, rich yellow flowers during mid- to late summer. The slightly hairy, mid-green leaves are divided into three coarsely scalloped leaflets. Good for the front of a border.

CULTIVATION *Grow in poor to fairly fertile soil that has good drainage. Choose a position in full sun.*

☼ ◊ Z 5-8 H 8-5   ‡6–12in (15–30cm) ↔6in (15cm)

POTENTILLA NEPALENSIS 'MISS WILMOTT'

A summer-flowering perennial that forms clumps of mid-green, divided leaves on wiry, red-tinged stems. The small pink flowers with cherry red centers are borne in loose clusters. Good for the front of a border or in cottage-style plantings.

CULTIVATION *Grow in any well-drained, poor to moderately fertile soil. Position in full sun or light dappled shade.*

☀☀ ◊ Z 5-8 H 8-5 ‡12–18in (30–45cm)
↔24in (60cm)

PRIMULA DENTICULATA

The drumstick primrose is a robust, clump-forming perennial bearing spherical clusters of small purple flowers with yellow centers. They are carried on stout, upright stalks from spring to summer above the basal rosettes of oblong to spoon-shaped, mid-green leaves. Thrives in damp but not waterlogged soil; ideal for a waterside planting.

CULTIVATION *Best in moist, organic, neutral to acid soil. Choose a site in partial shade, but it tolerates full sun where soil is reliably moist.*

☀☀ ◊ Z 2-8 H 8-1 ‡↔ 18in (45cm)

PRIMULA FLORINDAE

The giant cowslip is a deciduous, summer-flowering perennial that grows naturally by pools and streams. It forms clumps of oval, toothed, mid-green leaves that are arranged in rosettes at the base of the plant. Drooping clusters of up to 40 funnel-shaped, sweetly scented yellow flowers are borne well above the foliage on upright stems. Good in a bog garden or waterside setting.

CULTIVATION *Grow in deep, reliably moist, organic soil, in partial shade. Tolerates full sun if soil remains moist.*

☀◐ ◊ Z 3-8 H 8-1 ‡to 4ft (1.2m) ↔ 3ft (1m)

PRIMULA 'GUINEVERE'

A fast-growing, evergreen, clump-forming perennial, sometimes called *P.* 'Garryarde Guinevere', that bears clusters of pale purplish pink flowers. They have yellow centers, flat faces, and long throats and are carried above the deep bronze, oval leaves in spring. Excellent for damp, shady places.

CULTIVATION *Grow in moist, neutral to acid soil that is well-drained, in partial shade. Tolerates full sun, but only if the soil remains moist at all times.*

☀◐ ◊ Z 4-8 H 8-1 ‡5in (12cm) ↔ 10in (25cm)

CANDELABRA PRIMROSES (*PRIMULA*)

Candelabra primroses are robust, herbaceous perennials, so-called because their flowers are borne in tiered clusters that rise above the basal rosettes of broadly oval leaves in late spring or summer. Depending on the species, the foliage may be semi-evergreen, evergreen, or deciduous. The flowers have flat faces and long throats; as with most cultivated primroses, there is a wide choice of colors, from the brilliant red 'Inverewe' to the golden-yellow *P. prolifera*. Some flowers change color as they mature; those of *P. bulleyana* fade from crimson to orange. Candelabra primroses look most effective when grouped together in a bog garden or waterside setting.

CULTIVATION *Grow in deep, moist, neutral to acid, organic soil. Site in partial shade, although full sun is tolerated if the soil remains moist at all times. Divide and replant clumps in early spring.*

☼ ◐ ◊ Z 5-8 H 8-1

1 ↔ 24in (60cm)   **2** ↔ 24in (60cm)

3 ↕ 30in (75cm) ↔ 24in (60cm)   **4** ↕ to 3ft (1m) ↔ 24in (60cm)   **5** ↕ to 3ft (1m) ↔ 24in (60cm)

1 *P. bulleyana* **2** *P. prolifera* (syn. *P. helodoxa*) **3** *P.* 'Inverewe' **4** *P. pulverulenta*
5 *P. pulverulenta* Bartley Hybrids

PRIMULA ROSEA

A deciduous perennial that bears
rounded clusters of glowing pink,
long-throated flowers on upright
stalks in spring. Clumps of oval,
toothed, mid-green leaves emerge
after the flowers; these are tinted
red-bronze when young. Good for
a bog garden or waterside planting.

CULTIVATION *Grow in deep, reliably
moist, neutral to acid soil that is rich in
organic matter. Prefers partial shade
but tolerates full sun if the soil is moist
at all times.*

☀ ◐ ◊ Z 3-8 H 8-1   ‡↔ 8in (20cm)

PRIMULA VERIS

The cowslip is a semi-evergreen,
spring-flowering perennial with a
variable appearance. Stout flower
stems carry dense clusters of
small, funnel-shaped, sweetly
scented, nodding yellow flowers
above the clumps of lance-shaped,
crinkled leaves. Lovely naturalized
in moist grassy areas.

CULTIVATION *Best in deep, moist but
well-drained, fertile, organic soil, in
semi-shade or full sun, if soil remains
reliably moist.*

☀ ◑ ◊ Z 3-8 H 8-1   ‡↔ to 10in (25cm)

PRIMULA 'WANDA'

A very vigorous, semi-evergreen perennial that bears clusters of flat-faced, claret red flowers with yellow centers over a long period in spring. The oval, toothed, purplish green leaves are arranged in clumps at the base of the plant. Good in a waterside setting.

CULTIVATION *Best in deep, moist but well-drained, organic, fertile soil. Prefers partial shade, but tolerates full sun if soil remains damp.*

☼ ◐ ◊◊ Z 3-8 H 8-1   ‡4–6in (10–15cm)
↔12–16in (30–40cm)

PRUNELLA GRANDIFLORA 'LOVELINESS'

This vigorous, spreading perennial bears dense, upright spikes of light purple, tubular flowers in summer. The lance-shaped, deep-green leaves are arranged in clumps at ground level. Versatile groundcover when planted in groups. The flowers are attractive to beneficial insects.

CULTIVATION *Grow in any soil, in sun or partial shade. May swamp smaller plants, so allow room to expand. Divide clumps in spring or autumn to maintain vigor. Deadhead to prevent self-seeding.*

☼ ◐ ◊◊ Z 5-8 H 8-5   ‡6in (15cm
↔to 3ft (1m) or more

PRUNUS × *CISTENA*

An upright, slow-growing, deciduous shrub valued in particular for its foliage, which is red when young, maturing to red-purple. Bowl-shaped, pinkish white flowers open from mid- to late spring, sometimes followed by small, cherrylike, purple-black fruits. Good as a windbreak hedge.

CULTIVATION *Grow in any but water-logged soil, in full sun. Prune back overcrowded shoots after flowering. To grow as a hedge, prune the shoot tips of young plants then trim in mid-summer to encourage branching.*

☼ ◊◑ Z 4-8 H 8-1   ↨↔ 5ft (1.5m)

PRUNUS GLANDULOSA 'ALBA PLENA'

This small cherry is a neat, rounded, deciduous shrub producing dense clusters of pure white, bowl-shaped, double flowers during late spring. The narrowly oval leaves are pale to mid-green. Brings beautiful blossoms to a mixed or shrub border.

CULTIVATION *Grow in any moist but well-drained, moderately fertile soil, in sun. Can be pruned to a low framework each year after flowering to enhance the flowering performance.*

☼ ◊◑ Z 5-8 H 8-3   ↨↔ 5ft (1.5m)

PRUNUS 'KIKU-SHIDARE-ZAKURA'

Also known as 'Cheal's Weeping', this small deciduous cherry tree is grown for its weeping branches and clear pink blossoms. Dense clusters of large, double flowers are borne in mid- to late spring, with or before the lance-shaped, mid-green leaves, which are flushed bronze when young. Excellent in a small garden.

CULTIVATION *Best in any moist but well-drained, moderately fertile soil, in full sun. Tolerates alkaline soil. After flowering, prune out dead, diseased, or damaged wood; remove any shoots growing from the trunk as they appear.*

☀ ◑◔ Z 6-8 H 8-6   ↕↔ 10ft (3m)

PRUNUS LAUROCERASUS 'OTTO LUYKEN'

This compact cherry laurel is an evergreen shrub with dense, glossy dark green foliage. Abundant spikes of white flowers are borne in mid- to late spring and often again in autumn, followed by conical red fruits that ripen to black. Plant in groups as a low hedge or to cover bare ground.

CULTIVATION *Grow in any moist but well-drained, moderately fertile soil, in full sun. Prune in late spring or early summer to restrict size.*

☀ ◑◔ Z 6-9 H 9-6   ↕3ft (1m) ↔5ft (1.5m)

PRUNUS LUSITANICA
SUBSP. *AZORICA*

This Portugal laurel is a slow-growing, evergreen shrub bearing slender spikes of small, fragrant, white flowers in early summer. The oval, glossy dark green leaves have red stalks. Purple berries appear later in the season. Attractive year-round as a dense screen or hedge.

CULTIVATION *Grow in any moist but well-drained, fairly fertile soil, in sun with shelter from cold, drying winds. In late spring, prune to restrict size or to remove old or overcrowded shoots.*

☀ ◐◑ 7-9 H 9-7   ↕↔ to 70ft (20m)

PRUNUS SERRULA

A rounded, deciduous tree that is valued for its striking, glossy, copper-brown to mahogany red bark that peels with age. Small, bowl-shaped white flowers in spring are followed by little cherries in autumn. The leaves are lance-shaped and dark green, turning yellow in autumn. Best grown as a specimen tree.

CULTIVATION *Best in moist but well-drained, moderately fertile soil, in full sun. Remove dead or damaged wood after flowering, and remove any shoots growing from the trunk as they appear.*

☀ ◐◑ Z 6-8 H 8-6   ↕↔ 30ft (10m)

FLOWERING CHERRY TREES (*PRUNUS*)

Ornamental cherries are cultivated primarily for their white, pink, or red flowers which create a mass of blossoms, usually on bare branches, from late winter to late spring; cultivars of *P.* x *subhirtella* flower from late autumn. Most popular cultivars not only bear dense clusters of showy, double flowers but have other ornamental characteristics to extend their interest beyond the flowering season: *P. sargentii*, for example, has brilliant autumn foliage color, and some have shiny, colored bark. All of these features make flowering cherries superb specimen trees for small gardens.

CULTIVATION *Grow in any moist but well-drained, fairly fertile soil, in sun. Keep all pruning to an absolute minimum; restrict formative pruning to young plants only. Remove any damaged or diseased growth in mid-summer, and keep trunks clear of sprouting shoots.*

☼ ◐◑ Zones vary H 8-4

1 ‡ 70ft (20m) ↔ 30ft (10m)   **2** ‡↔ 40ft (12m)   **3** ‡ 30ft (10m) ↔ 25ft (8m)

4 ‡ 30ft (10m) ↔ 25ft (8m)   **5** ‡ 50ft (15m) ↔ 30ft (10m)   **6** ‡ 30ft (10m) ↔ 25ft (8m)

1 *P. avium* Z 4-8 **2** *P. avium* 'Plena' Z 4-8 **3** *P.* 'Kanzan' Z 6-8 **4** *P.* 'Okame' Z 5-8
5 *P. padus* 'Colorata' Z 4-8 **6** *P.* 'Pandora' Z 6-8

8 ↕↔ 25ft (8m)

9 ↕ to 70ft (20m) ↔ 50ft (15m)

7 ↕↔ 50ft (15m) ↔ 30ft (10m)

10 ↕ 25ft (8m) ↔ 30ft (10m)

11 ↕ 15ft (5m) ↔ 25ft (8m)

13 ↕ 30ft (10m) ↔ 20ft (6m)

14 ↕ 25ft (8m) ↔ 30ft (10m)

12 ↕↔ 25ft (8m)

15 ↕ 25ft (8m) ↔ 30ft (10m)

16 ↕ to 50ft (15m) ↔ 30ft (10m)

7 *P. padus* 'Watereri' Z 4-8 **8** *P.* 'Pink Perfection' Z 5-8 **9** *P. sargentii* Z 5-9 **10** *P.* 'Shirofugen' Z 6-8 **11** *P.* 'Shôgetsu' Z 6-8 **12** *P.* x *subhirtella* 'Autumnalis Rosea' Z 6-8 **13** *P.* 'Spire' Z 6-8 **14** *P.* 'Taihaku' Z 6-8 **15** *P.* 'Ukon' Z 6-8 **16** *P.* x *yedoensis* Z 6-8

PSEUDOPANAX LESSONII
'GOLD SPLASH'

This evergreen, upright to spreading shrub or tree bears yellow-splashed, deep green foliage. In summer, less conspicuous clusters of yellow-green flowers are carried among toothed leaves that are divided into teardrop-shaped leaflets. Purple-black fruits appear later in the season. Where not hardy, grow in a container as a foliage plant for a conservatory.

CULTIVATION *Best in well-drained, fertile soil or soil mix, in sun or partial shade. Prune to restrict spread in early spring. Minimum temperature 35°F (2°C).*

☼ ◑ ◊ H 12-7   ‡10–20ft (3–6m)
↔6–12ft (2–4m)

PULMONARIA
'LEWIS PALMER'

This lungwort, sometimes called *P*. 'Highdown', is a deciduous perennial that forms clumps of upright, flowering stems. These are topped by open clusters of pink then blue, funnel-shaped flowers in early spring. The coarse, softly hairy leaves, dark green with white spots, are arranged along the stems. Grow in a wild or woodland garden.

CULTIVATION *Best in moist but not waterlogged, fertile, organic soil, in deep or light shade. Every few years, divide and replant clumps after flowering.*

☼ ◑ ◊ Z 5-8 H 8-5 ‡14in (35cm) ↔18in (45cm

PULMONARIA OFFICINALIS 'SISSINGHURST WHITE'

A neat, clump-forming, evergreen perennial valued for its pure white spring flowers and white-spotted foliage. The elliptic, hairy, mid- to dark green leaves are carried on upright stems below funnel-shaped flowers that open from pale pink buds in early spring. Grow as a groundcover in a shady spot.

CULTIVATION *Grow in moist but not waterlogged, organic soil. Best in deep or light shade, but tolerates full sun. Divide and replant clumps every 2 or 3 years, after flowering.*

☀️◑◐ ♦ Z 6-8 H 8-6   ↕to 12in (30cm)
                             ↔18in (45cm)

PULSATILLA VULGARIS

The pasque flower is a compact perennial forming tufts of finely divided, light green foliage. Its bell-shaped, nodding, silky-hairy flowers are carried above the leaves in spring; they are deep to pale purple or occasionally red or white, with golden centers. Good in a rock garden, scree bed, or trough or between paving.

CULTIVATION *Best in fertile soil with very good drainage. Site in full sun where it will not be prone to excessive winter moisture. Do not disturb once planted.*

☀️ ◊ Z 5-7 H 7-5   ↕4–8in (10–20cm)
                            ↔8in (20cm)

PULSATILLA VULGARIS 'ALBA'

This clump-forming perennial, a white form of the pasque flower, bears nodding, bell-shaped, silky-hairy white flowers with bold yellow centers in spring. These are carried above the finely divided, light green foliage, which is hairy when young. Very pretty in a rock garden or scree bed.

CULTIVATION *Best in fertile soil with very good drainage. Grow in full sun; protect from excessive winter moisture. Resents disturbance once planted.*

☼ ◊ Z 5-7 H 7-5　　　‡↔8in (20cm)

PYRACANTHA 'ORANGE GLOW'

An upright to spreading, spiny, evergreen shrub bearing profuse clusters of tiny white flowers in late spring. Orange-red to dark orange berries follow in autumn and persist well into winter. The leaves are oval and glossy dark green. Excellent as a vandal-resistant barrier hedge that may also attract birds.

CULTIVATION *Grow in well-drained, fertile soil, in full sun to deep shade. Shelter from cold, drying winds. Prune in mid-spring, and trim new leafy growth again in summer to expose the berries.*

☼◐ ◊ Z 7-9 H 9-7　　　‡↔10ft (3m)

PYRACANTHA 'WATERERI'

A vigorous, upright, spiny shrub that forms a dense screen of evergreen foliage, ornamented by its abundance of white spring flowers and bright red berries in autumn. The leaves are elliptic and dark green. Good as a barrier hedge or in a shrub border; can also be trained against a wall. Attractive to birds.

CULTIVATION *Grow in well-drained, fertile soil, in sun or shade with shelter from wind. Cut back unwanted growth in mid-spring, and trim leafy growth in summer to expose the berries.*

☼ ◑ ◊ Z 7-9 H 9-7   ↔ 8ft (2.5m)

PYRUS CALLERYANA 'CHANTICLEER'

This thorny ornamental pear tree has a narrowly conical shape and makes a good specimen tree for smaller gardens. Attractive sprays of small white flowers in mid-spring are followed by tiny, spherical brown fruits in autumn. The oval, finely scalloped leaves are glossy dark green; they turn red before they fall. Tolerates urban pollution.

CULTIVATION *Grow in any well-drained, fertile soil, in full sun. Prune in winter to maintain a well-spaced crown.*

☼ ◊ Z 5-8 H 8-5   ↕50ft (15m) ↔20ft (6m)

PYRUS SALICIFOLIA 'PENDULA'

This weeping pear is a deciduous tree with silvery gray, willowlike leaves that are downy when young. Dense clusters of small, creamy white flowers appear during spring, followed by pear-shaped green fruits in autumn. A fine, pollution-tolerant tree for an urban garden.

CULTIVATION *Grow in fertile soil with good drainage, in sun. Prune young trees in winter to create a well-spaced, balanced framework of branches.*

☼ ◊ Z 5-9 H 9-5 ‡25ft (8m) ↔20ft (6m)

RAMONDA MYCONI

A tiny, neat, evergreen perennial with basal rosettes of dark green, slightly crinkled, broadly oval leaves. In late spring and early summer, heads of outward-facing, deep violet-blue flowers are borne above the foliage on short stems. Pink- and white-flowered variants also occur. Grow in a rock garden or in a dry wall.

CULTIVATION *Plant in moist but well-drained, moderately fertile, organic soil, in partial shade. Set plants at an angle to avoid water collecting in the rosettes and causing rot. Leaves wither if too dry, but they recover upon watering.*

◐ ◊◊ Z 5-7 H 7-5 ‡4in (10cm) ↔8in (20cm)

RANUNCULUS ACONITIFOLIUS 'FLORE PLENO'

White bachelor's buttons is a clump-forming, herbaceous perennial bearing small, almost spherical, fully double white flowers that last for a long time during late spring and early summer. The toothed leaves are deeply lobed and glossy dark green. Good for a woodland garden.

CULTIVATION *Grow in moist but well-drained soil that is rich in organic matter. Site in deep or partial shade.*

☀️ ◑ ◊◊ Z 5-9 H 9-5   ‡24in (60cm)
                              ↔18in (45cm)

RANUNCULUS CALANDRINIOIDES

This clump-forming perennial produces clusters of up to three cup-shaped, white or pink-flushed flowers from late winter to early spring. The lance-shaped, blue-green leaves emerge from the base in spring and die down in summer. Grow in a rock garden, scree bed, or alpine house.

CULTIVATION *Best in gritty, sharply drained, organic soil, in sun. Water sparingly when dormant in summer.*

☀️ ◊ Z 7-8 H 8-7   ‡8in (20cm) ↔6in (15cm)

RANUNCULUS GRAMINEUS

This clump-forming buttercup is a perennial that is equally at home in a herbaceous border or rock garden. Cup-shaped, lemon-yellow flowers are carried above the grasslike, finely hairy leaves in late spring and early summer.

CULTIVATION *Grow in moist but well-drained, fertile soil. Choose a position in full sun or partial shade.*

☼ ◑ ◊◊ Z 6-8 H 8-6   ↕to 12in (30cm) ↔to 6in (15cm)

RHAMNUS ALATERNUS 'ARGENTEOVARIEGATA'

This Italian buckthorn is a fast-growing, upright to spreading, evergreen shrub bearing oval, leathery, gray-green leaves with creamy white margins. Clusters of tiny, yellow-green flowers are borne in spring, followed by spherical red fruits that ripen to black.

CULTIVATION *Grow in any well-drained soil, in full sun. Prune out unwanted growth in early spring; remove any shoots with all-green leaves as seen.*

☼ ◊ Z 7-9 H 9-7   ↕15ft (5m) ↔12ft (4m

RHODANTHEMUM HOSMARIENSE

A spreading subshrub valued for its profusion of daisylike flowerheads with white petals and yellow eyes. These are borne from early spring to autumn, covering the silver, softly hairy, finely divided leaves. Grow at the base of a wall or in a rock garden. In an alpine house, it will flower year-round if deadheaded.

CULTIVATION *Grow in very well-drained soil, in a sunny position. Deadhead regularly to prolong flowering.*

☼ ◊ Z 9-10 H 12-7   ‡4–12in (10–30cm)
                        ↔12in (30cm)

RHODOCHITON ATROSANGUINEUS

An evergreen, slender-stemmed climber, also known as *R. volubilis*, that is grown as an annual or greenhouse plant. Hanging, tubular, black to purple flowers with red-purple, bell-shaped "skirts" are borne during summer and autumn among the heart-shaped, rich green leaves. Support larger plants with wiring or a trellis.

CULTIVATION *Grow in moist but well-drained, fertile, organic soil, in full sun; the roots must be in shade. Pinch out shoot tips to promote a bushy habit. Minimum temperature 37° F (3° C).*

☼ ◊◊ H 12-9   ‡10ft (3m)

EVERGREEN AND DECIDUOUS AZALEAS (*RHODODENDRON*)

Azaleas are rounded, shrubby plants valued for their showy, often scented flowers that are borne amid dark green foliage during spring. The individual flowers vary greatly in size and shape and are available in almost every color. Azaleas are suitable for a range of uses: dwarf or compact types, such as 'Beethoven' and 'Homebush', are excellent in containers or tubs on shaded patios; larger varieties, such as 'Cecile', will brighten up areas of the garden that are in shade. 'Hino-mayo',

R. luteum, 'Rose Bud', 'Vuyk's Rosyred', and 'Vuyk's Scarlet' thrive in sun, providing the soil is not allowed to dry out.

CULTIVATION *Grow in moist but well-drained, organic, acid soil, ideally in part-day shade. Shallow planting is essential. Little formative pruning is necessary, but older plants may become congested and require thinning in early summer.*

☼ ◐ ◊◊ Zones vary **H** 9-3

1 ↕↔ 4½ft (1.3m)

2 ↕↔ 2.2m (7ft)

3 ↕↔ 24in (60cm)

4 ↕↔ 5ft (1.5m)

5 ↕↔ 12ft (4m)

1 *R.* 'Beethoven' (Ev) Z 6-9 **2** *R.* 'Cecile' (De) Z 5-8 **3** *R.* 'Hino-mayo' (Ev) Z 7-9
4 *R.* 'Homebush' (De) Z 5-8 **5** *R. luteum* (De) Z 6-9

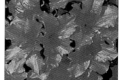

7 ‡↔ 6ft (2m)

6 ‡↔ 4ft (1.2m)

8 ‡↔ 4ft (1.2m)

‡↔ 24–36in (60–90cm)

10 ‡↔ 1.2m (4ft)

R. 'Palestrina' (Ev) Z 6-9 7 R. 'Persil' (De) Z 5-8 8 R. 'Vuyk's Scarlet' (Ev) Z 6-8
R. 'Rose Bud' (Ev) Z 6-9 10 R. 'Vuyk's Rosyred' (Ev) Z 6-8

LARGE RHODODENDRONS

These are large, woodland-suited rhododendrons that can reach treelike proportions and are grown primarily for their bright, sometimes fragrant, mostly spring flowers available in a wide spectrum of shapes and colors. They are ideal for adding color to shady areas or woodland gardens. Most leaves are oval and dark green, although the attractive young foliage of *R. bureavii* is light brown. Some cultivars, such as 'Cynthia' or 'Purple Splendour', are tolerant of direct sun (in reliably moist soil), making them more versatile than others; they make showy flowering screens or hedges for a large garden.

CULTIVATION *Grow in moist but well-drained, organic, acid soil. Most prefer dappled shade in sheltered woodland. Shallow planting is essential. Little formative pruning is necessary, although most can be renovated after flowering to leave a balanced framework of old wood.*

☼◑ ◊◊ Zones vary H 9-5

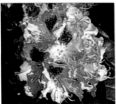

1 ↔ 10ft (3m)

2 ↔ 10ft (3m)

3 ↔ 11ft (3.5m)

1 'Blue Peter' Z 6-9 2 *R. bureavii* Z 6-9 3 'Crest' Z 7-9 4 'Cynthia' Z 6-9 5 *R. falconeri* Z 8-9

4 ↕↔ 20ft (6m)

5 ↕ to 40ft (12m) ↔ 15ft (5m)

6 ↕↔ 12ft (4m)

7 ↕↔ 10ft (3m)

8 ↕↔ 12ft (4m)

↕↔ 10ft (3m)

10 ↕↔ 10ft (3m)

11 ↕↔ 10ft (3m)

R. 'Fastuosum Flore Pleno' Z 5-8 **7** 'Furnivall's Daughter' Z 7-9 **8** 'Loderi King George' Z 7-9
'Purple Splendour' Z 6-9 **10** 'Sappho' Z 6-9 **11** 'Susan' Z 6-9

MEDIUM-SIZED RHODODENDRONS

These evergreen rhododendrons, between 5–10ft (1.5–3m) tall, are much valued for their attractive, often scented blooms; the flowers are carried among dark green foliage throughout spring. 'Yellow Hammer' will often produce an early show of flowers in autumn, and the foliage of 'Winsome' is unusual for its bronze tints when young. A vast number of different medium-sized rhododendrons is available, all suitable for shrub borders or grouped together in mass plantings. Some sun-tolerant varieties, especially low-growing forms such as 'May Day', are suitable for informal hedging.

CULTIVATION *Grow in moist but well-drained, organic, acid soil. Most prefer light, dappled shade. Shallow planting is essential. They require extra care in marginal areas; provide a thick winter mulch and avoid siting in a frost pocket. Trim after flowering, if necessary.*

☼ ◐ ◊◊ Zones vary H 9-7

1 ‡↔ 6ft (2m)   2 ‡↔ 5ft (1.5m)

1 *R.* 'Fabia' (Z 8-9) 2 *R.* 'Golden Torch' (Z 7-9)

3 ↕↔ 6ft (2m)

4 ↕↔ 5ft (1.5m)

5 ↕↔ 5ft (1.5m)

6 ↕↔ 6ft (2m)

↕↔ 6ft (2m)

8 ↕↔ 5ft (1.5m)

R. 'Fragrantissimum' (Z 9-10) **4** *R.* 'Hydon Dawn' (Z 7-9) **5** *R.* 'May Day' (Z 7-9)
R. 'Titian Beauty' (Z 7-9) **7** *R.* 'Yellow Hammer' (Z 7-9) **8** *R.* 'Winsome' (Z 7-9)

DWARF RHODODENDRONS

Dwarf rhododendrons are low-growing, evergreen shrubs with mid- to dark green, lance-shaped leaves. They flower throughout spring in a wide variety of showy colors and flower forms. If soil conditions are too alkaline for growing rhododendrons in the open garden, these compact shrubs are ideal in containers or barrels on shaded patios; 'Ptarmigan' is is particularly suited to this kind of planting, since it is able to tolerate periods without water. Dwarf rhododendrons are also effective in rock gardens. The earliest spring flowers may be vulnerable to cold and frost damage.

CULTIVATION *Grow in moist but well-drained, leafy, acid soil that is enriched with well-rotted organic matter. Site in sun or partial shade, but avoid the deep shade directly beneath a tree canopy. Best planted in spring or autumn; shallow planting is essential. Pruning is rarely necessary.*

☼◑ ◌◑ Zones vary H 9-6

1 ↔ 3½ft (1.1m)

2 ↔ 4ft (1.2m)

3 ↔ 24in (60cm)

4 ↔ 18–36in (45–90cm)

1 *R.* 'Cilpinense' (Z 8-9) **2** *R.* 'Doc' (Z 5-9) **3** *R.* 'Dora Amateis' (Z 6-9) **4** *R.* 'Ptarmigan' (Z 7-9)

RHUS TYPHINA 'DISSECTA'

Staghorn sumac is an upright, deciduous shrub with velvety red shoots that resemble antlers. This form has long leaves, divided into many finely cut leaflets, that turn a brilliant orange-red in autumn. Upright clusters of less significant, yellow-green flowers are produced in summer, followed by velvety clusters of deep crimson red fruits.

CULTIVATION *Grow in moist but well-drained, fairly fertile soil, in full sun to obtain best autumn color. Remove any suckering shoots arising from the ground around the base of the plant.*

☼ ◊◑ Z 3-8 H 8-1 ‡6ft (2m) ↔10ft (3m)

RIBES SANGUINEUM 'BROCKLEBANKII'

This slow-growing flowering currant is an upright, deciduous shrub with rounded, aromatic, yellow leaves, bright when young and fading in summer. The tubular, pale pink flowers, borne in hanging clusters in spring, are followed by small, blue-black fruits.

CULTIVATION *Grow in well-drained, fairly fertile soil. Site in sun, with shade during the hottest part of the day. Prune out some older stems after flowering. Cut back overgrown specimens in winter.*

☼☀ ◊ Z 6-8 H 8-6 ‡↔ 4ft (1.2m)

RIBES SANGUINEUM
'PULBOROUGH SCARLET'

This vigorous flowering currant, larger than 'Brocklebankii', (see previous page, bottom) is an upright, deciduous shrub, bearing hanging clusters of tubular, dark red flowers with white centers in spring. The aromatic, dark green leaves are rounded, with toothed lobes. Small blue-black fruits develop during the summer.

CULTIVATION *Grow in well-drained, moderately fertile soil, in full sun. Cut out some older stems after flowering; overgrown specimens can be pruned hard in winter or early spring.*

☼ ◊◖ Z 6-9 H 8-6 ‡6ft (2m) ↔ 8ft (2.5m)

ROBINIA HISPIDA

The bristly locust is an upright and arching, deciduous shrub with spiny shoots, useful for shrub borders on poor, dry soils. Deep rose-pink, pea-like flowers appear in hanging spikes during late spring and early summer; these are followed by brown seed pods. The large, dark green leaves are divided into several oval leaflets.

CULTIVATION *Grow in any but water-logged soil, in sun. Provide shelter from wind to avoid damage to the brittle branches. No pruning is necessary.*

☼ ◊ Z 6-10 H 12-6 ‡8ft (2.5m) ↔ 10ft (3m

ROBINIA PSEUDOACACIA 'FRISIA'

The black locust is a fast-growing, broadly columnar, deciduous tree bearing yellow-green foliage that is golden-yellow when young, turning orange-yellow in autumn. Hanging clusters of fragrant, pealike, small white flowers appear in mid-summer, but rarely in profusion. The divided leaves are borne on stems that are usually spiny.

CULTIVATION *Grow in moist but well-drained, fertile soil, in full sun. When young, maintain a single trunk by removing competing stems as soon as possible. Do not prune once established.*

☼ ◊◊ ◑ Z 4-9 H 9-1 ‡50ft (15m) ↔25ft (8m)

RODGERSIA PINNATA 'SUPERBA'

A clump-forming perennial that bears upright clusters of star-shaped, bright pink flowers. These are borne in mid- to late summer above bold, heavily veined, dark green foliage. The divided leaves, up to 36in (90cm) long, are purplish bronze when young. Good near water, in a bog garden, or for naturalizing at a woodland margin.

CULTIVATION *Best in moist, organic soil, in full sun or semi-shade. Provide shelter from wind. Will not tolerate prolonged drought.*

☼◐ ◑ Z 5-8 H 8-5 ‡4ft (1.2m) ↔30in (75cm)

MODERN BUSH ROSES

There are two types of modern bush rose, both grown for flowers that are borne in succession from summer to autumn. Hybrid tea (large-flowered) roses bear single blooms on tall stems; floribunda (cluster-flowered) roses carry up to up to 25 blooms per stem. All have deciduous, deep green leaves on upright, often thorny or prickly stems. The traditional use of bush roses in formal displays is still very popular, although a more restful mood is created if mixed with herbaceous plants and other shrubs; these will provide interest before and after the roses bloom. Most suit a small garden better than shrub roses (see page 386), since they are more compact.

CULTIVATION *Grow in moist but well-drained, fertile soil, in full sun. Cut flowered stems back to a leaf for repeat blooms. Prune main stems to about 10in (25cm) above ground in early spring, and remove any dead or diseased wood as necessary.*

☼ ◊◊ Z 5-9 H 9-1

1 ‡20in (50cm) ↔ 24in (60cm) **2** ‡3ft (1m) ↔ 24in (60cm) **3** ‡3½ft (1.1m) ↔ 30in (75cm)

4 ‡to 6ft (2m) ↔ 32in (80cm) **5** ‡4ft (1.2m) ↔ 3ft (1m)

HT = hybrid tea (large-flowered); F = floribunda (cluster-flowered)
1 *R.* AMBER QUEEN 'Harroony' (F) **2** *R.* 'Arthur Bell' (F) **3** *R.* BLESSINGS (HT)
4 *R.* ALEXANDER 'Harlex' (HT) **5** *R.* CHINATOWN (F) **6** *R.* ICEBERG 'Korbin' (F)

6 ‡32in (80cm) ↔ 26in (65cm)   **7** ‡30in (75cm) ↔ 28in (70cm ()   **8** ‡↔ 30in (75cm)

9 ‡32in (80cm) ↔ 24in (60cm)   **10** ‡4ft (1.2m) ↔ 30in (75cm)   **11** ‡4ft (1.2m) ↔ 1m (3ft)

12 ‡3ft (1m) ↔ 24in (60cm)

13 ‡3ft (1m) ↔ 30in (75cm)   **14** ‡3½ft (1.1m) ↔ 24in (60cm)

7 *R.* JUST JOEY (HT)   **8** *R.* MANY HAPPY RETURNS 'Harwanted' (F)   **9** *R.* MARGARET MERRIL 'Harkuly' (F)   **10** *R.* MOUNTBATTEN 'Harmantelle' (F)   **11** *R.* PEACE 'Madame A. Meilland' (HT) **12** *R.* REMEMBER ME 'Cocdestin' (HT)   **13** *R.* ROYAL WILLIAM 'Korzaun' (HT)   **14** *R.* SILVER JUBILEE (F)

CLIMBING ROSES

Climbing roses are often vigorous plants that will reach varying heights depending on the cultivar. All types have stiff, arching stems, usually with dense, glossy leaves divided into small leaflets. The frequently scented flowers are borne in summer, some in one exuberant flush, others having a lesser repeat flowering. They can be trained against walls or fences as decorative features in their own right, planted as a complement to other climbers (such as clematis), or allowed to scramble up into other wall-trained shrubs or even old trees. They are invaluable for disguising unsightly garden buildings or as a backdrop to a summer border.

CULTIVATION *Best in moist but well-drained, fairly fertile soil, in sun. Deadhead unless hips are wanted. As plants mature, prune back to within the allowed area, after flowering. Cut the oldest one or two stems back to the base in late winter to stimulate the production of new shoots.*

☼ ◊◊ mostly Z 5-9; H 9-1

1 ‡↔ to 20ft (6m)

2 ‡10ft (3m) ↔ 8ft (2.5m)

3 ‡↔ 7ft (2.2m)

4 ‡ to 30ft (10m) ↔ 20ft (6m)

5 ‡ to 15ft (5m) ↔ 12ft (4m)

1 *R. banksiae* 'Lutea' Z 8-9 **2** *R.* COMPASSION **3** *R.* DUBLIN BAY 'Macdub' **4** *R. filipes* 'Kiftsgate' Z 7-9
5 *R.* 'Gloire de Dijon' Z 6-9

6 ‡ to 10ft (3m) ↔ 6ft (2m)

7 ‡ 10ft (3m) ↔ 7ft (2.2m)

8 ‡↔ 8ft (2.5m)

9 ‡ 15ft (5m) ↔ 10ft (3m)

10 ‡ 10ft (3m) ↔ 8ft (2.5m)

11 ‡ to 20ft (6m) ↔ 12ft (4m)

12 ‡ to 10ft (3m) ↔ 6ft (2m)

5 *R.* GOLDEN SHOWERS **7** *R.* HANDEL 'Macha' **8** *R.* 'Maigold' **9** *R.* 'Madame Alfred Carrière'
10 *R.* 'New Dawn' **11** *R.* 'Madame Grégoire Staechelin' **12** *R.* 'Zéphirine Drouhin' Z 6-9

RAMBLING ROSES

Rambling roses are very similar to climbers (see page 380) but with more lax, flexible stems. These are easier to train onto complex structures such as arches, tunnels, and pergolas, or ropes and chains suspended between rigid uprights; most ramblers are vigorous. Unlike climbers, they can succumb to mildew, especially if trained against walls. All have divided, glossy green leaves, borne on thorny or prickly stems. Flowers are often scented, arranged singly or in clusters, and are borne during summer. Some bloom only once, while a few have a lesser repeat flowering later on.

CULTIVATION *Best in moist but well-drained, fertile soil, in full sun. Train stems of young plants onto a support to establish a permanent framework; prune back to this each year after flowering has finished, and remove any damaged wood as necessary.*

☼ ◊◊ Z 5-9 H 9-1

1 ‡to 15ft (5m) ↔ 10ft (3m)

2 ‡to 15ft (5m) ↔ 12ft (4m)

1 *R.* 'Albéric Barbier' **2** *R.* 'Albertine'

3 ‡ to 30ft (10m) ↔ 20ft (6m)

4 ‡ to 15ft (5m) ↔ to 12ft (4m)

5 ‡↔ 20ft (6m)

‡ to 20ft (6m) ↔ 12ft (4m)

7 ‡↔ to 12ft (4m)

8 ‡↔ 12ft (4m)

R. 'Bobbie James' **4** *R.* 'Félicité Perpétue' **5** *R.* 'Rambling Rector' **6** *R.* 'Seagull'
R. 'Sanders' White Rambler' **8** *R.* 'Veilchenblau'

PATIO ROSES

These small or miniature shrub roses, bred especially for their compact habit, greatly extend the range of garden situations in which roses can be grown. All have very attractive flowers in a wide range of colors, blooming over long periods from summer to autumn amid deciduous, glossy green leaves. With the exception of 'Ballerina', which grows to a height of about 5ft (1.5m), most are under 3ft (1m) tall, making them invaluable for confined, sunny spaces; planted in half barrels, other containers, or raised beds, they are also excellent for decorating patios and other hard-surface areas.

CULTIVATION *Grow in well-drained but moist, moderately fertile soil that is rich in well-rotted organic matter. Choose an open, sunny site. Remove all but the strongest shoots in late winter, then reduce these by about one-third of their height. Cut out any dead or damaged wood as necessary.*

☼ ◊◊ Z 5-9 H 9-1

1 ‡18in (45cm) ↔ 16in (40cm)

2 ‡to 5ft (1.5m) ↔ 4ft (1.2m)

3 ‡20in (50cm) ↔ 16in (40cm)

4 ‡16in (40cm) ↔ 24in (60cm)

5 ‡↔ 14in (35cm)

6 ‡↔ 24–36in (60–90cm)

1 *R.* ANNA FORD 'Harpiccolo' 2 *R.* 'Ballerina' 3 *R.* GENTLE TOUCH 'Diclulu'
4 *R.* QUEEN MOTHER 'Korquemu' 5 *R.* SWEET MAGIC 'Dicmagic' 6 *R.* 'The Fairy'

ROSES FOR GROUNDCOVER

Groundcover roses are low-growing, spreading, deciduous shrubs ideal for the front of a border, in both formal and informal situations. They produce beautiful flowers over long periods from summer into autumn amid divided, glossy green leaves, on thorny or prickly, sometimes trailing stems. Only those of really dense habit, such as SWANY 'Meiburenac', will provide weed-smothering cover, and even these are effective only if the ground is weed-free to begin with. Most give their best cascading over a low wall or when used to clothe a steep bank that is otherwise difficult to manage.

CULTIVATION *Best in moist but well-drained, reasonably fertile, organic soil, in full sun. Prune shoots back after flowering each year to well within the intended area of spread, removing any dead or damaged wood. Annual pruning will enhance flowering performance.*

☼ ◊◊ ◗ Z 5-9 H 9-1

1 ‡18in (45cm) ↔ 4ft (1.2m)

2 ‡30in (75cm) ↔ 4ft (1.2m)

3 ‡32in (80cm) ↔ 4ft (1.2m)

4 ‡to 30in (75cm) ↔ 5½ft (1.7m)

R. 'Nozomi'   2 R. RED BLANKET 'Intercell'   3 R. SURREY 'Korlanum'   4 R. SWANY 'Meiburenac'

SHRUB ROSES

Shrub roses, of which there is a bewildering choice, are all upright, deciduous plants much valued for their magnificent flowers, borne either in a single flush or repeatedly from summer to autumn amid divided, glossy leaves on thorny or prickly stems. Their charm is best exploited in informal plantings; they combine well with other shrubs, provided that they receive sufficient sun. Many are especially suited to open beds of traditional design, and a rose bed backed by a wall or a hedge allows for a layout of graduated height, with shrub roses at the back and compact bush roses (see page 378) at the front. They also make fine specimen plants.

CULTIVATION *Grow in well-drained but moist, fertile, organic soil, in full sun. Once established, remove a few old, unproductive stems in early spring, cutting flowered shoots back by one-third. Their form is easily spoiled by severe or careless pruning.*

☼ ◊◊ Z 5-9 H 9-1

1 ↕ 34in (85cm) ↔ 3½ft (1.1m)   **2** ↕↔ 4ft (1.2m)   **3** ↕ 5ft (1.5m) ↔ 4ft (1.2m)

4 ↕ 5ft (1.5m) ↔ 4ft (1.2m)   **5** ↕ 7ft (2.2m) ↔ 8ft (2.5m)   **6** ↕ 6ft (2m) ↔ 5ft (1.5m)

1 *R.* BONICA 'Meidomonac' **2** *R.* 'Buff Beauty' **3** *R.* 'Blanc Double de Coubert'
4 *R.* 'Céleste' **5** *R.* 'Complicata' **6** *R.* CONSTANCE SPRY **7** *R.* 'Cornelia'

7 ↕↔ 5ft (1.5m)

8 ↕ 5ft (1.5m) ↔ 4ft (1.2m)

9 ↕ 5ft (1.5m) ↔ 7ft (2.2m)

10 ↕ 5ft (1.5m) ↔ 3ft (1m)

11 ↕ 6ft (2m) ↔ 5ft (1.5m)

12 ↕ 4ft (1.2m) ↔ 5ft (1.5m)

13 ↕↔ 7ft (2.2m)

14 ↕ 5ft (1.5m) ↔ 4ft (1.2m)

15 ↕↔ 7ft (2.2m)

16 ↕ 7ft (2.2m) ↔ 5ft (2m)

17 ↕↔ 7ft (2.2m)

18 ↕ 10ft (3m) ↔ to 12ft (4m)

8 *R.* 'Fantin-Latour' **9** *R.* 'Felicia' **10** *R.* GERTRUDE JEKYLL 'Ausbord' **11** *R. glauca*
12 *R.* GRAHAM THOMAS 'Ausmas' **13** *R.* 'Marguerite Hilling' **14** *R.* 'Madame Hardy'
15 *R.* 'Nevada' **16** *R.* 'Roseraie de l'Haÿ' **17** *R.* 'William Lobb' **18** *R. xanthina* 'Canary Bird'

ROSMARINUS OFFICINALIS 'MISS JESSOP'S UPRIGHT'

This vigorous, upright rosemary is an evergreen shrub with aromatic foliage that can be used in cooking. From mid-spring to early summer whorls of small, purple-blue to white flowers are produced amid the narrow, dark green, white-felted leaves, often with a repeat show in autumn. Makes a good hedging plant for a kitchen garden.

CULTIVATION *Grow in well-drained, poor to moderately fertile soil. Choose a sunny, sheltered site. After flowering, trim any shoots that spoil the symmetry.*

☼ ◊ Z 8-10 H 12-8   ‡↔ 6ft (2m)

ROSMARINUS OFFICINALIS PROSTRATUS GROUP

These low-growing types of rosemary are aromatic, evergreen shrubs ideal for a rock garden or the top of a dry wall. Whorls of small, two-lipped, purple-blue to white flowers are produced in late spring, and often again in autumn. The dark green leaves have white-felted undersides and can be cut in for culinary use. Excellent in containers; protect during winter where not hardy.

CULTIVATION *Grow in well-drained, poor to moderately fertile soil, in full sun. Trim or lightly cut back shoots that spoil the symmetry, after flowering.*

☼ ◊ Z 8-10 H 12-8   ‡6in (15cm) ↔5ft (1.5m)

RUBUS 'BENENDEN'

This flowering raspberry is an
ornamental, deciduous shrub that
has spreading, arching, thornless
branches and peeling bark. It is
valued for its abundance of large,
saucer-shaped, roselike flowers with
glistening, pure white petals in late
spring and early summer. The lobed
leaves are dark green. Suitable for a
shrub border.

CULTIVATION *Grow in any rich, fertile
soil, in full sun or partial shade. After
flowering, remove the oldest stems to
relieve overcrowding and to promote
new growth.*

☼ ◑ ◊ Z 5-9 H 9-5   ‡↔ 10ft (3m)

RUBUS THIBETANUS

The ghost bramble, sometimes sold
with the cultivar name 'Silver Fern',
is an upright, summer-flowering,
deciduous shrub so named for its
conspicuously white-coated, prickly
stems in winter. The small, saucer-
shaped, red-purple flowers are
carried among the fernlike, white-
hairy, dark green leaves, followed
by spherical black fruits that also
have a whitish coating.

CULTIVATION *Grow in any fertile soil,
in sun or partial shade. Each spring,
cut all flowered stems back to the
ground, leaving the previous season's
new, unflowered shoots unpruned.*

☼ ◑ ◊ Z 7-9 H 9-7   ‡↔ 8ft (2.5m)

RUDBECKIA FULGIDA VAR. *SULLIVANTII* 'GOLDSTURM'

This black-eyed Susan is a clump-forming perennial valued for its strongly upright form and large, daisylike, golden-yellow flowerheads with cone-shaped, blackish brown centers. These appear above the substantial clumps of lance-shaped, mid-green leaves during late summer and autumn. It is a bold addition to a late summer border, and the cut flowers last reasonably well in water.

CULTIVATION *Grow in any moist but well-drained soil that does not dry out, in full sun or light shade.*

☼ ◑ ◊◊ Z 4-9 H 9-1   ↕ to 24in (60cm)
↔ 18in (45cm)

RUDBECKIA 'GOLDQUELLE'

A tall but compact perennial that bears large, fully double, bright lemon yellow flowers from mid-summer to mid-autumn. These are carried above loose clumps of deeply divided, mid-green leaves. The flowers are good for cutting.

CULTIVATION *Grow in any moist but well-drained soil, in full sun or light dappled shade.*

☼ ◑ ◊◊ Z 3-9 H 9-1   ↕ to 36in (90cm
↔ 18in (45cm

SALIX BABYLONICA VAR. *PEKINENSIS* 'TORTUOSA'

The dragon's claw willow is a fast-growing, upright, deciduous tree with curiously twisted shoots that are striking in winter. In spring, yellow-green catkins appear with the contorted, bright green leaves with gray-green undersides. Plant away from drains, since roots are invasive and water-seeking. Also sold as *S. matsudana* 'Tortuosa'.

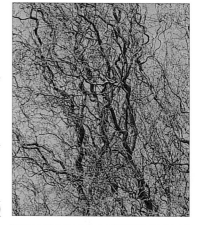

CULTIVATION *Grow in any but very dry or shallow, alkaline soil. Choose a sunny site. Thin occasionally in late winter to stimulate new growth, which most strongly exhibits the fascinating growth pattern.*

☼ ◑ Z 6-9 H 9-6 ‡50ft (15m) ↔25ft (8m)

SALIX 'BOYDII'

This tiny, very slow-growing, upright, deciduous shrub with gnarled branches is suitable for planting in a rock garden or trough. The small, almost rounded leaves are rough-textured, prominently veined, and grayish green. Catkins are produced only occasionally, in early spring.

CULTIVATION *Grow in any deep, moist but well-drained soil, in full sun; willows dislike shallow, alkaline soil. When necessary, prune in late winter to maintain a healthy framework.*

☼ ◐◑ Z 4-7 H 7-1‡12in (30cm) ↔8in (20cm)

SALIX CAPREA
'KILMARNOCK'

The Kilmarnock willow is a small, weeping, deciduous tree ideal for a small garden. It forms a dense, umbrella-like crown of yellow-brown shoots studded with silvery catkins in mid- and late spring, before the foliage appears. The broad, toothed leaves are dark green on top, and gray-green beneath.

CULTIVATION *Grow in any deep, moist but well-drained soil, in full sun. Prune annually in late winter to prevent the crown from becoming congested. Remove shoots that arise on the trunk.*

☼ ◐◖ Z 6-8 H 8-6 ‡6ft (2m) ↔6ft (2m)

SALIX HASTATA
'WEHRHAHNII'

This small, slow-growing, upright, deciduous shrub, with dark purple-brown stems and contrasting silvery gray, early spring catkins, makes a beautiful subject for providing winter color. The leaves are oval and bright green.

CULTIVATION *Grow in any moist soil, in sun; does not tolerate shallow, alkaline soils. Prune in spring to maintain a balance between young stems (which usually have the best winter color) and older wood with catkins.*

☼ ◖ Z 5-8 H 8-5 ↔3ft (1m

SALIX LANATA

The woolly willow is a rounded,
slow-growing, deciduous shrub with
stout shoots that have an attractive
white-woolly texture when young.
Large, upright, golden to gray-yellow
catkins emerge on older wood in late
spring among the dark green, broadly
oval, silver-gray, woolly leaves.

CULTIVATION *Grow in moist but well-
drained soil, in sun. Tolerates semi-
shade, but dislikes shallow, alkaline
soil. Prune occasionally in late winter
or early spring to maintain a balance
between old and young stems.*

☼◐ ◊◊ Z 3-5 H 5-1 ‡3ft (1m) ↔5ft (1.5m)

SALPIGLOSSIS
CASINO SERIES

These upright and compact,
weather-resistant annuals, ideal for
summer bedding, freely produce a
contrasting display of funnel-shaped
flowers throughout summer and
autumn. Colors range from blue and
purple to red, yellow, or orange,
often dramatically veined. The lance-
shaped, mid-green leaves have wavy
margins.

CULTIVATION *Grow in moist but well-
drained, fertile soil, in sun. Stems need
support. Deadhead regularly. Plant out
only after any risk of frost has passed.*

☼ ◊ annual H 6-1   ‡to 24in (60cm)
↔to 12in (30cm)

SALVIA ARGENTEA

This short-lived perennial forms large clumps of soft, felty-gray leaves around the base of the plant. Spikes of hooded, two-lipped, white or pinkish white flowers are borne in mid- and late summer on strong, upright stems. Removing the spike before it blooms may prolong the life of the plant.

CULTIVATION *Grow in light, well-drained soil, in a warm, sunny site. Protect from excessive winter moisture and slugs.*

☼ ◊ Z 5-8 H 8-5 ‡36in (90cm) ↔24in (60cm)

SALVIA FULGENS

An upright, evergreen, summer-flowering subshrub bearing spikes of tubular, two-lipped red flowers. The oval, toothed or notched leaves are rich green above and densely white-woolly beneath. Provides brilliant color for bedding or containers.

CULTIVATION *Grow in light, moist but well-drained, moderately fertile, organic soil. Site in full sun or semi-shade.*

☼◑ ◊ Z 9-10 H 12-3 ‡6in (15cm) ↔8in (20cm)

SALVIA OFFICINALIS 'ICTERINA'

A very attractive, yellow and green variegated form of sage with a mound-forming, subshrubby habit. The aromatic, evergreen, velvety leaves can be used in cooking. Less significant spikes of small, lilac-blue flowers appear in early summer. Ideal for an herb or kitchen garden.

CULTIVATION *Grow in moist but well-drained, organic, fairly fertile soil. Site in full sun or partial shade.*

☼ ◊ Z 7-8 H 8-5 ‡to 32in (80cm) ↔3ft (1m)

SALVIA PATENS 'CAMBRIDGE BLUE'

This upright perennial, with tall, loose spikes of pale blue flowers, is a useful addition to a herbaceous or mixed border, bedding, and large containers. The flowers are borne during mid-summer to mid-autumn above the oval, hairy, mid-green leaves. Where marginally hardy, shelter at the base of a warm wall.

CULTIVATION *Grow in well-drained soil, in full sun. Overwinter young plants in frost-free conditions.*

☼ ◊ Z 8-9 H 9-8 ‡18–24in (45–60cm) ↔18in (45cm)

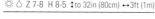

SALVIA PRATENSIS
HAEMATODES GROUP

A short-lived perennial, sometimes
sold as *S. haematodes*, forming basal
clumps of large, dark green leaves.
In early and mid-summer, spreading
spikes of massed blue-violet flowers,
with paler throats, emerge from the
center of the clumps. Provides color
for bedding, borders, or containers.

CULTIVATION *Grow in moist but well-
drained, moderately fertile, organic soil.
Site in full sun or light shade.*

☼ ◊ Z 3-9 H 9-1 ‡36in (90cm) ↔12in (30cm)

SALVIA SPLENDENS
'SCARLET KING'

This compact, bushy perennial, with
dense spikes of long-tubed, scarlet
flowers, is usually grown as an
annual, especially in cold climates.
The flowers are borne during
summer to autumn above the dark
green, toothed leaves. Its long-
lasting, brilliant flowers make an
invaluable addition to any bedding
or container display.

CULTIVATION *Grow in moist but well-
drained, organic, moderately fertile soil.
Choose a site in full sun.*

☼ ◊ annual H 12-1 ‡to 10in (25cm)
↔9–14in (23–35cm)

SALVIA × *SYLVESTRIS* 'MAINACHT'

A neat, clump-forming, pleasantly aromatic perennial bearing tall, dense, upright spikes of indigo blue flowers during early and mid-summer. The narrow, softly hairy, mid-green leaves are scalloped at the edges. Provides strong contrast when planted with silver-leaved plants in a herbaceous border.

CULTIVATION *Grow in well-drained, fertile soil, in sun. Tolerates drought. Cut back after the first flush of flowers to encourage a further set of blooms.*

☼ ◊ Z 5-9 H 9-3 ‡28in (70cm) ↔18in (45cm)

SALVIA ULIGINOSA

The bog sage is a graceful, upright perennial bearing spikes of clear blue flowers from late summer to mid-autumn. These are carried above lance-shaped, toothed, mid-green leaves, on branched stems. Good for moist borders; where not hardy, it can be grown outdoors as a tender perennial and overwintered under glass.

CULTIVATION *Needs moist but well-drained, fertile soil. Choose a sunny, sheltered position. Plants normally need a little support.*

☼ ◊ Z 8-10 H 12-8 ‡6ft (2m) ↔36in (90cm)

SAMBUCUS NIGRA
'GUINCHO PURPLE'

This attractive cultivar of the common
elderberry is an upright shrub with
dark green, divided leaves; these
turn black-purple then red in
autumn. In early summer, musk-
scented, pink-tinged white flowers
are borne in large, flattened clusters,
followed by small black fruits. Elders
are ideal in new gardens, because
they establish themselves quickly.

CULTIVATION *Grow in any fertile soil, in
sun or partial shade. For the best foliage
effect, either cut all stems to the ground
in winter or prune out old stems and
reduce length of young shoots by half.*

☼◑ ◊ Z 6-8 H 8-6   ↕↔ 20ft (6m)

SANTOLINA
CHAMAECYPARISSUS

Lavender cotton is a rounded,
evergreen shrub grown for its
foliage. The small, bright yellow
flowerheads in summer can be
removed to improve the foliage
effect. The slender, white-woolly
stems are densely covered with
narrow, gray-white, finely cut leaves.
Suitable for a mixed border or rock
garden or as low, informal hedging.

CULTIVATION *Grow in well drained,
poor to moderately fertile soil, in full
sun. Remove old flowerheads and
trim long shoots in autumn. Cut old,
straggly plants back hard each spring.*

☼ ◊ Z 6-9 H 9-6   ↕20in (50cm) ↔3ft (1m

SANTOLINA ROSMARINIFOLIA 'PRIMROSE GEM'

A dense, rounded, evergreen shrub, similar to *S. chamaecyparissus* (see facing page, below), but with bright green leaves and paler flowers. These are borne at the tips of slender stems in mid-summer above the finely cut aromatic leaves. Useful for filling gaps in a sunny border.

CULTIVATION *Grow in well drained, poor to moderately fertile soil, in full sun. In autumn, remove old flower-heads and prune long shoots. Cut old, straggly plants back hard each spring.*

☼ ◊ Z 6-9 H 9-6   ‡24in (60cm) ↔3ft (1m)

SAPONARIA OCYMOIDES

Rock soapwort is a sprawling, mat-forming perennial that carries a profusion of tiny, flat pink flowers from late spring into summer. The hairy, bright green leaves are small and oval. Excellent as part of a dry bank, scree, or rock garden, although it may swamp smaller, less vigorous plants.

CULTIVATION *Grow in gritty, sharply drained soil, in full sun. Cut back hard after flowering to keep compact.*

☼ ◊ Z 4-8 H 8-1   ‡3in (8cm)
↔18in (45cm) or more

SAPONARIA × OLIVANA

A cushion-forming, summer-flowering perennial that produces abundant clusters of small, pale pink flowers around the edge of a mound of small and narrow, mid-green leaves. Good for rock gardens, scree slopes, and dry banks.

CULTIVATION *Grow in sharply drained soil, in a sunny site. Top-dress the soil around the plant with grit or gravel.*

☼ ◊ Z 6-8 H 8-1   ↕2in (5cm) ↔6in (15cm)

SARCOCOCCA CONFUSA

Christmas box is a dense, evergreen shrub producing an unparalleled fragrance. Clusters of small white flowers appear in late winter, followed by small, glossy black fruits. The tiny, oval leaves are glossy and dark green. Excellent as a low hedge near a door or entrance. Tolerates atmospheric pollution, dry shade, and neglect.

CULTIVATION *Grow in moist but well-drained, fertile, organic soil. Site in deep or semi-shade with protection from cold, drying winds. Remove dead and damaged growth each year in spring.*

☼◐ ◊ Z 6-9 H 9-6   ↕6ft (2m) ↔3ft (1m)

SARCOCOCCA HOOKERIANA VAR. *DIGYNA*

This perfumed, evergreen shrub is very similar to *S. confusa* (see facing page, below), but it has a more compact and spreading habit. The tiny, fragrant white flowers, which are followed by small, black or blue-black fruits, have pink anthers; they are borne amid the slender, glossy leaves in late winter. The flowers are good for cutting.

CULTIVATION *Grow in moist but well-drained, fertile, organic soil, in shade. Dig up spreading roots in spring to confine it to its allotted space.*

☀️◐ ◊ Z 6-9 H 9-6 ‡5ft (1.5m) ↔6ft (2m)

SARRACENIA FLAVA

Yellow pitcher plant is a carnivorous perennial bearing nodding yellow flowers in spring. Some leaves are modified into large, upright, nectar-secreting, insect-catching pitchers. These are yellow-green and red-marked, with round mouths and hooded tops. Where not hardy, grow in a cool greenhouse or conservatory.

CULTIVATION *Grow in wet, rich, acid soil or soil mix, in sun. Irrigate plentifully with lime-free water, but keep slightly drier in winter.*

☀️ ◊◊ Z 7-10 H 12-7 ‡20–39in (50–100cm) ↔to 3ft (1m)

SAXIFRAGA 'JENKINSIAE'

This neat and slow-growing, evergreen perennial forms very dense cushions of gray-green foliage. It produces an abundance of solitary, cup-shaped, pale pink flowers with dark centers in early spring on short, slender red stems. Good for rock gardens or troughs.

CULTIVATION *Best in moist but sharply drained, moderately fertile, neutral to alkaline soil, in full sun. Provide shade from the hottest summer sun.*

☼ ◊ Z 6-7 H 7-6 ‡2in (5cm) ↔8in (20cm)

SAXIFRAGA 'SOUTHSIDE SEEDLING'

A mat-forming, evergreen perennial that is suitable for a rock garden. Open sprays of small, cup-shaped white flowers, spotted heavily with red, are borne in late spring and early summer. The oblong to spoon-shaped, pale green leaves form large rosettes close to soil level.

CULTIVATION *Grow in very sharply drained, moderately fertile, alkaline soil. Choose a position in full sun.*

☼ ◊ Z 4-6 H 6-1 ‡12in (30cm) ↔8in (20cm)

SCABIOSA CAUCASICA
'CLIVE GREAVES'

This delicate, perennial scabious, with solitary, lavender-blue flower-heads, is ideal for a cottage garden. The blooms have pincushion-like centers and are borne above the clumps of gray-green leaves during mid- to late summer. The flowerheads last well in flower arrangements.

CULTIVATION *Grow in well-drained, moderately fertile, neutral to slightly alkaline soil, in full sun. Deadhead to prolong flowering.*

☼ ◊ Z 4-9 H 9-1   ↕↔ 24in (60cm)

SCABIOSA CAUCASICA
'MISS WILLMOTT'

A clump-forming perennial that is very similar to 'Clive Greaves' (above) but with white flowerheads. These are borne in mid- to late summer and are good for cutting. The lance-shaped leaves are gray-green and arranged around the base of the plant. Perfect for a cottage garden.

CULTIVATION *Grow in well-drained, moderately fertile, neutral to slightly alkaline soil, in full sun. Deadhead to prolong flowering.*

☼ ◊ Z 4-9 H 9-1 ↕36in (90cm) ↔24in (60cm)

SCHIZOSTYLIS COCCINEA 'MAJOR'

A vigorous, robust, clump-forming perennial, often called *S. coccinea* 'Grandiflora', bearing gladiolus-like spikes of large red flowers. These appear in late summer on stiff and upright stems above the narrow, almost floppy, mid-green leaves. Good in sheltered spots, for a border front, or above water level in a waterside planting.

CULTIVATION *Grow in moist but well-drained, fertile soil, with a site in full sun. Plants rapidly become congested, but they are easily lifted and divided every few years in spring.*

☼ ◑ ◆ Z 7-9 H 9-7 ‡24in (60cm) ↔12in (30cm)

SCHIZOSTYLIS COCCINEA 'SUNRISE'

This clump-forming, vigorous perennial has the same general appearance, demands, and usage as 'Major' (above) but with upright spikes of salmon-pink flowers that open in autumn. The long leaves are sword-shaped and ribbed. When cut, the flowers last well in water.

CULTIVATION *Best in moist but well-drained, fertile soil, in sun. Naturally forms congested clumps, but these are easily lifted and divided in spring.*

☼ ◑ ◆ Z 7-9 H 9-7 ‡24in (60cm) ↔12in (30cm)

SCILLA BIFOLIA

A small, bulbous perennial bearing
early-spring flowers; it naturalizes
well under trees and shrubs or in
grass. The slightly one-sided spikes
of many star-shaped, blue to purple-
blue flowers are carried above the
clumps of narrow, basal leaves.

CULTIVATION *Grow in well-drained,
moderately fertile, organic soil, in full
sun or partial shade.*

☼ ◊ Z 3-8 H 8-1   ‡6in (15cm) ↔2in (5cm)

SCILLA MISCHTSCHENKOANA 'TUBERGENIANA'

This dwarf, bulbous perennial has
slightly earlier flowers than *S. bifolia*
(above); they are silvery blue with
darker stripes. They are grouped
together in elongating spikes,
appearing at the same time as the
semi-upright, narrow, mid-green
leaves. Naturalizes in thin grass.
Also known as *S. tubergeniana*.

CULTIVATION *Grow in well-drained,
moderately fertile soil that is rich in
well-rotted organic matter, in full sun.*

☼ ◊ Z 6-9 H 9-6   ‡6in (15cm) ↔2in (5cm)

SEDUM KAMTSCHATICUM 'VARIEGATUM'

This clump-forming, semi-evergreen perennial has eye-catching, fleshy leaves that are mid-green with pink tints and cream margins. During late summer, these contrast nicely with flat-topped clusters of small, star-shaped, yellow flowers that age to crimson later in the season. Suitable for rock gardens and borders.

CULTIVATION *Grow in well-drained, gritty, fertile soil. Choose a site in full sun, but it will tolerate light shade.*

☼ ◊ Z 4-9 H 9-1 ‡4in (10cm) ↔10in (25cm)

SEDUM 'RUBY GLOW'

This low-growing perennial is an ideal choice for softening the front of a mixed border. It bears masses of small, star-shaped, ruby red flowers from mid-summer to early autumn above clumps of fleshy, green-purple leaves. The nectar-rich flowers will attract bees, butterflies, and other beneficial insects.

CULTIVATION *Grow in well-drained, fertile soil that has adequate moisture in summer. Position in full sun.*

☼ ◊ Z 5-9 H 9-1 ‡10in (25cm) ↔18in (45cm)

SEDUM SPATHULIFOLIUM 'CAPE BLANCO'

A vigorous, evergreen perennial that forms a mat of silvery green foliage, often tinted bronze-purple, with a heavy bloom of white powder over the innermost leaves. Small clusters of star-shaped, bright yellow flowers are borne just above the leaves in summer. A very attractive addition to a trough or raised bed.

CULTIVATION *Grow in well-drained, moderately fertile, gritty soil. Position in full sun, but tolerates light shade.*

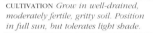

SEDUM SPATHULIFOLIUM 'PURPUREUM'

This fast-growing, summer-flowering perennial forms tight, evergreen mats of purple-leaved rosettes; the central leaves are covered with a thick, silvery bloom. Flat clusters of small, star-shaped, bright yellow flowers appear throughout summer. Suitable for a rock garden or the front of a sunny, well-drained border.

CULTIVATION *Grow in gritty, moderately fertile soil with good drainage, in sun or partial shade. Trim occasionally to prevent encroachment on other plants.*

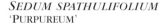

SEDUM SPECTABILE 'BRILLIANT'

This showy stonecrop with brilliant pink flowerheads is a clump-forming, deciduous perennial, excellent for the front of a border. The small, star-shaped flowers, packed into dense, flat clusters on fleshy stems, appear in late summer above the succulent, gray-green leaves. The flowerheads are attractive to bees and butterflies.

CULTIVATION *Grow in well-drained, fertile soil with adequate moisture during summer, in full sun.*

☼ ◊ Z 4-9 H 9-1   ‡↔ 18in (45cm)

SEDUM SPURIUM 'SCHORBUSER BLUT'

This vigorous, evergreen perennial forms mats of succulent, mid-green leaves that become purple-tinted when mature. Rounded clusters of star-shaped, deep pink flowers are borne during late summer. Suitable for a rock garden.

CULTIVATION *Grow in well-drained, moderately fertile, neutral to slightly alkaline soil, in full sun. Tolerates light shade. To improve flowering, divide the clumps or mats every 3 or 4 years.*

☼ ◑ ◊ Z 4-9 H 9-1 ‡4in (10cm) ↔24in (60cm)

SEDUM TELEPHIUM
SUBSP. *MAXIMUM*
'ATROPURPUREUM'

This clump-forming, deciduous perennial is valued for its very dark purple foliage, which contrasts well with other plants. During summer and early autumn, attractive pink flowers with orange-red centers are clustered above the oval, slightly scalloped leaves.

CULTIVATION *Grow in well-drained, moderately fertile, neutral to slightly alkaline soil, in full sun. Divide clumps every 3 or 4 years to improve flowering.*

☼ ◊ Z 4-9 H 9-1   ↕18–24in (45–60cm)
↔12in (30cm)

SELAGINELLA KRAUSSIANA

Trailing spikemoss is a mat-forming, evergreen perennial with a mosslike appearance. The trailing stems are clothed in tiny, scalelike, bright green leaves. An excellent foliage plant that can easily be grown in a greenhouse or conservatory.

CULTIVATION *Grow in moist, peaty soil, in semi-shade. Keep just moist in winter. Needs a humid atmosphere under glass;does well in a terrarium.*

☼ ◊ Z 10-11 H 12-10 ↕1in (2.5cm) ↔indefinite

SEMPERVIVUM ARACHNOIDEUM

The cobweb houseleek is a mat-forming, evergreen succulent, so-named because the foliage is webbed with white hairs. The small, fleshy, mid-green to red-tinted leaves are arranged in tight rosettes. In summer, flat clusters of star-shaped, reddish pink flowers appear on leafy stems. Suitable for growing in a wall crevice or trough.

CULTIVATION *Grow in gritty, sharply drained, poor to moderately fertile soil. Choose a position in full sun.*

☼ ◊ Z 5-8 Z 8-5 ‡3in (8cm) ↔12in (30cm)

SEMPERVIVUM CILIOSUM

A mat-forming, evergreen succulent carrying very hairy, dense rosettes of incurved, lance-shaped, gray-green leaves. It bears flat, compact heads of star-shaped, greenish yellow flowers throughout summer. The rosettes of leaves die after flowering but are rapidly replaced. Best in an alpine house in areas prone to wet winters.

CULTIVATION *Grow in gritty, sharply drained, poor to moderately fertile soil, in sun. Tolerates drought conditions, but dislikes winter moisture or climates that are warm and humid.*

☼ ◊ Z 7-10 H 12-7 ‡3in (8cm) ↔12in (30cm)

SEMPERVIVUM TECTORUM

The common hens and chicks is a vigorous, mat-forming, evergreen succulent with large, open rosettes of thick, oval, bristle-tipped, blue-green leaves, often suffused red-purple. In summer, dense clusters of star-shaped, red-purple flowers appear on upright, hairy stems. Very attractive growing in a strawberry jar or among terracotta fragments.

CULTIVATION *Grow in gritty, sharply drained, poor to moderately fertile soil. Choose a site in full sun.*

☼ ◊ Z 4-8 H 8-1 ‡6in (15cm) ↔20in (50cm)

SENECIO CINERARIA 'SILVER DUST'

This mound-forming, moderately fast-growing, evergreen shrub is usually grown as an annual for its attractive, lacy foliage. The almost white leaves are deeply cut and densely hairy. Plants kept into the second season bear loose heads of coarse, daisylike, mustard yellow flowerheads in mid-summer; many gardeners prefer to remove them. Ideal for creating massed foliage effects in summer bedding.

CULTIVATION *Grow in well-drained, fertile soil, in sun. Nip out flower buds if desired, or deadhead regularly.*

☼ ◊ Z 7-10 H 12-8   ‡↔ 12in (30cm)

SILENE SCHAFTA

A clump-forming, spreading, semi-evergreen perennial with floppy stems bearing small, bright green leaves. Profuse sprays of long-tubed, deep magenta flowers with notched petals are borne from late summer to autumn. Suitable for a raised bed or rock garden.

CULTIVATION *Grow in well-drained, neutral to slightly alkaline soil, in full sun or light dappled shade.*

☼◑ ◊ Z 5-7 H 7-4 ‡10in (25cm) ↔12in (30cm)

SKIMMIA × CONFUSA 'KEW GREEN'

A compact, dome-shaped, evergreen shrub producing aromatic, pointed, mid-green leaves. Conical spikes of fragrant, creamy white flowers open in spring. There are no berries, but it will pollinate female skimmias if they are planted nearby. Good in a shrub border or woodland garden.

CULTIVATION *Grow in moist but well-drained, moderately fertile, organic soil. Tolerates full sun to deep shade, atmospheric pollution, and neglect. Requires little or no pruning.*

☼◑ ◐ Z 6-9 H 9-6 ‡1½–10ft (0.5–3m) ↔5ft (1.5m)

SKIMMIA JAPONICA
'RUBELLA'

This tough, dome-shaped, evergreen shrub with dense foliage bears rounded spikes of dark red flower buds in autumn and winter. These open in spring to form fragrant heads of small white flowers. The oval leaves are dark green with red rims. No berries are produced, but it will pollinate female cultivars if planted nearby. Tolerant of urban pollution and coastal conditions.

CULTIVATION *Grow in moist, fertile, neutral to slightly acid soil, in partial or full shade. Requires little pruning, but cut back any shoots that spoil the shape.*

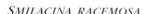 Z 7-9 H 9-7 ↕↔ to 20ft (6m)

SMILACINA RACEMOSA

False Solomon's seal is a clump-forming perennial bearing dense, feathery spikes of creamy white, often green-tinged flowers in mid- to late spring. These are followed by red berries. The lance-shaped, pale green, luxuriant leaves turn yellow in autumn. A beautiful subject for a woodland garden or shady border.

CULTIVATION *Grow in moist, neutral to acid, fertile soil that is rich in organic matter, in light or deep shade.*

Z 4-9 H 9-1 ↕ to 36in (90cm) ↔ 24in (60cm)

SOLANUM CRISPUM
'GLASNEVIN'

The long-flowering Chilean potato vine is a fast-growing, scrambling, woody-stemmed, evergreen climber. Fragrant, deep purple-blue flowers, borne in clusters at the tips of the stems during summer and autumn, are followed by small, yellow-white fruits. The leaves are oval and dark green. Where marginally hardy, grow on a warm, sunny wall.

CULTIVATION *Grow in any moist but well-drained, moderately fertile soil, in full sun or semi-shade. Cut back weak and badly placed growth in spring. Tie to a support as growth proceeds.*

☼◑ ◊◊ Z 9-10 H 12-1 ‡20ft (6m)

SOLANUM JASMINOIDES
'ALBUM'

This white-flowered potato vine is a scrambling, woody-stemmed, semi-evergreen climber. It produces broad clusters of fragrant, star-shaped, milk white flowers with prominent, lemon yellow anthers from summer to autumn. They are followed by black fruits. The leaves are dark green and oval.

CULTIVATION *Grow in any moist but well-drained, fertile soil, in full sun or semi-shade. Thin out shoots in spring. The climbing stems need support.*

☼◑ ◊◊ Z 8-10 H 12-1 ‡20ft (6m)

SOLIDAGO 'GOLDENMOSA'

This compact, vigorous goldenrod is a bushy perennial topped with bright golden-yellow flowerheads in late summer and early autumn. The leaves are wrinkled and mid-green. Valuable in a wild garden or for late summer color; the flowers are good for cutting. Can be invasive.

CULTIVATION *Grow in well-drained, poor to moderately fertile, preferably sandy soil, in full sun. Remove flowered stems to prevent self-seeding.*

☼ ◊ Z 5-9 H 9-5 ‡30in (75cm) ↔18in (45cm)

SOLLYA HETEROPHYLLA

The bluebell creeper is a twining, evergreen climber that must be grown in a cool conservatory in most regions. Clusters of nodding, bell-shaped blue flowers, followed by blue berries, are borne over a long period from early summer to autumn. The leaves are lance-shaped and deep green. Train over a trellis, a tepee of stakes, or an ornamental wire frame arch, or another plant.

CULTIVATION *Grow in moist but well-drained, moderately fertile, organic soil or soil mix, in a sunny, sheltered site. Water sparingly during winter and keep new growth trained to its support.*

☼ ◊◊ Z 10-11 H 12-1 ‡5–6ft (1.5–2m)

SORBUS ARIA 'LUTESCENS'

This compact whitebeam is a broadly columnar, deciduous tree, bearing oval and toothed, silvery gray foliage that turns russet and gold in autumn. Clusters of white flowers appear in late spring, followed by brown-speckled, dark red berries. It makes a beautiful specimen tree and is tolerant of a wide range of conditions.

CULTIVATION *Grow in moist but well-drained, fertile soil, in sun. Tolerates heavy clay soils, semi-shade, urban pollution, and exposed conditions. Remove any dead wood in summer.*

☼ ◐ ◊◊ Z 6-8 H 8-6 ‡30ft (10m) ↔25ft (8m)

SORBUS HUPEHENSIS VAR. *OBTUSA*

The Hubei mountain ash is an open and spreading tree that gives a fine display of autumn color. Broad clusters of white flowers in late spring are followed by round white berries; these ripen to dark pink later in the season. The blue-green leaves, divided into many leaflets, turn scarlet before they fall.

CULTIVATION *Grow in any moist but well-drained soil, preferably in full sun, but tolerates light shade. Remove any dead or diseased wood in summer.*

☼ ◐ ◊◊ Z 6-8 H 8-6 ‡↔ to 25ft (8m

SORBUS 'JOSEPH ROCK'

This broadly columnar, upright, deciduous tree has bright green leaves that are divided into many sharply toothed leaflets. These color attractively to orange, red, and purple in autumn. In late spring, white flowers appear in broad clusters, followed by round, pale yellow berries that ripen to orange-yellow.

CULTIVATION *Grow in moist but well-drained, fertile soil, in sun. Very prone to fireblight, the main sign of which is blackened leaves; affected growth must be pruned back in summer to at least 24in (60cm) below the diseased area.*

☼ ◊◊ Z 7-8 H 8-7 ‡30ft (10m) ↔22ft (7m)

SORBUS REDUCTA

A deciduous shrub that forms a low thicket of upright branches. Much-valued for its ornamental, dark green foliage that turns a rich red in autumn. Small, open clusters of white flowers appear in late spring, followed by white, crimson-flushed berries. Tolerates pollution.

CULTIVATION *Grow in well-drained, moderately fertile soil, in an open, sunny site. To thin congested plants, remove shoots that arise from the base while they are still young and soft.*

☼ ◊ Z 5-8 H 8-4 ‡3–5ft (1–1.5m) ↔6ft (2m)

SORBUS VILMORINII

A spreading shrub or small tree with elegant, arching branches bearing dark green leaves divided into many leaflets. The deciduous foliage gives a lovely display in autumn, turning orange- or bronze-red. Clusters of white flowers appear in late spring and early summer, followed later in the season by dark red berries that age to pink then white.

CULTIVATION *Grow in well-drained, moderately fertile, organic soil, in full sun or dappled shade. Remove any dead or diseased wood in summer.*

☼ ◐ ◊ Z 6-8 H 8-6   ↕↔ 15ft (5m)

SPARTIUM JUNCEUM

Spanish broom is an upright shrub with slender, dark green shoots that are almost leafless. A profusion of fragrant, pealike, rich golden-yellow flowers appear at the end of the stems from early summer to early autumn. These are followed by flattened, dark brown seed pods. Particularly useful on poor soils.

CULTIVATION *Grow in any but water-logged soil, in a warm, sunny site. When young, cut back main stems by half each spring to promote a bushy habit. Once established, trim every few years, but do not cut into old wood.*

☼ ◊◊ Z 8-10 H 12-8 ↕6in (15cm) ↔8in (20cm)

SPIRAEA JAPONICA
'ANTHONY WATERER'

A compact, deciduous shrub that
makes a good informal flowering
hedge. The lance-shaped, dark
green leaves, sometimes margined
with creamy white, are red when
young. Dense heads of tiny pink
flowers are borne among the foliage
in mid- to late summer.

CULTIVATION *Grow in any well-drained,
fairly fertile soil that does not dry out,
in full sun. On planting, cut back stems
to leave a framework 6in (15cm) high;
prune back close to this every other year
in spring. Deadhead after flowering.*

☼ ◊ Z 4-9 H 9-1   ↕↔ to 5ft (1.5m)

SPIRAEA JAPONICA
'GOLDFLAME'

This compact, deciduous, flowering
shrub bears pretty, bright yellow
leaves that are bronze-red when
young. Dense, flattened heads of
tiny, dark pink flowers appear at the
tips of slightly arching stems during
mid- and late summer. Ideal for a
rock garden.

CULTIVATION *Grow in well-drained soil
that does not dry out completely, in full
sun. On planting, cut back stems to a
framework 6in (15cm) high; prune
back close to this every other year in
spring. Deadhead after flowering.*

☼ ◊ Z 4-9 H 9-1   ↕↔ 30in (75cm)

SPIRAEA NIPPONICA 'SNOWMOUND'

This fast-growing and spreading, deciduous shrub has arching, reddish green stems. The dense clusters of small white flowers in mid-summer make an invaluable contribution to any shrub border. The rounded leaves are bright green when young, darkening as they age.

CULTIVATION *Grow in any moderately fertile soil that does not dry out too much during the growing season, in full sun. Cut back flowered stems in autumn, and remove any weak growth.*

☼ ◊ Z 4-8 H 8-1 ↕↔ 4–8ft (1.2–2.5m)

SPIRAEA × VANHOUTTEI

Bridal wreath is a fast-growing, deciduous shrub, more compact in habit than *S. nipponica* 'Snowmound' (above) but with similar mounds of white flowers during early summer. The diamond-shaped leaves are dark green above with blue-green undersides. Grow as an informal hedge or in a mixed border.

CULTIVATION *Grow in any well-drained, fertile soil that does not dry out, in sun. In autumn, cut back flowered stems, removing any weak or damaged growth.*

☼ ◊ Z 4-8 H 8-1 ↕6ft (2m) ↔5ft (1.5m)

STACHYURUS PRAECOX

This spreading, deciduous shrub
bears oval, mid-green leaves on
arching, red-purple shoots. Hanging
spikes of tiny, bell-shaped, pale
yellow-green flowers appear on the
bare stems in late winter and early
spring. Suitable for a shrub border,
and lovely in a woodland garden.

CULTIVATION *Grow in moist but well-
drained, organic, fertile, neutral to
acid soil. Prefers partial shade, but will
tolerate full sun if soil is kept reliably
moist. Regular pruning is unnecessary.*

 Z 7-9 H 9-7   ‡3–12ft (1–4m)
                            ↔10ft (3m)

STIPA GIGANTEA

Giant feather grass is a fluffy,
evergreen perennial forming dense
tufts of narrow, mid-green leaves. In
summer, these are topped by silvery
to purplish green flowerheads that
turn gold when mature and persist
well into winter. Makes an imposing
feature at the back of a border.

CULTIVATION *Grow in well-drained,
fertile soil, in full sun. Remove dead
leaves and flowerheads in early spring.*

 Z 8-10 H 12-8 ‡8ft (2.5m) ↔4ft (1.2m)

STYRAX JAPONICUS

Japanese snowbell is a gracefully spreading, deciduous tree bearing hanging clusters of fragrant, bell-shaped, dainty white flowers that are often tinged with pink. These appear during early to mid-summer amid oval, rich green leaves that may turn yellow or red in autumn. Ideal for a woodland garden.

CULTIVATION *Grow in moist but well-drained, neutral to acid soil, in full sun with shelter from wind. Tolerates dappled shade. Allow to develop naturally without much pruning.*

☼◑ ◊◊ Z 6-8 H 8-6 ‡30ft (10m) ↔25ft (8m)

STYRAX OBASSIA

The fragrant snowbell is a broadly columnar, deciduous tree bearing beautifully rounded, dark green leaves that turn yellow in autumn. Fragrant, bell-shaped white flowers are produced in long, spreading clusters in early and mid-summer.

CULTIVATION *Grow in moist but well-drained, fertile, organic, neutral to acid soil, in full sun or partial shade. Shelter from wind. Dislikes pruning; allow to develop naturally.*

☼◑ ◊◊ Z 6-8 H 8-6 ‡40ft (12m) ↔22ft (7m)

SYMPHYTUM × *UPLANDICUM* 'VARIEGATUM'

This upright, clump-forming, bristly perennial has large, lance-shaped, mid-green leaves with broad cream margins. Drooping clusters of pink-blue buds open into blue-purple flowers from late spring to late summer. Best suited to a wild garden or shady border. Less invasive than green-leaved types.

CULTIVATION *Grow in any moist soil, in sun or partial shade. For the best foliage effect, remove flowering stems before they bloom. Liable to form plain green leaves if grown in poor or infertile soil.*

☼ ◐ ◊ Z 3-9 H 9-1 ‡36in (90cm) ↔24in (60cm)

SYRINGA MEYERI 'PALIBIN'

This compact, slow-growing, deciduous shrub with a rounded shape is much valued for its abundant clusters of fragrant, lavender-pink flowers in late spring and early summer. The leaves are dark green and oval. Makes a bold contribution to any shrub border. Sometimes seen as *S. palibiniana*.

CULTIVATION *Grow in deep, moist but well-drained, fertile, preferably alkaline soil, in full sun. Deadhead for the first few years until established. Prune out weak and damaged growth in winter.*

☼ ◊◊ Z 4-7 H 7-1 ‡6ft (1.5–2m) ↔5ft (1.5m)

SYRINGA PUBESCENS
SUBSP. *MICROPHYLLA*
'SUPERBA'

This upright to spreading, conical,
deciduous shrub bears spikes of
very fragrant, rose-pink flowers at
the tips of slender branches. These
first appear in spring and continue
to open at irregular intervals until
autumn. The oval, mid-green leaves
are red-green when young. Makes a
good screen or informal hedge.

CULTIVATION *Grow in moist but well-
drained, fertile, organic, neutral to
alkaline soil, in full sun. Prune out any
weak or damaged growth in winter.*

☼ ◊◑ Z 5-8 H 8-3   ↕↔20ft (6m)

SYRINGA VULGARIS
'CHARLES JOLY'

This dark purple-flowered form of
common lilac is a spreading shrub
or small tree. Very fragrant, double
flowers appear during spring in
dense, conical clusters. The
deciduous leaves are heart-shaped
to oval and dark green. Use as a
backdrop in a shrub or mixed border.

CULTIVATION *Grow in moist but well-
drained, fertile, organic, neutral to
alkaline soil, in full sun. Young shrubs
require minimal pruning; old, lanky
stems can be cut back hard in winter.*

☼ ◊◑ Z 4-8 H 8-1   ↕↔22ft (7m)

SYRINGA VULGARIS
'KATHERINE HAVEMEYER'

A spreading lilac, forming a large
shrub or small tree, producing dense
clusters of very fragrant, double,
lavender-blue flowers. These open
from purple buds in spring. The
deciduous, mid-green leaves are
heart-shaped.

CULTIVATION *Grow in moist but well-
drained, fertile, organic, neutral to
alkaline soil, in sun. Mulch regularly.
Little pruning is necessary, but tolerates
hard pruning to renovate.*

☼ ◊◑ Z 4-8 H 8-1   ↕↔ 22ft (7m)

SYRINGA VULGARIS
'MADAME LEMOINE'

This lilac is very similar in form to
'Katherine Havemeyer' (above) but
has compact spikes of large, very
fragrant, double white flowers.
These are borne in spring amid the
deciduous, heart-shaped to oval,
mid-green leaves.

CULTIVATION *Grow in deep, moist but
well-drained, fertile, neutral to alkaline,
organic soil, in sun. Do not prune
young plants, but older shrubs can be
cut back hard in winter to renovate.*

☼ ◊◑ Z 4-8 H 8-1   ↕↔ 22ft (7m)

TAMARIX TETRANDRA

This large, arching shrub, with feathery foliage on purple-brown shoots, bears plumes of light pink flowers in mid- to late spring. The leaves are reduced to tiny, needle-like scales. Particularly useful in a shrub border on light, sandy soils; in warm but exposed areas, it can also be used as a windbreak or hedge, especially in coastal gardens.

CULTIVATION *Grow in well-drained soil, in full sun. Cut back young plants by almost half after planting. Prune each year after flowering, or the shrub may become top-heavy and unstable.*

☼ ◊ Z 5-9 H 9-5   ↔ 10ft (3m)

TANACETUM COCCINEUM 'BRENDA'

The painted daisy is a bushy, herbaceous perennial grown for its daisylike, bright magenta-pink, yellow-centered flowerheads in early summer. These are borne on upright stems above the aromatic, finely divided, gray-green foliage. The cut flowers last well in water.

CULTIVATION *Grow in well-drained, fertile, neutral to slightly acid soil, in an open, sunny site. Cut back after the first flush of flowers to encourage a second flowering later in the season.*

☼ ◊ Z 5-9 H 9-5   ↕ 28–32in (70–80cm)
↔ 18in (45cm)

TAXUS BACCATA

English yew is a slow-growing,
broadly conical, evergreen conifer.
The needlelike, dark green leaves
are arranged in two ranks along the
shoots. Male plants bear yellow
cones in spring, and female plants
produce cup-shaped, fleshy, bright
red fruits in autumn. Excellent as a
dense hedge, which can be clipped
to shape, and as a backdrop to
colorful plants. All parts are toxic.

CULTIVATION *Grow in any well-drained,
fertile soil, in sun to deep shade. Tolerates
alkaline or acidic soils. Plant both sexes
together for berries. Trim or cut back in
summer or early autumn to renovate.*

 ☼ ◑ ◊ Z 7-8 H 8-5 ‡70ft (20m) ↔30ft (10m)

TAXUS BACCATA
'DOVASTONII AUREA'

This slow-growing, evergreen conifer
has wide-spreading, horizontally
tiered branches that weep at the
tips. It is smaller than the English
yew (above) and has yellow-
margined to golden-yellow foliage.
Fleshy, bright red fruits appear in
autumn. All parts of this plant are
poisonous if eaten.

CULTIVATION *Grow in any well-drained,
fertile soil, in sun or deep shade. Tolerates
alkaline or acidic conditions. Plant
close to male yews for a reliable display
of berries. Trim or cut back in summer
or early autumn to renovate.*

☼ ◑ ◊ Z 7-8 H 8-5 ‡15ft (5m) ↔6ft (2m)

TAXUS BACCATA 'FASTIGIATA'

Irish yew is a dense, strongly upright, evergreen conifer that becomes columnar with age. The dark green leaves are not two-ranked like other yews but stand out all around the shoots. All are female, bearing fleshy, berrylike, bright red fruits in late summer. All parts are toxic if eaten.

CULTIVATION *Grow in any reliably moist soil, but tolerates most conditions including very dry, alkaline soils, in full sun or deep shade. Plant with male yews for a reliable crop of berries. Trim or cut back to renovate, in summer or early autumn, if necessary.*

☼☀ ◊◊ Z 7-8 H 8-5 ‡30ft (10m) ↔12ft (4m)

THALICTRUM DELAVAYI 'HEWITT'S DOUBLE'

An upright, clump-forming perennial that produces upright sprays of long-lasting, pomponlike, rich mauve flowers from mid-summer to early autumn. The large, finely divided, mid-green leaves are carried on slender stems, which are shaded dark purple. An excellent foil in a herbaceous border to plants with bolder leaves and flowers.

CULTIVATION *Grow in moist but well-drained, organic soil, in sun or light shade. Divide clumps and replant every few years to maintain vigor.*

☼☀ ◊◊ Z 5-9 H 9-4 ‡4ft (1.2m) or more ↔24in (60cm)

THALICTRUM FLAVUM SUBSP. *GLAUCUM*

This subspecies of yellow meadow
rue is a summer-flowering, clump-
forming perennial that bears large,
upright heads of fragrant, sulfur
yellow flowers. These are carried
above mid-green, divided leaves.
Good at the margins of woodland.

CULTIVATION *Best in moist, organic soil,
in partial shade. Tolerates sun and dry
soil. Flower stems may need staking.*

☼ ◐ ◊◊ Z 6-9 H 9-6 ‡3ft (1m) ↔24in (60cm)

THUJA OCCIDENTALIS 'HOLMSTRUP'

This shrublike form of arborvitae
is a slow-growing conifer with a
conical shape. The dense, mid-green
leaves are distinctively scented and
arranged in vertical sprays. Small
oval cones appear amid the foliage.
Plant alone as a specimen tree, or
use as a hedge.

CULTIVATION *Grow in deep, moist but
well-drained soil, in full sun. Shelter
from cold, drying winds. Trim as
necessary in spring and late summer.*

☼ ◊◊ Z 2-7 H 7-1 ‡to 12ft (4m) ↔10–15ft (3–5m)

THUJA OCCIDENTALIS
'RHEINGOLD'

This bushy, spreading, slow-growing conifer is valued for its golden-yellow foliage, which is pink-tinted when young and turns bronze in winter. Small, oval cones are carried amid the billowing sprays of scented, scalelike leaves.
Good as a specimen tree.

CULTIVATION *Grow in deep, moist but well-drained soil, in a sheltered, sunny site. Trim in spring and late summer, but be careful not to spoil the form.*

☼ ◊◊ Z 2-7 H 7-1   ↕3–6ft (1–2m)
↔10–15ft (3–5m)

THUJA ORIENTALIS
'AUREA NANA'

This dwarf Oriental arborvitae is an oval-shaped conifer with fibrous, red-brown bark. The yellow-green foliage, which fades to bronze over winter, is arranged in flat, vertical sprays. Flask-shaped cones are borne amid the foliage. Good in a rock garden.

CULTIVATION *Grow in deep, moist but well-drained soil, in sun with shelter from cold, drying winds. Trim in spring and again in late summer as necessary.*

☼ ◊◊ Z 6-9 H 9-6   ↕↔ to 24in (60cm)

THUJA PLICATA
'STONEHAM GOLD'

This slow-growing, dwarf form of
western red cedar is a conical conifer
with fissured, red-brown bark and
flattened, irregularly arranged sprays
of bright gold, aromatic foliage; the
tiny, scalelike leaves are very dark
green within the plant. The cones
are small and elliptic. Ideal for a
larger rock garden.

CULTIVATION *Grow in deep, moist but
well-drained soil, in full sun with
shelter from cold, drying winds. Trim
in spring and again in late summer.*

☼ ◊◊ Z 6-8 H 8-6   ↕↔ to 6ft (2m)

THUNBERGIA
GRANDIFLORA

The blue trumpet vine is a vigorous,
woody-stemmed, evergreen climber
that can be grown as an annual
in cold climates. Lavender- to violet-
blue, sometimes white, trumpet-
shaped flowers with yellow throats
appear in hanging clusters during
summer. The oval to heart-shaped,
dark green leaves are softly hairy.

CULTIVATION *Grow in moist but well-
drained, fertile soil or soil mix, in sun.
Provide shade during the hottest part of
the day. Give the climbing stems support.
Minimum temperature 50°F (10°C).*

☼ ◊◊ H 12-10   ↕15–30ft (5–10m)

THUNBERGIA MYSORENSIS

A spring-flowering, fast-growing, woody-stemmed climber bearing hanging spikes of large yellow flowers with brownish red to purple tubes. The narrow, evergreen leaves are dark green with prominent veins. Must be grown in a warm conservatory or heated greenhouse in most areas.

CULTIVATION *Grow in moist but well-drained, fertile, organic soil or soil mix with shade from midday sun. Give the climbing stems support. Minimum temperature 59°F (15°C).*

☼ ◑◗ H 12-10   ‡to 20ft (6m)

THYMUS × CITRIODORUS 'BERTRAM ANDERSON'

A low-growing, rounded, evergreen shrub carrying small, narrow, gray-green leaves, strongly suffused with yellow. They are aromatic and can be used in cooking. Heads of pale lavender-pink flowers are borne above the foliage in summer. Lovely in an herb garden. Sometimes sold as 'Anderson's Gold'.

CULTIVATION *Best in well-drained, neutral to alkaline soil, in full sun. Trim after flowering, and remove sprigs for cooking as they are needed.*

☼ ◊ Z 6-9 H 9-6   ‡to 12in (30cm)
                          ↔to 10in (25cm)

THYMUS × CITRIODORUS 'SILVER QUEEN'

This rounded, evergreen shrub is similar to 'Bertram Anderson' (see facing page, below) but with silver-white foliage. Masses of oblong, lavender-pink flowerheads are borne throughout summer. Plant in an herb garden; the aromatic leaves can be used in cooking.

CULTIVATION *Grow in well-drained, neutral to alkaline soil, in full sun. Trim after flowering, and remove sprigs for cooking as needed.*

☼ ◊ Z 6-9 H 9-6   ‡to 12in (30cm)
↔to 10in (25cm)

THYMUS SERPYLLUM VAR. *COCCINEUS*

A mat-forming, evergreen subshrub with finely hairy, trailing stems bearing tiny, aromatic, mid-green leaves. Crimson-pink flowers are borne in congested whorls during summer. Suitable for planting in paving crevices, where the foliage will release its fragrance when stepped on. May also be seen as *T. praecox* 'Coccineus'.

CULTIVATION *Grow in well-drained, neutral to alkaline, gritty soil. Choose a position in full sun. Trim lightly after flowering to keep the plant neat.*

☼ ◊ Z 4-9 H 9-1 ‡10in (25cm) ↔18in (45cm)

TIARELLA CORDIFOLIA

This vigorous, summer-flowering perennial is commonly known as foam flower, getting its common name from the tiny, star-shaped, creamy white flowers. These are borne in a profusion of upright sprays above lobed, pale green leaves that turn bronze-red in autumn. Ideal as a groundcover in a woodland garden.

CULTIVATION *Best in cool, moist, organic soil, in deep or light shade. Tolerates a wide range of soil types.*

☼ ◐ ● ◊ Z 3-7 H 7-1 ‡4–12in (10–30cm)
↔to 12in (30cm)

TOLMIEA MENZIESII
'TAFF'S GOLD'

A spreading, clump-forming, semi-evergreen perennial carrying ivy-like, long-stalked, pale lime green leaves that are mottled with cream and pale yellow. An abundance of tiny, nodding, slightly scented, green and chocolate brown flowers appear in slender, upright spikes during late spring and early summer. Plant in groups to cover the ground in a woodland garden.

CULTIVATION *Grow in moist but well-drained, organic soil, in partial or deep shade. Sun will scorch the leaves.*

☼ ◐ ● ◊◊ Z 6-9 H 9-6 ‡12–24in (30–60cm)
↔3ft (1m

TRACHELOSPERMUM JASMINOIDES

Star jasmine is an evergreen, woody-stemmed climber with attractive, oval, glossy dark green leaves. The very fragrant flowers, creamy white aging to yellow, have five twisted petal lobes. They are borne during mid- to late summer and are followed by long seed pods. Where marginally hardy, grow in the shelter of a warm wall with a deep mulch around the base of the plant.

CULTIVATION *Grow in any well-drained, moderately fertile soil, in full sun or partial shade. Tie in young growth.*

☼☀ ◊ Z 9-10 H 12-9 ‡28ft (9m)

TRADESCANTIA × ANDERSONIANA 'J.C. WEGUELIN'

This tufted, clump-forming perennial bears large, pale blue flowers with three wide-open, triangular petals. These appear from early summer to early autumn in paired clusters at the tips of branching stems. The slightly fleshy, mid-green leaves are long, pointed, and arching. Effective in a mixed or herbaceous border.

CULTIVATION *Grow in moist, fertile soil, in sun or partial shade. Deadhead to encourage repeat flowering.*

☼☀ ◊ Z 5-9 H 9-5 ‡24in (60cm) ↔18in (45cm)

TRADESCANTIA × *ANDERSONIANA* 'OSPREY'

This clump-forming perennial bears clusters of large white flowers on the tips of the upright stems from early summer to early autumn. Each flower has three triangular petals, surrounded by two leaflike bracts. The mid-green leaves are narrow and often purple-tinted. A long-flowering plant for a mixed or herbaceous border.

CULTIVATION *Grow in moist but well-drained, fertile soil, in sun or partial shade. Deadhead to prevent self-seeding.*

☀:◑: ◊◊ Z 5-9 H 9-5   ‡24in (60cm)
                        ↔18in (45cm)

TRICYRTIS FORMOSANA

An upright, herbaceous perennial grown for its white, purple-spotted, star-shaped flowers on zig-zagging, softly hairy stems. These appear in early autumn above lance-shaped, dark green leaves that clasp the stems. An unusual plant for a shady border or open woodland garden.

CULTIVATION *Grow in moist, organic soil. Choose a sheltered site in deep or partial shade. Where marginally hardy, provide a deep winter mulch where there is unlikely to be much snow cover.*

☀:◑: ◊ Z 6-9 H 9-6   ‡to 32in (80cm)
                       ↔18in (45cm)

TRILLIUM GRANDIFLORUM

The great white trillium is a vigorous, clump-forming perennial grown for its large, three-petaled, pure white flowers that often fade to pink. These are carried in spring on slender stems and above a whorl of three large, dark green, almost circular leaves. Effective in the company of hostas.

CULTIVATION *Grow in moist but well-drained, leafy, neutral to acid soil, in deep or light shade. Provide an annual mulch of leaf mold in autumn.*

☼ ◐ ◖◗ Z 5-8 H 8-5 ↕ to 16in (40cm)
↔ 12in (30cm)

TRILLIUM LUTEUM

An upright, clump-forming perennial valued for its sweet-scented, golden- or bronze-green flowers in spring. These are produced above a whorl of oval, pointed, mid-green leaves that are heavily marked with paler green. Very attractive in a moist, shady border.

CULTIVATION *Grow in moist but well-drained, organic, preferably acid to neutral soil, in deep or partial shade. Mulch with leaf mold each autumn.*

☼ ◐ ◖◗ Z 5-8 H 8-5 ↕ to 16in (40cm)
↔ to 12in (30cm)

TROLLIUS × *CULTORUM* 'ORANGE PRINCESS'

This globeflower is a robust, clump-forming perennial with orange-gold flowers. These are held above the mid-green foliage in late spring and early summer. The leaves are deeply cut with five rounded lobes. Good for bright color beside a pond or stream or in a damp border.

CULTIVATION *Best in heavy, moist, fertile soil, in full sun or partial shade. Cut stems back hard after the first flush of flowers to encourage further blooms.*

☀️ ◑ ◊ Z 5-8 H 8-3 ‡to 36in (90cm) ↔18in (45cm)

TROPAEOLUM MAJUS 'HERMINE GRASSHOF'

This double-flowered nasturtium is a strong-growing, often scrambling, annual climber. Long-spurred, bright red flowers appear during summer and autumn above the light green, wavy-margined leaves. Excellent for hanging baskets and other containers.

CULTIVATION *Grow in moist but well-drained, fairly poor soil, in full sun. The climbing stems need support. Propagate from cuttings.*

☀️ ◊ annual H 12-1 ‡3–10ft (1–3m) ↔5–15ft (1.5–5m)

TROPAEOLUM SPECIOSUM

The flame nasturtium is a slender, herbaceous climber producing long-spurred, bright vermilion flowers throughout summer and autumn. These are followed by small, bright blue fruits. The mid-green leaves are divided into several leaflets. Effective growing through dark-leaved hedging plants, which contrast well with its flowers.

CULTIVATION *Grow in moist, organic, neutral to acid soil, in full sun or partial shade. Provide shade at the roots, and support the climbing stems.*

☼ ◐ ◊◊ Z 8-10 H 12-1   ‡to 10ft (3m)

TSUGA CANADENSIS 'JEDDELOH'

This dwarf form of the Canada hemlock is a small, vase-shaped conifer with deeply furrowed, purplish gray bark. The bright green foliage is made up of needlelike leaves, which are arranged in two ranks along the stems. An excellent small specimen tree for shady places; also popular for bonsai training.

CULTIVATION *Grow in moist but well-drained, organic soil, in full sun or partial shade. Provide shelter from cold, drying winds. Trim during summer.*

☼ ◐ ◊◊ Z 4-8 H 8-1 ‡5ft (1.5m) ↔6ft (2m)

TULIPA CLUSIANA
VAR. CHRYSANTHA

The yellow-flowered lady tulip is a bulbous perennial that flowers in early to mid-spring. The bowl- to star-shaped flowers, tinged red or brownish purple on the outsides, are produced in clusters of up to three per stem above the linear, gray-green leaves. Suitable for a raised bed or rock garden.

CULTIVATION *Grow in well-drained, fertile soil, in full sun with shelter from strong winds. Deadhead and remove any fallen petals after flowering.*

☼ ◊ Z 4-7 H 8-1 ↕12in (30cm)

TULIPA LINIFOLIA

This slender, variable, bulbous perennial bears bowl-shaped red flowers in early and mid-spring. These are carried above the linear, gray-green leaves with wavy red margins. The petals have yellow margins and black-purple marks at the base. Good for a rock garden.

CULTIVATION *Grow in sharply drained, fertile soil, in full sun with shelter from strong winds. Deadhead and remove any fallen petals after flowering.*

☼ ◊ Z 4-7 H 8-1 ↕8in (20cm)

TULIPA LINIFOLIA
BATALINII GROUP

Slender, bulbous perennials, often
sold as *T. batalinii*, bearing solitary,
bowl-shaped, pale yellow flowers
with dark yellow or bronze marks
on the insides. These appear from
early to mid-spring above linear,
gray-green leaves with wavy red
margins. Use in spring bedding; the
flowers are good for cutting.

CULTIVATION *Grow in sharply drained,*
fertile soil, in full sun with shelter from
strong winds. Deadhead and remove
any fallen petals after flowering.

☼ ◊ Z 4-7 H 8-1   ↕14in (35cm)

TULIPA TURKESTANICA

This bulbous perennial produces up
to 12 star-shaped white flowers per
stem in early and mid-spring. They
are flushed with greenish gray on
the outsides and have yellow or
orange centers. The linear, gray-
green leaves are arranged beneath
the flowers. Grow in a rock garden
or sunny border away from paths or
seating areas: the flowers have an
unpleasant scent.

CULTIVATION *Grow in well-drained,*
fertile soil, in full sun with shelter from
strong winds. Deadhead and remove
any fallen petals after flowering.

☼ ◊ Z 4-7 H 8-1   ↕12in (30cm)

TULIP CULTIVARS

These cultivated varieties of tulip are spring-flowering, bulbous perennials, with a wider range of flower color than any other spring bulbs, from the buttercup yellow 'Hamilton' to the violet-purple 'Blue Heron' and the multicolored red, white, and blue 'Union Jack'. This diversity makes them invaluable for bringing variety into the garden, either massed together in large containers or beds or planted in a mixed border. Flower shape is also varied; as well as the familiar cup-shaped blooms, as in 'Dreamland', there are also conical, goblet-, and star-shaped forms. The flowers are good for cutting.

CULTIVATION *Grow in well-drained, fertile soil, in sun with shelter from strong winds and excessive moisture. Remove spent flowers. You can lift bulbs once the leaves have died down, then store over summer. Replant the largest bulbs in autumn.*

☼ ◊ Z 4-7 H 8-1

1 ‡6in (15cm) **2** ‡24in (60cm) **3** ‡20in (50cm)

4 ‡16in (40cm) **5** ‡20in (50cm) **6** ‡12in (30cm)

1 *T.* 'Ancilla' **2** *T.* 'Blue Heron' **3** *T.* 'China Pink' **4** *T.* 'Don Quichotte' **5** *T.* 'Hamilton'
6 *T.* 'Oriental Splendour'

7 ↕24in (60cm) 8 ↕12in (30cm)

9 ↕14in (35cm) 10 ↕24in (60cm) 11 ↕8in (20cm)

12 ↕16in (40cm) 13 ↕24in (60cm) 14 ↕20in (50cm)

7 *T.* 'Dreamland' 8 *T.* 'Keizerskroon' 9 *T.* 'Prinses Irene' 10 *T.* 'Queen of Sheba'
11 *T.* 'Red Riding Hood' 12 *T.* 'Spring Green' 13 *T.* 'Union Jack' 14 *T.* 'West Point'

UVULARIA GRANDIFLORA

Large merrybells is a slow-spreading, clump-forming perennial bearing solitary or paired, narrowly bell-shaped, sometimes green-tinted yellow flowers. They hang gracefully from slender, upright stems during mid- to late spring above the downward-pointing, lance-shaped, mid-green leaves. Excellent for a shady border or woodland garden.

CULTIVATION *Grow in moist but well-drained, fertile soil that is rich in organic matter, in partial shade.*

☼☼ ◊◊ Z 3-7 H 7-1 ↕to 30in (75cm)
↔12in (30cm)

VACCINIUM CORYMBOSUM

The highbush blueberry is a dense, deciduous, acid soil-loving shrub with slightly arching shoots. The oval leaves are mid-green, turning yellow or red in autumn. Hanging clusters of small, often pink-tinged white flowers appear in late spring and early summer, followed by sweet, edible, blue-black berries. Best in a woodland garden in acid soil.

CULTIVATION *Grow in moist but well-drained, peaty or sandy, acid soil, in sun or light shade. Trim in winter.*

☼☼ ◊◊ Z 3-7 H 7-1 ↕↔ 5ft (1.5m)

VACCINIUM GLAUCOALBUM

A mound-forming, dense, evergreen shrub bearing elliptic, leathery, dark green leaves with bright bluish white undersides. Very small, pink-tinged white flowers appear in hanging clusters during late spring and early summer, followed by edible, white-bloomed, blue-black berries. Good for a acid woodland garden.

CULTIVATION *Grow in open, moist but well-drained, peaty or sandy, acid soil, in sun or partial shade. Trim in spring.*

☼◐ ◊◊ Z 3-7 H 12-9 ↕20–48in (50–120cm) ↔3ft (1m)

VACCINIUM VITIS-IDAEA KORALLE GROUP

These heavy-fruiting cowberries are creeping, evergreen shrubs with oval, glossy dark green leaves, shallowly notched at the tips. In late spring and early summer, small, bell-shaped, white to deep pink flowers appear in dense, nodding clusters. These are followed by a profusion of round, bright red berries that are edible but taste acidic. Makes a good groundcover for an acid, woodland garden.

CULTIVATION *Best in peaty or sandy, moist but well-drained, acid soil, in full sun or partial shade. Trim in spring.*

☼◐ ◊◊ Z 2-6 H 6-2 ↕10in (25cm) ↔indefinite

VERBASCUM
'GAINSBOROUGH'

This short-lived, semi-evergreen perennial is valued for its spires of saucer-shaped, soft yellow flowers, borne throughout summer. Most of the oval, gray-green leaves are arranged in rosettes around the base of the stems. A very beautiful, long-flowering plant for a herbaceous or mixed border.

CULTIVATION *Grow in well-drained, fertile soil, in an open, sunny site. Often short-lived, but easily propagated by root cuttings taken in winter.*

☼ ◊ Z 5-9 H 9-3 ‡4ft (1.2m) ↔12in (30cm)

VERBASCUM
DUMULOSUM

This evergreen subshrub forms small, spreading domes of felted, gray or gray-green leaves on white-downy stems. In late spring and early summer, clusters of small, saucer-shaped yellow flowers with red-purple eyes appear amid the foliage. Where marginal, grow in small crevices of a warm, sunny wall.

CULTIVATION *Best in gritty, sharply drained, moderately fertile, preferably alkaline soil, in full sun. Shelter from excessive winter moisture.*

☼ ◊ Z 6-9 H 9-4 ‡to 10in (25cm) ↔to 16in (40cm)

VERBASCUM 'HELEN JOHNSON'

This evergreen perennial produces spikes of saucer-shaped flowers in an unusual light pink-brown during early to late summer. The oval, wrinkled, finely downy, gray-green leaves are arranged in rosettes around the base of the stems. Naturalizes well in a wild garden.

CULTIVATION *Grow in well-drained, poor, alkaline soil, in full sun. Flower stems will need staking in fertile soil, where it grows larger.*

☼ ◊ Z 6-9 H 9-5   ↕36in (90cm)
↔12in (30cm) or more

VERBASCUM 'LETITIA'

This dense, rounded, evergreen subshrub produces a continuous abundance of small, clear yellow flowers with reddish purple centers throughout summer. The lance-shaped, irregularly toothed, gray-green leaves are carried beneath the clustered flowers. Suitable for a raised bed or rock garden. Where marginally hardy, grow in crevices of a drystone wall.

CULTIVATION *Best in sharply drained, fairly fertile, alkaline soil, in sun. Shelter from excessive winter moisture.*

☼ ◊ Z 5-9 H 9-5   ↕to 10in (25cm)
↔to 12in (30cm)

VERBENA 'SISSINGHURST'

A mat-forming perennial bearing rounded heads of small, brilliant magenta-pink flowers that appear from late spring to autumn – most prolifically in summer. The dark green leaves are cut and toothed. Excellent for edging a path or growing in a barrel.

CULTIVATION *Grow in moist but well-drained, moderately fertile soil or soil mix. Choose a site in full sun.*

☼ ◊ Z 7-11 H 12-1   ‡ to 8in (20cm)
↔ to 3ft (1m)

VERONICA GENTIANOIDES

This early summer-flowering, mat-forming perennial bears shallowly cup-shaped, pale blue or white flowers. These are carried in upright spikes that arise from rosettes of glossy, broadly lance-shaped, dark green leaves at the base of the plant. Excellent for the edge of a border.

CULTIVATION *Grow in moist but well-drained, moderately fertile soil, in full sun or light shade.*

☼ ◑ ◊ Z 4-7 H 7-1   ‡↔ 18in (45cm)

VERONICA PROSTRATA

The prostrate speedwell is a dense,
mat-forming perennial. In early
summer, it produces upright spikes
of saucer-shaped, pale to deep blue
flowers at the tips of sprawling
stems. The small, bright to mid-
green leaves are narrow and
toothed. Good in a rock garden.

CULTIVATION *Best in moist but well-
drained, poor to moderately fertile soil.
Choose a position in full sun.*

☼ ◊ Z 5-8 H 8-4   ↕to 6in (15cm)
                  ↔to 16in (40cm)

VERONICA SPICATA
SUBSP. *INCANA*

The silver speedwell is an entirely
silver-hairy, mat-forming perennial
with upright flowering stems. These
are tall spikes of star-shaped, purple-
blue flowers, borne from early to
late summer. The narrow leaves are
silver-hairy and toothed. Ideal for a
rock garden.

CULTIVATION *Grow in well-drained,
moderately fertile soil, in full sun.
Protect from excessive winter moisture.*

☼ ◊ Z 3-8 H 8-1   ↕↔ 12in (30cm)

VIBURNUM ×
BODNANTENSE 'DAWN'

A strongly upright, deciduous shrub carrying toothed, dark green leaves that are bronze when young. From late autumn to spring, when the plant has no leaves, small, tubular, heavily scented, dark pink flowers, which age to white, are borne in clustered heads. These are followed by small, blue-black fruits.

CULTIVATION *Grow in any deep, moist but well-drained, fertile soil, in full sun. On mature plants, relieve overcrowding by cutting the oldest stems back to the base after flowering.*

☼ ◐◊ Z 7-8 H 8-7　‡10ft (3m) ↔6ft (2m)

VIBURNUM ×
CARLCEPHALUM

This vigorous, rounded, deciduous shrub has broadly heart-shaped, irregularly toothed, dark green leaves that turn red in autumn. Rounded heads of small, fragrant white flowers appear amid the foliage during late spring. Good in a shrub border or a woodland garden.

CULTIVATION *Grow in deep, moisture-retentive, fertile soil. Tolerates sun or semi-shade. Little pruning is necesary.*

☼◐ ◊ Z 6-8 H 8-6　‡↔ 10ft (3m

VIBURNUM DAVIDII

A compact, evergreen shrub that
forms a dome of dark green foliage
consisting of oval leaves with three
distinct veins. In late spring, tiny,
tubular white flowers appear in
flattened heads; female plants bear
tiny but decorative, oval, metallic
blue fruits, later in the season. Looks
good planted in groups.

CULTIVATION *Best in deep, moist but
well-drained, fertile soil, in sun or semi-
shade. Grow several specimens together
for reliable fruiting. Keep neat, if
desired, by cutting wayward stems
back to strong shoots, or to the base
of the plant, in spring.*

☼☀ ◊◊ Z 8-9 H 9-8   ↔ 3–5ft (1–1.5m)

VIBURNUM FARRERI

This strongly upright, deciduous
shrub has oval, toothed, dark green
leaves that are bronze when young
and turn red-purple in autumn.
During mild periods in winter and
early spring, small, fragrant, white or
pink-tinged flowers are borne in
dense clusters on the bare stems.
These are occasionally followed by
tiny, bright red fruits.

CULTIVATION *Grow in any reliably
moist but well-drained, fertile soil, in
full sun or partial shade. Thin out old
shoots after flowering.*

☼☀ ◊◊ Z 6-8 H 8-6 ↕10ft (3m) ↔8ft (2.5m)

VIBURNUM OPULUS 'XANTHOCARPUM'

A vigorous, deciduous shrub bearing maplelike, lobed, mid-green leaves that turn yellow in autumn. Flat heads of showy white flowers are produced in late spring and early summer, followed by large bunches of spherical, bright yellow berries.

CULTIVATION *Grow in any moist but well-drained soil, in sun or semi-shade. Cut out older stems after flowering to relieve overcrowding.*

☼ ◑ ◊◊ Z 4-8 H 8-1 ‡15ft (5m) ↔12ft (4m)

VIBURNUM PLICATUM 'MARIESII'

A spreading, deciduous shrub bearing distinctly tiered branches. These are clothed in heart-shaped, toothed, dark green leaves that turn red-purple in autumn. In late spring, saucer-shaped white flowers appear in spherical, lacecaplike heads. Few berries are produced.

CULTIVATION *Grow in any well-drained, fairly fertile soil, in sun or semi-shade. Requires little pruning, other than to remove damaged wood after flowering; be careful not to spoil the form.*

☼ ◑ ◊ Z 4-8 H 8-1 ‡10ft (3m) ↔12ft (4m

VIBURNUM TINUS 'EVE PRICE'

This very compact, evergreen shrub has dense, dark green foliage. Over a long period from late winter to spring, pink flower buds open to tiny, star-shaped white flowers, carried in flattened heads; they are followed by small, dark blue-black fruits. Can be grown as an informal hedge.

CULTIVATION *Grow in any moist but well-drained, moderately fertile soil, in sun or partial shade. Train or clip after flowering to maintain desired shape.*

☼◐ ◊◊ Z 8-10 H 12-8　↔ 10ft (3m)

VINCA MAJOR 'VARIEGATA'

This variegated form of the greater periwinkle, also known as 'Elegantissima', is an evergreen subshrub with long, slender shoots bearing oval, dark green leaves that have creamy white margins. Dark violet flowers are produced over a long period from mid-spring to autumn. Useful as a groundcover for a shady bank, but may be invasive. Widely grown in containers, especially hanging baskets and windowboxes.

CULTIVATION *Grow in any moist but well-drained soil. Tolerates deep shade, but flowers best with part-day sun.*

☼◑◐ ◊◊ Z 7-11 H 12-7　‡18in (45cm) ↔indefinite

VINCA MINOR
'ATROPURPUREA'

This dark-flowered creeping myrtle is a mat-forming, groundcover subshrub with long trailing shoots. Dark plum-purple flowers are produced over a long period from mid-spring to autumn among the oval, dark green leaves.

CULTIVATION *Grow in any but very dry soil, in full sun for best flowering, but tolerates partial shade. Restrict growth by cutting back hard in early spring.*

☼ ◐ ◊◊ Z 4-9 H 9-1 ‡4–8in (10–20cm)
↔indefinite

VIOLA CORNUTA

The horned violet is a spreading, evergreen perennial that produces an abundance of slightly scented, spurred, violet to lilac-blue flowers; the petals are widely separated, with white markings on the lower ones. The flowers are borne amid the mid-green, oval leaves from spring to summer. Suitable for a rock garden.

CULTIVATION *Grow in moist but well-drained, poor to moderately fertile soil, in sun or partial shade. Cut back after flowering to keep compact.*

☼ ◐ ◊◊ Z 7-9 H 7-1 ‡to 6in (15cm
↔to 16in (40cm

VIOLA 'JACKANAPES'

A robust, clump-forming, evergreen perennial bearing spreading stems with oval and toothed, bright green leaves. Spurred, golden-yellow flowers with purple streaks appear in late spring and summer; the upper petals are deep brownish purple. Good for containers or bedding.

CULTIVATION *Grow in moist but well-drained, fairly fertile soil, in full sun or semi-shade. Often short-lived, but easily grown from seed sown in spring.*

☼◐ ◊◊ Z 4-8 H 8-1   ↕to 5in (12cm)
    ↔to 12in (30cm)

VIOLA 'NELLIE BRITTON'

This clump-forming, evergreen perennial with spreading stems produces an abundance of spurred, pinkish mauve flowers over long periods in summer. The oval, mid-green leaves are toothed and glossy. Suitable for the front of a border.

CULTIVATION *Best in well-drained but moist, moderately fertile soil, in full sun or partial shade. Deadhead frequently to prolong flowering.*

☼◐ ◊◊ Z 5-7 H 7-1   ↕to 6in (15cm)
    ↔to 12in (30cm)

VITIS COIGNETIAE

The crimson glory vine is a fast-growing, deciduous climber with large, heart-shaped, shallowly lobed, dark green leaves that turn bright red in autumn. Small, blue-black grapelike fruits appear in autumn. Train against a wall or on a trellis.

CULTIVATION *Grow in well-drained, neutral to alkaline soil, in sun or semi-shade. Autumn color is best on poor soils. Pinch out the growing tips after planting and allow the strongest shoots to form a permanent framework. Prune back to this each year in mid-winter.*

☼ ◑ ◊ Z 5-9 H 9-1   ↕50ft (15m)

VITIS VINIFERA 'PURPUREA'

The purpleleaf grape is a woody, deciduous climber bearing rounded, lobed, toothed leaves; these are white-hairy when young, turning plum purple, then dark purple, before they fall. Tiny, pale green summer flowers are followed by small purple grapes in autumn. Grow over a robust fence or pergola or through a large shrub or tree.

CULTIVATION *Grow in well-drained, slightly alkaline soil, in sun or semi-shade. Autumn color is best on poor soils. Prune back to an established framework each year in mid-winter.*

☼ ◑ ◊ Z 6-9 H 9-6   ↕22ft (7m)

WEIGELA FLORIDA
'FOLIIS PURPUREIS'

A compact, deciduous shrub with
arching shoots that produce clusters
of funnel-shaped, dark pink flowers
with pale insides in late spring and
early summer. The bronze-green
foliage is made up of oval, tapered
leaves. Pollution-tolerant, so it is
ideal for urban gardens.

CULTIVATION *Best in well-drained,
fertile, organic soil, in full sun. Prune
out some older branches at ground
level each year after flowering.*

☼ ◊ Z 5-8 H 8-1   ‡3ft (1m) ↔5ft (1.5m)

WEIGELA
'FLORIDA VARIEGATA'

A dense, deciduous shrub that
produces abundant clusters of
funnel-shaped, dark pink flowers
with pale insides. These are borne
in late spring and early summer
amid attractive, gray-green leaves
with white margins. Suitable for a
mixed border or open woodland.
Tolerates urban pollution.

CULTIVATION *Grow in any well-drained,
fertile, organic soil, in full sun. Prune
out some of the oldest branches each
year after flowering.*

☼ ◊ Z 5-8 H 8-1   ‡6–8ft (2–2.5m)

WISTERIA FLORIBUNDA 'ALBA'

This white-flowered Japanese wisteria is a fast-growing, woody climber with bright green, divided leaves. The fragrant, pealike flowers appear during early summer in very long, drooping spikes; beanlike, velvety green seed pods usually follow. Train against a wall, up into a tree, or over a well-built arch.

CULTIVATION *Grow in moist but well-drained, fertile soil, in sun or partial shade. Prune back new growth in summer and in late winter to control spread and promote flowering.*

☼ ☀ ◊◊ Z 5-9 H 9-1 ‡28ft (9m) or more

WISTERIA FLORIBUNDA 'MULTIJUGA'

This lilac-blue-flowered Japanese wisteria is a vigorous, woody-stemmed climber. Long, hanging flower clusters open during early summer, usually followed by bean-like, velvety green seed pods. Each mid-green leaf is composed of many oval leaflets. Train against a wall or up into a tree.

CULTIVATION *Grow in moist but well-drained, fertile soil, in full sun or partial shade. Trim in mid-winter, and repeatedly in summer.*

☼ ☀ ◊◊ Z5-9 H 9-1 ‡28ft (9m) or more

WISTERIA SINENSIS

Chinese wisteria is a vigorous, deciduous climber that produces long, hanging spikes of fragrant, pealike, lilac-blue to white flowers. These appear amid the bright green, divided leaves in spring, usually followed by beanlike, velvety green seed pods.

CULTIVATION *Grow in moist but well-drained, fertile soil, in sun or partial shade. Cut back long shoots to 2 or 3 buds throughout the growing season.*

☼ ◑ ◊◊ Z 5-8 H 8-1   ‡28ft (9m) or more

YUCCA FILAMENTOSA 'BRIGHT EDGE'

An almost stemless, clump-forming shrub with basal rosettes of rigid, lance-shaped, dark green leaves, to 30in (75cm) long, with broad yellow margins. Tall spikes, to 6ft (2m) or more, of nodding, bell-shaped white flowers, tinged with green or cream, are borne in mid-summer.
An architectural specimen for a border or courtyard.

CULTIVATION *Grow in any well-drained soil, in full sun to partial shade. Remove the large spikes of faded flowers at the end of the bloom season.*

☼ ◊ Z 5-10 H 12-1 ‡30in (75cm) ↔5ft (1.5m)

YUCCA FLACCIDA 'IVORY TOWER'

An almost stemless, evergreen shrub that forms a dense, basal clump of swordlike leaves. Tall spikes, to 5ft (1.5m) or more, of nodding, bell-shaped white flowers are borne in mid-summer. The lance-shaped, dark blue-green leaves, fringed with curly or straight threads, are arranged in basal rosettes. Thrives in coastal gardens and on sandy soils.

CULTIVATION *Grow in any well-drained soil, but needs a hot, dry position in full sun to flower well. Remove the large spikes of faded flowers after bloom.*

☼ ◊ Z 5-9 H 9-1 ‡22in (55cm) ↔5ft (1.5m)

ZANTEDESCHIA AETHIOPICA

This relatively small-flowered calla lily is a clump-forming perennial. Almost upright, cream-yellow flowers are borne in succession from late spring to mid-summer, followed by long, arrow-shaped leaves, evergreen in mild areas. May be used as a waterside plant in shallow water, where hardiness is improved.

CULTIVATION *Best in moist but well-drained, fertile, organic soil. Choose a site in full sun or partial shade. Mulch deeply for winter where marginally hardy.*

☼☀ ◊● Z 8-10 H 7-1 ‡36in (90cm) ↔24in (60cm)

ZANTEDESCHIA AETHIOPICA 'GREEN GODDESS'

This green-flowered calla lily is a clump-forming, robust perennial that is evergreen in mild climates. Upright and white-centered flowers appear from late spring to mid-summer above the dull green, arrow-shaped leaves. Grows well in shallow water.

CULTIVATION *Grow in moist, organic, fertile soil. Choose a site in full sun or partial shade. Mulch deeply for winter where marginally hardy.*

☀☀ ◐◆ Z 8-10 H 7-1 ‡36in (90cm) ↔24in (60cm)

ZAUSCHNERIA CALIFORNICA 'DUBLIN'

This deciduous California fuchsia, sometimes called 'Glasnevin', is a clump-forming perennial bearing a profusion of tubular, bright red flowers during late summer and early autumn. The gray-green leaves are lance-shaped and hairy. Provides spectacular, late-season color for a dry stone wall or border. Where marginally hardy, grow at the base of a wall.

CULTIVATION *Best in well-drained, moderately fertile soil, in full sun. Provide shelter from cold, drying winds.*

☀ ◊ Z 8-10 H 12-8   ‡to 10in (25cm)
↔to 12in (30cm)

THE PLANTING GUIDE

CHOOSING PLANTS THAT are just right for
any given part of your garden is the secret
of success. The *Planting Guide* provides
"shopping lists" of plants for a variety of
purposes, whether for awkward or
problem sites – such as damp,
shady places – or to create special effects
or plant groupings such as a wildlife
garden or a color-themed foliage
display. Plants that also have illustrated
A–Z entries have cross-references to their
picture and description.

CONTAINER PLANTS FOR SPRING COLOR

A large pot of evergreens and bright spring flowers and bulbs brings cheer to a front door or patio on a chilly early spring day. Tailor the soil to suit the plants: camellias and rhododendrons can be grown in acidic soil mix, for example. Keep containers in a sheltered place for earlier flowers, water in winter if necessary, and give liquid fertilizer as growth begins in spring.

AGAPANTHUS CAMPANULATUS 'ALBOVITTATUS'
Perennial, Z 7-10 H 12-7 Soft blue flowers in large heads above white-striped leaves.
‡3ft (90cm) ↔ 18in (45cm)

AJUGA REPTANS 'CATLIN'S GIANT'
Perennial, Z 3-9 H 9-1 Clumps of green leaves and spikes of blue flowers.
‡8in (20cm) ↔ 24–36in (60–90cm)

BERGENIA PURPURASCENS 'BALLAWLEY'
Perennial   page 72

CAMELLIA JAPONICA 'ADOLPHE AUDUSSON'
Evergreen shrub   page 84

CAMELLIA × *WILLIAMSII* 'DONATION'
Evergreen shrub   page 86

CHAENOMELES 'GEISHA GIRL'
Shrub, Z 5-8 H 8-3 Soft apricot, semi-double flowers.
‡3ft (1m) ↔ 4ft (1.2m)

CHAMAECYPARIS LAWSONIANA 'MINIMA GLAUCA'
Evergreen shrub, Z 5-9 H 9-4 A small conifer of neat habit with blue-green leaves.
‡24in (60cm)

CHIONODOXA FORBESII 'PINK GIANT'
Bulb, Z 3-9 H 9-1 Starry, white-centered pink flowers. ‡4–8in (10–20cm) ↔ 1¼in (3cm)

CHIONODOXA SARDENSIS
Bulb, Z 5-9 H 9-3 Bright blue, starry flowers in early spring.
‡4–8in (10–20cm) ↔ 1¼in (3cm)

CROCUS CHRYSANTHUS 'LADYKILLER'
Bulb, Z 3-8 H 8-1 White, scented flowers with purple stripes outside.
‡3in (7cm) ↔ 2in (5cm)

ERICA CARNEA 'MYRETOUN RUBY'
Evergreen shrub, Z 5-7 H 7-3 Spreading habit, with pink flowers that deepen as they age. ‡6in (15cm) ↔ 18in (45cm)

HEDERA HELIX 'KOLIBRI'
Evergreen climber, Z 5-10 H 12-3 Trailing stems with leaves variegated white and green. ‡18in (45cm)

HYACINTHUS ORIENTALIS 'CITY OF HAARLEM'
Bulb   page 225

HYACINTHUS ORIENTALIS 'GIPSY QUEEN'
Bulb, Z 5-9 H 9-5 Orange-pink, scented flowers. ‡10in (25cm)

HYACINTHUS ORIENTALIS 'HOLLYHOCK'
Bulb, Z 5-9 H 9-5 Spikes of double red flowers. ‡8in (20cm)

HYACINTHUS ORIENTALIS 'VIOLET PEARL'
Bulb, Z 5-9 H 9-5 Spikes of scented, amethyst-violet flowers with paler petal edges. ‡10in (25cm)

ILEX × *ALTACLERENSIS* 'GOLDEN KING'
Evergreen shrub, Z 7-9 H 9-7 A compact female holly with variegated leaves. Suitable for a large container for several years. ‡↔ 20ft (6m)

MYOSOTIS 'BLUE BALL'
Biennial, Z 5-9 H 7-1 Compact plant with azure blue flowers.
‡15cm (6in) ↔ 20cm (8in)

NARCISSUS 'CEYLON'
Bulb page **298**

NARCISSUS 'CHEERFULNESS'
Bulb page **298**

NARCISSUS SMALL DAFFODILS
Bulbs pages **296–297**

PIERIS 'FOREST FLAME'
Evergreen shrub page **340**

PIERIS FORMOSA VAR. *FORRESTII* 'WAKEHURST'
Evergreen shrub page **340**

PIERIS JAPONICA 'PURITY'
Evergreen shrub, Z 6-8 H 8-6 A compact variety with white flowers and pale young growth. ‡↔ 3ft (1m)

PRIMULA 'GUINEVERE'
Perennial page **351**

RHODODENDRON CILPINENSE GROUP
Evergreen shrub page **374**

RHODODENDRON 'CURLEW'
Evergreen shrub, Z 7-9 H 9-7 Small trusses of bright yellow flowers.
‡↔ 24in (60cm)

RHODODENDRON 'DOC'
Evergreen shrub page **374**

RHODODENDRON 'HOMEBUSH'
Shrub page **368**

RHODODENDRON 'MOTHER'S DAY'
Evergreen shrub, Z 6-8 H 9-5 Bright red-flowered evergreen azalea.
‡↔ 5ft (1.5m)

RHODODENDRON 'PTARMIGAN'
Evergreen shrub page **374**

RHODODENDRON 'SUSAN'
Evergreen shrub page **371**

TULIPA 'APRICOT BEAUTY'
Bulb, Z 4-7 H 8-1 Pastel, salmon-pink flowers of great beauty.
‡14in (35cm)

TULIPA 'CAPE COD'
Bulb, Z 4-7 H 8-1 Yellow flowers striped with red above prettily marked leaves.
‡8in (20cm)

TULIPA 'CARNAVAL DE NICE'
Bulb, Z 4-7 H 8-1 Red and white-striped blooms resemble double peonies.
‡16in (40cm)

TULIPA CLUSIANA VAR. *CHRYSANTHA*
Bulb page **440**

TULIPA CULTIVARS
Bulbs pages **442–443**

TULIPA PRAESTANS 'UNICUM'
Bulb, Z 4-7 H 8-1 Cream-edged leaves and one to four scarlet flowers per stem.
‡12in (30cm)

TULIPA 'TORONTO'
Bulb, Z 4-7 H 8-1 Multiheaded tulips with three to five flowers of deep coral pink.
‡10in (25cm)

VIOLA UNIVERSAL SERIES
Biennial, Z 4-8 H 7-1 Wide range of colors with flowers throughout spring.
‡6in (15cm) ↔ to 12in (30cm)

VIOLA 'VELOUR BLUE'
Biennial, Z 4-8 H 7-1 Compact plants with masses of small, light blue flowers.
‡6in (15cm) ↔ 8in (20cm)

CONTAINER PLANTS FOR SUMMER COLOR

Containers can bring color to areas that have no soil; they can be filled with permanent plants or used to add extra color when filled with annuals and tender perennials. In a large pot, combine the two with a shrub, augmented by lower, temporary plants. There is a huge choice, but every container will need regular watering and feeding if it is to look its best.

ABUTILON 'CANARY BIRD'
Shrub, Z 9-10 H 12-1 Bushy plant with pendulous yellow flowers.
‡↔ to 10ft (3m)

ABUTILON MEGAPOTAMICUM
Shrub page 30

AGAPANTHUS CAMPANULATUS SUBSP. PATENS
Perennial page 39

ARGYRANTHEMUM 'VANCOUVER'
Perennial page 53

CLEMATIS 'DOCTOR RUPPEL'
Climber page 109

CROCOSMIA 'LUCIFER'
Perennial page 130

CUPHEA IGNEA
Perennial page 133

DIASCIA BARBERAE 'BLACKTHORN APRICOT'
Perennial page 146

DIASCIA VIGILIS
Perennial, Z 7-9 H 9-7 The creeping stems carry loose spikes of pink flowers with yellow centers.
‡ 12in (30cm) ↔ 24in (60cm)

FUCHSIA 'ANNABEL'
Shrub page 185

FUCHSIA 'CELIA SMEDLEY'
Shrub page 185

FUCHSIA 'DISPLAY'
Shrub, Z 8-10 H 7-1 Upright plant with carmine and pink flowers.
‡ 24–30in (60–75cm) ↔ 18–24in (45–60cm)

FUCHSIA 'NELLIE NUTTALL'
Shrub page 185

FUCHSIA 'SNOWCAP'
Shrub, Z 8-10 H 7-1 Bushy plant with red and white flowers.
‡ 24in (60cm) ↔ 18in (45cm)

FUCHSIA 'SWINGTIME'
Shrub page 185

FUCHSIA 'THALIA'
Shrub page 185

FUCHSIA 'WINSTON CHURCHILL'
Shrub, Z 8-10 H 7-1 Pink and lavender, double flowers.
‡↔ 18–30in (45–75cm)

GAZANIA CHANSONETTE SERIES
Perennial page 191

HOSTA 'FRANCEE'
Perennial page 222

HYDRANGEA MACROPHYLLA 'AYESHA'
Shrub, Z 6-9 H 9-2 Unusual because the blooms are cupped, resembling *Syringa* (lilac) flowers.
‡ 5ft (1.5m) ↔ 6ft (2m)

LILIUM FORMOSANUM VAR. *PRICEI*
Perennial page 265

LILIUM LONGIFLORUM
Perennial page 266

LILIUM MONADELPHUM
Perennial   page **267**

LOTUS MACULATUS
Perennial, min. 40ºF (5ºC) H 12-1 Narrow,
silvery leaves contrast with orange,
clawlike flowers on trailing shoots.
‡ 8in (20cm) ↔ indefinite

NICOTIANA LANGSDORFII
Annual H 12-1 Airy spikes of small, green,
tubular flowers with flaring trumpets.
‡ to 5ft (1.5m) ↔ to 14in (35cm)

OSTEOSPERMUM 'BUTTERMILK'
Perennial   page **308**

OSTEOSPERMUM 'PINK WHIRLS'
Perennial, Z 10-11 H 6-1 Well-branched
plant flowering all summer, with
pinched petals.
‡ ↔ 24in (60cm)

PELARGONIUM 'ATTAR OF ROSES'
Perennial, min. 36ºF (2ºC) H 12-1 Rose-
scented leaves and small pale mauve
flowers. ‡ 20–24in (50–60cm) ↔ 10–12in (25–30cm)

PELARGONIUMS, FLOWERING
Perennials   pages **320–321**

PENSTEMON 'ANDENKEN AN
FRIEDRICH HAHN'
Perennial   page **322**

PENSTEMON 'HEWELL PINK BEDDER'
Perennial, Z 8-10 H 9-11 A free-flowering,
bushy plant with tubular, pink flowers.
‡ 18in (45cm) ↔ 12in (30cm)

PETUNIA 'LAVENDER STORM'
Annual H 12-1 Compact, ground-covering
plants with large blooms.
‡ 12in (30cm) ↔ 16in (40cm)

PETUNIA 'MILLION BELLS BLUE'
Annual H 12-1 Masses of small flowers on
bushy, compact plants.
‡ 10in (25cm)

PETUNIA 'PRISM SUNSHINE'
Annual H 12-1 A reliable, large-flowered
yellow petunia.
‡ 15in (38cm)

PLUMBAGO AURICULATA
Scrambling shrub   page **345**

ROSA 'ANNA FORD'
Patio rose   page **384**

ROSA 'GENTLE TOUCH'
Patio rose   page **384**

ROSA 'QUEEN MOTHER'
Patio rose   page **384**

ROSA 'SWEET MAGIC'
Patio rose   page **384**

ROSA 'THE FAIRY'
Patio rose   page **384**

SALVIA PATENS 'CAMBRIDGE BLUE'
Perennial   page **395**

SCAEVOLA AEMULA
'BLUE WONDER'
Perennial, min 40ºF (5ºC) H 9-1 Blue,
fan-shaped flowers on a sprawling,
vigorous bush.
‡ 6in (15cm) ↔ 5ft (1.5m)

TROPAEOLUM MAJUS
'HERMINE GRASSHOF'
Annual climber   page **438**

VERBENA 'LAWRENCE JOHNSTON'
Perennial, Z 8-10 H 12-1
Bright green foliage with intense,
fiery red flowers.
‡ 18in (45cm) ↔ 24in (60cm)

VERBENA 'SISSINGHURST'
Annual H 12-1 Spreading plant with fine
leaves and magenta-pink flowers.
‡ to 8in (20cm) ↔ to 3 ft (1m)

CONTAINER PLANTS FOR AUTUMN INTEREST

Autumn is a season of great change as the leaves of deciduous plants become brilliant before they fall. Most annuals have finished their display, but some plants, especially tender perennials such as cannas, dahlias, and heliotrope, continue to provide splashes of colorful flowers. Evergreens, both needle and broadleaved, form a strong and solid background for all garden displays.

ARGYRANTHEMUM
'JAMAICA PRIMROSE'
Perennial   page 53

BRASSICA 'OSAKA'
Annual H 8-1 Frilled ornamental cabbage in shades of pink and red; cold-tolerant.
‡↔ 12in (30cm)

CANNA 'LUCIFER'
Tender perennial H 12-1 Dwarf cultivar with green leaves and red, yellow-edged flowers.
‡ 24in (60cm) ↔ 20in (50cm)

CHAMAECYPARIS LAWSONIANA
'ELLWOOD'S GOLD'
Conifer   page 99

CLEMATIS 'MADAME JULIA CORREVON'
Climber   page 111

ESCALLONIA LAEVIS 'GOLD BRIAN'
Evergreen shrub, Z 8-9 H 9-8 Pink flowers held against bright yellow leaves.
‡↔ 3ft (1m)

GAULTHERIA MUCRONATA
'CRIMSONIA'
Evergreen shrub, Z 8-9 H 9-8 Acid-loving fine-leaved shrub with showy, deep pink berries.
‡↔ 4ft (1.2m)

HIBISCUS SYRIACUS
'WOODBRIDGE'
Shrub   page 221

HYPERICUM × *MOSERIANUM*
'TRICOLOR'
Shrub, Z 7-9 H 9-7 Variegated narrow leaves flushed pink, plus yellow flowers.
‡ 12in (30cm) ↔ 24in (60cm)

JUNIPERUS COMMUNIS
'COMPRESSA'
Conifer   page 247

MYRTUS COMMUNIS
Evergreen shrub   page 294

NANDINA DOMESTICA
'FIREPOWER'
Shrub, Z 6-9 H 9-3 Compact plant with red autumn color and berries.
‡ 18in (45cm) ↔ 24in (60cm)

OSMANTHUS HETEROPHYLLUS
'VARIEGATUS'
Evergreen shrub, Z 7-9 H 9-7 Hollylike cream-edged leaves and fragrant, white flowers in autumn.
‡↔ 15ft (5m)

RUDBECKIA HIRTA 'TOTO'
Annual H 7-1 Orange flowers with black centers on very compact plants.
‡↔ 8in (20cm)

THUJA ORIENTALIS
'AUREA NANA'
Conifer   page 430

VIBURNUM TINUS
'VARIEGATUM'
Evergreen shrub, Z 8-10 H 12-8 The leaves are broadly margined with creamy yellow.
‡ 10ft (3m)

CONTAINER PLANTS FOR WINTER INTEREST

Few plants flower during cold winter months; use those that do in containers by doors and windows, where they can be seen from the comfort of indoors. Many evergreens, especially variegated ones, look cheery when other plants are bare. Plant shrubs out in the garden after a few years in pots. To protect roots and pots, wrap pots with bubblewrap or layers of burlap.

AUCUBA JAPONICA 'CROTONIFOLIA'
Evergreen shrub   page 64

CYCLAMEN COUM
Bulb, Z 5-9 H 9-4 Deep green heart-shaped leaves and pink flowers.
‡ 2–3in (5–8cm) ↔ 4in (10cm)

ERICA CARNEA 'SPRINGWOOD WHITE'
Evergreen shrub   page 159

ERICA × DARLEYENSIS 'ARTHUR JOHNSON'
Evergreen shrub, Z 7-8 H 7-3 The upright stems have deep green leaves and bear pink flowers in winter.
‡ 75cm (30in) ↔ 60cm (42in)

EUONYMUS FORTUNEI 'HARLEQUIN'
Evergreen shrub, Z 5-9 H 9-3 Compact shrub. Young leaves heavily splashed with white. ‡↔ 16in (40cm)

FATSIA JAPONICA 'VARIEGATA'
Evergreen shrub, Z 8-10 H 12-8 Large, lobed leaves, edged with white; creamy white flowers on mature plants.
‡↔ 6ft (2m)

FESTUCA GLAUCA 'BLAUFUCHS'
Ornamental grass   page 179

GAULTHERIA MUCRONATA 'MULBERRY WINE'
Evergreen shrub   page 190

HEDERA HELIX 'EVA'
Evergreen climber, Z 5-10 H 12-5 Small gray-green leaves edged white.
‡ 4ft (1.2m)

ILEX AQUIFOLIUM 'FEROX ARGENTEA'
Evergreen shrub   page 233

JUNIPERUS COMMUNIS 'HIBERNICA'
Conifer, Z 2-6 H 6-1 Compact, upright plant with gray-green needles.
‡ 10–15ft (3–5m) ↔ 12in (30cm)

LAMIUM MACULATUM 'BEACON SILVER'
Perennial, Z 4-8 H 8-1 Bright silver-gray foliage and magenta-pink flowers.
‡ 8in (20cm) ↔ 3ft (1m)

LAURUS NOBILIS
Evergreen shrub/small tree   page 256

LIRIOPE MUSCARI 'JOHN BURCH'
Perennial, Z 6-10 H 12-1 Grasslike plant with gold-striped leaves and violet flowers.
‡ 12in (30cm) ↔ 18in (45cm)

SKIMMIA JAPONICA 'RUBELLA'
Evergreen shrub   page 413

VIBURNUM DAVIDII
Evergreen shrub   page 451

VIOLA 'FLORAL DANCE'
Annual H 8-1 Winter pansies in mixed colors. ‡ 6in (15cm) ↔ 12in (30cm)

VIOLA 'MELLO 21'
Annual H 8-1 Pansy mixture of 21 colors.
‡ 6in (15cm) ↔ 12in (30cm)

YUCCA GLORIOSA 'VARIEGATA'
Evergreen shrub, Z 7-10 H 12-1 Erect shrub with sharp, pointed leaves edged with yellow. ‡↔ 6ft (2m)

PLANTS FOR CONTAINERS IN SUNNY SITES

A sunny position where pots can be placed allows the cultivation of a huge range of plants. Apart from most bedding, many tender plants that must spend cold winters under glass should thrive in a sheltered sunny position and bring a touch of the exotic. Specimen plants are best grown in their own containers; simply group them together to create masterful associations.

BRACHYSCOME 'STRAWBERRY MIST'
Annual H 12-1 Low, spreading plant with feathery foliage and pink daisylike flowers.
‡ 10in (25cm) ↔ 18in (45cm)

CORDYLINE AUSTRALIS 'ALBERTII'
Evergreen shrub page **115**

CORREA BACKHOUSEANA
Evergreen shrub page **118**

ERICA ERIGENA 'IRISH DUSK'
Evergreen shrub, Z 8-9 H 9-8 Deep pink flowers are produced from autumn to spring on plants with grayish green leaves.
‡ 24in (60cm) ↔ 18in (45cm)

FELICIA AMELLOIDES 'SANTA ANITA'
Subshrub page **178**

FUSCHIA 'MADAME CORNÉLLISSEN'
Shrub, Z 8-10 H 12-1 Upright, with masses of red and white single flowers.
‡↔ 24in (60cm)

GAZANIA 'DAYBREAK RED STRIPE'
Perennial, Z 8-10 H 12-1 Raise from seed for showy yellow blooms striped with red.
‡ to 8in (20cm) ↔ to 10in (25cm)

GERANIUM 'ANN FOLKARD'
Perennial page **194**

GERANIUM CINEREUM VAR. *SUBCAULESCENS*
Perennial page **195**

GERANIUM PALMATUM
Perennial, Z 7-9 H 9-1 Bold clumps of foliage with large mauve flowers in summer.
‡↔ to 4ft (1.2m)

HEBE ALBICANS
Evergreen shrub, Z 9-10 H 12-9 Compact, with grayish leaves and short spikes of white flowers in early summer.
‡ 24in (60cm) ↔ 36in (30cm)

HEBE 'MRS. WINDER'
Evergreen shrub, Z 9-10 H 12-9 Dark foliage, flushed purple, and violet flowers in late summer.
‡ 3ft (1m) ↔ 4ft (1.2m)

HOSTA 'KROSSA REGAL'
Perennial, Z 3-8 H 8-1 A magnificent cultivar with upright gray leaves and tall spikes of lilac flowers.
‡ 28in (70cm) ↔ 30in (75cm)

IMPATIENS SUPER ELFIN SERIES
Annuals page **235**

IPOMOEA 'HEAVENLY BLUE'
Annual climber page **237**

JASMINUM MESNYI
Climber page **245**

LATHYRUS ODORATUS 'JAYNE AMANDA'
Annual climber page **255**

LATHYRUS ODORATUS 'NOEL SUTTON'
Annual climber page **255**

LATHYRUS ODORATUS 'WHITE SUPREME'
Annual climber page **255**

LEPTOSPERMUM SCOPARIUM 'RED DAMASK'
Evergreen shrub, Z 9-10 H 12-3 Plant with tiny leaves and double, deep pink flowers.
‡↔ 10ft (3m)

LOBELIA ERINUS 'KATHLEEN MALLARD'
Annual H 12-1 Neat-growing, unusual
double-flowered blue lobelia.
‡4in (10cm) ↔ 12in (30cm)

MIMULUS AURANTIACUS
Evergreen shrub   page 291

MYRTUS COMMUNIS SUBSP.
TARENTINA
Evergreen shrub   page 295

OSTEOSPERMUM 'SILVER SPARKLER'
Perennial, Z 10-11 H 6-1 White daisylike
flowers and bright, variegated leaves.
‡↔ 18in (45cm)

PASSIFLORA 'AMETHYST'
Climber, min 40°F (5°C) H 12-1 Fast-
growing climber producing beautiful
lavender flowers all summer.
‡12ft (4m)

PELARGONIUM 'CLORINDA'
Perennial, min 36°F (2°C) H 12-1 Rough,
scented foliage and quite large, bright pink
flowers. ‡18–20in (45–50cm) ↔ 8–10in (20–25cm)

PELARGONIUM 'DEACON MOONLIGHT'
Perennial, min 36°F (2°C) H 12-1 Pale lilac
double flowers above neat foliage on
compact plants.
‡8in (20cm) ↔ 10in (25cm)

PELARGONIUM 'DOLLY VARDEN'
Perennial   page 321

PELARGONIUM 'VISTA DEEP ROSE'
Perennial, min 36°F (2°C) H 12-1 Single
color in this seed-raised F2 series.
‡↔ 12in (30cm)

PENSTEMON 'APPLE BLOSSOM'
Perennial   page 322

PENSTEMON 'OSPREY'
Perennial, Z 7-9 H 8-1 Spikes of white
flowers edged with pink on an upright
plant. ‡↔ 45cm (18in)

PETUNIA 'DUO PEPPERMINT'
Annual H 12-1 Double, pink flowers, quite
weather-resistant in wet summers.
‡8in (20cm) ↔ 12in (30cm)

PHORMIUM 'SUNDOWNER'
Perennial, Z 9-10 H 12-2 Upright, evergreen
leaves that are deep green, striped with
pink and cream.
‡↔ 6ft (2m)

REHMANNIA GLUTINOSA
Perennial, Z 9-10 H 12-9 Slightly sticky
leaves on tall stems that carry dusky pink,
foxglove-like flowers.
‡6–12in (15–30cm) ↔ to 12in (30cm)

RHODOCHITON ATROSANGUINEUS
Evergreen climber   page 367

SEMPERVIVUM ARACHNOIDEUM
Succulent   page 410

SOLENOPSIS AXILLARIS
Perennial, min 45°F (7°C) H 12-1 Dome-
shaped and feathery with delicate but
showy star-shaped, blue flowers.
‡↔ 12in (30cm)

THYMUS × *CITRIODORUS*
'AUREUS'
Evergreen shrub, Z 6-9 H 9-6 Low-growing
bush, scented of lemon, with gold leaves
and pink flowers.
‡12in (30cm) ↔ to 10in (25cm)

TROPAEOLUM MAJUS
'MARGARET LONG'
Annual H 12-1 Compact, trailing plant with
double, soft orange flowers.
‡↔ 12in (30cm)

TWEEDIA CAERULEA
Perennial, min 39°F (3°C) H 12-1
A straggly, twining plant with gray leaves
and starry, turquoise blue flowers.
‡24–36in (60cm–1m)

PLANTS FOR CONTAINERS IN SHADE

A shady site can be a difficult place to grow plants – the soil is often dry – but a wide range of interesting plants can be grown in containers. Remember that rain may not reach plants under trees;

regular watering is needed all year, plus feeding in summer. Add bulbs for spring color and flowering plants in summer. Combine plants for form and texture as well as color.

ACER PALMATUM 'CRIMSON QUEEN'
Shrub, Z 6-8 H 8-2 Arching shoots with finely toothed purple leaves.
‡10ft (3m) ↔ 12ft (4m)

AGERATUM 'SOUTHERN CROSS'
Annual H 12-1 Neat, bushy plants with white and blue fluffy flowers.
‡↔ 10in (25cm)

AJUGA REPTANS 'MULTICOLOR'
Perennial, Z 3-9 H 9-1 Mats of bronze leaves marked pink and cream, and blue flowers. ‡6in (15cm) ↔ 18in (45cm)

BEGONIA NONSTOP SERIES
Perennials, min 50ºF (10ºC) H 7-1 Compact plants with double flowers in many colors.
‡↔ 12in (30cm)

CAMELLIA JAPONICA 'LAVINIA MAGGI'
Evergreen shrub, Z 7-8 H 10-3 Vigorous cultivar with white flowers variably striped with red and pink.
‡10ft (3m) ↔ 6ft (2m)

DRYOPTERIS ERYTHROSORA
Fern, Z 6-9 H 9-6 Colorful fern with copper-red young fronds and red spots underneath. ‡24in (60cm) ↔ 15in (38cm)

DRYOPTERIS WALLICHIANA
Fern   page **152**

X *FATSHEDERA LIZEI* 'ANNEMIEKE'
Evergreen shrub, Z 8-10 H 12-1 Procumbent stems and leaves with bright gold centers. Sometimes sold as 'Lemon and Lime'. ‡4–8ft (1.2–2m) or more ↔ 10ft (3m)

FATSIA JAPONICA
Evergreen shrub   page **178**

FUCHSIA 'DOLLAR PRINCESS'
Shrub, Z 8-10 H 12-1 A robust plant with small, red and purple, double flowers.
‡12–18in (30–45cm) ↔ 18–24in (45–60cm)

HEDERA HELIX 'IVALACE'
Evergreen climber   page **210**

HEDERA HELIX 'MANDA'S CRESTED'
Evergreen climber, Z 5-10 H 12-5 Uneven, curled and twisted, fingered leaves.
‡4ft (1.2m)

HOSTA 'ROYAL STANDARD'
Perennial   page **223**

ILEX CRENATA 'CONVEXA'
Evergreen shrub   page **234**

IMPATIENS 'BLACKBERRY ICE'
Annual H 12-1 Double purple flowers and white-variegated foliage.
‡to 28in (70cm)

IMPATIENS SUPER ELFIN SERIES
Annuals   page **235**

IPHEION UNIFLORUM 'WISLEY BLUE'
Bulbous perennial   page **236**

PIERIS JAPONICA 'LITTLE HEATH'
Evergreen shrub, Z 6-8 H 9-6 Compact, acid soil-loving, with white-edged leaves flushed pink in spring.
‡↔ 24in (60cm)

RHODODENDRON 'VUYK'S SCARLET'
Evergreen shrub   page **369**

VIOLA 'IMPERIAL ANTIQUE SHADES'
Annual H 12-5 Large flowers in pink, cream, and parchment colors.
‡6in (15cm) ↔ 8in (25cm)

FOLIAGE PLANTS FOR HANGING BASKETS

Although flowering plants are the most popular choice for hanging baskets, they can often be enhanced with attractive foliage plants. Silver-leaved plants are the most widely grown foil for flowers, but there are trailing plants that have gold, green, and red leaves, and it is not difficult to plant a beautiful basket using solely plants chosen for their colorful and contrasting leaves.

AJUGA REPTANS 'BURGUNDY GLOW'
Perennial   page **41**

ASPARAGUS DENSIFLORUS 'MYERSII'
Perennial   page **56**

BEGONIAS, FOLIAGE
Perennials   page **67**

CHLOROPHYTUM COMOSUM 'VITTATUM'
Perennial, min 45°F (7°C) H 12-1 Variegated narrow leaves; arching stems bear spidery plantlets. ‡ 6–8in (15–20cm) ↔ 6–12in (15–30cm)

GLECHOMA HEDERACEA 'VARIEGATA'
Perennial, Z 6-8 H 8-6 Long, pendent stems with grey-green leaves edged with white. ↔ trailing to 6ft (2m)

HEDERA HELIX 'GOLDCHILD'
Evergreen climber   page **210**

HELICHRYSUM PETIOLARE
Evergreen shrub   page **214**

HELICHRYSUM PETIOLARE 'LIMELIGHT'
Evergreen shrub, Z 10-11 H 12-1 Arching stems with pale green leaves, yellow in sun. ‡ 3ft (1m) ↔ indefinite

HELICHRYSUM PETIOLARE 'VARIEGATUM'
Evergreen shrub   page **215**

LAMIUM MACULATUM 'AUREUM'
Perennial, Z 4-8 H 8-1 Creeping, with bright yellow leaves marked white. ‡ 8in (20cm) ↔ 3ft (1m)

LOTUS BERTHELOTII
Subshrub   page **276**

LYSIMACHIA CONGESTIFLORA 'OUTBACK SUNSET'
Perennial, Z 6-9 H 12-1 Semi-trailing, with green, cream, and bronze leaves and clusters of yellow flowers.
‡ 6in (15cm) ↔ 12in (30cm)

LYSIMACHIA NUMMULARIA 'AUREA'
Perennial   page **279**

PELARGONIUM 'L'ELEGANTE'
Perennial   page **319**

PELARGONIUM 'SWANLAND LACE'
Perennial, min 36°F (2°C) H 9-1 Trailing plant with pink flowers; leaves veined with yellow. ‡ 12in (30cm)

PLECTRANTHUS FORSTERI 'MARGINATUS'
Perennial, min 50°F (10°C) H 12-1 Scented foliage, edged with white. New growth arches strongly
‡ 10in (25cm) ↔ 3ft (1m)

SAXIFRAGA STOLONIFERA 'TRICOLOR'
Perennial, Z 6-9 H 9-6 Round leaves edged white and flushed pink; strings of plantlets.
‡↔ to 12in (30cm)

SELAGINELLA KRAUSSIANA
Perennial   page **409**

TROPAEOLUM ALASKA SERIES
Annuals H 12-1 Easily raised, bushy nasturtiums with white-splashed leaves.
‡ to 12in (30cm) ↔ to 18in (45cm)

FLOWERING PLANTS FOR HANGING BASKETS

Most gardens, and houses or apartments without gardens, can be brightened by a few hanging baskets. They are easy to plant, and there are lots of cheerful plants to choose from, all with a long flowering season and a low or trailing habit. Baskets require regular watering and feeding to grow and flower well all summer. Automatic irrigation systems take the worry out of vacation watering.

ABUTILON MEGAPOTAMICUM
Shrub   page **30**

ACALYPHA REPTANS
Perennial, Z 10-11 H 12-1 Spreading plant with short red-hot cats'-tails.
‡6in (15cm) ↔ 24in (60cm)

ANAGALLIS MONELLI
Perennial, Z 7-8 H 8-7 Spreading plant with small leaves and bright, intense, deep blue flowers.
‡4–8in (10–20cm) ↔ 16in (40cm)

ANTIRRHINUM 'CANDELABRA LEMON BLUSH'
Perennial, Z 9-10 H 12-1 Bushy habit with trailing flower stems carrying pale yellow flowers, flushed with pink.
‡↔ 15in (38cm)

BEGONIA FUCHSIOIDES
Perennial, min 50ºF (10ºC) H 12-1 Arching stems set with tiny, glossy leaves bear pendent pink or red flowers.
‡30in (75cm) ↔ 18in (45cm)

BEGONIA 'ILLUMINATION ORANGE'
Perennial   page **66**

BEGONIA 'IRENE NUSS'
Perennial   page **66**

BEGONIA SUTHERLANDII
Perennial, min 50ºF (10ºC) H 12-1 Reddish, arching stems carry pale green leaves and masses of small, orange flowers.
‡4 ft (1.2m) ↔ 18in (45cm)

BIDENS FERULIFOLIA
Perennial   page **74**

CONVOLVULUS SABATIUS
Perennial   page **114**

DIASCIA 'LILAC BELLE'
Perennial, Z 8-9 H 9-8 Loose spikes of mauve–pink flowers on low plants.
‡8in (20cm) ↔ 12in (30cm)

FUCHSIA 'GOLDEN MARINKA'
Shrub   page **186**

FUCHSIA 'LENA'
Shrub   page **186**

FUCHSIA 'JACK SHAHAN'
Shrub   page **186**

FUCHSIA 'LA CAMPANELLA'
Shrub   page **186**

IMPATIENS TEMPO SERIES
Annuals   page **235**

LOBELIA CASCADE SERIES
Annual H 6-1 Trailing stems with flowers in shades of blue, pink, and white.
‡6in (15cm)

LOBELIA RICHARDSONII
Perennial, Z 4-9 H 9-1 Bushy but rather sparse, trailing stems with small leaves and bright lilac-blue flowers.
‡6in (15cm) ↔ 12in (30cm)

MIMULUS AURANTIACUS
Evergreen shrub   page **291**

PAROCHETUS COMMUNIS
Perennial, Z 8-10 H 12-8 A fast-growing trailer with cloverlike leaves and pale blue, pea-like flowers.
‡4in (10cm) ↔ 12in (30cm)

PELARGONIUM 'AMETHYST'
Perennial   page 320

PELARGONIUM 'THE BOAR'
Perennial   page 321

PELARGONIUM 'L'ELÉGANTE'
Perennial   page 319

PELARGONIUM 'LILAC MINI CASCADE'
Perennial, min 36ºF (2ºC) H 12-1 Single, pink flowers on a compact but vigorous plant. ‡ 18–20in (45–50cm) ↔ 6–8in (15–20cm)

PELARGONIUM 'MADAME CROUSSE'
Perennial, min 36ºF (2ºC) H 10-1 Trailing plant with semi-double pink flowers.
‡ 20-24in (50-60cm) ↔ 6–8in (15–20cm)

PELARGONIUM 'OLDBURY CASCADE'
Perennial, min 36ºF (2ºC) H 10-1 Rich red flowers on a compact plant with cream-variegated leaves.
‡ 18in (45cm) ↔ 12in (30cm)

PELARGONIUM 'ROULETTA'
Perennial, min 36ºF (2ºC) H 10-1 Double white flowers, heavily margined with red.
‡ 20–24in (50–60cm) ↔ 6–8in (15–20cm)

PELARGONIUM 'VILLE DE PARIS'
Perennial, min 36ºF (2ºC) H 10-1 Single, pink flowers produced in profusion on a pendulous plant.
‡ 24in (60cm) ↔ 18in (45cm)

PELARGONIUM 'YALE'
Perennial, min 36ºF (2ºC) H 10-1 The trailing stems carry clusters of semi-double bright red flowers.
‡ 8–10in (20–25cm) ↔ 6–8in (15–20cm)

PETUNIA DADDY SERIES
Annuals H 12-1 Large flowers, heavily veined with darker shades.
‡ to14in (35cm) ↔ 12–36in (30–90cm)

PETUNIA 'MARCO POLO ADVENTURER'
Annual H 12-1 Large, double flowers of bright rose pink on trailing plants.
‡ ↔ 15in (38cm)

PETUNIA 'SURFINIA PASTEL PINK'
Annual H 12-1 Large flowers of mid-pink on a strong plant that trails attractively.
‡ 9–16in (23–40cm) ↔ 12–36in (30–90cm)

SUTERA CORDATA 'KNYSNA HILLS'
Perennial, min 40ºF (5ºC) H 12-6 Bushy plant with massed heads of tiny, pale pink flowers.
‡ 20cm (8in) ↔ 60cm (24in)

SUTERA CORDATA 'SNOWFLAKE'
Perennial, Zones 9-10 H 12-6 Spreading, small-leafed plant with tiny, five-petaled white flowers. May be offered as *Bacopa*.
‡ 4in (10cm) ↔ 24in (60cm)

VERBENA 'IMAGINATION'
Annual H 12-1 Loosely branched, spreading plants with small, deep violet flowers. ‡ ↔ 15in (38cm)

VERBENA 'TAPIEN PINK'
Annual H 12-1 Trailing stems with clusters of small pink flowers.
‡ ↔ 15in (38cm)

VIOLA 'SUNBEAM'
Annual H 6-1 Semi-trailing plant with small yellow flowers.
‡ ↔ 12in (30cm)

SPRING-FLOWERING BULBS

The first signs that winter is giving way to spring are usually the flowers of spring bulbs. From tiny winter aconites that open as the leaves push through the soil to majestic crown imperials, there are bulbs for every situation. Most are tolerant of a wide range of soils, and many can be grown in the shade of trees. Grown in pots, they can be brought into the home to be enjoyed.

ALLIUM CRISTOPHII   page 42

ANEMONE BLANDA
'WHITE SPLENDOUR'   page 46

CAMASSIA CUSICKII
Z 3-10 H 12-1 Sheaves of narrow leaves and tall racemes of blue starlike blooms.
↕ 24–32in (60–80cm) ↔ 4in (10cm)

CHIONODOXA LUCILIAE   page 102

CHIONODOXA SARDENSIS
Z 5-9 H 9-5 Deep blue starry flowers on slender stems.
↕ 4–8in (10–20cm) ↔ 1¼in (3cm)

CORYDALIS FLEXUOSA
Z 6-8 H 8-6 Clumps of delicate foliage and nodding bright blue flowers.
↕ 6–12in (15–30cm) ↔ 8in (20cm)

CORYDALIS SOLIDA 'GEORGE BAKER'
  page 120

CROCUS ANGUSTIFOLIUS
Z 3-8 H 8-1 Clusters of bronze-marked orange-yellow flowers in spring.
↕ 2in (5cm)

CROCUS CHRYSANTHUS
'BLUE PEARL'
Z 3-8 H 8-1 Lilac-blue flowers with white and yellow centers.
↕ 3in (8cm) ↔ 1½in (4cm).

CROCUS CHRYSANTHUS
'E. A. BOWLES'   page 131

CROCUS SIEBERI 'HUBERT EDELSTEIN'
  page 131

CROCUS SIEBERI 'TRICOLOR'
  page 131

CROCUS TOMMASINIANUS
Z 3-8 H 8-1 An early-flowering crocus with slender, silvery lilac flowers.
↕ 3-4in (8-10cm) ↔ 1in (2.5cm)

ERANTHIS HYEMALIS   page 157

ERYTHRONIUM CALIFORNICUM
'WHITE BEAUTY'
Z 3-9 H 9-1 The recurved, white flowers are held above mottled leaves.
↕ 6-14in (15-35cm) ↔ 4in (10cm)

ERYTHRONIUM 'PAGODA'
  page 166

FRITILLARIA ACMOPETALA
  page 182

FRITILLARIA IMPERIALIS
'AUREOMARGINATA'
Z 5-9 H 9-5 Tall stems carrying heads of orange flowers, with yellow-margined leaves. ↕ 5ft (1.5m) ↔ 10–12in (25–30cm)

FRITILLARIA PALLIDIFLORA
  page 183

GALANTHUS NIVALIS
Z 3-9 H 9-5 The common but easily grown snowdrop, best planted while in leaf.
↕ 4in (10cm)

HERMODACTYLUS TUBEROSUS
Z 7-9 H 9-7 Straggly leaves almost hide the velvety green and black irislike flowers.
↕ 20–40cm (8–16in) ↔ 5cm (2in)

HYACINTHUS 'BLUE JACKET'

HYACINTHUS ORIENTALIS
'ANNA MARIE'
Z 5-9 H 9-5 Spikes of scented, pale pink flowers.
↕ 8in (20cm) ↔ 3in (8cm)

IPHEION UNIFLORUM 'FROYLE MILL'
Z 6-9 H 9-6 Vigorous, clump-forming plant with onion-scented leaves and violet, star-shaped flowers.
↕ 6–8in (15–20cm)

IRIS BUCHARICA

IRIS RETICULATA 'CANTAB'
Z 5-8 H 8-5 Pale blue flowers with deeper falls. Long leaves develop after flowering.
↕ 4–6in (10–15cm)

MUSCARI LATIFOLIUM
Z 4-8 H 8-1 Broad leaves and bicolored spikes of flowers in pale and dark blue.
↕ 8in (20cm) ↔ 2in (5cm)

NARCISSUS 'ACTAEA'

NARCISSUS BULBOCODIUM

NARCISSUS 'FEBRUARY GOLD'

NARCISSUS 'HAWERA'

NARCISSUS 'ICE FOLLIES'

NARCISSUS 'LITTLE WITCH'
Z 3-9 H 9-1 Golden yellow flowers with reflexed petals.
↕ 9in (22cm)

NARCISSUS MINOR

NARCISSUS 'PASSIONALE'

NARCISSUS TRIANDRUS

SCILLA BIFOLIA

SCILLA MISCHTSCHENKOANA
'TUBERGENIANA'

SCILLA SIBIRICA
Z 5-8 H 8-5 Bell-shaped flowers of cobalt blue above bright green leaves.
↕ 4-8in (10-20cm) ↔ 2in (5cm)

TULIPA 'APELDOORN'S ELITE'
Z 4-7 H 8-1 Rich yellow flowers feathered with red to give a subtle effect.
↕ 24in (60cm)

TULIPA 'BALLADE'
Z 4-7 H 8-1 Elegant flowers of rich pink with white petal edges and tips.
↕ 20in (50cm)

TULIPA 'CHINA PINK'

TULIPA 'MAUREEN'
Z 4-7 H 8-1 Oval flowers of ivory white.
↕ 20in (50cm)

TULIPA 'MRS. JOHN T. SCHEEPERS'
Z 4-7 H 8-1 Large flowers of crisp, pale yellow. ↕ 24in (60cm)

TULIPA 'RED SURPRISE'
Z 4-7 H 8-1 Bright red flowers that open to produce starry blooms.
↕ 8in (20cm)

SUMMER-FLOWERING BULBS

Summer-flowering bulbs bring sparkle to gardens with their bright colors and exotic shapes. Unfortunately, many are not hardy in most regions, but they are not expensive, and most can be lifted in autumn and kept in a frost-free place. Dahlias and gladioli are familiar to everyone, but modern lilies are easy to grow, too, and tigridias and hedychiums are even more exotic.

ALLIUM CERNUUM   page 42

ALLIUM GIGANTEUM   page 42

ALLIUM KARATAVIENSE   page 42

ALLIUM 'PURPLE SENSATION'
Z 4-9 H 12-1 Globular heads of small, deep purple flowers.
‡3ft (1m) ↔ 4in (10cm)

BLETILLA STRIATA
Z 5-8 H 8-5 Terrestrial orchid: a leafy plant with spikes of 1–6 small, magenta flowers.
‡↔ 12–24in (30–60cm)

CRINUM × *POWELLII*
Z 7-10 H 12-7 Huge bulbs produce large leaves and long trumpet flowers in pink.
‡5ft (1.5m) ↔ 12in (30cm)

CROCOSMIA 'EMILY MCKENZIE'
Z 6-9 H 9-6 Sword-shaped leaves and bright orange flowers marked with bronze.
‡24in (60cm) ↔ 3in (8cm)

DAHLIA 'BISHOP OF LLANDAFF'   page 138

DAHLIA 'GLORIE VAN HEEMSTEDE'
Z 8-10 H 12-1 Medium-sized bright yellow flowers shaped like waterlilies.
‡4½ft (1.3m) ↔ 2ft (60cm)

DAHLIA 'JESCOT JULIE'
Z 8-10 H 12-1 Long-petaled flowers of orange and red.
‡36in (1m) ↔ 18in (45cm)

DAHLIA 'PEARL OF HEEMSTEDE'
Z 8-10 H 12-1 This waterlily dahlia has flowers of silvery pink.
‡3ft (1m) ↔ 18in (45cm)

DRACUNCULUS VULGARIS
Z 8-10 H 12-1 Spotted stems support interesting leaves and huge, purple, unpleasantly scented spathes.
‡ to 5ft (1.5m) ↔ 24in (60cm)

EREMURUS 'CLEOPATRA'
Z 6-9 H 9-6 Rosettes of straplike leaves and tall spikes of small, soft orange flowers.
‡5ft (1.5m) ↔ 24in (60cm)

EUCOMIS BICOLOR
Z 8-10 H 12-1 Rosettes of broad leaves below spikes of starry cream blooms edged purple, topped with a leafy topknot.
‡ 12–24in (30–60cm) ↔ 8in (20cm)

GLADIOLUS CALLIANTHUS   page 199

GLADIOLUS COMMUNIS SUBSP. *BYZANTINUS*   page 200

GLADIOLUS 'GREEN WOODPECKER'
Z 8-10 H 12-1 Striking greenish yellow flowers with red markings.
‡5ft (1.5m) ↔ 5in (12cm)

HEDYCHIUM COCCINEUM
Z 8-10 H 12-8 An exotic-looking plant with spikes of tubular, scented flowers in orange, pink, or cream.
‡10ft (3m) ↔ 3ft (1m)

HEDYCHIUM COCCINEUM 'TARA'
Z 8-10 H 12-8 This has deeper-colored flowers. ‡10ft (3m) ↔ 3ft (1m)

HEDYCHIUM GARDNERIANUM   page 523

IXIA VIRIDIFLORA
Z 10-11 H 12-7 Unusual pale turquoise-green flowers on tall, wiry stems.
↕ 12–24in (30–60cm)

LEUCOJUM AESTIVUM 'GRAVETYE GIANT'
page 261

LILIUM 'BLACK DRAGON'
Z 4-8 H 8-1 Tall stems carry pure white, scented flowers that are marked deep maroon on the outside.
↕ 1.5m (5ft)

LILIUM 'EVEREST'
Z 5-8 H 8-1 Large white flowers, heavily scented, with dark spots, on tall stems.
↕ 5ft (1.5m)

LILIUM HENRYI
page 265

LILIUM 'KAREN NORTH'
Z 4-8 H 8-1 Elegant flowers with reflexed petals of orange-pink with deeper spots.
↕ 3–4½ft (1–1.3m)

LILIUM MARTAGON VAR. *ALBUM*
page 266

LILIUM PYRENAICUM
page 268

LILIUM REGALE
page 268

NECTAROSCORDUM SICULUM
Z 6-10 H 12-6 Plants smell strongly of garlic and produce loose umbels of pendulous cream flowers.
↕ to 4ft (1.2m) ↔ 4in (10cm)

RHODOHYPOXIS BAURII 'TETRA RED'
Z 9-10 H 12-9 Forms clumps or mats of bright, squat, starry flowers.
↕↔ 4in (10cm)

TIGRIDIA PAVONIA
min 46°F (8°C) H 12-3 Broad, spotted flowers in shades of red, yellow, and white, each lasting a single day.
↕ 5ft (1.5m) ↔ 4in (10cm)

TROPAEOLUM POLYPHYLLUM
Z 8-10 H 12-1 Trailing stems with finely divided gray leaves and bright yellow flowers.
↕ 2–3in (5–8cm) ↔ to 3ft (1m)

ZANTEDESCHIA AETHIOPICA 'GREEN GODDESS'
page 461

AUTUMN-FLOWERING BULBS

Some bulbs and corms provide color and interest when most plants are dying down. Most require full sun and well-drained soil to produce their flowers during the last fine days of the year.

Many do not fit easily with bulb production cycles and do not flower well until they are established in the garden, so it may take some extra effort to find these in nurseries or catalogs.

ALLIUM CALLIMISCHON
Z 5-9 H 9-5 Slender stems with white or pale pink flowers for dry soils.
‡4–14in (8–35cm) ↔ 2in (5cm)

× *AMARYGIA PARKERI*
Z 9-10 H 12-9 This uncommon hybrid produces large pink trumpet flowers.
‡3ft (1m) ↔ 12in (30cm)

AMARYLLIS BELLADONNA
Z 7-10 H 12-7 The dark stems support beautiful pink trumpets.
‡24in (60cm) ↔ 4in (10cm)

COLCHICUM SPECIOSUM 'ALBUM'
page **113**

COLCHICUM 'WATERLILY'
Z 4-9 H 9-1 Beautiful white goblets that appear without leaves.
‡7in (18cm) ↔ 4in (10cm)

CRINUM × *POWELLII* 'ALBUM'
page **129**

CROCUS BANATICUS
page **132**

CROCUS BORYI
Z 4-8 H 8-1 Each corm produces up to four pale lilac and cream flowers.
‡3in (8cm) ↔ 2in (5cm)

CROCUS GOULIMYI   page **132**

CROCUS KOTSCHYANUS   page **132**

CROCUS MEDIUS   page **132**

CROCUS OCHROLEUCUS   page **132**

CROCUS PULCHELLUS   page **132**

CROCUS SPECIOSUS
Z 3-8 H 8-1 Violet-blue, scented flowers with orange stigmas.
‡6in (15cm)

CYCLAMEN HEDERIFOLIUM
page **134**

LEUCOJUM AUTUMNALE   page **261**

MERENDERA MONTANA
Z 6-9 H 9-6 Starry lilac flowers; needs well-drained soil.
‡↔ 2in (5cm)

NERINE BOWDENII   page **300**

STERNBERGIA LUTEA
Z 7-9 H 9-7 Deep green leaves and bright yellow crocuslike flowers.
‡6in (15cm) ↔ 3in (8cm)

TROPAEOLUM TUBEROSUM 'KEN ASLET'
Z 8-10 H 12-1 Clambering stems with small leaves and yellow, hooded flowers.
‡6–12ft (2–4m)

ZEPHYRANTHES CANDIDA
Z 9-10 H 12-1 Clumps of narrow leaves and white, crocuslike flowers over many weeks.
‡4–8in (10–20cm) ↔ 3in (8cm)

SPRING BEDDING

When the last bedding plants of the season die down, it is time to replace them with plants that will survive the winter then flower in spring. Most of these are biennials, such as Canterbury bells, sweet Williams, and wallflowers. Add winter-flowering pansies for early color, especially in containers. Plant spring bulbs among the bedding plants for extra interest.

BELLIS PERENNIS 'POMPONETTE'
page 68

CAMPANULA MEDIUM 'CALYCANTHEMA'
Biennial, Z 5-8 H 8-5 Cup-and-saucer Canterbury bells in pink, blue, and white.
‡ to 30in (75cm)

DIANTHUS BARBATUS
'AURICULA-EYED MIXED'
Biennial, Z 3-9 H 8-1 Traditional sweet Williams with flowers zoned in white, pink, and maroon.
‡ to 24in (60cm)

ERYSIMUM CHEIRI 'CLOTH OF GOLD'
Biennial, Z 3-7 H 7-1 Yellow, scented flowers. ‡ 18in (45cm)

ERYSIMUM CHEIRI
'FIREKING IMPROVED'
Biennial, Z 3-7 H 7-1 Reliable wallflower with orange-red flowers.
‡ 18in (45cm)

ERYSIMUM CHEIRI
'PRINCE PRIMROSE YELLOW'
Biennial, Z 3-7 H 7-1 Dwarf, with large flowers. ‡ 12in (30cm)

HYACINTHUS ORIENTALIS 'FONDANT'
Bulb, Z 5-9 H 9-5 Flowers of clean, pure pink with no hint of blue.
‡ 10in (25cm)

HYACINTHUS ORIENTALIS 'OSTARA'
Bulb
page 225

HYACINTHUS ORIENTALIS 'PINK PEARL'
Bulb
page 226

HYACINTHUS ORIENTALIS 'VIOLET PEARL'
Bulb, Z 5-9 H 9-5 Amethyst-colored flowers.
‡ 10in (25cm)

MYOSOTIS 'SPRING SYMPHONY BLUE'
Biennial, Z 5-9 H 9-5 The blue flowers associate well with most spring bulbs.
‡ 6in (15cm)

TULIPA 'HALCRO'
Bulb, Z 4-7 H 8-1 Large flowers of deep salmon-red.
‡ 28in (70cm)

TULIPA 'ORANJE NASSAU'
Bulb, Z 4-7 H 8-1 Fiery flowers in shades of red and scarlet.
‡ 12in (30cm)

TULIPA 'SPRING GREEN'
Bulb
page 443

VIOLA 'FELIX'
Annual H 12-1 Yellow and purple, "whiskered" flowers on tufted plants.
‡ 6in (15cm)

VIOLA 'RIPPLING WATERS'
Annual H 12-1 Large flowers of dark purple edged with white.
‡ 6in (15cm)

VIOLA ULTIMA SERIES
Annual H 12-1 Wide range of colors on plants that flower through mild spells.
‡ 6in (15cm)

SUMMER BEDDING

Although bedding out on the grand scale will probably never be as popular as it was in Victorian times, most gardeners can manage to find room for plants that grow and flower quickly once planted out. Many of these are annuals, while others are tender perennials grown as annuals in most areas. Most have a long flowering period within a given season.

AGERATUM HOUSTONIANUM 'PACIFIC'
Annual H 12-1 Compact plants with dense heads of purple-blue flowers.
‡8in (20cm)

ANTIRRHINUM SONNET SERIES
Annuals   page **50**

BEGONIA COCKTAIL SERIES
Tender perennials   page **66**

BEGONIA 'PIN UP'
Tender perennials   page **66**

BEGONIA SEMPERFLORENS OLYMPIA SERIES
Tender perennials H 12-1 Compact, large-flowered bedding begonias.
‡↔8in (20cm)

DAHLIA 'COLTNESS GEM' GROUP
Tender perennials H 12-1 Reliable, single-flowered dahlias in clear, bright colors.
‡↔18in (45cm)

DIASCIA RIGESCENS
Tender perennial   page **146**

HELIOTROPIUM ARBORESCENS 'PRINCESS MARINA'
Tender perennial   page **216**

IMPATIENS DECO SERIES
Annuals H 12-1 Large, bright flowers on plants with dark green leaves.
‡↔ to 8in (20cm)

LOBELIA 'CRYSTAL PALACE'
Annual   page **272**

LOBELIA 'COMPLIMENT SCARLET'
Perennial, Z 3-8 H 8-3 Bold plant with green foliage and scarlet flowers on tall spikes. ‡30in (75cm) ↔ 12in (30cm)

LOBELIA ERINUS 'MRS. CLIBRAN'
Annual H 6-1 A compact plant with white-eyed, bright blue flowers.
‡4-6in (10-15cm)

NICOTIANA 'LIME GREEN'
Annual   page **300**

NICOTIANA X *SANDERAE* 'DOMINO SALMON PINK'
Annual H 12-1 Upward-facing flowers of salmon-pink on compact plants.
‡12–18in (30–45cm)

NICOTIANA SYLVESTRIS
Tender perennial   page **301**

NIGELLA 'MISS JEKYLL'
Annual   page **301**

PELARGONIUM MULTIBLOOM SERIES
Tender perennials   page **321**

PELARGONIUM VIDEO SERIES
Tender perennials   page **321**

PENSTEMON 'BEECH PARK'
Perennial, Z 7-10 H 12-3 Large pink and white trumpets throughout summer. Sometimes sold as 'Barbara Barker'.
‡30in (75cm) ↔ 18in (45cm)

PENSTEMON 'BURGUNDY'
Perennial, Z 7-10 H 12-3 Deep wine-red flowers above dark green leaves.
‡36in (90cm) ↔ 18in (45cm)

PENSTEMON 'MAURICE GIBBS'
Perennial, Z 7-10 H 12-3 The large-leaved
plants bear spikes of bright cerise flowers
with white throats.
‡30in (75cm) ↔ 18in (45cm)

PENSTEMON 'MYDDELTON GEM'
Perennial, Z 7-10 H 12-3 Long-flowering
plant with pale green leaves and deep
pink, tubular flowers.
‡30in (75cm) ↔ 18in (45cm)

PETUNIA CARPET SERIES
Annuals page 326

PETUNIA 'MIRAGE REFLECTIONS'
Annual H 12-1 Weather-resistant multiflora
petunias with pastel colors highlighted
by darker veins.
‡12in (30cm) ↔ 24in (60cm)

PHLOX DRUMMONDII 'TAPESTRY'
Annual H 12-1 Wide range of pastel colors
and bicolors on bushy plants.
‡20in (50cm) ↔ 15in (38cm)

POLEMONIUM 'LAMBROOK MAUVE'
Perennial page 346

PORTULACA GRANDIFLORA
SUNDIAL SERIES
Annuals H 12-1 Sun-loving plants with
brilliant flowers, with petals like satin.
‡4in (10cm) ↔ 6in (15cm)

RUDBECKIA HIRTA 'RUSTIC DWARFS'
Annual H 7-1 Mixture of autumnal shades
on large, dark-eyed flowers.
‡to 24in (60cm)

SALPIGLOSSIS CASINO SERIES
Annuals page 393

SALVIA COCCINEA 'LADY IN RED'
Annual H 12-1 Bushy plants bear slender
spikes of small but showy red flowers all
summer. ‡16in (40cm)

SALVIA FARINACEA 'VICTORIA'
Annual H 12-1 The small, deep blue
flowers are crowded on spikes held well
above the leaves.
‡to 24in (60cm) ↔ 12in (30cm)

SALVIA FULGENS
Subshrub page 394

SALVIA PRATENSIS HAEMATODES
GROUP
Perennial page 396

SALVIA SPLENDENS 'SCARLET KING'
Perennial page 396

SALVIA SPLENDENS SIZZLER SERIES
Annuals H 12-1 Early-flowering plants
with blooms in colors from red to
lavender and white.
‡10–12in (25–30cm)

TAGETES 'DISCO ORANGE'
Annual H 12-1 Weather-resistant, single
flowers.
‡8-10in (20-25cm)

TAGETES 'SAFARI SCARLET'
Annual H 12-1 Large, bright double
flowers.
‡8-10in (20-25cm)

TAGETES 'ZENITH RED'
Annual H 12-1 Afro-French marigold with
double red flowers.
‡12in (30cm)

VERBENA × HYBRIDA
'PEACHES AND CREAM'
Annual H 12-1 Seed-raised spreading
plants with peach-colored flowers
that fade to cream.
‡12in (30cm) ↔ 18in (45cm)

VERBENA × HYBRIDA 'SILVER ANNE'
Tender perennial H 12-1 Sweetly scented
pink flowers that fade almost to white,
above divided foliage.
‡12in (30cm) ↔ 24in (60cm)

HERBACEOUS PLANTS WITH VARIEGATED LEAVES

Variegation may be restricted to a narrow rim around the edge of a leaf, or it may be more spectacular. Regular patterning with white, cream, or gold may help define the shape of large leaves, but random streaks and splashes can make some plants look messy. Remember that plants may revert back to their plain form: always remove any shoots with plain green leaves.

AQUILEGIA VULGARIS 'VERVAENEANA GROUP'
Perennial, Z 3-8 H 7-1 Leaves are marbled and splashed with yellow and green, below white, pink, or blue flowers.
‡36in (90cm) ↔ 18in (45cm)

ARABIS PROCURRENS 'VARIEGATA'
Perennial   page **51**

ARMORACIA RUSTICANA 'VARIEGATA'
Perennial, Z 4-8 H 8-1 Deep-rooted plants with large leaves heavily splashed with white, especially in spring.
‡3ft (1m) ↔ 18in (45cm)

ASTRANTIA 'SUNNINGDALE VARIEGATED'
Perennial   page **63**

BRUNNERA MACROPHYLLA 'HADSPEN CREAM'
Perennial   page **76**

COREOPSIS 'CALYPSO'
Perennial, Z 4-9 H 9-1 Narrow leaves edged with gold, and yellow flowers with a red zone.
‡ ↔ 15in (38cm)

GAURA LINDHEIMERI 'CORRIE'S GOLD'
Perennial, Z 6-9 H 9-6 White flowers on thin stems, and small leaves edged with gold. ‡to 5ft (1.5m) ↔ 36in (90cm)

HEMEROCALLIS FULVA 'KWANZO VARIEGATA'
Perennial, Z 3-10 H 12-1 Arching leaves with bright white stripes, and occasional double orange flowers. ‡30in (75cm)

HOSTA 'FORTUNEI ALBOPICTA'
Perennial   page **222**

HOSTA 'GOLDEN TIARA'
Perennial   page **222**

HOSTA 'GREAT EXPECTATIONS'
Perennial, Z 3-8 H 9-2 Glaucous-green, puckered leaves with broad yellow centers and grayish white flowers.
‡22in (55cm) ↔ 34in (85cm)

HOSTA 'SHADE FANFARE'
Perennial   page **223**

HOSTA SIEBOLDII VAR. *ELEGANS*
Perennial   page **223**

HOSTA 'HALCYON'
Perennial   page **223**

HOSTA 'UNDULATA UNIVITTATA'
Perennial, Z 3-8 H 9-2 This popular plant produces clumps of twisted leaves with a central cream splash.
‡18in (45cm) ↔ 28in (70cm)

HOSTA VENUSTA
Perennial   page **223**

HOSTA 'WIDE BRIM'
Perennial   page **223**

HOUTTUYNIA CORDATA 'CHAMELEON'
Perennial, Z 6-11 H 12-6 Leaves in shades of cream, green, and red, and white flowers. ‡to 6–12in (15–30cm) or more ↔ indefinite

IRIS LAEVIGATA 'VARIEGATA'
Perennial   page **238**

IRIS PALLIDA 'VARIEGATA'
Perennial   page 242

LYSIMACHIA PUNCTATA 'ALEXANDER'
Perennial, Z 4-8 H 8-1 Creeping plant with
spires of yellow flowers and white-edged
foliage, tinged pink in spring.
↕3ft (1m) ↔ 2ft (60cm)

MIMULUS LUTEUS 'VARIEGATUS'
Perennial, Z 7-9 H 9-7 Creeping plant with
yellow flowers and pale green leaves
edged with white.
↕12in (30cm) ↔ 18in (45cm)

MOLINIA CAERULEA 'VARIEGATA'
Ornamental grass   page 292

PERSICARIA VIRGINIANA 'PAINTER'S
PALETTE'
Perennial, Z 5-9 H 9-5 Bright foliage
splashed with white and marked with red
and brown, on red stems. Can become
weedy. ↕16–48in (40–120cm) ↔ 24–56in (60–140cm)

PHALARIS ARUNDINACEA 'PICTA'
Ornamental grass   page 327

PHLOX PANICULATA 'PINK POSIE'
Perennial, Z 4-8 H 8-1 Compact phlox with
white-edged leaves and pink flowers.
↕30in (75cm) ↔ 24in (60cm)

PHORMIUM COOKIANUM SUBSP.
HOOKERI 'TRICOLOR'
Evergreen perennial   page 334

PHYSOSTEGIA VIRGINIANA
'VARIEGATA'
Perennial, Z 4-8 H 8-1 Upright plant with
grayish leaves edged with white, and
deep pink flowers.
↕30in (75cm) ↔ 24in (60cm)

PLEIOBLASTUS AURICOMUS
Bamboo   page 344

PULMONARIA RUBRA 'DAVID WARD'
Perennial, Z 5-8 H 8-5 Coral-red flowers in
spring, and leaves margined with white.
↕to 16in (40cm) ↔ 36in (90cm)

SAXIFRAGA STOLONIFERA
'TRICOLOR'
Perennial, Z 6-9 H 9-3 A spreading
plant with round leaves edged with
white and pink.
↕12in (30cm) ↔ indefinite

SISYRINCHIUM STRIATUM
'AUNT MAY'
Perennial, Z 7-8 H 8-7 Upright fans of
narrow, gray leaves edged with cream, and
spikes of cream flowers.
↕↔ to 20in (50cm)

SYMPHYTUM × *UPLANDICUM*
'VARIEGATUM'
Perennial   page 423

VERONICA GENTIANOIDES
'VARIEGATA'
Perennial, Z 4-7 H 7-1 Mats of deep green
leaves margined with white, and spikes of
small, pale blue flowers.
↕↔ 18in (45cm)

VINCA MAJOR 'VARIEGATA'
Perennial   page 453

VARIEGATED SHRUBS AND TREES

While flowers usually have a short season, foliage provides color for at least half the year – and all year if evergreen. Variegated plants increase that interest with their bright coloring, and some have flowers that complement the foliage. Many variegated evergreens are useful to brighten shady areas and are good in pots and containers; they are also popular with flower arrangers.

ACER CAMPESTRE 'CARNIVAL'
Tree, Z 5-8 H 8-6 A tree that can be pruned to keep it smaller, with pink-splashed leaves. ↕25ft (8m) ↔ 15ft (5m)

ACER NEGUNDO 'FLAMINGO'
Tree   page 33

ACER PALMATUM 'BUTTERFLY'
Shrub or small tree   page 34

ACER PLATANOIDES 'DRUMMONDII'
Tree, Z 3-7 H 7-1 The leaves are boldly edged with white: watch out for reversion to plain green, and remove these shoots. ↕30-40ft (10-12m)

ACER PSEUDOPLATANUS 'LEOPOLDII'
Tree, Z 4-7 H 7-1 The leaves are pink at first in spring, then speckled with yellow. ↕30ft (10m)

ARALIA ELATA 'VARIEGATA'
Shrub, Z 4-9 H 9-1 Huge leaves divided into many leaflets, each edged with white, on tall, lanky stems. ↕15ft (5m)

BERBERIS THUNBERGII 'ROSE GLOW'
Shrub   page 70

BUDDLEJA DAVIDII 'HARLEQUIN'
Shrub, Z 6-9 H 9-5 Striking leaves edged with white, and purple flowers. ↕↔8ft (2.5m)

BUDDLEJA DAVIDII 'SANTANA'
Shrub, Z 6-9 H 9-5 Mottled foliage in shades of green and yellow, and purple flowers. ↕↔8ft (2.5m)

BUXUS SEMPERVIRENS 'ELEGANTISSIMA'
Evergreen shrub   page 79

CAMELLIA × *WILLIAMSII* 'GOLDEN SPANGLES'
Evergreen shrub, Z 7-8 H 10-8 Shrub with bright pink flowers and gold-splashed leaves. ↕↔8ft (2.5m)

CEANOTHUS 'PERSHORE ZANZIBAR'
Evergreen shrub, Z 8-10 H 10-8 Shrub with fluffy blue flowers in late spring, and lemon-yellow and bright green foliage. ↕↔8ft (2.5m)

CORNUS ALBA 'ELEGANTISSIMA'
Shrub, Z 2-8 H 8-1 Dark red stems with gray-green leaves, edged with white, that turn pink in autumn. ↕↔10ft (3m)

CORNUS ALBA 'SPAETHII'
Shrub   page 116

CORNUS ALTERNIFOLIA 'ARGENTEA'
Shrub, Z 4-8 H 8-1 Tiers of horizontal branches, clothed with small leaves that are edged in white. ↕10ft (3m) ↔ 8ft (2.5m)

CORNUS MAS 'VARIEGATA'
Shrub, Z 5-8 H 8-4 After yellow flowers in spring the plant is bright with white-edged leaves.
‡ 8ft (2.5m) ↔ 6ft (2m)

COTONEASTER ATROPURPUREUS 'VARIEGATUS'
Shrub   page 123

ELAEAGNUS PUNGENS 'MACULATA'
Evergreen shrub   page 154

EUONYMUS FORTUNEI 'SILVER QUEEN'
Evergreen shrub   page 172

FUCHSIA MAGELLANICA VAR. *GRACILIS* 'VARIEGATA'
Shrub, Z 6-9 H 9-7 The leaves are colored in smoky pinks and grays, with small red and purple flowers.
‡ to 10ft (3m) ↔ 6–10ft (2–3m)

FUCHSIA MAGELLANICA VAR. *MOLINAE* 'SHARPITOR'
Shrub, Z 6-9 H 9-7 Pretty plant with white-edged leaves and pale pink flowers.
‡ to 10ft (3m) ↔ 6–10ft (2–3m)

HEDERA HELIX 'GLACIER'
Evergreen climber   page 210

HIBISCUS SYRIACUS 'MEEHANII'
Shrub, Z 5-9 H 9-5 Sun-loving, with purple-blue flowers; leaves with broad white edges. ‡ 10ft (3m) ↔ 6ft (2m)

HYDRANGEA MACROPHYLLA 'TRICOLOR'
Shrub, Z 6-9 H 9-5 Gray-green leaves marked with white, and pale pink flowers.
‡ 5ft (1.5m) ↔ 4ft (1.2m)

ILEX × *ALTACLERENSIS* 'LAWSONIANA'
Evergreen shrub   page 232

LIGUSTRUM LUCIDUM 'EXCELSUM SUPERBUM'
Evergreen shrub   page 264

OSMANTHUS HETEROPHYLLUS 'VARIEGATUS'
Evergreen shrub, Z 7-9 H 9-7 Hollylike leaves with broad yellow margins, and fragrant, tiny flowers in autumn.
‡ 8ft (2.5m)

PHILADELPHUS 'INNOCENCE'
Shrub Z 5-8 H 8-5 Arching shrub with creamy yellow leaves and semidouble white flowers.
‡ 10ft (3m) ↔ 6ft (2m)

PHILADELPHUS CORONARIUS 'VARIEGATUS'
Shrub   page 329

PIERIS 'FLAMING SILVER'
Evergreen shrub, Z 6-8 H 8-6 Acid-loving plant with narrow foliage, edged white, that is pink in spring.
‡ ↔ 8ft (2.5m)

PITTOSPORUM TENUIFOLIUM 'IRENE PATERSON'
Evergreen shrub, Z 9-10 H 12-9 Slow-growing shrub with white-speckled leaves.
‡ 4ft (1.2m) ↔ 2ft (60cm)

PSEUDOPANAX LESSONII 'GOLD SPLASH'
Evergreen shrub   page 360

RHAMNUS ALATERNUS 'ARGENTEOVARIEGATA'
Evergreen shrub   page 366

RHODODENDRON 'PRESIDENT ROOSEVELT'
Evergreen shrub, Z 7-9 H 9-7 Weakly branching, acid-loving shrub with gold-splashed leaves and red flowers.
‡ ↔ 6ft (2m)

SAMBUCUS NIGRA 'PULVERULENTA'
Shrub, Z 6-8 H 8-6 Slow-growing shrub for part shade with young leaves heavily splashed with white.
‡ ↔ 6ft (2m)

WEIGELA FLORIDA 'VARIEGATA'
Shrub   page 457

GOLD-LEAVED PLANTS

Gold-leaved plants bring a splash of sunshine to the garden. In contrast to plants with variegated leaves, most fully gold-leaved plants are rather prone to scorch in full sun so are best in light shade. But avoid dark shade, or the leaves may become lime green. Some plants are gold for only a part of their growth; their young, gold tips fade to green, but this contrast is still pleasing.

ACER CAPPADOCICUM 'AUREUM'
Tree, Z 6-8 H 8-6 The leaves unfurl yellow in spring, turn green in summer, then become gold in autumn.
‡50ft (15m) ↔ 30ft (10m)

ACER SHIRASAWANUM 'AUREUM'
Tree, Z 5-7 H 7-5 The bright yellow leaves turn red in autumn.
‡↔ 20ft (6m)

CALLUNA VULGARIS 'BEOLEY GOLD'
Evergreen shrub   page 82

CAREX ELATA 'AUREA'
Ornamental grass   page 91

CAREX HACHIJOENSIS 'EVERGOLD'
Ornamental grass   page 91

CHAMAECYPARIS LAWSONIANA 'MINIMA AUREA'
Conifer, Z 5-9 H 9-5 Small evergreen, conical shrub with green and gold foliage.
‡3ft (1m)

CHAMAECYPARIS LAWSONIANA 'STARDUST'
Conifer, Z 5-9 H 9-5 The foliage is yellow and fernlike.
‡50ft (15m) ↔ 25ft (8m)

CHAMAECYPARIS OBTUSA 'CRIPPSII'
Conifer, Z 4-8 H 8-1 A slow-growing tree with showy gold foliage.
‡50ft (15m) ↔ 25ft (8m)

CHOISYA TERNATA 'SUNDANCE'
Evergreen shrub   page 103

CORNUS ALBA 'AUREA'
Shrub, Z 2-8 H 8-1 Beautiful soft gold foliage that is prone to scorch on dry soils.
‡↔ 3ft (1m)

CORTADERIA SELLOANA 'AUREOLINEATA'
Ornamental grass   page 119

ERICA ARBOREA 'ALBERT'S GOLD'
Evergreen shrub, Z 9-10 H 12-9 Attractive, upright habit, with gold foliage but few flowers. ‡6ft (2m) ↔ 32in (80cm)

ERICA CARNEA 'FOXHOLLOW'
Evergreen shrub   page 159

ERICA CARNEA 'WESTWOOD YELLOW'
Evergreen shrub, Z 5-7 H 7-5 Upright habit, with yellow foliage, and pale pink flowers in winter.
‡8in (20cm) ↔ 12in (30cm)

ERICA × *STUARTII* 'IRISH LEMON'
Evergreen shrub   page 161

FAGUS SYLVATICA 'DAWYCK GOLD'
Tree, Z 5-7 H 7-5 An upright, narrow, compact tree with bright yellow leaves.
‡60ft (18m) ↔ 22ft (7m)

FRAXINUS EXCELSIOR 'JASPIDEA'
Tree, Z 5-8 H 8-5 The winter shoots are yellow, as are the leaves in spring and autumn.
‡100ft (30m) ↔ 70ft (20m)

FUCHSIA 'GENII'
Shrub   page 184

GLEDITSIA TRIACANTHOS 'SUNBURST'
Tree   page 200

HAKONECHLOA MACRA 'AUREOLA'
Ornamental grass   page 203

HEDERA HELIX 'BUTTERCUP'
Evergreen climber   page 210

HOSTA 'SUM AND SUBSTANCE'
Perennial, Z 3-8 H 8-1 Huge leaves of pale
green or gold, with pale lavender flowers.
‡ 30in (75cm) ↔ 4ft (1.2m)

HUMULUS LUPULUS 'AUREUS'
Climbing perennial   page 224

ILEX CRENATA 'GOLDEN GEM'
Evergreen shrub, Z 5-7 H 7-5 Compact,
small-leaved shrub with bright gold leaves
and sparse black berries.
‡ 3ft (1m) ↔ 4–5ft (1.2–1.5m)

IRIS PSEUDACORUS 'VARIEGATUS'
Perennial, Z 5-8 H 8-5 Pale green and
yellow striped foliage that is green by
midsummer.
‡ ↔ 3–5ft (1–1.5m)

LAURUS NOBILIS 'AUREA'
Evergreen shrub   page 256

LONICERA NITIDA
'BAGGESEN'S GOLD'
Evergreen shrub   page 273

ORIGANUM VULGARE 'AUREUM'
Perennial herb   page 306

PHYSOCARPUS OPULIFOLIUS
'DART'S GOLD'
Shrub   page 337

RIBES SANGUINEUM
'BROCKLEBANKII'
Shrub   page 375

ROBINIA PSEUDOACACIA 'FRISIA'
Tree   page 377

SAMBUCUS RACEMOSA
'SUTHERLAND GOLD'
Shrub, Z 3-7 H 7-5 Finely divided foliage
of bright yellow that is best when plants
are regularly cut back.
‡ ↔ 2m (6ft)

SPIRAEA JAPONICA 'GOLDFLAME'
Shrub   page 419

DARK AND PURPLE FOLIAGE

The primary value of dark foliage in the garden is as a foil to other plants, though many are very beautiful in their own right. An adjacent purple-leaved plant makes gold, variegated, and silver plants look even more brilliant and is the perfect foil for white, pink, yellow, and orange flowers. Most purple-leaved plants develop their best color in full sun, looking dull and greenish in shade.

ACER PLATANOIDES 'CRIMSON KING'
Tree, Z 3-7 H 7-1 The bold leaves are deep purple, brighter when young.
‡ 80ft (25m) ↔ 50ft (15m)

AEONIUM ARBOREUM 'ZWARTKOP'
Succulent subshrub, min 50°F (10°C) H 12-1 This remarkable plant has rosettes of deep purple, almost black leaves on long stems.
‡ ↔ 6ft (2m)

AJUGA REPTANS 'ATROPURPUREA'
Perennial page 40

BERBERIS THUNBERGII F. *ATROPURPUREA*
Shrub, Z 5-8 H 8-5 The deep purple foliage turns bright red in autumn before it falls, revealing the spiny stems.
‡ 6ft (2m) ↔ 8ft (2.5m)

BERBERIS THUNBERGII 'RED CHIEF'
Shrub, Z 5-8 H 8-5 Deep reddish purple foliage on an upright shrub.
‡ 5ft (1.5m) ↔ 24in (60cm)

CERCIS CANADENSIS 'FOREST PANSY'
Tree, Z 5-9 H 9-5 Pink flowers on bare twigs in early spring are followed by beautiful purple foliage.
‡ ↔ 30ft (10m)

CIMICIFUGA SIMPLEX 'BRUNETTE'
Perennial, Z 4-8 H 8-1 Coarsely divided purple foliage, and dark stems with white fluffy flowers in autumn.
‡ 3–4ft (1–1.2m) ↔ 24in (60cm)

CLEMATIS MONTANA 'TETRAROSE'
Climber page 108

CORYLUS MAXIMA 'PURPUREA'
Shrub page 121

COTINUS COGGYGRIA 'ROYAL PURPLE'
Shrub page 122

COTINUS 'GRACE'
Shrub page 123

CRYPTOTAENIA JAPONICA F. *ATROPURPUREA*
Biennial, Z 5-7 H 9-6 Three-lobed leaves on upright stems, wholly colored with purple, and tiny flowers.
‡ ↔ 24in (60cm)

ERICA CARNEA 'VIVELLII'
Evergreen shrub page 159

EUPHORBIA DULCIS 'CHAMELEON'
Perennial, Z 4-9 H 9-4 Purple foliage on bushy plants with lime green tinted bracts when in flower.
‡ ↔ 12in (30cm)

FAGUS SYLVATICA 'DAWYCK PURPLE'
Tree, Z 5-7 H 7-5 This columnar tree has deep purple leaves.
‡ 70ft (20m) ↔ 15ft (5m)

FAGUS SYLVATICA 'PURPUREA PENDULA'
Tree, Z 5-7 H 7-5 The deep purple leaves hang from pendent branches on this small, dome-shaped tree.
‡ ↔ 10ft (3m)

GERANIUM SESSILIFLORUM SUBSP.
NOVAE-ZELANDIAE 'NIGRICANS'
Perennial, Z 8-9 H 9-8 Small, mat-forming
plant with dull, bronze-purple foliage and
small white flowers.
↕ 3in (8cm) ↔ 6in (15cm)

HEBE 'MRS. WINDER'
Evergreen shrub, Z 9-10 H 12-9 A compact
shrub with dark leaves that are purple
when young, and violet-blue flowers.
↕ 3ft (1m) ↔ 4ft (1.2m)

HEDERA HELIX 'ATROPURPUREA'
Evergreen climber   page 210

HEUCHERA MICRANTHA VAR.
DIVERSIFOLIA 'PALACE PURPLE'
Perennial   page 219

OPHIOPOGON PLANISCAPUS
'NIGRESCENS'
Perennial   page 305

PENSTEMON DIGITALIS
'HUSKER RED'
Perennial, Z 2-8 H 10-7 Semi-evergreen
perennial with red and purple foliage and
pink-marked white flowers.
↕ 20–30in (50–75cm) ↔ 12in (30cm)

PHYSOCARPUS OPULIFOLIUS
'DIABLO'
Shrub, Z 3-7 H 7-1 Deep purple, almost
brown leaves and clusters of small pink
flowers.
↕ 6ft (2m) ↔ 3ft (1m)

RHEUM PALMATUM
'ATROSANGUINEUM'
Perennial, Z 5-9 H 9-5 Scarlet buds open to
reveal large, architectural, crimson-purple
leaves that mature to deep green.
↕ 6ft (2m)

SALVIA OFFICINALIS
PURPURASCENS GROUP
Evergreen shrub, Z 7-8 H 8-5 Dull purple,
fragrant leaves on a spreading plant; best
color when pruned back hard in spring.
↕ 30in (75cm) ↔ 3ft (1m)

SAMBUCUS NIGRA
'GUINCHO PURPLE'
Shrub   page 398

SEDUM TELEPHIUM SUBSP.
MAXIMUM 'ATROPURPUREUM'
Perennial   page 409

TRADESCANTIA PALLIDA
'PURPUREA'
Perennial, min 50°F (10°C) H 12-1 This
sprawling plant has rich purple leaves
and small pink flowers.
↕ 8in (20cm) ↔ 16in (40cm)

VIBURNUM SARGENTII 'ONONDAGA'
Shrub, Z 4-7 H 7-1 Upright-growing shrub
with purple leaves that turn red in autumn,
and pale pink and white flowers.
↕ 6ft (2m)

VIOLA RIVINIANA 'PURPUREA'
Perennial, Z 5-8 H 8-5 Low-growing plant
with small purple leaves and flowers.
Seeds profusely.
↕ 4–8in (10–20cm) ↔ 8–16cm (20–40cm)

VITIS VINIFERA 'PURPUREA'
Climber   page 456

WEIGELA FLORIDA
'FOLIIS PURPUREIS'
Shrub   page 457

SILVER FOLIAGE

Most plants that have silver leaves have adapted to hot, sunny climates, and these are plants for full sun in the garden. They are also adapted to low rainfall in many cases, so they can form the basis of a dry garden or gravel garden. Their color makes them ideal to associate with pink and white flowers and with purple foliage. In addition, many have fragrant leaves.

ACACIA BAILEYANA
Shrub, Z 10-11 H 12-10 The foliage is less fine than *A. dealbata* but is steely gray, and the flowers are bright yellow.
‡ 15–25ft (5–8m) ↔ 10–20ft (3–6m)

ACCA SELLOWIANA
Evergreen shrub, Z 8-10 H 12-8 Green leaves with silver reverses; flowers with fleshy red and white, edible petals.
‡ 6ft (2m) ↔ 8ft (2.5m)

ANAPHALIS TRIPLINERVIS
Perennial, Z 3-8 H 8-1 Clump-forming plant with silver-gray leaves, and white flowers in late summer.
‡ 32–36in (80–90cm) ↔ 18–24in (45–60cm)

ANAPHALIS TRIPLINERVIS 'SOMMERSCHNEE'
Perennial   page 44

ANTENNARIA MICROPHYLLA
Perennial   page 49

ANTHEMIS PUNCTATA SUBSP. *CUPANIANA*
Perennial   page 49

ARTEMISIA ABSINTHIUM 'LAMBROOK SILVER'
Perennial   page 55

ARTEMISIA ALBA 'CANESCENS'
Perennial, Z 4-8 H 8-1 Very finely divided gray leaves that form a feathery mass.
‡ 18in (45cm) ↔ 12in (30cm)

ARTEMISIA LUDOVICIANA 'SILVER QUEEN'
Perennial   page 55

ARTEMISIA PONTICA
Evergreen perennial, Z 4-8 H 8-1 A creeping, invasive perennial that has masses of upright stems with feathery leaves that form a mounded clump, then it spreads.
‡ 16–32in (40–80cm) ↔ indefinite

ATRIPLEX HALIMUS
Shrub, Z 7-9 H 9-7 Wind-tolerant, fast-growing plant with small, shiny, silvery leaves. ‡ 6ft (2m) ↔ 8ft (2.5m)

BRACHYGLOTTIS 'SUNSHINE'
Evergreen shrub   page 75

CEDRUS ATLANTICA F. *GLAUCA*
Conifer, Z 6-9 H 9-6 The blue Atlas cedar forms an imposing specimen tree with blue-gray foliage.
‡ 130ft (40m) ↔ 30ft (10m)

CONVOLVULUS CNEORUM
Evergreen shrub   page 114

CYTISUS BATTANDIERI
Shrub   page 135

DIANTHUS 'BECKY ROBINSON'
Perennial, Z 5-9 H 9-5 Hummocks of gray foliage and ruby-red and pink, laced flowers.
‡ 15in (38cm) ↔ indefinite

DIANTHUS 'HAYTOR WHITE'
Perennial   page 145

ECHEVERIA AGAVOIDES
Succulent   page 153

ELAEAGNUS 'QUICKSILVER'
Evergreen shrub   page 155

ERICA TETRALIX 'ALBA MOLLIS'
Evergreen shrub   page 161

EUCALYPTUS GUNNII
Evergreen tree   page 169

HALIMIUM 'SUSAN'
Evergreen shrub   page 205

HEBE 'RED EDGE'
Evergreen shrub, Z 9-10 H 10-9 Spreading, low shrub with gray leaves edged with red.
‡ 18in (45cm) ↔ 24in (60cm)

HEBE PIMELEOIDES 'QUICKSILVER'
Evergreen shrub, Z 9-10 H 10-9 Ground-hugging shrub with tiny silver leaves and pale lilac flowers.
‡ 12in (30cm) ↔ 24in (60cm)

HEBE PINGUIFOLIA 'PAGEI'
Evergreen shrub   page 208

HELIANTHEMUM 'WISLEY PRIMROSE'
Evergreen shrub   page 213

HELICHRYSUM SPLENDIDUM
Perennial   page 215

HELICTOTRICHON SEMPERVIRENS
Ornamental grass, Z 4-9 H 9-1 A tufted perennial forming a mound of gray-blue leaves, with taller flower stems in early summer. ‡ 4½ft (1.4m) ↔ 2ft (60cm)

PYRUS SALICIFOLIA 'PENDULA'
Tree   page 364

ROMNEYA COULTERI
Perennial, Z 7-8 H 8-7 Vigorous, suckering plant with coarsely toothed silver leaves and white, yellow-centered flowers.
‡ 6ft (2m) ↔ indefinite

SALIX 'BOYDII'
Shrub   page 391

SALIX LANATA
Shrub   page 393

SALVIA ARGENTEA
Perennial   page 394

SANTOLINA CHAMAECYPARISSUS
Evergreen shrub   page 398

SEDUM SPATHULIFOLIUM 'CAPE BLANCO'
Perennial   page 407

SENECIO CINERARIA 'SILVER DUST'
Evergreen shrub   page 411

SENECIO CINERARIA 'WHITE DIAMOND'
Evergreen shrub H 12-8 The almost white leaves resemble oak leaves in shape.
‡ 12–16in (30–40cm) ↔ 12in (30cm)

SENECIO VIRAVIRA
Shrub, Z 8-10 H 12-8 The finely divided leaves are carried on sprawling stems that produce creamy, pompon flowers.
‡ 24in (60cm) ↔ 3ft (1m)

TREES, SHRUBS, AND PERENNIALS FOR SPRING

Spring is a frantic time in the garden, and at times it seems that every plant is trying to flower. The earliest flowers are demure and adapted to survive any snows, sleet, and wind, but by April, flowers are bigger and bolder, and the yellows, blues, and white of spring bulbs are joined by masses of pink cherry blossoms, showy magnolias, rhododendrons, clematis, and wisteria.

ACER PSEUDOPLATANUS
'BRILLIANTISSIMUM'
Tree page 35

BERGENIA PURPURASCENS
Perennial, Z 3-8 H 8-1 The bold, leathery leaves turn red in cold weather; clusters of bright, purplish flowers open in spring.
‡ 18in (45cm) ↔ 12in (30cm)

CALTHA PALUSTRIS
Perennial page 83

CAMELLIA × *WILLIAMSII* CULTIVARS
Shrubs pages 86–87

CHAENOMELES SPECIOSA
'MOERLOOSEI'
Shrub page 97

CLEMATIS ALPINA
Climber, Z 6-9 H 9-6 The blue, bell-shaped flowers have white centers and are followed by fluffy seedheads.
‡ 6–10ft (2–3m)

CLEMATIS ALPINA 'FRANCES RIVIS'
Climber, Z 6-9 H 9-6 Bell-shaped flowers with four twisted, deep blue petals.
‡ 6–10ft (2–3m)

CLEMATIS MACROPETALA
'MARKHAM'S PINK'
Climber page 108

CLEMATIS MONTANA VAR. *RUBENS*
Climber page 108

CORYDALIS SOLIDA
Bulbous perennial, Z 5-7 H 7-5 Tubular pink flowers are held above feathery, gray foliage. ‡ 10in (25cm) ↔ 8in (20cm)

CORYLOPSIS PAUCIFLORA
Shrub page 120

DAPHNE TANGUTICA
Evergreen shrub, Z 7-9 H 9-7 The tips of shoots are studded with fragrant, pink and white flowers in late spring.
‡ ↔ 3ft (1m)

DICENTRA 'LUXURIANT'
Perennial, Z 4-8 H 8-1 Deeply lobed leaves and clusters of red flowers over a long season. ‡ 12in (30cm) ↔ 18in (45cm)

DODECATHEON MEADIA
Perennial, Z 4-8 H 8-1 A clump-forming plant with clusters of magenta-pink flowers that resemble cyclamen.
‡ 16in (40cm) ↔ 10in (25cm)

EPIMEDIUM × *RUBRUM*
Perennial page 156

EPIMEDIUM × *VERSICOLOR*
'SULPHUREUM'
Perennial, Z 5-9 H 9-5 Evergreen, clump-forming plant with divided leaves and pretty, pale yellow flowers.
‡ ↔ 12in (30cm)

EUPHORBIA × *MARTINII*
Evergreen subshrub page 174

EUPHORBIA POLYCHROMA
Perennial page 175

FORSYTHIA × *INTERMEDIA*
'LYNWOOD'
Shrub page 180

FOTHERGILLA MAJOR
Shrub page 181

HEPATICA NOBILIS
Perennial   page **219**

MAGNOLIA CAMPBELLII 'CHARLES RAFFILL'
Shrub   page **282**

MAGNOLIA 'ELIZABETH'
Shrub   page **282**

MAGNOLIA × LOEBNERI 'MERRILL'
Shrub   page **282**

MAGNOLIA × SOULANGEANA 'LENNEI'
Tree, Z 5-9 H 9-5 Beautiful tree of spreading habit with large, deep purple flowers.
‡↔ 20ft (6m)

MAGNOLIA STELLATA
Shrub or small tree   page **283**

MALUS FLORIBUNDA
Tree   page **286**

PIERIS JAPONICA 'MOUNTAIN FIRE'
Evergreen shrub, Z 6-8 H 8-6 Acid-loving shrub with white flowers and red new growth that becomes bronze, then green.
‡12ft (4m) ↔ 10ft (3m)

PRIMULA VERIS
Perennial   page **353**

PRIMULA VIALII
Perennial, Z 5-8 H 8-5 Short-lived, with dense heads of lilac flowers and red buds.
‡12–24in (30–60cm) ↔ 12in (30cm)

PRUNUS AVIUM 'PLENA'
Tree   page **358**

PRUNUS GLANDULOSA 'ALBA PLENA'
Shrub   page **355**

PRUNUS 'KANZAN'
Tree   page **358**

PRUNUS PADUS 'COLORATA'
Tree   page **358**

PRUNUS PADUS 'WATERERI'
Tree   page **358**

PRUNUS 'PANDORA'
Tree   page **358**

PRUNUS 'PINK PERFECTION'
Tree   page **359**

PRUNUS 'SHIROFUGEN'
Tree   page **359**

PRUNUS 'SHŌGETSU'
Tree   page **359**

PRUNUS 'SPIRE'
Tree   page **359**

PRUNUS × SUBHIRTELLA 'AUTUMNALIS ROSEA'
Tree   page **359**

PRUNUS 'UKON'
Tree   page **359**

PRUNUS × YEDOENSIS
Tree   page **359**

PULMONARIA RUBRA
Perennial, Z 5-8 H 8-5 Unspotted leaves and coral-red flowers.
‡16in (40cm) ↔ 3ft (1m)

RHODODENDRON SPECIES AND CULTIVARS
Shrubs   pages **368–374**

SAXIFRAGA 'TUMBLING WATERS'
Alpine, Z 6-7 H 7-6 Rosettes of silvery green leaves produce tall, arching stems bearing hundreds of tiny white flowers.
‡18in (45cm) ↔ 12in (30cm)

VIOLA 'MAGGIE MOTT'
Perennial, Z 5-8 H 8-5 Dainty blue and white flowers on bushy plants.
‡6in (15cm) ↔ 10in (25cm)

WISTERIA FLORIBUNDA 'MACROBOTRYS'
Climber   page **458**

WISTERIA FLORIBUNDA 'ROSEA'
Climber, Z 5-9 H 9-5 Long racemes of pale pink flowers cascade from this vigorous plant.
‡28ft (9m)

PLANTS FOR SUMMER COLOR

In gardens the summer months are often dominated by annuals, but there are many bright-flowered perennials, too, at their best. There are fewer shrubs in flower in midsummer than in spring, but an important exception is the rose, without which gardens would be much plainer. There are roses for every part of the garden, from climbers to groundcover.

ANCHUSA AZUREA
'LODDON ROYALIST'
Perennial   page **45**

AQUILEGIA VULGARIS
'NORA BARLOW'
Perennial   page **51**

BUDDLEJA DAVIDII 'DARTMOOR'
Shrub, Z 6-9 H 9-5 The narrow leaves are deeply toothed, and the large flower clusters are a richreddish purple.
‡10ft (3m) ↔ 15ft (5m)

BUDDLEJA GLOBOSA
Shrub   page **78**

CAMPANULA LACTIFLORA
'LODDON ANNA'
Perennial   page **89**

CLEMATIS 'BEES' JUBILEE'
Climber, Z 4-9 H 9-1 Large pink flowers with a dark band through each petal, on a compact plant.
‡8ft (2.5m)

CLEMATIS × *DURANDII*
Perennial, Z 6-9 H 9-5 Nonclimbing hybrid that sprawls through other plants, with large, blue flowers.
‡3–6ft (1–2m)

CLEMATIS 'GIPSY QUEEN'
Climber, Z 4-9 H 9-1 Velvety purple flowers with red anthers, throughout summer.
‡10ft (3m)

CLEMATIS 'PERLE D'AZUR'
Climber   page **111**

DEUTZIA × *HYBRIDA* 'MONT ROSE'
Shrub   page **144**

DICENTRA 'LANGTREES'
Perennial, Z 4-8 H 8-4 Pale, pearly white flowers are held on glossy stems above the feathery gray foliage.
‡12in (30cm) ↔ 18in (45cm)

DIGITALIS LANATA
Perennial, Z 4-9 H 9-1 Leafy stems with densely packed, small cream or fawn flowers. ‡24in (60cm) ↔ 12in (30cm)

ERICA CINEREA 'VELVET NIGHT'
Evergreen shrub, Z 6-8 H 8-6 Exceptionally dark foliage is highlighted by deep purple flowers.
‡24in (60cm) ↔ 32in (80cm)

ERICA VAGANS 'LYONESSE'
Evergreen shrub   page **161**

ERICA VAGANS 'MRS D. F. MAXWELL'
Evergreen shrub   page **161**

EUPHORBIA SCHILLINGII
Perennial   page **175**

FUCHSIA HARDY TYPES
Shrubs   page **184**

FUCHSIA 'PHYLLIS'
Shrub, Z 8-10 H 12-8 The semidouble cerise flowers are carried on an upright plant. ‡3–5ft (1–1.5m) ↔ 30–36in (75–90cm)

GERANIUMS, HARDY, LARGE
Perennials   pages **196–197**

HEBE 'GREAT ORME'
Evergreen shrub   page **207**

HEMEROCALLIS CULTIVARS
Perennials page **218**

HYDRANGEA SERRATA 'BLUEBIRD'
Shrub page **230**

HYPERICUM 'HIDCOTE'
Shrub page **231**

IRIS LAEVIGATA
Perennial page **238**

JASMINUM HUMILE 'REVOLUTUM'
Shrub, Z 7-9 H 9-7 Fragrant, bright yellow flowers are set against divided foliage for most of summer.
‡ 8ft (2.5m) ↔ 10ft (3m)

LATHYRUS LATIFOLIUS
'WHITE PEARL'
Climber, Z 5-9 H 9-5 This herbaceous perennial has white, scentless flowers.
‡ 6ft (2m)

OENOTHERA FRUTICOSA
'FYRVERKERI'
Perennial page **302**

PENSTEMON CULTIVARS
Perennials pages **322–323**

PHOTINIA × *FRASERI* 'RED ROBIN'
Evergreen shrub page **335**

PHYGELIUS AEQUALIS 'YELLOW
TRUMPET'
Evergreen shrub page **335**

PLATYCODON GRANDIFLORUS
Perennial page **344**

POTENTILLA 'GIBSON'S SCARLET'
Perennial page **349**

ROSA 'JUST JOEY'
Hybrid tea rose page **379**

ROSA 'MANY HAPPY RETURNS'
Floribunda rose page **379**

ROSA 'MOUNTBATTEN'
Floribunda rose page **379**

ROSA 'SWEET DREAM'
Floribunda rose, Z 5-9 H 9-1 Dense clusters of peach-pink, double flowers.
‡ 16in (40cm) ↔ 24in (60cm)

ROSA 'TEQUILA SUNRISE'
Hybrid tea rose Z 5-9 H 9-1 Bright yellow flowers heavily edged with scarlet.
‡ 30in (75cm) ↔ 24in (60cm)

ROSES, RAMBLER
Cimbers pages **382–3**

SALVIA × *SYLVESTRIS* 'MAINACHT'
Perennial page **397**

THALICTRUM DELAVAYI
'HEWITT'S DOUBLE'
Perennial page **428**

TRADESCANTIA × *ANDERSONIANA*
'J. C. WEUGELIN'
Perennial page **435**

TRADESCANTIA × *ANDERSONIANA*
'OSPREY'
Perennial page **436**

Plants for Autumn Color

Autumn is a season of great change in the garden, and although many annuals and perennials continue their summer display, it is the colors of leaves and fruits (see also pp.502–3) that most capture the imagination. This should be the most spectacular time of all in the garden, as borders erupt in fiery orange and red shades before the somber displays of winter.

ACER PALMATUM 'BLOODGOOD'
Small tree   page 34

ACER PALMATUM 'GARNET'
Shrub   page 34

ACER PALMATUM 'OSAKAZUKI'
Shrub or small tree   page 34

ACER GROSSERI VAR. *HERSII*
Tree   page 32

AMELANCHIER LAMARCKII
Large shrub   page 44

ANEMONE HUPEHENSIS
'HADSPEN ABUNDANCE'
Perennial   page 47

ANEMONE HUPEHENSIS
'SEPTEMBER CHARM'
Perennial, Z 4-8 H 8-1 Pale pink flowers on neat growth.
‡ 24–36in (60–90cm) ↔ 16in (40cm)

ASTER AMELLUS 'KING GEORGE'
Perennial   page 58

ASTER ERICOIDES 'PINK CLOUD'
Perennial, Z 5-8 H 8-3 Bushy plants are covered with small pink flowers in autumn.
‡ 3ft (1m) ↔ 12in (30cm)

ASTER LATERIFOLIUS 'HORIZONTALIS'
Perennial   page 59

BERBERIS WILSONIAE
Shrub   page 71

CEANOTHUS × *DELILEANUS*
'GLOIRE DE VERSAILLES'
Shrub   page 95

CLEMATIS 'ALBA LUXURIANS'
Climber   page 110

CLEMATIS 'DUCHESS OF ALBANY'
Climber   page 110

CLEMATIS × *TRITERNATA*
'RUBROMARGINATA'
Climber, Z 6-8 H 9-6 Strong shoots bear masses of small, cross-shaped deep pink and white flowers.
‡ 15ft (5m)

CORNUS KOUSA VAR. *CHINENSIS*
Tree   page 117

CORTADERIA SELLOANA
'SUNNINGDALE SILVER'
Ornamental grass   page 119

COTONEASTER MICROPHYLLUS
Evergreen shrub, Z 6-8 H 8-6 An arching shrub with pinkish red berries in autumn.
‡ 3ft (1m) ↔ 5ft (1.5m)

DAHLIA CULTIVARS
Perennials   page 119

EUCRYPHIA × *NYMANSENSIS*
'NYMANSAY'
Evergreen tree   page 170

EUONYMUS ALATUS
Shrub   page 170

EUONYMUS EUROPAEUS
'RED CASCADE'
Shrub   page 171

FUCHSIA 'MRS. POPPLE'
Shrub   page 184

GENTIANA SEPTEMFIDA
Perennial   page 193

GINKGO BILOBA
Tree, Z 5-9 H 9-5 This deciduous conifer relative has broad leaves that turn bright yellow before they drop in autumn.
‡ to 100ft (30m) ↔ 25ft (8m)

HELIANTHUS 'LODDON GOLD'
Perennial   page 213

HIBISCUS SYRIACUS 'OISEAU BLEU'
Shrub   page 220

INDIGOFERA AMBLYANTHA
Shrub, Z 7-9 H 9-7 Slender stems bear feathery leaves and upright stems of small pink flowers.
‡ 6ft (2m) ↔ 8ft (2.5m)

LIRIODENDRON TULIPIFERA
Tree   page 270

LIRIOPE MUSCARI
Perennial   page 271

MALUS 'JOHN DOWNIE'
Tree   page 286

NANDINA DOMESTICA
Shrub   page 295

PARTHENOCISSUS TRICUSPIDATA
Climber   page 317

PHYGELIUS CAPENSIS
Shrub, Z 8-9 H 9-8 Upright stems bear large, loose clusters of tubular orange flowers.
‡ 4ft (1.2m) ↔ 5ft (1.5m)

PRUNUS SARGENTII
Tree   page 359

PRUNUS × SUBHIRTELLA 'AUTUMNALIS ROSEA'
Tree   page 359

PSEUDOLARIX AMABILIS
Tree, Z 5-9 H 9-5 A deciduous conifer that is grown for its attractive conical shape and golden autumn color.
‡ 50–70ft (15–20m) ↔ 20–40ft (6–12m)

RHUS TYPHINA 'DISSECTA'
Shrub   page 375

RUDBECKIA FULGIDA VAR. *DEAMII*
Perennial, Z 4-9 H 9-1 Daisylike flowers of orange, with black centers.
‡ 24in (60cm) ↔ 18in (45cm)

RUDBECKIA 'GOLDQUELLE'
Perennial   page 390

SALVIA ULIGINOSA
Perennial   page 397

SCHIZOSTYLIS COCCINEA 'MAJOR'
Perennial   page 404

SEDUM 'RUBY GLOW'
Perennial   page 406

SEDUM SPECTABILE 'ICEBERG'
Perennial, Z 4-9 H 9-5 Fleshy, pale-leaved plant with pure white flowers.
‡ 12–18in (30–45cm) ↔ 14in (35cm)

SORBUS REDUCTA
Shrub   page 417

SORBUS VILMORINII
Shrub or small tree   page 418

TRICYRTIS FORMOSANA
Perennial, Z 6-9 H 9-6 Erect stems with glossy leaves and pale pink, starry flowers with darker spots.
‡ 32in (80cm) ↔ 18in (45cm)

VIBURNUM PLICATUM 'MARIESII'
Shrub   page 452

VITIS COIGNETIAE
Climber   page 456

PLANTS FOR WINTER INTEREST

Gardeners who think that nothing of interest happens in gardens in winter miss out on some of the most exciting plants of all. Delicate scents and brightly colored flowers may appear in all but the coldest climates. Many grow happily in shady positions: this is a good place to plant a winter garden, preferably by a door or where it can be seen from a window.

ACER GRISEUM
Tree   page **32**

ASPLENIUM SCOLOPENDRIUM
CRISTATUM GROUP
Evergreen fern, Z 6-8 H 8-6 Erect, leathery fronds with broadened, irregular tips, which look bold in winter.
‡ 18in (45cm) ↔ 24in (60cm)

AUCUBA JAPONICA 'CROTONIFOLIA'
Evergreen shrub   page **64**

BERGENIA PURPURASCENS
'BALLAWLEY'
Perennial   page **72**

CALLUNA VULGARIS 'ROBERT
CHAPMAN'
Evergreen shrub   page **82**

CHAMAECYPARIS OBTUSA
'NANA AUREA'
Conifer, Z 4-8 H 8-1 This dwarf conifer is rounded with a flat top and yellow foliage.
‡ 6ft (2m)

CHIMONANTHUS PRAECOX
'GRANDIFLORUS'
Shrub   page **102**

CLEMATIS CIRRHOSA VAR.
BALEARICA
Climber, Z 7-9 H 9-7 This evergreen climber has pale cream, bell-shaped, fragrant flowers.
‡ 2.5-3m (8-10ft)

CORNUS ALBA 'SIBIRICA'
Shrub   page **115**

CORNUS MAS
Shrub or small tree   page **117**

CORNUS MAS 'AUREA'
Shrub to small tree, Z 5-8 H 8-5 Masses of tiny yellow flowers in late winter followed by chartreuse spring foliage that matures to green in summer.
‡↔ 15ft (5m)

CYCLAMEN COUM PEWTER GROUP
Hardy bulb   page **134**

DAPHNE BHOLUA 'GURKHA'
Shrub   page **140**

ERICA CARNEA 'ANN SPARKES'
Evergreen shrub   page **159**

ERICA CARNEA 'PINK SPANGLES'
Evergreen shrub, Z 5-7 H 8-6 This bright heath has pink flowers that are pink and white as they first open.
‡ 6in (15cm) ↔ 18in (45cm)

ERICA CARNEA 'VIVELLII'
Evergreen shrub   page **159**

ERICA × *DARLEYENSIS* 'FURZEY'
Evergreen shrub, Z 7-8 H 8-7 This small shrub has dark foliage and deep pink flowers. ‡ 12in (30cm) ↔ 24in (60cm)

ERICA × *DARLEYENSIS* 'J. W. PORTER'
Evergreen shrub, Z 7-8 H 8-7 Deep green foliage tipped with cream and red in spring, and deep pink flowers.
‡ 12in (30cm) ↔ 24in (60cm)

HAMAMELIS × *INTERMEDIA*
'ARNOLD PROMISE'
Shrub   page **205**

HAMAMELIS × INTERMEDIA 'JELENA'
Shrub, Z 5-9 H 9-5 Leaves turn red before
falling in autumn, then spidery, bronze-
orange flowers appear in late winter.
‡↔ 12ft (4m)

HELLEBORUS ARGUTIFOLIUS
Perennial page **216**

HELLEBORUS FOETIDUS
Perennial page **217**

HELLEBORUS NIGER
Perennial page **217**

HELLEBORUS × NIGERCORS
Perennial, Z 6-9 H 9-6 Clump-forming plant
with short, branched stems of white
flowers flushed green and pink.
‡ 30cm (12in) ↔ 1m (3ft)

ILEX AQUIFOLIUM 'GOLDEN
MILKBOY'
Holly page **233**

ILEX × MESERVEAE 'BLUE PRINCESS'
Holly page **234**

IRIS UNGUICULARIS
Perennial page **243**

JUNIPERUS COMMUNIS 'REPANDA'
Conifer, Z 2-6 H 6-1 The foliage of this
ground-hugging conifer is bronze in
winter. ‡ 8in (20cm) ↔ 36in (1m)

LONICERA × PURPUSII
'WINTER BEAUTY'
Shrub page **275**

MAHONIA × MEDIA
'LIONEL FORTESCUE'
Evergreen shrub, Z 8-9 H 9-8 Divided
leaves with leaflets like holly leaves and
upright spikes of bright yellow flowers.
‡ 15ft (5m) ↔ 12ft (4m)

MAHONIA × MEDIA 'WINTER SUN'
Evergreen shrub, Z 8-9 H 9-8 The appeal
of this prickly, upright shrub lies in its
scented yellow winter flowers.
‡ 15ft (5m) ↔ 12ft (4m)

RUBUS THIBETANUS
Shrub page **389**

SALIX BABYLONICA VAR. *PEKINENSIS*
'TORTUOSA'
Tree page **391**

SALIX HASTATA 'WEHRHAHNII'
Shrub page **392**

SKIMMIA JAPONICA 'NYMANS'
Evergreen shrub, Z 7-9 H 9-7 This
spreading shrub is female and bears
showy clusters of red berries.
‡ 3ft (1m) ↔ 6ft (2m)

STACHYURUS PRAECOX
Shrub page **421**

SYMPHORICARPUS × DOORENBOSII
'WHITE HEDGE'
Shrub, Z 4-7 H 7-4 Suckering shrub of
upright habit with white berries.
‡ 6ft (2m) ↔ indefinite

VIBURNUM × BODNANTENSE 'DAWN'
Shrub page **450**

VIBURNUM FARRERI
Shrub page **451**

VIBURNUM TINUS 'EVE PRICE'
Evergreen shrub page **453**

BERRYING PLANTS

If birds do not enjoy the feast as soon as they ripen, berries can enhance the garden for many months. Red berries are most common, but there are black, white, yellow, pink, blue, and even purple berries to be included in almost any garden. Pale berries look best against a dark background such as an evergreen hedge, and red berries are attractive against a clear blue sky.

ACTAEA ALBA
Perennial, Z 4-9 H 9-1 Clump-former with divided leaves and fluffy flowers followed by pearly white berries with black eyes.
↕ 36in (90cm) ↔ 18–24in (45–60cm)

ARBUTUS UNEDO
'RUBRA'
Evergreen tree, Z 7-9 H 9-7 The pink flowers and red, globular fruits are both at their best in autumn.
↕↔ 25ft (8m)

ARUM ITALICUM 'MARMORATUM'
Perennial, Z 6-9 H 9-6 Evergreen, marbled foliage and spikes of red berries in autumn when the leaves die down.
↕ 12in (30cm) ↔ 6in (15cm)

BERBERIS DICTYOPHYLLA
Shrub, Z 6-9 H 9-6 This deciduous shrub is at its best in winter when the white shoots are studded with red berries.
↕ 6ft (2m) ↔ 5ft (1.5m)

BERBERIS × STENOPHYLLA
'CORALLINA COMPACTA'
Evergreen shrub   page 69

BERBERIS VERRUCULOSA
Evergreen shrub   page 71

CALLICARPA BODINIERI VAR.
GIRALDII 'PROFUSION'
Shrub   page 80

CELASTRUS ORBICULATUS
Climber, Z 4-8 H 8-1 Strong-growing climber with yellow autumn color and yellow fruits opening to reveal red seeds.
↕ 45ft (14m)

CLERODENDRON TRICHOTOMUM
VAR. *FARGESII*
Shrub, Z 7-9 H 9-7 Fast-growing plant with fragrant white flowers and turquoise berries set against red calyces.
↕↔ 15ft (5m)

CORIARIA TERMINALIS VAR.
XANTHOCARPA
Shrub, Z 9-10 H 12-9 Arching subshrub with small leaves and clusters of translucent yellow berries.
↕ 3ft (1m) ↔ 6ft (2m)

CORNUS 'NORMAN HADDEN'
Evergreen tree, Z 6-8 H 8-6 Some leaves turn yellow and drop each autumn, when the cream and pink flowers are followed by large red fruits.
↕↔ 25ft (8m)

COTONEASTER CONSPICUUS
'DECORUS'
Evergreen shrub   page 124

COTONEASTER 'ROTHSCHILDIANUS'
Evergreen shrub, Z 6-8 H 8-6 An arching shrub with golden yellow berries in autumn after white flowers in summer.
↕↔ 15ft (5m)

EUONYMUS PLANIPES
Shrub, Z 5-9 H 9-5 The foliage is bright red in autumn and falls to reveal red capsules containing orange seeds.
↕↔ 10ft (3m)

GAULTHERIA MUCRONATA
'WINTERTIME'
Evergreen shrub   page 190

HIPPOPHAE RHAMNOIDES
Shrub   page **221**

ILEX AQUIFOLIUM 'J. C. VAN TOL'
Evergreen shrub   page **233**

ILEX × MESERVEAE 'BLUE ANGEL'
Evergreen shrub, Z 5-9 H 9-5 Compact,
slow-growing shrub with glossy, dark,
bluish green leaves and red berries.
↕ 12ft (4m) ↔ 6ft (2m)

ILEX VERTICILLATA 'WINTER RED'
Shrub, Z 5-8 H 8-5 Deciduous shrub with
white flowers in spring and masses of
small red berries in winter.
↕ 8–10ft (2.5–3m) ↔ 10ft (3m)

LEYCESTERIA FORMOSA
Shrub, Z 9-10 H 12-9 Tall, arching stems
tipped with white flowers within maroon
bracts, followed by purple berries.
↕ ↔ 6ft (2m)

LONICERA NITIDA 'BAGGESEN'S
GOLD'
Evergreen shrub   page **273**

LONICERA PERICLYMENUM
'GRAHAM THOMAS'
Climber   page **274**

PHYSALIS ALKEKENGI
Perennial, Z 5-8 H 8-5 Spreading plant with
upright stems; orange lanterns containing
orange berries follow white flowers.
↕ 24–30in (60–75cm) ↔ 36in (90cm)

PYRACANTHA 'CADROU'
Evergreen shrub, Z 7-8 H 9-6 Spiny shrub
with white flowers and red berries.
↕ ↔ 6ft (2m)

ROSA 'FRU DAGMAR HASTRUP'
Shrub rose, Z 2-9 H 9-1 Rugosa rose
with large, single pink flowers and
large red hips.
↕ 1m (3ft) ↔ 1.2m (4ft)

ROSA MOYESII 'GERANIUM'
Shrub rose, Z 4-9 H 9-1 Arching, prickly
stems with neat red flowers and large,
long red hips.
↕ 8ft (2.5m) ↔ 5ft (1.5m)

ROSA 'SCHARLACHGLUT'
Shrub rose, Z 4-9 H 9-1 Vigorous long-
stemmed rose that can be trained as a
climber, with showy scarlet flowers and
scarlet hips.
↕ 10ft (3m) ↔ 6ft (2m)

SAMBUCUS RACEMOSA
'PLUMOSA AUREA'
Shrub, Z 3-7 H 7-1 Divided yellow leaves in
summer and clusters of small, red berries.
↕ ↔ 10ft (3m)

SKIMMIA JAPONICA 'FRUCTU ALBO'
Evergreen shrub, Z 7-9 H 9-7 Neat
evergreen with white flowers and
bright white fruits.
↕ 24in (60cm) ↔ 3ft (1m)

SORBUS ARIA 'LUTESCENS'
Tree   page **416**

SORBUS HUPEHENSIS VAR. *OBTUSA*
Tree   page **416**

TROPAEOLUM SPECIOSUM
Perennial climber   page **439**

VIBURNUM DAVIDII
Evergreen shrub   page **451**

VIBURNUM OPULUS
'XANTHOCARPUM'
Shrub   page **452**

CONIFERS FOR SMALL GARDENS

Conifers provide an amazing range of shapes, sizes, colors, and textures. They can be used to give upright accents in borders, as dense screens, and for evergreen groundcover. They tolerate a wide range of soils but most, except yew, need sun. Many change color with the seasons and are especially attractive in late spring when new growth contrasts with older foliage.

ABIES BALSAMEA F. *HUDSONIA*
Conifer, Z 3-6 H 6-1 This very dwarf form grows into an irregularly rounded shrub, but it does not bear cones.
‡ 24in (60cm) ↔ 3ft (1m)

ABIES KOREANA 'SILBERLOCKE'
Conifer, Z 5-6 H 6-5 Attractive twisted foliage that reveals the silver reverse to the needles, plus attractive cones.
‡ 30ft (10m) ↔ 20ft (6m)

ABIES LASIOCARPA 'COMPACTA'
Conifer, Z 5-6 H 6-5 Slow-growing conical tree with blue-gray leaves.
‡ 10–15ft (3–5m) ↔ 6–10ft (2–3m)

ABIES NORDMANNIANA 'GOLDEN SPREADER'
Conifer, Z 4-6 H 6-4 Dwarf, slow-growing plant with bright gold foliage.
‡ 3ft (1m) ↔ 5ft (1.5m)

CHAMAECYPARIS LAWSONIANA 'CHILWORTH SILVER'
Conifer, Z 5-9 H 9-5 Slow-growing conical shrub with silver-gray foliage.
‡ 5ft (1.5m)

CHAMAECYPARIS LAWSONIANA 'ELLWOOD'S GOLD'
Conifer page **99**

CHAMAECYPARIS OBTUSA 'NANA GRACILIS'
Conifer page **100**

CHAMAECYPARIS OBTUSA 'TETRAGONA AUREA'
Conifer page **101**

CRYPTOMERIA JAPONICA 'ELEGANS COMPACTA'
Conifer page **133**

CRYPTOMERIA JAPONICA 'VILMORINIANA'
Conifer, Z 6-9 H 9-6 Forms a tight ball of stiff foliage that is green in summer and bronze in winter.
‡ ↔ 18in (45cm)

JUNIPERUS CHINENSIS 'BLAAUW'
Conifer, Z 3-9 H 9-1 Forms a dense, upright shrub with blue-gray leaves.
‡ 4ft (1.2m) ↔ 3ft (1m)

JUNIPERUS CHINENSIS 'OBELISK'
Conifer, Z 3-9 H 9-1 Grows slowly into an interesting, upright shape with bluish green leaves.
‡ 8ft (2.5m) ↔ 24in (60cm)

JUNIPERUS COMMUNIS 'COMPRESSA'
Conifer page **247**

JUNIPERUS × *PFITZERIANA* 'PFITZERIANA'
Conifer page **247**

JUNIPERUS PROCUMBENS 'NANA'
Conifer page **248**

JUNIPERUS SCOPULORUM 'BLUE HEAVEN'
Conifer, Z 4-7 H 7-1 Neat in habit, with blue leaves and a conical shape.
‡ 6ft (2m) ↔ 24in (60cm)

JUNIPERUS SQUAMATA 'BLUE STAR'
Conifer page **248**

JUNIPERUS SQUAMATA 'HOLGER'
Conifer, Z 5-8 H 8-5 Spreading evergreen
with bluish foliage that contrasts with the
yellowish new growth.
↕ ↔ 6ft (2m)

MICROBIOTA DECUSSATA
Conifer, Z 3-7 H 7-1 Spreading conifer with
fine foliage that turns bronze in winter.
↕ 3ft (1m) ↔ indefinite

PICEA ABIES 'NIDIFORMIS'
Conifer, Z 3-8 H 8-1 This slow-growing
plant grows outward to forms a "nest" in
the center of the plant.
↕ 5ft (1.5m) ↔ 10–12ft (3–4m)

PICEA GLAUCA VAR. *ALBERTIANA*
'CONICA'
Conifer   page 338

PICEA MARIANA 'NANA'
Conifer   page 339

PICEA PUNGENS 'KOSTER'
Conifer   page 339

PINUS MUGO 'MOPS'
Conifer   page 342

PINUS PARVIFLORA
'ADCOCK'S DWARF'
Conifer, Z 6-9 H 9-6 A dwarf cultivar of the
Japanese white pine, with grayish leaves.
↕ 6ft (2m)

PINUS SYLVESTRIS 'BEUVRONENSIS'
Conifer, Z 3-7 H 7-1 A rounded, dwarf
cultivar of the Scots pine.
↕ 3ft (1m)

TAXUS BACCATA 'DOVASTONII AUREA'
Conifer   page 427

TAXUS BACCATA
'FASTIGIATA AUREOMARGINATA'
Conifer, Z 7-8 H 8-7 Upright accent plant
with leaves margined in yellow, and red-
fleshed (poisonous) berries.
↕ 10–15ft (3–5m) ↔ 3–8ft (1–2.5m)

TAXUS BACCATA 'FASTIGIATA'
Conifer   page 428

TAXUS BACCATA 'REPENS AUREA'
Conifer, Z 7-8 H 8-7 This spreading form of
English yew has golden leaves.
↕ 3–5ft (1–1.5m)

THUJA OCCIDENTALIS 'HOLMSTRUP'
Conifer   page 429

THUJA OCCIDENTALIS 'RHEINGOLD'
Conifer   page 430

THUJA OCCIDENTALIS 'SMARAGD'
Conifer, Z 2-7 H 7-1 A dwarf, conical bush
with bright green leaves.
↕ 3ft (1m) ↔ 32in (80cm)

THUJA ORIENTALIS 'AUREA NANA'
Conifer   page 430

THUJA PLICATA 'STONEHAM GOLD'
Conifer   page 431

TSUGA CANADENSIS 'JEDDELOH'
Conifer   page 439

TREES FOR SMALL GARDENS

Trees add shade and character to gardens, but large forest trees should never be planted in small gardens or too near homes. Maples, oaks, and ashes may be cheap to buy, but it is best to look for smaller trees that will give interest over a long period during the year. Consider the shade they will cast: evergreens can create areas that are dry and dark where little will grow.

ACER DAVIDII 'ERNEST WILSON'
Deciduous tree, Z 5-7 H 7-5 Unlobed leaves turn orange in autumn before falling to show the green, white-streaked branches.
‡ 25ft (8m) ↔ 30ft (10m)

ACER PALMATUM CULTIVARS
Deciduous trees or large shrubs page 34

AMELANCHIER × GRANDIFLORA 'BALLERINA'
Deciduous tree page 43

BETULA UTILIS VAR. *JACQUEMONTII*
Deciduous tree page 74

CERCIS SILIQUASTRUM
Deciduous tree page 97

CORNUS 'EDDIE'S WHITE WONDER'
Deciduous tree, Z 5-8 H 8-5 Multistemmed tree that bears deep purple, small flowers surrounded by large white bracts.
‡ 20ft (6m) ↔ 15ft (5m)

CRATAEGUS LAEVIGATA 'PAUL'S SCARLET'
Deciduous tree page 127

GENISTA AETNENSIS
Deciduous tree or large shrub page 191

GLEDITSIA TRIACANTHOS 'RUBYLACE'
Deciduous tree, Z 3-7 H 7-1 Elegant divided foliage that is bright wine-red when young, maturing to bronzed green.
‡ 12m (40ft) ↔ 10m (30ft)

LABURNUM × WATERERI 'VOSSII'
Deciduous tree page 252

LIGUSTRUM LUCIDUM
Evergreen tree or large shrub page 263

MAGNOLIA 'HEAVEN SCENT'
Deciduous tree, Z 6-9 H 9-6 Goblet-shaped pink flowers with white interiors in spring and early summer.
‡ ↔ 30ft (10m)

MAGNOLIA × LOEBNERI 'LEONARD MESSEL'
Deciduous tree page 283

MALUS CORONARIA 'CHARLOTTAE'
Tree, Z 4-7 H 8-1 Spreading tree with fragrant, semidouble, pale pink flowers in spring. ‡ ↔ 28ft (9m)

MALUS TSCHONOSKII
Deciduous tree page 287

PRUNUS SERRULA
Deciduous tree page 357

PYRUS CALLERYANA 'CHANTICLEER'
Deciduous tree page 363

SALIX CAPREA 'KILMARNOCK'
Deciduous tree page 392

SALIX 'ERYTHROFLEXUOSA'
Deciduous tree, Z 5-9 H 9-5 Semiweeping tree with twisted, orange-yellow shoots.
‡ ↔ 5m (15ft)

SORBUS 'JOSEPH ROCK'
Deciduous tree page 417

STYRAX JAPONICUS
Deciduous tree page 422

STYRAX OBASSIA
Deciduous tree page 422

HEDGE PLANTS WITH ATTRACTIVE FOLIAGE

Hedge plants must be tolerant of regular clipping. Those that have one flush of growth each year, such as yew, need clipping only once a season, unlike privet that may require trimming twice or three times. Evergreens are most popular, but deciduous plants still reduce wind speed and are often cheaper to buy. (Dimensions below are ultimate sizes for unclipped plants.)

BUXUS SEMPERVIRENS 'ELEGANTISSIMA'
Evergreen shrub   page **79**

BUXUS SEMPERVIRENS 'SUFFRUTICOSA'
Evergreen shrub   page **79**

CHAMAECYPARIS LAWSONIANA 'FLETCHERI'
Conifer, Z 5-9 H 9-5 Dense, gray foliage on an erect, compact shrub.
‡ 40ft (12m)

CHAMAECYPARIS LAWSONIANA 'LANE'
Conifer   page **99**

CHAMAECYPARIS LAWSONIANA 'PEMBURY BLUE'
Conifer   page **99**

X *CUPRESSOCYPARIS LEYLANDII*
Conifer, Z 6-9 H 9-6 Very vigorous plant that can be managed if trimmed at an early stage, and then regularly.
‡ 120ft (35m) ↔ 15ft (5m)

X *CUPRESSOCYPARIS LEYLANDII* 'HAGGERSTON GREY'
Conifer, Z 6-9 H 9-6 The most popular form of this fast-growing conifer, with gray-green foliage.
‡ 120ft (35m) ↔ 15ft (5m)

X *CUPRESSOCYPARIS LEYLANDII* 'ROBINSON'S GOLD'
Conifer, Z 6-9 H 9-6 The best gold form, with foliage that is bronze when young.
‡ 120ft (35m) ↔ 15ft (5m)

FAGUS SYLVATICA
Deciduous tree, Z 5-7 H 7-5 European beech and its purple retain their dead leaves in winter if trimmed to 6ft (2m).
‡ 80ft (25m) ↔ 50ft (15m)

LIGUSTRUM OVALIFOLIUM 'AUREUM'
Evergreen shrub, Z 6-8 H 6-6 Good choice where a bright yellow hedge is required and regular clipping is practical.
‡ ↔ 12ft (4m)

PRUNUS X *CISTENA*
Deciduous shrub   page **355**

PRUNUS LAUROCERASUS
Evergreen shrub, Z 6-9 H 8-6 Cherry laurel requires careful pruning, but it can be quite attractive and withstands hard pruning well.
‡ 25ft (8m) ↔ 30ft (10m)

PRUNUS LAUROCERASUS 'OTTO LUYKEN'
Evergreen shrub   page **356**

PRUNUS LUSITANICA
Evergreen shrub, Z 7-9 H 9-7 Pleasant evergreen with dark green leaves on red stalks, and white flowers if not clipped.
‡ ↔ 70ft (20m)

TAXUS BACCATA
Evergreen tree   page **427**

FLOWERING HEDGES

Flowering hedges add much more than structural elements and security to the garden: they can become a focus of attention. Many flowering shrubs that tolerate pruning can be used, but, because of the pruning regime required to maintain flowering at its best, they may not be suitable for very formal hedges or boundary hedges where year-round screening is required.

ESCALLONIA 'APPLE BLOSSOM'
Evergreen shrub   page 166

FORSYTHIA × *INTERMEDIA* 'LYNWOOD'
Shrub   page 180

FUCHSIA 'RICCARTONII'
Shrub   page 184

HEBE 'MIDSUMMER BEAUTY'
Evergreen shrub, Z 9-10 H 12-9 Bright green leaves and purple flowers, fading to white, on short spikes in summer.
‡3ft (1m) ↔ 4ft (1.2m)

HYPERICUM 'ROWALLANE'
Shrub, Z 7-9 H 9-7 Semievergreen, bearing clusters of yellow, cupped flowers in summer on arching stems.
‡6ft (2m) ↔ 3ft (1m)

LAVANDULA ANGUSTIFOLIA 'HIDCOTE'
Evergreen shrub   page 257

OSMANTHUS × *BURKWOODII*
Evergreen shrub   page 307

PHILADELPHUS CORONARIUS 'AUREUS'
Shrub, Z 5-8 H 8-3 Golden yellow foliage that may scorch in full sun on poor soil, and fragrant white flowers.
‡8ft (2.5m) ↔ 5ft (1.5m)

POTENTILLA FRUTICOSA 'PRIMROSE BEAUTY'
Shrub   page 307

PRUNUS × *CISTENA*
Shrub   page 355

PRUNUS LUSITANICA SUBSP. *AZORICA*
Shrub   page 357

RHODODENDRON 'HINO-MAYO'
Evergreen shrub   page 368

RIBES SANGUINEUM 'PULBOROUGH SCARLET'
Shrub   page 376

ROSA 'BUFF BEAUTY'
Shrub rose   page 386

ROSA 'CHINATOWN'
Cluster-flowered bush rose   page 378

ROSA 'FELICIA'
Shrub rose   page 387

SPIRAEA × *VANHOUTTEI*
Shrub   page 420

SYRINGA PUBESCENS SUBSP. *MICROPHYLLA* 'SUPERBA'
Shrub   page 424

VIBURNUM TINUS 'GWENLLIAN'
Evergreen shrub, Z 8-10 H 10-8 Dense shrub with pinkish flowers that open from deep pink buds.
‡↔ 10ft (3m)

SPINY HEDGES

There are places in the garden, usually around the edges, where the physical barrier of a hedge is not enough, and plants with spines are needed to ensure privacy and prevent the access of animals. Though these plants have many advantages, pruning and clipping must be carefully done, and be on the lookout for spiny fragments of twigs when weeding at the base.

BERBERIS DARWINII
Evergreen shrub page **68**

BERBERIS × OTTAWENSIS 'SUPERBA'
Shrub page **69**

BERBERIS × STENOPHYLLA
Evergreen shrub, Z 6-9 H 9-6 Long, arching shoots are covered with small orange flowers in spring.
↕ 10ft (3m) ↔ 15ft (5m)

BERBERIS THUNBERGII
Shrub, Z 5-8 H 8-5 Spiny stems have purple leaves that turn red before they fall in autumn.
↕ 3ft (1m) ↔ 8ft (2.5m)

CRATAEGUS MONOGYNA
Tree, Z 5-7 H 7-5 The singleseed hawthorn makes a quick-growing, spiny hedge, but it is not as attractive as some.
↕ 30ft (10m) ↔ 25ft (8m)

ILEX AQUIFOLIUM
Evergreen tree, Z 7-9 H 9-7 English holly makes a dense, impenetrable hedge, but its fallen leaves are a painful nuisance.
↕ 80ft (25m) ↔ 25ft (8m)

ILEX AQUIFOLIUM 'MADAME BRIOT'
Tree page **233**

MAHONIA JAPONICA
Evergreen shrub page **284**

MAHONIA × MEDIA 'BUCKLAND'
Evergreen shrub page **285**

PONCIRUS TRIFOLIATA
Shrub, Z 5-9 H 9-5 Angular green shoots with vicious spines, fragrant white flowers, and orangelike fruits in autumn.
↕ ↔ 15ft (5m)

PRUNUS SPINOSA
Tree, Z 5-9 H 9-5 The blackthorn is a dense shrub with white spring flowers and sloes (edible black fruit) in autumn.
↕ 15ft (5m) ↔ 12ft (4m)

PYRACANTHA 'ORANGE GLOW'
Evergreen shrub page **362**

PYRACANTHA 'WATERERI'
Evergreen shrub page **363**

ROSA GLAUCA
Shrub rose page **387**

ROSA RUGOSA 'ALBA'
Shrub rose, Z 2-9 H 9-1 Thickets of prickly stems and white flowers followed by large red hips.
↕ ↔ 3–8ft (1–2.5m)

GROUNDCOVER PLANTS FOR SUN

Many plants with creeping, trailing, or clump-forming habits can be planted as groundcovers in sunny gardens. However, most will suppress only new weeds, and very few will actively smother existing weeds, so clear the soil of all perennial weeds before you plant. When planting, mix different plants to create interest, and add a few taller plants to prevent a flat effect.

ALCHEMILLA MOLLIS
Perennial   page **41**

ARTEMISIA STELLERIANA
'BOUGHTON SILVER'
Perennial, Z 3-7 H 7-1 Divided, evergreen, silver foliage that forms dense mats.
‡ 6in (15cm) ↔ 12–18in (30–45cm)

CAMPANULA GLOMERATA 'SUPERBA'
Perennial   page **88**

CEANOTHUS THYRSIFLORUS VAR.
REPENS
Evergreen shrub   page **95**

CORNUS CANADENSIS
Perennial   page **116**

DICENTRA 'STUART BOOTHMAN'
Perennial   page **148**

ERICA X DARLEYENSIS 'JENNY
PORTER'
Evergreen shrub   page **159**

GERANIUM 'JOHNSON'S BLUE'
Perennial   page **195**

GERANIUM X OXONIANUM
'WARGRAVE PINK'
Perennial   page **197**

HOSTA FORTUNEI VAR.
AUREOMARGINATA
Perennial   page **222**

JUNIPERUS SQUAMATA 'BLUE CARPET'
Conifer, Z 5-8 H 8-5 Relatively low-growing juniper with shoots that lift from the ground at a gentle angle.
‡ 12–18in (30–45cm) ↔ 5–6ft (1.5–1.8m)

LAMIUM MACULATUM
'WHITE NANCY'
Perennial   page **253**

OSTEOSPERMUM JUCUNDUM
Perennial   page **309**

PERSICARIA VACCINIFOLIA
Perennial   page **326**

PHALARIS ARUNDINACEA 'PICTA'
Perennial grass   page **327**

PHLOMIS RUSSELIANA
Perennial   page **330**

PHLOX SUBULATA 'MCDANIEL'S
CUSHION'
Alpine, Z 3-8 H 8-1 The mossy foliage is covered with starry pink flowers in late spring. ‡ 2–6in (5–15cm) ↔ 20in (50cm)

POTENTILLA MEGALANTHA
Perennial   page **349**

ROSA GROUNDCOVER TYPES
Shrubs   page **385**

ROSMARINUS OFFICINALIS
'SEVERN SEA'
Evergreen shrub, Z 8-10 H 12-8 A mound-forming plant with arching branches and bright blue flowers.
‡ 3ft (1m) ↔ 5ft (1.5m)

SEMPERVIVUM CILIOSUM
Alpine   page **410**

VERONICA GENTIANOIDES
Perennial   page **448**

VIOLA 'NELLIE BRITTON'
Perennial   page **455**

GROUNDCOVER PLANTS FOR SHADE

Shade is often considered to be a problem, but there are lots of plants to use as groundcover that do not need full sun. However, the more dense the shade, the less choice there is. Luckily, those that tolerate some of the worst conditions are evergreen though slow growing. In less hostile conditions, many of these plants will spread quickly, making them excellent alternatives to grass.

AJUGA REPTANS 'CATLIN'S GIANT'
Perennial, Z 3-9 H 9-1 Very large, purple leaves and tall, blue flower spikes.
‡ 8in (20cm) ↔ 24–36in (60–90cm)

BERGENIA 'SILBERLICHT'
Perennial   page **72**

CONVALLARIA MAJALIS
Perennial   page **113**

COTONEASTER DAMMERI
Evergreen shrub, Z 6-8 H 8-6 Spreading shrub with white flowers and red berries.
‡ 8in (20cm) ↔ 6ft (2m)

EPIMEDIUM X *PERRALCHICUM*
Perennial   page **156**

EUONYMUS FORTUNEI 'EMERALD GAIETY'
Evergreen shrub, Z 5-9 H 9-5 Bushy, with white-edged leaves tinted pink in winter.
‡ 3ft (1m) ↔ 5ft (1.5m)

EUPHORBIA AMYGDALOIDES VAR. *ROBBIAE*
Perennial   page **172**

GAULTHERIA PROCUMBENS
Evergreen shrub, Z 3-8 H 8-1 Creeping, with leaves scented of wintergreen, pale pink flowers, and red berries.
‡ 6in (15cm) ↔ 3ft (1m)

GERANIUM MACRORRHIZUM 'CZAKOR'
Perennial, Z 4-8 H 8-1 Mats of scented foliage tinted with purple in autumn, and magenta flowers in summer.
‡ 20in (50cm) ↔ 24in (60cm)

GERANIUM SYLVATICUM 'ALBUM'
Perennial, Z 4-8 H 8-1 Deeply lobed leaves and small, white flowers. For moist soil.
‡ 30in (75cm) ↔ 24in (60cm)

HEDERA HIBERNICA
Evergreen climber   page **211**

HEUCHERA 'RED SPANGLES'
Perennial   page **220**

HOSTA 'FRANCES WILLIAMS'
Perennial   page **222**

OMPHALODES CAPPADOCICA
Perennial   page **303**

PACHYSANDRA TERMINALIS
Perennial   page **310**

POLYSTICHUM SETIFERUM
Fern   page **347**

SANGUINARIA CANADENSIS 'PLENA'
Perennial, Z 3-9 H 9-1 For moist soil, with large glaucous leaves and double white flowers. ‡ 6in (15cm) ↔ 12in (30cm)

TIARELLA CORDIFOLIA
Perennial   page **434**

TOLMIEA 'TAFF'S GOLD'
Perennial   page **434**

TRACHYSTEMON ORIENTALIS
Perennial, Z 6-8 H 8-6 Large, rough, heart-shaped leaves and boragelike flowers.
‡ 12in (30cm) ↔ 3ft (1m)

VINCA MINOR 'ARGENTEOVARIEGATA'
Perennial, Z 4-9 H 9-1 Pale blue flowers among gray-green and cream leaves.
‡ 6in (15cm) ↔ 36in (1m)

PLANTS WITH SCENTED FOLIAGE

While flowers tend to have sweet, fruity perfumes, leaf scents tend to be more spicy or resinous, though some, especially scented geraniums, mimic other plants. Some plants waft their perfume onto the air, and others need gentle stroking. It is likely that these plants evolved their scents to make themselves less appealing to insect pests; gardeners find them irresistible.

ALOYSIA TRIPHYLLA
Shrub, Z 8-11 H 12-8 Shrub with narrow, slightly matte leaves that have an intense aroma of lemon when touched.
‡↔ 10ft (3m)

AMICIA ZYGOMERIS
Perennial, Z 8-10 H 12-8 Unusual plant, related to beans, with gray-green foliage that smells of cucumber when crushed.
‡ 7ft (2.2m) ↔ 4ft (1.2m)

CALOCEDRUS DECURRENS
Conifer, Z 5-8 H 8-5 A columnar tree with foliage that is sweetly scented when crushed.
‡ 70–130ft (20–40m) ↔ 6–28ft (2–9m)

CALYCANTHUS OCCIDENTALIS
Shrub, Z 6-9 H 9-6 Large leaves with a spicy scent and brick-red flowers that smell of fruit and spice and vinegar.
‡ 10ft (3m) ↔ 12ft (4m)

CERCIDIPHYLLUM JAPONICUM
Tree, Z 4-8 H 8-1 In autumn the leaves of this graceful tree turn orange and red and smell like burnt sugar.
‡ 70ft (20m) ↔ 50ft (15m)

CHAMAEMELUM NOBILE 'TRENEAGUE'
Perennial, Z 6-9 H 9-6 This nonflowering form of chamomile hugs the soil, and its foliage smells fruity when gently crushed.
‡ 4in (10cm) ↔ 18in (45cm)

CISTUS × HYBRIDUS
Evergreen shrub page **107**

CISTUS LADANIFER
Evergreen shrub, Z 8-10 H 12-8 The dark green leaves are sticky and fragrant; the flowers are white with a yellow eye.
‡ 6ft (2m) ↔ 5ft (1.5m)

HELICHRYSUM ITALICUM
Evergreen shrub, Z 7-10 H 12-7 Narrow, gray foliage that smells of curry.
‡ 24in (60cm) ↔ 3ft (1m)

HOUTTUYNIA CORDATA 'FLORE PLENO'
Perennial, Z 6-11 H 12-3 An invasive, creeping plant with purplish leaves that have a strong citrus fragrance when crushed, and semi-double flowers.
‡ 6–12in (15–30cm) ↔ indefinite

LAVANDULA ANGUSTIFOLIA 'TWICKEL PURPLE'
Evergreen shrub page **257**

LAVANDULA STOECHAS
Shrub, Z 8-9 H 9-8 The purple flowerheads are topped with purple bracts.
‡↔ 24in (60cm)

MELISSA OFFICINALIS 'AUREA'
Perennial, Z 3-7 H 7-1 Form of lemon balm with yellow splashes on the leaves.
‡ 3ft (1m) ↔ 18in (45cm)

MENTHA SUAVEOLENS 'VARIEGATA'
Perennial, Z 6-9 H 9-6 Variegated apple mint has a pleasant fragrance and showy leaves.
‡ 3ft (1m) ↔ indefinite

MONARDA 'CAMBRIDGE SCARLET'
Perennial page **292**

MONARDA 'SCORPION'
Perennial, Z 4-9 H 9-1 Whorls of bracts and violet flowers on tall, leafy stems.
↕ 5ft (1.5m) ↔ 3ft (1m)

ORIGANUM LAEVIGATUM
Perennial   page 305

ORIGANUM LAEVIGATUM 'HERRENHAUSEN'
Perennial   page 306

PELARGONIUM CRISPUM 'VARIEGATUM'
Tender perennial   page 319

PELARGONIUM 'LADY PLYMOUTH'
Tender perennial   page 319

PELARGONIUM 'MABEL GREY'
Tender perennial   page 319

PELARGONIUM TOMENTOSUM
Tender perennial   page 319

PERILLA FRUTESCENS VAR. *CRISPA*
Annual   page 324

PEROVSKIA ATRIPLICIFOLIA
Subshrub, Z 6-9 H 9-6 The upright stems carry tiny blue flowers in autumn, but the grayish leaves are fragrant all summer.
↕ 4ft (1.2m) ↔ 3ft (1m)

PEROVSKIA 'BLUE SPIRE'
Subshrub   page 324

PROSTANTHERA CUNEATA
Evergreen shrub, Z 9-10 H 12-9 A bushy plant with small, mint-scented leaves and pretty white flowers in summer.
↕↔ 12–36in (30–90cm)

PROSTANTHERA ROTUNDIFOLIA
Shrub, Z 9-10 H 12-9 In late spring the small mint-scented leaves are smothered in lilac flowers.
↕ 6–12ft (2–4m) ↔ 3–10ft (1–3m)

PSEUDOTSUGA MENZIESII
Conifer, Z 5-7 H 7-5 A large tree with resinous foliage and interesting cones.
↕ 80–160ft (25–50m) ↔ 20–30ft (6–10m)

PTELEA TRIFOLIATA 'AUREA'
Tree, Z 5-9 H 9-5 The gold foliage and bark of this small tree are strongly scented.
↕ 15ft (5m)

ROSA EGLANTERIA
Shrub rose, Z 4-9 H 9-4 Arching shoots with small pink flowers, and foliage that is scented of cooking apples when wet.
↕↔ 2.5m (8ft)

ROSMARINUS OFFICINALIS 'SILVER SPIRES'
Evergreen shrub, Z 8-10 H 12-8 The culinary rosemary but with silver-variegated foliage on an upright plant.
↕ 3ft (1m) ↔ 24in (60cm)

SALVIA DISCOLOR
Shrub, Z 9-10 H 12-3 Attractive green leaves with silver reverses, which smell of blackcurrants, and small, dark flowers.
↕ 18in (45cm) ↔ 12in (30cm)

SALVIA OFFICINALIS 'ICTERINA'
Subshrub   page 395

SKIMMIA × *CONFUSA* 'KEW GREEN'
Evergreen shrub   page 412

PLANTS WITH SCENTED FLOWERS

Fragrance is too often forgotten when planting a garden. Yet there are as many shades of fragrance as there are of colors: they can affect mood, take you back to your childhood, or whisk you off to a far-off land with a single sniff. The most strongly scented flowers are often white or insignificant in appearance, but they have evolved to make their presence felt in other ways.

ABELIA CHINENSIS
Shrub, Z 7-9 H 9-7 Spreading, with heads of small pale pink flowers in late summer.
‡5ft (1.5m) ↔ 8ft (2.5m)

BUDDLEJA ALTERNIFOLIA
Shrub   page **76**

CAMELLIA 'INSPIRATION'
Evergreen shrub   page **83**

CAMELLIA JAPONICA
'ALEXANDER HUNTER'
Evergreen shrub   page **84**

CAMELLIA JAPONICA
'ELEGANS'
Evergreen shrub   page **85**

CHIMONANTHUS PRAECOX
'LUTEUS'
Shrub, Z 7-9 H 9-7 Pale yellow flowers scent the late winter air.
‡12ft (4m) ↔ 10ft (3m)

CHOISYA 'AZTEC PEARL'
Evergreen shrub, Z 9-10 H 12-9 Narrowly divided, deep green leaves and white, pink-tinged flowers in spring and autumn.
‡↔ 8ft (2.5m)

CLEMATIS MONTANA
F. *GRANDIFLORA*
Climber   page **108**

DAPHNE BHOLUA 'GURKHA'
Shrub   page **140**

DAPHNE TANGUTICA RETUSA GROUP
Evergreen shrub   page **141**

DIANTHUS 'DORIS'
Perennial   page **145**

ERICA ERIGENA
'GOLDEN LADY'
Evergreen shrub   page **159**

HAMAMELIS MOLLIS
Shrub, Z 5-9 H 9-5 Spidery, powerfully fragrant yellow flowers appear on the bare twigs in late winter.
‡↔ 12ft (4m)

HOSTA 'HONEYBELLS'
Perennial   page **223**

JASMINUM OFFICINALE
Climber, Z 9-10 H 12-9 A strong, twining climber with white flowers in summer, which have an intense, sweet scent.
‡40ft (12m)

JASMINUM OFFICINALE
'ARGENTEOVARIEGATUM'
Climber   page **246**

LILIUM PINK PERFECTION GROUP
Bulb   page **267**

LONICERA CAPRIFOLIUM
Climber, Z 6-9 H 9-6 The Italian honeysuckle produces pink and cream, fragrant flowers in summer.
‡20ft (6m)

LONICERA PERICLYMENUM 'BELGICA'
Climber, Z 5-9 H 9-5 In early summer this honeysuckle produces creamy yellow flowers streaked with maroon.
‡22ft (7m)

LONICERA PERICLYMENUM 'GRAHAM THOMAS'
Climber   page **274**

MAGNOLIA GRANDIFLORA 'GOLIATH'
Evergreen tree page **281**

MAHONIA × *MEDIA* 'CHARITY'
Evergreen shrub page **285**

OSMANTHUS DELAVAYI
Evergreen shrub page **307**

PAEONIA LACTIFLORA 'DUCHESSE DE NEMOURS'
Perennial page **312**

PHILADELPHUS 'BEAUCLERK'
Shrub page **328**

PHILADELPHUS 'BELLE ETOILE'
Shrub page **328**

PHLOX PANICULATA 'WHITE ADMIRAL'
Perennial, Z 4-8 H 8-1 Large heads of pure white flowers with a sweet, peppery scent, borne in summer.
↕3ft (1m)

PITTOSPORUM TENUIFOLIUM
Evergreen shrub page **342**

PITTOSPORUM TOBIRA
Evergreen shrub or small tree page **343**

PRIMULA FLORINDAE
Perennial page **351**

ROSA 'ALBERTINE'
Rambler rose page **382**

ROSA 'ARTHUR BELL'
Floribunda rose page **378**

ROSA 'BLESSINGS'
Hybrid tea rose page **378**

ROSA 'CLIMBING ICEBERG '
Climbing rose, Z 5-9 H 9-5 This fine rose has many pure white flowers all summer.
↕8ft (2.5m)

ROSA 'COMPASSION'
Climbing rose page **380**

ROSA 'GRAHAM THOMAS'
English shrub rose page **387**

ROSA 'JUST JOEY'
Hybrid tea rose page **379**

ROSA 'MARGARET MERRIL'
Floribunda rose page **379**

ROSA 'PEACE'
Hybrid tea rose page **379**

ROSA 'PENELOPE'
Shrub rose, Z 6-9 H 9-6 Large clusters of creamy pink flowers have a pronounced, sweet fragrance.
↕↔3½ft (1.1m)

ROSA 'REMEMBER ME'
Hybrid tea rose page **379**

SARCOCOCCA HOOKERIANA VAR. *DIGYNA*
Evergreen shrub page **401**

SKIMMIA JAPONICA 'RUBELLA'
Evergreen shrub page **413**

SMILACINA RACEMOSA
Perennial page **413**

SYRINGA MEYERI 'PALIBIN'
Shrub page **423**

SYRINGA VULGARIS 'MADAME LEMOINE'
Shrub page **425**

ULEX EUROPAEUS 'FLORE PLENO'
Evergreen shrub, Z 6-8 H 8-6 The spiny bushes have at least a few of the coconut-scented double flowers almost all year.
↕8ft (2.5m) ↔6ft (2m)

VIBURNUM × *BURKWOODII* 'PARK FARM HYBRID'
Evergreen shrub, Z 4-8 H 8-1 Upright shrub with bronze new leaves and deep pink, scented flowers in late spring.
↕10ft (3m) ↔6ft (2m)

VIBURNUM CARLESII 'AURORA'
Shrub, Z 5-8 H 8-5 Shrub with pink flowers in late spring, opening from red buds.
↕↔6ft (2m)

PLANTS FOR PAVING CRACKS AND GRAVEL BEDS

Plants help break up large expanses of paving or gravel. The clean surface also helps prevent the delicate flowers of small plants from becoming splashed with soil and reflects heat back up to sun-loving plants. Few plants tolerate much foot traffic; use only the toughest, such as thymes and chamomile, where there is heavy use. Less busy areas can be home to dwarf shrubs and alpines.

ACAENA 'BLUE HAZE'
Perennial, Z 7-9 H 9-7 A vigorous, spreading perennial with divided, gray-blue leaves and round, white flowerheads that are followed by red burrs.
‡ 4-6in (10-15cm) ↔ 3ft (1m)

ACAENA MICROPHYLLA
Perennial   page **31**

AETHIONEMA 'WARLEY ROSE'
Shrub   page **38**

AJUGA REPTANS 'ATROPURPUREA'
Perennial   page **40**

ANTHEMIS PUNCTATA SUBSP.
CUPANIANA
Perennial   page **49**

ARENARIA MONTANA
Perennial   page **52**

ARMERIA JUNIPERIFOLIA
Subshrub   page **54**

CAMPANULA COCHLEARIFOLIA
Perennial   page **88**

CHAMAEMELUM NOBILE
'TRENEAGUE'
Perennial, Z 6-9 H 9-6 This nonflowering form of chamomile hugs the soil, and its foliage smells fruity when gently crushed.
‡ 4in (10cm) ↔ 18in (45cm)

DIANTHUS 'PIKE'S PINK'
Perennial, Z 5-8 H 8-5 Small alpine pink with sweetly scented pink flowers.
‡ 6in (15cm)

DIASCIA 'JOYCE'S CHOICE'
Perennial, Z 8-9 H 9-8 Early-flowering plant with long spikes of pale, apricot-pink flowers in summer.
‡ 30cm (12in) ↔ 45cm (18in)

ERIGERON KARVINSKIANUS
Perennial   page **162**

ERINUS ALPINUS
Perennial   page **162**

HELIANTHEMUM 'RHODANTHE
CARNEUM'
Evergreen shrub   page **212**

LYSIMACHIA NUMMULARIA 'AUREA'
Perennial   page **279**

PENSTEMON RUPICOLA
Dwarf shrub, Z 4-9 H 9-1 Evergreen, with leathery leaves and small, tubular, deep pink flowers in early summer. Tiny when compared with border penstemons:
‡ 4in (10cm) ↔ 18in (45cm)

PHLOX DOUGLASII 'CRACKERJACK'
Perennial, Z 5-7 H 7-5 A compact, evergreen perennial phlox with narrow, stiff leaves and magenta flowers in late summer.
‡ 5in (12cm) ↔ 8in (20cm)

PHLOX DOUGLASII 'RED ADMIRAL'
Perennial   page **332**

PRATIA PEDUNCULATA
Perennial, Z 5-7 H 7-5 Mildly invasive, creeping plant with tiny leaves and star-shaped, pale blue flowers in summer.
‡ ½in (1.5cm) ↔ indefinite

SAPONARIA OCYMOIDES
Perennial   page 399

SEDUM ACRE 'AUREUM'
Perennial, Z 4-9 H 9-1 Rather invasive
succulent with tiny shoots and leaves that
are yellow when young; yellow flowers.
‡2in (5cm) ↔ 24in (60cm)

SEDUM KAMTSCHATICUM
'VARIEGATUM'
Perennial   page 406

SEDUM SPATHULIFOLIUM
'PURPUREUM'
Perennial   page 407

SEDUM SPURIUM 'SCHORBUSER BLUT'
Perennial   page 408

SOLEIROLIA SOLEIROLII 'AUREA'
Perennial, Z 10-11 H 12-10 Small but
surprisingly invasive plant with shiny
lime green, tiny leaves that rapidly form
mounds and mats.
‡2in (5cm) ↔ 3ft (1m)

THYMUS × CITRIODORUS
'BERTRAM ANDERSON'
Evergreen subshrub   page 432

THYMUS × CITRIODORUS
'SILVER QUEEN'
Evergreen subshrub, Z 6-9 H 9-6 The
leaves of this cultivar are variegated, and
look good with the lavender-pink flowers.
‡30cm (12in) ↔ 25cm (10in)

THYMUS 'PINK CHINTZ'
Subshrub, Z 4-9 H 9-1 Trailing stems that
root as they grow, with grayish leaves and
pink flowers loved by bees.
‡10in (25cm) ↔ 18in (45cm)

THYMUS POLYTRICHUS SUBSP.
BRITANNICUS 'ALBUS'
Subshrub, Z 5-9 H 9-5 A mat-forming
woody plant with hairy leaves and white
flowers.
‡2in (5cm) ↔ 24in (60cm)

THYMUS SERPYLLUM VAR.
COCCINEUM
Subshrub   page 433

VIOLA 'JACKANAPES'
Perennial   page 455

ARCHITECTURAL PLANTS

Every garden needs plants that are larger than life, with the sort of shape or texture that cannot be ignored. With their bold leaves and spiky shapes, using too many of these plants will give a "busy" effect, but when carefully placed among less extraordinary plants, they become the focus of a view in the border. Make use of light and shade to emphasize bold silhouettes.

ACANTHUS SPINOSUS
Perennial page **31**

AESCULUS PARVIFLORA
Shrub page **38**

AGAVE AMERICANA
Succulent, min 40°F (5°C) H 12-1 Viciously spiny plant with steely gray leaves that curve to make a magnificent rosette.
‡6ft (2m) ↔ 10ft (3m)

AILANTHUS ALTISSIMA
Tree, Z 4-8 H 8-1 This can be a tall tree but will produce divided leaves 4ft (1.2m) long if cut back hard every year. Weedy but tough. ‡80ft (25m) ↔ 50ft (15m)

BETULA NIGRA
Tree page **73**

BETULA PENDULA 'YOUNGII'
Tree page **73**

CATALPA BIGNONIOIDES 'AUREA'
Tree, Z 5-9 H 9-5 A large, spreading tree, which can be pruned hard annually to produce large, gold leaves.
‡↔ 30ft (10m)

CHAMAECYPARIS NOOTKATENSIS 'PENDULA'
Conifer page **100**

CHAMAECYPARIS PISIFERA 'FILIFERA AUREA'
Conifer, Z 4-8 H 8-1
A broad, arching shrub with whiplike, golden shoots.
‡40ft (12m) ↔ 15ft (5m)

CORYLUS AVELLANA 'CONTORTA'
Shrub page **121**

CROCOSMIA MASONIORUM
Perennial page **130**

ERYNGIUM GIGANTEUM
Biennial, Z 5-8 H 8-5 Rosettes of deep green leaves produce spiny, white stems and flowerheads in the second year.
‡36in (90cm) ↔ 12in (30cm)

EUCALYPTUS PAUCIFLORA SUBSP. *NIPHOPHILA*
Evergreen tree page **169**

EUPHORBIA CHARACIAS
Perennial page **173**

FAGUS SYLVATICA 'PENDULA'
Tree, Z 5-7 H 7-5 A tree of huge proportions with horizontal and arching branches cascading to the ground.
‡50ft (15m) ↔ 70ft (20m)

FARGESIA NITIDA
Ornamental grass page **177**

GUNNERA MANICATA
Perennial page **201**

HELIANTHUS 'MONARCH'
Perennial page **214**

KNIPHOFIA CAULESCENS
Perennial, Z 6-9 H 9-6 An evergreen redhot poker with blue-gray leaves and pale orange flowers in fat spikes.
‡4ft (1.2m) ↔ 2ft (60cm)

MACLEAYA × *KEWENSIS* 'KELWAY'S CORAL PLUME'
Perennial page **280**

MELIANTHUS MAJOR
Shrub   page 290

PAEONIA DELAVAYI
Shrub   page 311

PAULOWNIA TOMENTOSA
Tree, Z 5-8 H 8-5 If allowed to grow
naturally this has lilac flowers, but it makes
a bold foliage plant if cut back hard.
‡ 40ft (12m) ↔ 30ft (10m)

PHORMIUM TENAX
Perennial, Z 9-10 H 12-1 Upright, evergreen
leaves that are narrow and leathery and
surround tall, arching flower spikes.
‡ 12ft (4m) ↔ 6ft (2m)

PHORMIUM TENAX PURPUREUM
GROUP
Perennials   page 334

*PHYLLOSTACHYS AUREOSULCATA
VAR. AUREOCAULIS*
Bamboo, Z 6-10 H 12-6 Large bamboo with
bright golden canes and narrow leaves.
‡ 10–20ft (3–6m) ↔ indefinite

PHYLLOSTACHYS NIGRA
Bamboo   page 336

*PHYLLOSTACHYS NIGRA VAR.
HENONIS*
Bamboo   page 337

PLEIOBLASTUS VARIEGATUS
Bamboo   page 345

PRUNUS 'AMANOGAWA'
Tree, Z 6-8 H 8-6 Very slender, upright
growth, resembling a Lombardy poplar,
with semi-double pink flowers in spring.
‡ 25ft (8m) ↔ 12ft (4m)

PRUNUS 'KIKU-SHIDARE-ZAKURA'
Tree   page 356

RODGERSIA AESCULIFOLIA
Perennial, Z 5-8 H 8-5 Creeping rhizomes
produce clumps of large leaves like those
of horse chestnuts, and pink flowers.
‡ 2m (6ft) ↔ 1m (3ft)

SORBARIA TOMENTOSA VAR.
ANGUSTIFOLIA
Shrub, Z 8-10 H 12-8 A spreading shrub
with feathery leaves, red stems, and fluffy,
white flowerheads.
‡ 10ft (3m)

STIPA GIGANTEA
Ornamental grass   page 421

TRACHYCARPUS FORTUNEI
Palm, Z 9-10 H 12-9 Slow-growing but
fairly cold-tolerant palm with fan-shaped
leaves and a furry trunk with age.
‡ 70ft (20m) ↔ 8ft (2.5m)

VIBURNUM PLICATUM 'PINK BEAUTY'
Shrub, Z 4-8 H 8-1 A spreading shrub with
horizontal tiers of branches covered
with white flowers turning to pink.
‡ 10ft (3m) ↔ 12ft (4m)

WOODWARDIA RADICANS
Fern, Z 8-9 H 9-8 A large, evergreen fern
with huge, arching fronds.
‡ 6ft (2m) ↔ 10ft (3m)

YUCCA FILAMENTOSA
Evergreen shrub, Z 5-10 H 12-5 A clump-
forming, essentially stemless plant with
swordlike leaves and spires of creamy
flowers.
‡ 30in (75cm) ↔ 5ft (1.5m)

YUCCA FILAMENTOSA 'BRIGHT EDGE'
Shrub   page 459

YUCCA FLACCIDA 'IVORY TOWER'
Shrub   page 460

YUCCA GLORIOSA
Evergreen shrub, Z 7-10 H 12-7 Erect
trunks with narrow, sharp-tipped gray-
green leaves, and large clusters
of white flowers.
‡ ↔ 6ft (2m)

Shrubs and Climbers for Cold Walls

Cold walls or fences are sunless nearly all year, but the even temperatures and often moist soil suits ivies, climbing hydrangeas, and some shrubs. Walls that receive only morning sun can be a problem in areas experiencing frost: rapid thawing can damage shoots and flowers, as with camellias. However, this is the perfect site for some clematis, roses, *Chaenomeles*, and honeysuckles.

AKEBIA QUINATA
Semievergreen climber, Z 5-9 H 9-5
Twining stems with dark green, divided leaves and spicy-scented, purple flowers in spring.
‡ 30ft (10m)

CAMELLIA × WILLIAMSII 'Francis Hanger'
Evergreen shrub, Z 7-9 H 10-8 Glossy leaves form a good foil to the white, golden-centered flowers.
‡ 5ft (1.5m)

CHAENOMELES SPECIOSA 'Geisha Girl'
Shrub, Z 5-8 H 8-5 Bushy plant with semidouble flowers of pale apricot pink.
‡ 5ft (1.5m)

CLEMATIS 'Carnaby'
Midseason clematis, Z 4-9 H 9-5 Compact climber with large pink flowers, with a deeper center to each petal.
‡ 2.5m (8ft) ↔ 1m (3ft)

CLEMATIS 'Helsingborg'
Early clematis, Z 6-9 H 9-6 Masses of dainty, deep purple-blue flowers are followed by fluffy seedheads.
‡ 2-3m (6-10ft) ↔ 1.5m (5ft)

CLEMATIS 'Henryi'
Midseason clematis   page 109

CLEMATIS 'Minuet'
Late-season clematis   page 111

CLEMATIS 'Nelly Moser'
Midseason clematis   page 109

CLEMATIS 'Niobe'
Midseason clematis, Z 4-9 H 9-1 Single, large flowers of deep red with contrasting yellow anthers.
‡ 6-10ft (2-3m) ↔ 3ft (1m)

CLEMATIS 'Venosa Violacea'
Late-season clematis   page 111

CODONOPSIS CONVOLVULACEA
Perennial climber   page 112

CORYLOPSIS PAUCIFLORA
Shrub   page 120

COTONEASTER HORIZONTALIS
Shrub   page 124

DAPHNE ODORA 'Aureomarginata'
Evergreen shrub, Z 7-9 H 9-7 Low-growing, mounded shrub with pale pink, fragrant flowers, and leaves edged with gold.
‡ 5ft (1.5m)

EUONYMUS FORTUNEI 'Emerald 'n' Gold'
Evergreen shrub   page 171

FORSYTHIA SUSPENSA
Shrub   page 181

GARRYA ELLIPTICA 'James Roof'
Evergreen shrub   page 189

HEDERA CANARIENSIS 'Gloire de Marengo'
Evergreen climber, Z 6-10 H 12-6 Silvery green leaves variegated with white and tinged pink in winter.
‡ 12ft (4m)

HEDERA COLCHICA
'DENTATA'
Evergreen climber   page **209**

HEDERA COLCHICA
'SULPHUR HEART'
Evergreen climber   page **209**

HEDERA HELIX 'GOLDHEART'
Evergreen climber, Z 5-10 H 12-5 Reddish
stems with deep green leaves marked with
a central gold splash.
‡25ft (8m)

HYDRANGEA ANOMALA SUBSP.
PETIOLARIS
Climber   page **226**

JASMINUM HUMILE
Evergreen shrub, Z 7-9 H 9-7 Sparsely
branched, arching shrub with bright yellow
flowers
in summer.
‡8ft (2.5m)

JASMINUM NUDIFLORUM
Shrub   page **245**

KERRIA JAPONICA 'PLENIFLORA'
Shrub, Z 4-9 H 9-1 Vigorous, upright plant
with slender, green stems and double
orange-gold flowers.
‡10ft (3m)

LONICERA JAPONICA 'HALLIANA'
Evergreen climber, Z 4-10 H 12-1 Strong-
growing, often invasive climber with highly
scented white flowers that age to yellow.
‡30ft (10m)

MUEHLENBECKIA COMPLEXA
Climber, Z 8-10 H 12-8 Masses of threadlike
dark, twisting stems with tiny violin-
shaped leaves.
‡10ft (3m)

PARTHENOCISSUS HENRYANA
Climber   page **317**

PARTHENOCISSUS QUINQUEFOLIA
Climber, Z 3-9 H 9-1 Vigorous, deciduous
climber with leaves divided into five
leaflets. Turns vivid red shades in autumn.
‡50ft (15m)

PILEOSTEGIA VIBURNOIDES
Evergreen climber, Z 7-10 H 12-7 Oblong,
dark green leaves and clusters of fluffy,
satr-shaped white flowers.
‡20ft (6m)

PYRACANTHA 'HARLEQUIN'
Evergreen shrub, Z 7-9 H 9-7 Prickly shrub
with white-variegated leaves, white
flowers, and red berries.
‡5ft (1.5m) ↔ 6ft (2m)

ROSA 'ALBÉRIC BARBIER'
Rambler rose   page **382**

ROSA 'DUBLIN BAY'
Climbing rose   page **380**

ROSA 'HANDEL'
Climbing rose   page **381**

ROSA 'MERMAID'
Climbing rose, Z 6-9 H 9-6 Strong, thorny
climber with dark, shiny leaves and single,
primrose yellow flowers.
‡20ft (6m)

SCHIZOPHRAGMA INTEGRIFOLIUM
Climber, Z 5-9 H 9-5 Large climber with
toothed, dark green leaves and showy
white flower clusters.
‡40ft (12m)

PLANTS FOR WARM WALLS

Reserve the warmest, sunniest garden walls to grow plants that are slightly tender in your climate. However, these sites can also be very dry, especially if the border is narrow and in the shadow of a roof, and it may be difficult to establish plants. Walls that receive only the afternoon sun are less suitable for many plants because they receive only the strongest and hottest sun.

ABELIA 'EDWARD GOUCHER'
Shrub   page 28

ABELIA FLORIBUNDA
Evergreen shrub   page 28

ABELIA × *GRANDIFLORA*
Shrub   page 29

ABELIA × *GRANDIFLORA* 'FRANCIS MASON'
Evergreen shrub, Z 6-9 H 9-6 Yellow-marked leaves; pale pink flowers in late summer. ‡6ft (1.5m)

ABUTILON 'KENTISH BELLE'
Shrub   page 29

ACACIA DEALBATA
Evergreen tree, Z 9-10 H 12-9 An open-growing, tree with feathery gray-green foliage and fragrant yellow spring flowers. ‡50-100ft (15-30m)

ACTINIDIA KOLOMIKTA
Climber   page 37

CALLISTEMON CITRINUS 'SPLENDENS'
Evergreen shrub   page 81

CAMPSIS × *TAGLIABUANA* 'MADAME GALEN'
Climber   page 90

CARPENTERIA CALIFORNICA
Evergreen shrub   page 92

CEANOTHUS 'AUTUMNAL BLUE'
Evergreen shrub   page 94

CEANOTHUS 'CONCHA'
Evergreen shrub, Z 9-10 Dark blue flowers. ‡10ft (3m)

CESTRUM PARQUI
Shrub, Z 8-10 H 12-8 Weak-stemmed bush with narrow leaves and clusters of lime green, tubular, night-scented flowers in summer. ‡6ft (2m)

CLEMATIS CIRRHOSA 'FRECKLES'
Early clematis, Z 7-9 H 9-7 Purple tinted, cream-spotted leaves, and bell-shaped flowers in winter. ‡8-10ft (2.5-3m) ↔ 5ft (1.5m)

CLEMATIS 'LASURSTERN'
Midseason clematis   page 109

CLEMATIS 'ETOILE VIOLETTE'
Late-season clematis   page 110

CLEMATIS 'JACKMANNII'
Late-season clematis   page 111

CLEMATIS REHDERIANA
Late-season clematis   page 111

CLEMATIS 'THE PRESIDENT'
Midseason clematis   page 109

CLEMATIS VITICELLA 'PURPUREA PLENA ELEGANS'
Late-season clematis   page 111

CLIANTHUS PUNICEUS
Evergreen shrub   page 112

CYTISUS BATTANDIERI
Semievergreen shrub   page 135

ECCREMOCARPUS SCABER
Climber   page 152

ESCALLONIA 'LANGLEYENSIS'
Evergreen shrub   page 167

FREMONTODENDRON 'CALIFORNIA GLORY'
Shrub   page **182**

HEDYCHIUM GARDNERIANUM
Perennial, Z 9-10 H 12-9 Large heads of spidery, sweetly scented cream flowers.
‡ 6-7ft (2-2.2m)

IPOMOEA INDICA
Climber   page **237**

JASMINUM × STEPHANENSE
Climber, Z 8-10 H 12-8 Fast-growing, with clusters of pink, fragrant flowers in summer.
‡ 15ft (5m)

JOVELLANA VIOLACEA
Semievergreen shrub, Z 9-10 H 12-9 Weak shrub with fine foliage and bell-like, pale violet flowers in summer.
‡ 24in (60cm) ↔ 3ft (1m)

LAPAGERIA ROSEA
Climber   page **253**

LONICERA × ITALICA
Climber   page **273**

LONICERA × TELLMANNIANA
Climber   page **275**

MAGNOLIA GRANDIFLORA 'EXMOUTH'
Evergreen tree   page **280**

PASSIFLORA CAERULEA
Climber   page **318**

PHYGELIUS AEQUALIS 'YELLOW TRUMPET'
Shrub   page **335**

PHYGELIUS × RECTUS 'AFRICAN QUEEN'
Shrub   page **336**

PITTOSPORUM TENUIFOLIUM 'SILVER QUEEN'
Evergreen shrub, Z 9-10 H 12-9 Wiry black twigs support gray-green, white-edged leaves, and purple, scented flowers in autumn. ‡ 3-12ft (1-4m) ↔ 6ft (2m)

RIBES SPECIOSUM
Shrub, Z 7-9 H 9-7 Spiny shrub with bristly stems, small glossy leaves, and pendulous red flowers resembling fuchsias.
‡ 6ft (2m)

RHODANTHEMUM HOSMARIENSE
Subshrub   page **367**

ROSES, CLIMBING
Climbers   pages **380–381**

SOLANUM CRISPUM 'GLASNEVIN'
Climber   page **414**

SOLANUM JASMINOIDES 'ALBUM'
Climber   page **414**

THUNBERGIA GRANDIFLORA
Climber   page **431**

TRACHELOSPERMUM JASMINOIDES
Evergreen climber   page **435**

VESTIA FOETIDA
Shrub, Z 8-10 H 12-8 A short-lived plant with unpleasantly scented leaves and prolific, pendulous yellow flowers.
‡ 6ft (2m) ↔ 5ft (1.5m)

VITIS 'BRANT'
Climber, Z 5-9 H 9-5 An ornamental grape vine with green leaves that turn red in autumn, and black, edible grapes.
‡ 22ft (7m)

WISTERIA FLORIBUNDA 'ALBA'
Climber   page **458**

WISTERIA SINENSIS
Climber   page **459**

WISTERIA SINENSIS 'SIERRA MADRE'
Climber, Z 5-8 H 8-5 Attractive cultivar with bicolored, fragrant flowers.
‡ 28ft (9m)

ZAUSCHNERIA CALIFORNICA 'DUBLIN'
Perennial   page **461**

PLANTS FOR BEES AND BUTTERFLIES

Plants that will attract these fascinating and useful garden visitors usually have simple, tubular or daisylike flowers, especially in pinks and purples; avoid double-flowered varieties. Butterflies also like fruity scents. Remember that their caterpillar stage needs different food plants. Milkweeds are well known as the food of monarchs, but long grass and other weeds support many species.

AJUGA REPTANS 'BRAUNHERZ'
Perennial, Z 3-9 H 9-1 Creeping plant with purplish leaves, and blue flowers in spring.
‡6in (15cm) ↔ 36in (90cm)

ALLIUM SCHOENOPRASUM 'FORESCATE'
Perennial, Z 3-9 H 9-1 An ornamental form of chives with heads of pink flowers.
‡24in (60cm)

ASCLEPIAS INCARNATA
Perennial, Z 3-8 H 8-1 Thick, upright stems support small heads of curious pale pink flowers that produce interesting seed heads.
‡4ft (1.2m) ↔ 24in (60cm)

ASTER 'ANDENKEN AN ALMA PÖTSCHKE'
Perennial   page 58

ASTER AMELLUS 'SONIA'
Perennial, Z 5-8 H 8-5 A hairy, leafy plant that becomes covered with pale pink, yellow-centered flowers.
‡24in (60cm) ↔ 18in (45cm)

ASTER × FRIKARTII 'MÖNCH'
Perennial   page 59

ASTER TURBINELLUS
Perennial, Z 4-8 H 8-1 Wiry, almost black stems with small leaves and diffuse heads of lilac flowers in late summer.
‡4ft (1.2m) ↔ 2ft (60cm)

BUDDLEJA AURICULATA
Evergreen shrub, Z 8-9 H 9-8 Small clusters of white and orange, scented flowers are produced in autumn.
‡3m (10ft)

BUDDLEJA DAVIDII 'BLACK KNIGHT'
Shrub, Z 6-9 H 9-6 Spikes of deep purple flowers. Prune hard as growth begins.
‡10ft (3m) ↔ 15ft (5m)

BUDDLEJA 'LOCHINCH'
Shrub   page 78

CALLUNA VULGARIS 'WICKWAR FLAME'
Evergreen shrub, Z 5-7 H 7-5 Gold leaves turn red in winter; pink flowers in summer.
‡20in (50cm) ↔ 26in (65cm)

CARYOPTERIS × CLANDONENSIS 'HEAVENLY BLUE'
Shrub   page 92

CEANOTHUS 'PUGET BLUE'
Evergreen shrub, Z 8-10 H 12-8 Billowing mass of fine foliage covered with mid-blue flowers. ‡2.2m (7ft)

CYTISUS × BEANII
Shrub   page 136

DAHLIA MERCKII
Perennial, Z 8-10 H 12-1 Tuberous-rooted plant with slender, translucent stems and pale mauve, often nodding flowers.
‡6ft (2m) ↔ 3ft (1m)

DIGITALIS PURPUREA 'SUTTON'S APRICOT'
Biennial, Z 4-8 H 8-1 Tall-stemmed foxglove with pale apricot-pink flowers in summer. ‡3-6ft (1-2m)

ECHINACEA PURPUREA
Perennial, Z 3-9 H 9-1 Stems carry large, daisylike flowers with purplish pink petals.
‡3ft (1m) ↔ 18in (45cm)

ECHIUM VULGARE 'BLUE BEDDER'
Biennial H 8-1 Bushy plant with bristly, grayish green leaves and soft blue flowers.
‡ 18in (45cm)

ERICA VAGANS 'BIRCH GLOW'
Evergreen shrub page **161**

ERICA VAGANS 'VALERIE PROUDLEY'
Evergreen shrub, Z 7-9 H 9-7 Gold foliage, and white flowers in summer.
· ‡ 6in (15cm) ↔ 12in (30cm ()

ERICA × *VEITCHII* 'EXETER'
Evergreen page **158**

ERYNGIUM PLANUM
Perennial, Z 5-9 H 9-5 Branched stems of steely blue, with small, light blue, spiky flower heads emerging from evergreen leaf rosettes. ‡ 36in (90cm) ↔ 45cm (18in)

HELIOTROPIUM 'PRINCESS MARINA'
Shrub page **216**

HYSSOPUS OFFICINALIS
Evergreen shrub, 6-9 H 9-6 Green leaves and spikes of blue flowers in summer.
‡ 24in (60cm) ↔ 3ft (1m)

LAMIUM ORVALA
Perennial, Z 4-8 H 8-1 A choice, clump-forming plant that does not creep and has large leaves and purplish flowers in spring.
‡ 24in (60cm) ↔ 12in (30cm)

LAVANDULA ANGUSTIFOLIA 'LODDON PINK'
Evergreen shrub, Z 5-8 H 8-5 Compact; gray leaves and spikes of pink flowers.
‡ 18in (45cm) ↔ 24in (60cm)

LUNARIA REDIVIVA
Perennial, Z 6-9 H 9-6 Pale lilac, fragrant flowers followed by translucent seedheads.
‡ 24–36in (60–90cm) ↔ 12in (30cm)

MENTHA LONGIFOLIA BUDDLEJA MINT GROUP
Perennial, Z 6-9 H 9-6 Tall stems of grayish leaves; heads of tightly packed pink flowers.
‡ 3ft (1m)

MONARDA 'CROFTWAY PINK'
Perennial page **293**

ORIGANUM LAEVIGATUM 'HERRENHAUSEN'
Perennial page **306**

PAPAVER ORIENTALE 'CEDRIC MORRIS'
Perennial page **315**

PAPAVER RHOEAS 'MOTHER OF PEARL'
Annual H 12-1 An easy annual that can be sown in spring or autumn, with delicate flowers in pastel shades.
‡ 36in (90cm) ↔ 12in (30cm)

PENSTEMON 'SOUR GRAPES'
Perennial, Z 7-10 H 12-7 Intriguing flowers in shades of grayish blue, pink, and mauve on spikes above large, green leaves.
‡ 24in (60cm) ↔ 18in (45cm)

PRUNELLA GRANDIFLORA 'LOVELINESS'
Perennial page **354**

ROSMARINUS OFFICINALIS 'MISS JESSOP'S UPRIGHT'
Evergreen shrub page **388**

SEDUM 'HERBSTFREUDE'
Perennial, Z 3-10 H 12-1 Upright, unbranched stems with pale green, fleshy leaves, and deep pink flowers in flat heads in late summer. Often sold as 'Autumn Joy'.
‡ ↔ 24in (60cm)

TAGETES 'NAUGHTY MARIETTA'
Annual H 12-1 Bushy plants with single, yellow flowers marked with red.
‡ 12–16in (30–40cm)

TRACHELIUM CAERULEUM
Annual H 12-9 This wiry, upright plant produces flat heads of small purple flowers in summer.
‡ 3ft (1m) ↔ 12in (30cm)

PLANTS TO ATTRACT GARDEN BIRDS

Many birds feed on a wide variety of plants, and it is possible to grow plants with berries and seeds to attract a wide range of birds to your garden. Unfortunately, their feeding necessarily means that the food source – and the attractive autumn display – may not last long, so it is worth planting a variety of plants and providing extra food on a regular basis.

ATRIPLEX HORTENSIS VAR. *RUBRA*
Annual H 9-7 Vigorous plant with deep red leaves that contrast well with other plants; its seeds are loved by birds.
‡4ft (1.2m) ↔ 12in (30cm)

BERBERIS THUNBERGII
Shrub, Z 5-8 H 8-5 Green leaves and small yellow flowers in summer become red leaves and berries in autumn.
‡6ft (2m) ↔ 8ft (2.5m)

CORTADERIA SELLOANA 'PUMILA'
Ornamental grass, Z 7-10 H 12-7
A compact pampas grass with short flower spikes.
‡5ft (1.5m) ↔ 4ft (1.2m)

COTONEASTER LACTEUS
Evergreen shrub   page 125

COTONEASTER SIMONSII
Shrub   page 125

CRATAEGUS × *LAVALLEI* 'CARRIEREI'
Tree   page 128

CYNARA CARDUNCULUS
Perennial   page 135

DAPHNE MEZEREUM
Shrub, Z 5-8 H 8-5 Small shrub with upright branches, fragrant pink flowers in spring, and red berries in autumn.
‡4ft (1.2m) ↔ 3ft (1m)

HEDERA HELIX
Evergreen climber, Z 5-10 H 12-5 When ivy reaches its flowering stage, the black berries are attractive to many birds.
‡10ft (3m)

HELIANTHUS ANNUUS 'MUSIC BOX'
Annual H 12-1 Multicolored sunflowers that produce heads of seeds that may be harvested to feed birds in later months.
‡28in (70cm) ↔ 24in (60cm)

ILEX AQUIFOLIUM 'HANDSWORTH NEW SILVER'
Evergreen tree or large shrub   page 233

LONICERA PERICLYMENUM 'SEROTINA'
Climber   page 274

MAHONIA AQUIFOLIUM
Evergreen shrub, Z 6-9 H 9-6 A suckering shrub with gently spiny leaves and yellow flowers followed by black berries.
‡3ft (1m) ↔ 5ft (1.5m)

MALUS ZUMI 'GOLDEN HORNET'
Tree   page 287

MISCANTHUS SINENSIS
Ornamental grass, Z 4-9 H 9-1 This grass forms clumps of long, arching leaves and silver or pink flowerheads in late summer.
‡8ft (2.5m) ↔ 4ft (1.2m)

ONOPORDUM ACANTHIUM
Biennial, Z 6-9 H 9-6 A large, silvery, prickly plant with thistlelike purple flowers.
‡8ft (2.5m) ↔ 3ft (1m)

PAPAVER SOMNIFERUM 'WHITE CLOUD'
Annual H 12-1 White, double flowers and pretty seedpods that contain seeds attractive to some birds.
‡3ft (1m) ↔ 12in (30cm)

PRUNUS PADUS
Tree, Z 4-8 H 8-1 A spreading tree with pendent spikes of small white flowers followed by black cherries.
‡ 50ft (15m) ↔ 30ft (10m)

PYRACANTHA 'MOHAVE'
Evergreen shrub, Z 6-9 H 9-6 Dense, spiny growth with dark green leaves and long-lasting, bright red berries.
‡ 12ft (4m) ↔ 15ft (5m)

RIBES ODORATUM
Shrub, Z 5-8 H 8-5 Shrub with fresh green leaves, yellow scented flowers in spring, and black berries in summer.
‡ ↔ 6ft (2m)

ROSA FILIPES 'KIFTSGATE'
Climbing rose   page 380

ROSA PIMPINELLIFOLIA
Species shrub rose, Z 3-9 H 9-1 This very spiny bush has single white flowers followed by purplish black hips.
‡ 3ft (1m) ↔ 4ft (1.2m)

ROSA 'SCABROSA'
Rugosa shrub rose, Z 2-9 H 9-1 Deep pink flowers and bright red hips on a mounded bush with deeply veined foliage.
‡ ↔ 5½ft (1.7m)

SAMBUCUS NIGRA 'AUREOMARGINATA'
Shrub, Z 6-8 H 8-6 Fast-growing plant for any soil, with yellow-edged leaves, white flowers, and heads of black elderberries.
‡ ↔ 20ft (6m)

SILYBUM MARIANUM
Biennial, Z 6-9 H 9-6 Rosettes of spiny leaves, veined with white; prickly mauve seedheads and thistle-like seeds.
‡ 5ft (1.5m) ↔ 24–36in (60–90cm)

SORBUS AUCUPARIA 'FASTIGIATA'
Tree, Z 4-7 H 7-1 Broadly conical tree bearing red berries in late summer after white spring flowers.
‡ 25ft (8m) ↔ 15ft (5m)

VIBURNUM BETULIFOLIUM
Shrub, Z 5-8 H 8-5 Spectacular displays of red berries follow white flowers in summer when several plants are grown together.
‡ ↔ 10ft (3m)

VIBURNUM OPULUS
Shrub, Z 4-8 H 8-1 Strong-growing shrub with white flowers in summer, bright autumn color, and red berries.
‡ 15ft (5m) ↔ 12ft (4m)

VITIS VINIFERA 'PURPUREA'
Climber   page 456

FLOWERS FOR CUTTING

It is useful to be able to cut flowers from the garden, either to use on their own or to add to bought flowers. Many annuals are grown especially for cutting, but other garden plants can supply flowers for the house without spoiling the display. To produce more stems for cutting, pinch out the shoots of free-branching plants such as asters and chrysanthemums in early summer.

ACHILLEA 'CORONATION GOLD'
Perennial Z 3-9 H 9-1 Clumps of silvery leaves and small, gold flowers in flat, rounded heads.
‡ 30–36in (75–90cm) ↔ 18in (45cm)

ACONITUM 'BRESSINGHAM SPIRE'
Perennial   page 36

AGAPANTHUS
Perennials   page 39

ALSTROEMERIA LIGTU HYBRIDS
Perennials   page 43

ANEMONE
Perennials   page 47

AQUILEGIA VULGARIS
Perennial   page 50

ASTER PRINGLEI 'MONTE CASSINO'
Perennial Z 4-8 H 8-1 Thin stems of narrow, upright habit, forming a dense "bush" with needle-like leaves and small white flowers.
‡ 3ft (1m) ↔ 12in (30cm)

ASTILBE
Perennials   page 60

ASTRANTIA MAJOR 'SHAGGY'
Perennial Z 4-7 H 7-1 The showy bracts around the clusters of flowers are longer than in most.
‡ 12–36in (30–90cm) ↔ 18in (45cm)

BAPTISIA AUSTRALIS
Perennial   page 65

BRUNNERA MACROPHYLLA
Perennial   page 76

CALLISTEPHUS MILADY SUPER MIXED
Annuals   page 81

CAMPANULA PERSICIFOLIA 'CHETTLE CHARM'
Perennial Z 3-8 H 8-1 Mats of deep green foliage and thin stems with white, blue-edged flowers.
‡ 3ft (1m) ↔ 12in (30cm)

CHRYSANTHEMUM
Perennials   page 104

CROCOSMIA × *CROCOSMIIFLORA* 'SOLFATERRE'
Perennial   page 129

DAHLIA
Perennials   page 138

DELPHINIUM
Perennials   page 142

DIANTHUS
Perennials   page 145

DICENTRA
Perennials   page 147

DICTAMNUS ALBUS
Perennial   page 148

ERYNGIUM
Perennials and biennials   page 163

GAILLARDIA 'DAZZLER'
Perennial   page 187

GERANIUM
Perennials   page 196

GEUM 'MRS J. BRADSHAW'
Perennial Z 5-9 H 9-5 Hairy basal leaves, wiry branched stems, and very showy double scarlet flowers.
‡ 16–24in (40–60cm) ↔ 24in (60cm)

GYPSOPHILA
Perennials page **202**

HELIANTHUS
Perennials and annuals page **213**

HOSTA
Perennials page **222**

HYDRANGEA
Shrubs page **227**

IRIS
Perennials page **238**

KNIPHOFIA
Perennials page **250**

LATHYRUS
Annuals and perennials page **254**

LAVANDULA
Perennials page **257**

LEUCANTHEMUM × *SUPERBUM*
Perennial page **260**

LILIUM
Bulbs page **264**

LIRIOPE MUSCARI
Perennial page **271**

LYSIMACHIA CLETHROIDES
Perennial page **278**

MONARDA
Perennials page **292**

MUSCARI
Bulbs page **293**

NARCISSUS
Bulbs page **296**

PAEONIA
Perennials page **311**

PENSTEMON
Perennials page **322**

PHILADELPHUS
Shrubs page **328**

PHLOX PANICULATA
Perennials page **333**

PHYSOSTEGIA VIRGINIANA 'VIVID'
Perennial page **338**

ROSA
Shrubs page **378**

RUDBECKIA
Perennials page **390**

SCABIOSA CAUCASICA
Perennial page **403**

SEDUM SPECTABILE 'BRILLIANT'
Perennial page **408**

SOLIDAGO 'GOLDENMOSA'
Perennial page **415**

× *SOLIDASTER LUTEUS* 'LEMORE'
Perennial Z 5-8 H 8-5 This generic hybrid between a goldenrod and an aster produces heads of yellow flowers.
‡ 3ft (90cm) ↔ 12in (30cm)

SYRINGA VULGARIS
Shrub page **424**

TANACETUM COCCINEUM 'BRENDA'
Perennial page **426**

TULIPA
Bulbs page **442**

VERONICA SPICATA SUBSP. *INCANA*
Perennial page **449**

ZANTEDESCHIA AETHIOPICA
Perennial page **460**

FLOWERS FOR DRYING

Dried flowers prolong the beauty of summer throughout the year. Many are easy to grow and can be dried by simply hanging them upside down in a shady, airy position. If dried in silica gel then kept in a dry atmosphere, almost any flowers can be used. Select young, unblemished flowers that are not fully open, and remove the leaves before putting them into the silica gel.

ACHILLEA FILIPENDULINA
'GOLD PLATE'
Perennial, Z 3-9 H 9-1 Heads of gold flowers held above the grayish foliage.
‡4ft (1.2m) ↔ 18in (45cm)

ACHILLEA 'MOONSHINE'
Perennial   page **35**

AMARANTHUS HYPOCHONDRIACUS
'GREEN THUMB'
Annual H 12-1 Plants produce upright, branched spikes of pale green flowers.
‡24in (60cm) ↔ 12in (30cm)

ASTRANTIA MAXIMA
Perennial   page **62**

BRACTEANTHA BRIGHT BIKINI SERIES
Annuals   page **75**

CATANANCHE CAERULEA 'MAJOR'
Perennial, Z 3-8 H 12-1 Cornflower-like flowers of papery texture on wiry stems above narrow, grayish leaves.
‡20–36in (50–90cm) ↔ 12in (30cm)

CENTAUREA CYANUS 'FLORENCE PINK'
Annual H 12-1 Upright-growing annual with a bushy habit and pink flowers.
‡14in (35cm) ↔ 18in (45cm)

CONSOLIDA AJACIS GIANT IMPERIAL SERIES
Annual H 9-3 Larkspur producing elegant spires of flowers resembling delphiniums.
‡2–3ft (60–100cm) ↔ 14in (35cm)

CORTADERIA SELLOANA
'SUNNINGDALE SILVER'
Ornamental grass   page **119**

ECHINOPS RITRO
Perennial   page **153**

GOMPHRENA HAAGEANA
'STRAWBERRY FIELDS'
Annual   page **201**

HYDRANGEA MACROPHYLLA
CULTIVARS
Shrubs   page **228**

HYDRANGEA SERRATA 'BLUEBIRD'
Shrub   page **230**

LAGURUS OVATUS
Ornamental grass   page **252**

LIMONIUM SINUATUM 'ART SHADES'
Annual H 7-1 Crispy flowers in shades of pink, salmon, orange, pink, and blue.
‡24in (60cm) ↔ 12in (30cm)

LIMONIUM SINUATUM 'FOREVER GOLD'
Perennial   page **269**

NIGELLA DAMASCENA 'MULBERRY ROSE'
Annual H 12-1 Feathery foliage and flowers in shades of purplish pink, plus inflated seed pods.
‡18in (45cm) ↔ 9in (23cm)

RHODANTHE MANGLESII 'SUTTON'S ROSE'
Annual H 12-1 Wiry plants with grayish leaves and white or pink flowers with a strawlike texture.
‡24in (60cm) ↔ 6in (15cm)

PLANTS WITH ORNAMENTAL SEEDHEADS

Although they may lack the bright colors of the flowers, there is much beauty to be enjoyed in the seedheads of plants. Some may be cut and preserved to decorate the home, while others can be left in the garden to bring straw or bronze tones to the winter scene and look especially good when covered with frost or snow, until birds pull them apart in their hunt for food.

ALLIUM CRISTOPHII
Bulb page 42

ASTILBE CHINENSIS VAR. *PUMILA*
Perennial, Z 4-8 H 8-2 Chubby pink flower spikes become rust-brown as they age.
‡ 10in (25cm) ↔ 8in (20cm)

CLEMATIS 'BILL MACKENZIE'
Climber page 110

CLEMATIS MACROPETALA 'WHITE SWAN'
Climber, Z 6-9 H 9-6 A very compact, early-flowering clematis with white blooms and silver seedheads.
‡ 3ft (1m)

COTINUS COGGYGRIA
Shrub, Z 5-8 H 8-5 Green leaves in summer that turn scarlet in autumn, with feathery, smokelike seedheads.
‡↔ 15ft (5m)

HYDRANGEA PANICULATA 'GRANDIFLORA'
Shrub page 229

HYOSCYAMUS NIGER
Annual H 7-1 Extremely poisonous plant with sinister, veined flowers and beautiful seedheads resembling shuttlecocks.
‡ 2–4ft (0.6–1.4m) ↔ 3ft (1m)

IRIS FOETIDISSIMA
Perennial, Z 7-9 H 9-7 Pale blue and brown flowers lead to green pods that split in autumn to reveal orange seeds.
‡ 12–36in (30–90cm) ↔ 12in (30cm)

IRIS 'SHELFORD GIANT'
Perennial, Z 6-9 H 9-6 Sheaves of long, green leaves and tall stems of yellow and white flowers, plus distinctive ribbed seedheads.
‡ 6ft (1.8m) ↔ 24in (60cm)

NIGELLA ORIENTALIS 'TRANSFORMER'
Annual H 12-1 Bushy annual with finely divided leaves and small yellow flowers that produce umbrella-like seed pods.
‡ 18in (45cm) ↔ 9–12in (22–30cm)

PAEONIA LUTEA VAR. *LUDLOWII*
Shrub page 313

PAPAVER SOMNIFERUM 'HENS AND CHICKENS'
Annual H 8-1 The single flowers are followed by curious pods that are surrounded by a ring of smaller pods.
‡ 4ft (1.2m) ↔ 12in (30cm)

PHYSALIS ALKEKENGI
Perennial, Z 5-8 H 8-5 Vigorous, suckering perennial with bright orange, "Chinese lantern" fruits in autumn.
‡ 24–30in (60–75cm) ↔ 1m (90cm)

SCABIOSA STELLATA 'DRUMSTICK'
Annual H 9-1 Wiry-stemmed, hairy annual with pale lilac flowers and round, satellite-like seedheads.
‡ 12in (30cm) ↔ 9in (23cm)

COTTAGE GARDEN-STYLE PLANTS

The idealized image of an English cottage garden is in summer, with bees lazily buzzing around roses, lilies, hollyhocks, and peonies, but in fact the authentic cottage garden was a glorious mixture of old-fashioned flowers discarded by wealthier gardeners. Cottage garden flowers are often scented, usually herbaceous, and achievable in North America.

ACONITUM 'SPARK'S VARIETY'
Perennial page **36**

ALCEA ROSEA 'NIGRA'
Biennial, Z 3-9 H 9-1 The "black" hollyhock.
‡6ft (2m) ↔ 24in (60cm)

CALENDULA 'FIESTA GITANA'
Annual page **80**

CAMPANULA 'BURGHALTII'
Perennial, Z 4-8 H 8-1 A hybrid that forms mounds of mid-green leaves and large, tubular flowers of grayish blue.
‡2ft (60cm) ↔ 12in (30cm)

CAMPANULA PERSICIFOLIA 'WHITE CUP AND SAUCER'
Perennial, Z 3-8 H 8-1 Pure white flowers are bell-shaped with a white circular disk, like a saucer, below the bell.
‡36in (90cm) ↔ 12in (30cm)

CAMPANULA PORTENSCHLAGIANA
Perennial page **89**

DELPHINIUM CULTIVARS
Perennials page **142**

DIANTHUS 'GRAN'S FAVOURITE'
Perennial page **145**

DICENTRA SPECTABILIS
Perennial page **147**

ERYNGIUM ALPINUM
Perennial page **163**

ESCHSCHOLZIA CALIFORNICA
Annual page **168**

GERANIUM MACRORRHIZUM 'ALBUM'
Perennial, Z 4-8 H 8-1 Scented, evergreen leaves and white flowers in summer.
‡20in (50cm) ↔ 24in (60cm)

GERANIUM × *OXONIANUM* 'A. T. JOHNSON'
Perennial, Z 4-8 H 8-1 This clump-forming plant has silvery pink flowers.
‡12in (30cm)

GERANIUM SANGUINEUM 'ALBUM'
Perennial, Z 4-8 H 8-1 A compact plant with divided leaves and white flowers.
‡8in (20cm) ↔ 12in (30cm)

GERANIUM SYLVATICUM 'MAYFLOWER'
Perennial page **197**

GEUM 'LADY STRATHEDEN'
Perennial page **198**

KNIPHOFIA TRIANGULARIS
Perennial page **251**

LILIUM CANDIDUM
Bulb page **264**

LUPINUS POLYPHYLLUS 'BAND OF NOBLES'
Perennial, Z 5-8 H 8-5 A good seed mixture with tall spikes of bicolored flowers.
‡5ft (1.5m) ↔ 30in (75cm)

LUPINUS 'THE CHATELAINE'
Perennial, Z 5-8 H 8-5 Tall spires of bicolored flowers in deep pink and white.
‡36in (90cm) ↔ 30in (75cm)

LYCHNIS CHALCEDONICA
Perennial   page 277

PAEONIA LACTIFLORA 'BOWL OF BEAUTY'
Perennial   page 311

PAEONIA OFFICINALIS 'RUBRA PLENA'
Perennial   page 313

PAPAVER ORIENTALE 'BEAUTY OF LIVERMERE'
Perennial   page 314

PAPAVER ORIENTALE 'MRS. PERRY'
Perennial, Z 4-9 H 9-1 Salmon-pink flowers with petals like satin above coarse foliage.
‡ 30in (75cm) ↔ 24–36in (60–90cm)

PAPAVER RHOEAS SHIRLEY MIXED
Annuals   page 315

PHLOX 'KELLY'S EYE'
Perennial   page 332

PHLOX PANICULATA 'BRIGADIER'
Perennial   page 333

PHLOX PANICULATA 'EVENTIDE'
Perennial   page 333

PHLOX PANICULATA 'FUJIYAMA'
Perennial   page 333

PHLOX PANICULATA 'MOTHER OF PEARL'
Perennial   page 333

PRIMULA 'WANDA'
Perennial   page 345

ROSA 'BALLERINA'
Patio rose   page 384

ROSA 'FANTIN-LATOUR'
Centifolia shrub rose   page 387

ROSA 'GERTRUDE JEKYLL'
English shrub rose   page 387

ROSA XANTHINA 'CANARY BIRD'
Shrub rose   page 387

SAXIFRAGA × URBIUM
Perennial, Z 6-7 H 7-6 Mats of evergreen leaf rosettes and sprays of dainty white flowers in late spring.
‡ 12in (30cm) ↔ indefinite

SCABIOSA CAUCASICA 'MISS WILLMOTT'
Perennial   page 403

SCHIZOSTYLIS COCCINEA 'SUNRISE'
Perennial   page 404

VERBASCUM 'PINK DOMINO'
Perennial, Z 5-9 H 9-1 Dark green leaves give rise to unbranched stems of rounded, deep pink flowers.
‡ 4ft (1.2m) ↔ 12in (30cm)

VIOLA CORNUTA
Perennial   page 454

PLANTS FOR THE ROCK GARDEN

Rock gardens are good places to grow small plants, raising them closer to observers' eyes. But the raised beds also allow the soil to be tailored to suit these plants, which often require perfect drainage or specific soil mixes. Most of the plants below are easily grown and require no special treatment, making them yet more attractive: rock gardening can become an addictive hobby.

ADIANTUM PEDATUM
Fern   page **37**

ALLIUM MOLY
Bulbous perennial   page **42**

ANCHUSA CESPITOSA
Alpine, Z 5-7 H 7-5 White-eyed blue
flowers appear between narrow leaves
in spring. ‡ 2–4in (5–10cm) ↔ 6–8in (15–20cm)

ANDROSACE CARNEA SUBSP. *LAGGERI*
Perennial   page **45**

ANDROSACE SEMPERVIVOIDES
Alpine, Z 5-7 H 7-5 Leaf rosettes form loose
mats; pink flowers open in late spring.
‡ 1–2in (2.5–5cm) ↔ 6–8in (15–20cm)

ARENARIA MONTANA
Perennial   page **52**

ARMERIA MARITIMA 'VINDICTIVE'
Perennial, Z 3-9 H 9-1 Hummocks of
narrow leaves; slender stems of deep pink
flowers. ‡ 6in (15cm) ↔ 8in (20cm)

AUBRIETA X *CULTORUM*
'BRESSSINGHAM PINK'
Perennial, Z 5-7 H 7-5 Cushions of green
leaves covered with double, pink flowers
in spring. ‡ 2in (5cm) ↔ 24in (60cm)

AURINIA SAXATILIS
Perennial   page **64**

BERBERIS THUNBERGII 'BAGATELLE'
Shrub   page **70**

CAMPANULA 'BIRCH HYBRID'
Perennial, Z 4-7 H 7-1 A spreading plant
with deep blue bellflowers.
‡ 4in (10cm) ↔ 40in (50cm)

CAMPANULA CHAMISSONIS 'SUPERBA'
Alpine, Z 2-6 H 6-1 The rosettes of pale
green leaves disappear under pale blue
flowers in early summer.
‡ 2in (5cm) ↔ 8in (20cm)

CROCUS CORSICUS
Spring bulb   page **131**

DAPHNE PETRAEA 'GRANDIFLORA'
Evergreen shrub   page **140**

DIANTHUS 'LA BOURBOULE'
Perennial   page **145**

DIASCIA 'RUBY FIELD'
Perennial, Z 8-9 H 9-8 Mats of heart-shaped
leaves are covered with deep salmon-
pink flowers in summer.
‡ 10in (25cm) ↔ 24in (60cm)

DRYAS OCTOPETALA
Evergreen subshrub, Z 3-6 H 6-1 Mats of
deep green leaves with white flowers in
spring, then fluffy seedheads.
‡ 4in (10cm) ↔ 36in (1m)

GENTIANA ACAULIS
Perennial   page **192**

GERANIUM CINEREUM 'BALLERINA'
Perennial   page **194**

GEUM MONTANUM
Perennial   page **198**

GYPSOPHILA 'ROSENSCHLEIER'
Perennial   page **203**

HELIANTHEMUM 'FIRE DRAGON'
Shrub   page **211**

HELIANTHEMUM 'HENFIELD BRILLIANT'
Shrub page 212

IRIS CRISTATA
Perennial, Z 4-8 H 8-1 In moist soil the creeping stems produce dainty fans of foliage and lilac-blue and white flowers in late spring.
‡4in (10cm)

IRIS 'KATHARINE HODGKIN'
Bulbous perennial page 241

IRIS LACUSTRIS
Perennial page 242

LATHYRUS VERNUS
Perennial page 254

LEPTOSPERMUM SCOPARIUM 'KIWI'
Shrub page 260

LEWISIA COTYLEDON
Perennial page 262

LEWISIA TWEEDYI
Perennial page 262

LINUM 'GEMMELL'S HYBRID'
Perennial page 270

MUSCARI AUCHERI
Bulbous perennial page 294

NARCISSUS 'HAWERA'
Bulb page 297

OMPHALODES CAPPADOCICA 'CHERRY INGRAM'
Perennial page 304

OXALIS ADENOPHYLLA
Bulbous perennial page 310

OXALIS ENNEAPHYLLA 'ROSEA'
Bulb, Z 6-9 H 9-6 Clumps of frilly, gray-green leaves; pink flowers in early summer.
‡3in (8cm) ↔ 6in (15cm)

PHLOX DIVARITICA 'CHATTAHOOCHEE'
Perennial page 331

PHLOX DOUGLASII 'BOOTHMAN'S VARIETY'
Perennial page 331

PHLOX NANA 'MARY MASLIN'
Perennial, Z 7-8 H 8-7 Spreading stems with bright scarlet flowers in summer.
‡8in (20cm) ↔ 12in (30cm)

PITTOSPORUM TENUIFOLIUM 'TOM THUMB'
Evergreen shrub page 343

RAMONDA MYCONI
Perennial page 364

RANUNCULUS CALANDRINOIDES
Perennial page 365

RANUNCULUS GRAMINEUS
Perennial page 366

ROSMARINUS OFFICINALIS PROSTRATUS GROUP
Shrub page 388

SAPONARIA × *OLIVANA*
Perennial page 400

SAXIFRAGA 'JENKINSIAE'
Alpine page 402

SAXIFRAGA 'SOUTHSIDE SEEDLING'
Perennial page 402

SEMPERVIVUM TECTORUM
Perennial page 411

SILENE SCHAFTA
Perennial page 412

TULIPA LINIFOLIA BATALINII GROUP
Bulb page 441

TULIPA TURKESTANICA
Bulb page 441

VERBASCUM 'LETITIA'
Subshrub page 447

VERONICA PROSTRATA
Perennial page 449

VERONICA SPICATA SUBSP. *INCANA*
Perennial page 449

PLANTS FOR WHITE GARDENS

Single-color gardens are popular with many gardeners, and the most planted are white gardens, perhaps because so many white flowers are also scented. Consider also leaf color and foliage, including variegated-, silver-, and gray-leaved plants. To relieve the sameness of the design, it is often helpful to add a few cream or pale blue flowers – these will actually enhance the effect.

ANEMONE BLANDA 'WHITE SPLENDOUR'
Bulb   page **46**

ANEMONE × HYBRIDA 'HONORINE JOBERT'
Perennial   page **47**

ASTILBE 'IRRLICHT'
Perennial, Z 4-9 H 8-1 The coarsely cut dark foliage is a good contrast to the upright, fluffy white flowers.
↕↔ 18in (50cm)

CLEMATIS 'MARIE BOISSELOT'
Climber, Z 4-9 H 9-1 The large flowers are white with cream anthers and produced in late summer into autumn.
↕ 10ft (3m)

COSMOS BIPINNATUS 'SONATA WHITE'
Annual   page **122**

CRAMBE CORDIFOLIA
Perennial   page **127**

CROCUS SIEBERI 'ALBUS'
Bulb   page **131**

DAHLIA 'HAMARI BRIDE'
Perennial, Z 8-10 H 12-1 This semi-cactus dahlia has pure white flowers and is popular for cutting and exhibition.
↕ 4ft (1.2m) ↔ 2ft (60cm)

DELPHINIUM 'SANDPIPER'
Perennial   page **143**

DEUTZIA SETCHUENENSIS VAR. *CORYMBIFLORA*
Shrub, Z 6-8 H 8-6 Masses of white flowers produced on a bush with brown, peeling bark.
↕ 6ft (2m) ↔ 5ft (1.5m)

DICENTRA SPECTABILIS 'ALBA'
Perennial   page **147**

DICTAMNUS ALBUS
Perennial   page **148**

DIGITALIS PURPUREA F. *ALBIFLORA*
Biennial   page **150**

ECHINACEA PURPUREA 'WHITE LUSTRE'
Perennial, Z 3-9 H 9-1 The stiff stems have creamy white flowers with golden cones.
↕ 32in (80cm) ↔ 18in (45cm)

ERICA CARNEA 'SPRINGWOOD WHITE'
Evergreen shrub   page **159**

ERICA TETRALIX 'ALBA MOLLIS'
Evergreen shrub   page **161**

GILLENIA TRIFOLIATA
Perennial   page **199**

GYPSOPHILA PANICULATA 'BRISTOL FAIRY'
Perennial   page **202**

HYDRANGEA ARBORESCENS 'ANNABELLE'
Shrub   page **227**

HYDRANGEA PANICULATA 'FLORIBUNDA'
Shrub   page **229**

HYDRANGEA QUERCIFOLIA
Shrub   page 230

IRIS CONFUSA
Bulbous perennial   page 239

IRIS SIBIRICA 'WHITE SWIRL'
Perennial   page 243

IRIS 'SKATING PARTY'
Perennial Z 3-9 H 9-3 The ruffled, white
flowers have matching white beards.
‡ 36in (1m) ↔ indefinite

JASMINUM POLYANTHUM
Climber   page 246

LUNARIA ANNUA VAR. *ALBIFLORA*
Biennial, Z 5-9 H 9-5 The white-flowered
form of common honesty or money plant.
‡ 3ft (90cm) ↔ 12in (30cm)

MALVA MOSCHATA F. *ALBA*
Perennial   page 288

NARCISSUS 'EMPRESS OF IRELAND'
Bulb   page 298

PAEONIA OBOVATA VAR. *ALBA*
Perennial, Z 5-8 H 8-5 A choice plant with
rounded, grayish leaflets and pure white
flowers, most attractive in bud.
‡ ↔ 24–28in (60–70cm)

PAPAVER ORIENTALE 'BLACK AND
WHITE'
Perennial   page 314

PARAHEBE CATARRACTAE
Subshrub   page 316

PHYSOSTEGIA VIRGINIANA
'SUMMER SNOW'
Perennial, Z 4-8 H 8-1 Pure white flowers
in spikes on upright stems above abundant
mid-green foliage.
‡ 4ft (1.2m) ↔ 24in (60cm)

PULMONARIA OFFICINALIS
'SISSINGHURST WHITE'
Perennial   page 361

PULSATILLA VULGARIS 'ALBA'
Perennial   page 362

RANUNCULUS ACONITIFOLIUS
'FLORE PLENO'
Perennial   page 365

ROSA 'ICEBERG'
Floribunda rose   page 379

ROSA 'MADAME HARDY'
Shrub rose   page 387

ROSA 'MARGARET MERRIL'
Floribunda rose   page 379

ROSA 'RAMBLING RECTOR'
Rambler rose   page 383

RUBUS 'BENENDEN'
Shrub   page 389

TULIPA 'PURISSIMA'
Bulb, Z 4-7 H 8-1 The compact stems
carry very large, pure white flowers in
midspring.
‡ 14in (35cm)

ZANTEDESCHIA AETHIOPICA
'CROWBOROUGH'
Perennial   page 460

PLANTS FOR CLAY SOIL

Clay soil is difficult to dig, either wet or dry. It is prone to harbor slugs, and it is slow to warm up in spring; it is often described as a cold soil. However, it is usually rich in nutrients, and if plenty of organic matter is added it can be very fertile. Plants to avoid are those from upland areas, such as alpines, or those on the borderline of hardiness in your climate.

CAMPANULA LATILOBA 'HIDCOTE AMETHYST'
Perennial, Z 4-8 H 7-5 Stocky stems of mauve-purple, cup-shaped flowers in midsummer. ‡36in (90cm) ↔ 18in (45cm)

CLEMATIS 'POLISH SPIRIT'
Climber, Z 5-9 H 9-5 Late-flowering, with small, single, purple flowers with red anthers. ‡5m (15ft) ↔ 2m (6ft)

CORNUS STOLONIFERA 'FLAVIRAMEA'
Shrub page **118**

COTONEASTER × WATERERI 'JOHN WATERER'
Evergreen shrub page **126**

DEUTZIA × ELEGANTISSIMA 'ROSEALIND'
Shrub page **144**

DIGITALIS GRANDIFLORA
Perennial page **149**

FILIPENDULA PURPUREA
Perennial page **179**

GERANIUM PSILOSTEMON
Perennial page **197**

HEMEROCALLIS 'STELLA DE ORO'
Perennial page **218**

HYDRANGEA PANICULATA 'KYUSHU'
Shrub, Z 4-8 H 8-1 Erect-growing cultivar with glossy leaves and creamy white flowers. ‡10–22ft (3–7m) ↔ 8ft (2.5m)

IRIS SIBIRICA 'SHIRLEY POPE'
Perennial, Z 4-9 H 9-1 Deep blue and white flowers above narrow, grassy leaves. ‡34in (85cm)

LONICERA NITIDA 'SILVER LINING'
Evergreen shrub, Z 6-9 H 9-6 Each small leaf of this mound-shaped shrub has a thin, white margin. ‡↔ 1.5m (5ft)

MAHONIA AQUIFOLIUM 'APOLLO'
Evergreen shrub page **284**

NARCISSUS 'JUMBLIE'
Bulb page **297**

PERSICARIA CAMPANULATA
Perennial, Z 5-8 H 8-5 Clusters of pink, bell-shaped flowers on spreading stems. ‡↔ 36in (90cm)

PHILADELPHUS 'MANTEAU D'HERMINE'
Shrub page **329**

POTENTILLA FRUTICOSA 'TANGERINE'
Shrub, Z 3-7 H 7-1 Twiggy, with yellow flowers flushed red throughout summer. ‡3ft (1m) ↔ 5ft (1.5m)

ROSA 'AMBER QUEEN'
Floribunda rose page **378**

SPIRAEA JAPONICA 'ANTHONY WATERER'
Shrub page **419**

SYMPHYTUM 'GOLDSMITH'
Perennial, Z 5-9 H 9-5 This spreading plant has heart-shaped leaves edged in gold, with pale blue, cream, and pink flowers. ‡↔ 12in (30cm)

SYRINGA VULGARIS 'KATHERINE HAVEMEYER'
Shrub page **425**

PLANTS FOR SANDY SOIL

The advantages of sandy soils include the ability to dig, hoe, and prepare them during much of the year because they drain quickly after rain. However, water drains through quickly, taking nutrients with it, so it is important to dig in organic matter to improve the soil structure, retain moisture, and improve fertility. Silver-leaved and slightly tender plants are very suitable.

BUDDLEJA DAVIDII 'WHITE PROFUSION'
Shrub page 77

CALLUNA VULGARIS 'DARKNESS'
Evergreen shrub page 82

CERATOSTIGMA WILLMOTTIANUM
Shrub page 96

ECHINOPS BANNATICUS 'TAPLOW BLUE'
Perennial, Z 5-9 H 9-5 A robust, thistlelike plant with globular blue flowerheads.
‡4ft (1.2m) ↔ 2ft (60cm)

ERICA CINEREA 'EDEN VALLEY'
Evergreen shrub page 160

ERYNGIUM × *OLIVERIANUM*
Perennial page 163

ESCALLONIA 'PEACH BLOSSOM'
Evergreen shrub, Z 8-9 H 9-8 Arching, with peach-pink and white flowers in late spring.
‡8ft (2.5m)

EUCALYPTUS DALRYMPLEANA
Evergreen tree, Z 9-10 H 10-9 A fast-growing tree with green adult leaves and white bark. ‡70ft (20m) ↔ 25ft (8m)

GENISTA HISPANICA
Shrub, Z 7-9 H 9-7 Small, spiny, covered with small yellow flowers in early summer.
‡30in (75cm) ↔ 5ft (1.5m)

GLADIOLUS COMMUNIS SUBSP. *BYZANTINUS*
Bulb page 200

KNIPHOFIA 'LITTLE MAID'
Perennial page 205

LAVATERA ARBOREA 'VARIEGATA'
Biennial, Z 8-10 H 10-8 An evergreen, slightly tender, intensely variegated plant with purple flowers in the second year.
‡10ft (3m) ↔ 5ft (1.5m)

LAVATERA 'ROSEA'
Shrub page 259

LIMNANTHES DOUGLASII
Annual page 269

OENOTHERA MACROCARPA
Perennial page 302

PENSTEMON 'HIDCOTE PINK'
Perennial, Z 7-10 H 10-4 A bedding penstemon; spikes of tubular, pink flowers.
‡24–30in (60–75cm) ↔ 18in (45cm)

PENSTEMON PINIFOLIUS 'MERSEA YELLOW'
Evergreen shrub, Z 4-10 H 10-4 Dwarf, spreading, with narrow yellow flowers in summer.
‡16in (40cm) ↔ 10in (25cm)

PERSICARIA AFFINIS 'SUPERBA'
Perennial page 325

PERSICARIA BISTORTA 'SUPERBA'
Perennial page 325

POTENTILLA FRUTICOSA 'DAYDAWN'
Shrub page 348

POTENTILLA NEPALENSIS 'MISS WILLMOTT'
Perennial page 350

SANTOLINA ROSMARINIFOLIA 'PRIMROSE GEM'
Evergreen shrub page 399

PLANTS FOR ALKALINE SOILS

The majority of plants will grow in soil that is neutral or slightly acidic or alkaline, but some positively prefer alkaline soil. These include plants that are just as important as rhododendrons and camellias of acidic soils and include delphiniums, clematis, and dianthus. Quality of soil is important: it must be improved with organic matter, and poor, thin, alkaline soils are difficult to work.

AQUILEGIA VULGARIS 'NIVEA'
Perennial page 50

BUDDLEJA DAVIDII 'PINK DELIGHT'
Shrub, Z 6-9 H 9-6 Bright pink flowers are produced on thick, conical spikes.
‡10ft (3m) ↔ 15ft (5m)

BUDDLEJA DAVIDII 'ROYAL RED'
Shrub page 77

BUDDLEJA × WEYERIANA 'SUNGOLD'
Shrub, Z 6-8 H 8-6 An attractive hybrid with spikes of golden flowers in summer.
‡4m (12ft) ↔ 3m (10ft)

CERCIS SILIQUASTRUM
Tree page 97

CHAENOMELES SPECIOSA 'NIVALIS'
Shrub, Z 5-8 H 8-5 A variety of flowering quince with pure white flowers in spring.
‡8ft (2.5m) ↔ 15ft (5m)

CLEMATIS 'COMTESSE DE BOUCHAUD'
Climber page 111

CLEMATIS × JOUINIANA 'PRAECOX'
Climber, Z 4-9 H 9-4 This unusual hybrid is a scrambler, with a frothy mass of tiny white and lilac-blue flowers.
‡6–10ft (2–3m)

CLEMATIS 'MISS BATEMAN'
Climber, Z 4-9 H 9-1 The white flowers have contrasting red anthers and are borne freely in early summer.
‡8ft (2.5m) ↔ 3ft (1m)

CONVALLARIA MAJALIS VAR. *ROSEA*
Perennial, Z 2-7 H 7-1 This variety has dusky pink flowers with the familiar scent.
‡9in (23cm) ↔ 12in (30cm)

COTONEASTER STERNIANUS
Evergreen shrub page 126

DELPHINIUM 'BLUE NILE'
Perennial, Z 3-7 H 7-1 The tall spikes of deep blue flowers have white eyes.
‡6ft (2m) ↔ 24–36in (60–90cm)

DEUTZIA SCABRA 'PRIDE OF ROCHESTER'
Shrub, Z 6-8 H 8-6 Stems have attractive, peeling, brown bark, but the chief merit is the scented, double, pale pink flowers.
‡10ft (3m) ↔ 6ft (2m)

DIANTHUS ALPINUS
Perennial, Z 3-8 H 8-1 Cushions of gray foliage produce scented pink flowers.
‡3in (8cm) ↔ 4in (10cm)

DIANTHUS DELTOIDES
Perennial, Z 3-10 H 12-1 Mats of deep green leaves are covered with small pink flowers for several weeks in summer.
‡8in (20cm) ↔ 12in (30cm)

DIANTHUS 'MONICA WYATT'
Perennial page 145

EUONYMUS EUROPAEUS 'RED CASCADE'
Shrub page 171

FRAXINUS ORNUS
Tree, Z 6-9 9-8 Bushy, round-headed tree with showy white flowers and purple autumn color.
‡↔ 50ft (15m)

FUCHSIA 'HEIDI ANN'
Shrub, Z 8-10 H 12-1 An upright, bushy plant with double lilac and cerise flowers.
‡↔ 18in (45cm)

FUCHSIA 'PROSPERITY'
Shrub, Z 8-10 H 12-8 A vigorous, hardy plant with crimson and pink double flowers.
‡↔ 18in (45cm)

GALANTHUS 'MAGNET'
Bulb page **188**

HELIANTHEMUM 'JUBILEE'
Shrub, Z 6-8 H 8-6 This small shrub has bright green leaves and double yellow flowers.
‡ 8in (20cm) ↔ 12in (30cm)

HELLEBORUS ORIENTALIS
Perennial, Z 4-9 H 9-1 Nodding flowers in shades of pink, white, and green are produced in early spring.
‡↔ 18in (45cm)

ILEX AQUIFOLIUM 'SILVER QUEEN'
Evergreen tree page **233**

MAGNOLIA × *KEWENSIS* 'WADA'S MEMORY'
Shrub page **283**

MAGNOLIA 'RICKI'
Shrub page **283**

MAGNOLIA SALICIFOLIA
Shrub page **283**

MAGNOLIA × *SOULANGEANA* 'RUSTICA RUBRA'
Shrub page **283**

MAGNOLIA WILSONII
Shrub page **283**

MORUS NIGRA
Tree, Z 5-9 H 9-5 This is a tough, long-lived, picturesque tree with tasty fruit.
‡ 40ft (12m) ↔ 50ft (15m)

PRUNUS 'OKAME'
Tree page **358**

PRUNUS 'TAIHAKU'
Tree page **359**

PRUNUS TENELLA 'FIRE HILL'
Shrub, Z 6-8 H 8-6 Deep pink, single flowers cover the upright branches in spring.
‡↔ 5ft (1.5m)

PULSATILLA VULGARIS
Perennial page **361**

SYRINGA VULGARIS 'CHARLES JOLY'
Shrub page **424**

PLANTS FOR ACIDIC SOIL

Acidic soils contain low quantities of calcium, a plant nutrient found in limestone, but some of the most beautiful plants, including kalmias, rhododendrons, and pieris, have adapted to grow well only in soils where it is deficient. Most also benefit from light shade and rich soil. Where soil is not ideal, grow plants in large containers of acidic soil mix.

ACER JAPONICUM 'ACONITIFOLIUM'
Shrub   page 33

ACER PALMATUM VAR. *DISSECTUM*
Shrub, Z 6-8 H 8-6 The finely cut leaves turn yellow in autumn.
‡6ft (2m) ↔ 10ft (3m)

ACER PALMATUM 'SEIRYU'
Shrub, Z 6-8 H 8-6 An upright shrub with divided leaves that turn orange in autumn.
‡6ft (2m) ↔ 4ft (1.2m)

CAMELLIA 'LEONARD MESSEL'
Evergreen shrub   page 85

CAMELLIA × *WILLIAMSII* 'DEBBIE'
Evergreen shrub, Z 7-8 H 12-8 The semidouble flowers are deep pink.
‡6–15ft (2–5m) ↔ 3–10ft (1–3m)

CAMELLIA SASANQUA 'NARUMIGATA'
Evergreen shrub, Z 7-8 H 12-7 Small, fragrant, pale pink flowers in autumn.
‡20ft (6m) ↔ 10ft (3m)

CASSIOPE 'EDINBURGH'
Evergreen shrub   page 93

CRINODENDRON HOOKERIANUM
Evergreen shrub   page 128

DABOECIA CANTABRICA 'BICOLOR'
Evergreen shrub   page 137

DABOECIA CANTABRICA 'WILLIAM BUCHANAN'
Evergreen shrub   page 137

ENKIANTHUS CAMPANULATUS
Shrub   page 155

ERICA ARBOREA VAR. *ALPINA*
Evergreen shrub   page 158

ERICA ARBOREA 'ESTRELLA GOLD'
Evergreen shrub, Z 9-10 H 12-9 Fragrant white flowers appear among the lime green foliage and yellow shoot tips.
‡4ft (1.2m) ↔ 30in (75cm)

ERICA 'C. D. EASON'
Shrub   page 160

ERICA CILIARIS 'CORFE CASTLE'
Shrub   page 160

ERICA CILIARIS 'DAVID MCLINTOCK'
Shrub   page 160

ERICA ERIGENA 'W. T. RATCLIFF'
Evergreen shrub, Z 8-9 H 9-8 A compact plant with green foliage and white flowers.
‡30in (75cm) ↔ 22in (55cm)

ERICA 'FIDDLER'S GOLD'
Shrub   page 160

ERICA 'WINDLEBROOKE'
Shrub   page 160

EUCRYPHIA NYMANSENSIS 'NYMANSAY'
Evergreen shrub   page 170

HAMAMELIS × *INTERMEDIA* 'PALLIDA'
Shrub   page 206

HYDRANGEA MACROPHYLLA 'BLUE WAVE'
Shrub, Z 6-9 H 9-6 This lacecap variety gives a delicate but showy display with large and small blue flowers in each head.
‡5ft (1.5m) ↔ 6ft (2m)

RHODODENDRON 'GINNY GEE'
Dwarf rhododendron, Z 6-9 H 9-6 A compact plant bearing pink flowers that fade almost to white with age.
↕ ↔ 24–36in (60–90cm)

RHODODENDRON IMPEDITUM
Dwarf rhododendron, Z 5-8 H 8-5 Gray-green leaves are almost hidden by lavender-blue flowers in spring.
↕ ↔ 24in (60cm)

PLANTS FOR POOR SOIL

While it is true that most plants grow better in well-prepared soil, there are some that grow well in poor soil that has not had much preparation or cultivation. Many annuals evolved to take advantage of open sites, disappearing as the soil improves and larger plants invade the area, so they are a good choice, but there are shrubs and perennials that will also survive.

ACHILLEA 'MOONSHINE'
Perennial page **35**

ARTEMISIA ABROTANUM
Shrub, Z 5-8 H 8-5 This small shrub has green, finely divided, pleasantly fragrant leaves. ‡↔ 3ft (1m)

BUDDLEJA DAVIDII 'EMPIRE BLUE'
Shrub page **77**

CEANOTHUS 'BLUE MOUND'
Evergreen shrub page **94**

CYTISUS PRAECOX 'ALLGOLD'
Shrub page **136**

CYTISUS PRAECOX 'WARMINSTER'
Shrub, Z 6-9 H 9-6 Arching shoots, thickly set with creamy yellow flowers in spring. ‡4ft (1.2m) ↔ 5ft (1.5m)

CISTUS × PURPUREUS
Evergreen shrub page **107**

ERYSIMUM CHEIRI 'HARPUR CREWE'
Perennial page **165**

ESCHSCHOLZIA CAESPITOSA 'SUNDEW'
Annual H 12-5 Low-growing, with divided gray leaves and pale yellow flowers. ‡↔ 6in (15cm)

FALLOPIA BALDSCHUANICA
Climber page **176**

FESTUCA GLAUCA 'BLAUFUCHS'
Ornamental grass page **179**

GAILLARDIA 'DAZZLER'
Perennial page **187**

GENISTA LYDIA
Shrub page **192**

HEBE OCHRACEA 'JAMES STIRLING'
Evergreen shrub, Z 8-10 H 10-8 Like a yellow dwarf conifer until white flowers appear. ‡18in (45cm) ↔ 24in (60cm)

IBERIS SEMPERVIRENS
Evergreen shrub page **232**

KOLKWITZIA AMABILIS 'PINK CLOUD'
Shrub page **251**

LATHYRUS LATIFOLIUS
Climber page **254**

LAVANDULA ANGUSTIFOLIA 'TWICKEL PURPLE'
Evergreen shrub page **257**

LAVATERA 'BARNSLEY'
Shrub page **258**

PHLOMIS FRUTICOSA
Evergreen shrub page **330**

POTENTILLA FRUTICOSA 'ELIZABETH'
Shrub page **348**

ROBINIA HISPIDA
Shrub page **376**

SANTOLINA CHAMAECYPARISSUS 'LEMON QUEEN'
Evergreen shrub, Z 6-9 H 9-6 Silvery, feathery foliage, and small, pale yellow flowers. ‡↔ 12in (60cm)

THYMUS VULGARIS 'SILVER POSIE'
Evergreen shrub, Z 4-9 H 9-4 Thyme with variegated leaves and pink flowers. ‡6–12in (15–30cm) ↔ 16in (40cm)

PLANTS FOR WET SOIL

Waterlogged, badly drained soils are inhospitable places for most plants. Roots need to breathe; if all the air spaces within the soil are filled with water, most roots will rot and only marginal or aquatic plants will survive. However, if the soil is permanently moist there are many beautiful plants that will thrive, and many may survive flooding if it is only for a few days.

ASTILBE × *CRISPA* 'PERKEO'
Perennial page **61**

ASTILBE 'SPRITE'
Perennial page **61**

ASTILBE 'STRAUSSENFEDER'
Perennial page **62**

CARDAMINE PRATENSE 'FLORE PLENO'
Perennial, Z 5-8 H 8-5 Double-flowered lady's smock with lilac-pink flowers in spring. ‡ ↔ 8in (20cm)

CHAMAECYPARIS PISIFERA 'BOULEVARD'
Conifer page **101**

CIMICIFUGA RACEMOSA
Perennial page **106**

CORNUS ALBA 'SIBIRICA'
Shrub page **115**

DARMERA PELTATA
Perennial page **141**

EUPHORBIA GRIFFITHII 'DIXTER'
Perennial, Z 4-9 H 9-1 Orange bracts in autumn. ‡30in (75cm) ↔ 3ft (1m)

FILIPENDULA RUBRA 'VENUSTA'
Perennial page **180**

FRITILLARIA MELEAGRIS
Bulb page **183**

IRIS FORRESTII
Perennial page **240**

IRIS PSEUDACORUS
Perennial page **238**

IRIS × *ROBUSTA* 'GERALD DARBY'
Perennial page **238**

IRIS VERSICOLOR
Perennial page **238**

LIGULARIA 'GREGYNOG GOLD'
Perennial page **263**

LOBELIA 'QUEEN VICTORIA'
Perennial page **272**

LYSICHITON AMERICANUS
Perennial page **277**

LYSICHITON CAMTSCHATCENSIS
Perennial page **278**

LYSIMACHIA CLETHROIDES
Perennial page **278**

LYSIMACHIA NUMMULARIA 'AUREA'
Perennial page **279**

LYTHRUM SALICARIA 'FEUERKERZE'
Perennial page **279**

MATTEUCCIA STRUTHIOPTERIS
Hardy fern page **288**

MIMULUS CARDINALIS
Perennial page **291**

OSMUNDA REGALIS
Hardy fern page **308**

PRIMULA CANDELABRA TYPES
Perennials page **352**

PRIMULA DENTICULATA
Perennial page **350**

PRIMULA ROSEA
Perennial page **353**

RODGERSIA PINNATA 'SUPERBA'
Perennial page **377**

Plants for Hot, Dry Sites

As problems of water supply become more acute, consider plants that have low water requirements. Often these have silvery or small leaves, and some are fragrant, so the garden can still be interesting through the year. They look attractive growing through gravel, an effective mulch to retain soil moisture. In addition, many establish quickly and are evergreen and low maintenance.

ABUTILON VITIFOLIUM 'VERONICA TENNANT'
Shrub   page 30

AGAVE VICTORIAE-REGINA
Succulent   page 40

ALLIUM × HOLLANDICUM
Bulb, Z 4-10 H 12-1 Tall stems bear round heads of purple flowers in early summer.
‡3ft (1m)

ALSTROEMERIA LIGTU HYBRIDS
Perennial   page 43

ARMERIA JUNIPERIFOLIA 'BEVAN'S VARIETY'
Perennial   page 54

ARTEMISIA 'POWIS CASTLE'
Perennial   page 56

ARTEMISIA SCHMIDTIANA 'NANA'
Perennial, Z 5-8 H 8-5 An evergreen that forms a feathery, silvery carpet with tiny yellow flowerheads in summer.
‡3in (8cm) ↔ 12in (30cm)

BALLOTA PSEUDODICTAMNUS
Evergreen shrub   page 65

CEANOTHUS ARBOREUS 'TREWITHEN BLUE'
Shrub   page 93

CEANOTHUS 'CASCADE'
Evergreen shrub, Z 9 10 H 12-9 The arching branches bear masses of powder blue flowers in late spring.
‡↔ 12ft (4m)

CEDRONELLA CANARIENSIS
Perennial, min 40°F (5°C) H 12-8
The slightly sticky leaves are aromatic; produces small clusters of mauve flowers in late summer.
‡4ft (1.2m) ↔ 24in (60cm)

CERATOSTIGMA PLUMBAGINOIDES
Perennial   page 96

CISTUS × AGUILARII 'MACULATUS'
Evergreen shrub   page 106

CONVOLVULUS CNEORUM
Evergreen shrub   page 114

CYTISUS BATTANDIERI
Shrub   page 135

CYTISUS × KEWENSIS
Shrub, Z 6-8 H 8-6 Arching stems are covered with cream flowers in spring.
‡12in (30cm) ↔ 5ft (1.5m)

CYTISUS MULTIFLORUS
Shrub, Z 7-8 H 8-7 An upright shrub at first, then spreading, with masses of small white flowers.
‡10ft (3m) ↔ 8ft (2.5m)

DIANTHUS 'HAYTOR WHITE'
Perennial   page 145

DICTAMNUS ALBUS VAR. *PURPUREUS*
Perennial   page 149

DIERAMA PULCHERRIMUM
Perennial, Z 8-10 H 12-8 Clumps of grasslike leaves produce arching stems of pendent, pink, bell-shaped flowers.
‡3–5ft (1–1.5m) ↔ 24in (60cm)

ERYNGIUM BOURGATII
Perennial, Z 5-9 H 9-5 Silver-veined spiny
leaves form clumps with branching stems
of steely blue prickly flowerheads.
‡ 6–18in (15–45cm) ↔ 12in (30cm)

ERYSIMUM 'BOWLES' MAUVE'
Evergreen shrub   page 164

ERYSIMUM 'WENLOCK BEAUTY'
Perennial   page 165

ESCHSCHOLZIA CAESPITOSA
Annual   page 168

EUPHORBIA CHARACIAS
Perennial   page 173

EUPHORBIA CHARACIAS SUBSP.
WULFENII 'JOHN TOMLINSON'
Perennial   page 173

EUPHORBIA MYRSINITES
Perennial   page 174

GERANIUM MADERENSE
Perennial, Z 8-9 H 9-8 An imposing, large
plant with divided leaves and a colorful
display of mauve flowers in summer.
‡ ↔ 24in (60cm)

GYMNOCALYCIUM ANDREAE
Cactus   page 202

X *HALIMIOCISTUS SAHUCII*
Evergreen shrub   page 204

HALIMIOCISTUS WINTONENSIS
Evergreen shrub, Z 7-9 H 9-7 Pale cream
flowers with maroon centers are produced
in clusters above woolly leaves.
‡ 24in (60cm) ↔ 36in (90cm)

HALIMIUM LASIANTHUM
Evergreen shrub, Z 9-10 H 12-9 Pale
yellow, purple-blotched flowers are
produced on a grayish green bush.
‡ 3ft (1m) ↔ 5ft (1.5m)

HEBE MACRANTHA
Evergreen shrub, Z 9-10 H 12-9 Unlike
most hebes, the flowers are produced in
clusters of 3, but they are large and white.
‡ 24in (60cm) ↔ 36in (90cm)

HEBE RAKAIENSIS
Evergreen shrub   page 208

HIBISCUS SYRIACUS 'WOODBRIDGE'
Shrub   page 221

LAVANDULA STOECHAS SUBSP.
PEDUNCULATA
Evergreen shrub   page 258

PARAHEBE PERFOLIATA
Evergreen shrub   page 316

ROSMARINUS OFFICINALIS
'BENENDEN BLUE'
Evergreen shrub, Z 8-10 H 12-8 Upright,
with deep green leaves and vivid blue
flowers. ‡ ↔ 5ft (1.5m)

SPARTIUM JUNCEUM
Shrub   page 418

TULIPA LINIFOLIA
Bulb   page 440

TULIPA TARDA
Bulb, Z 4-7 H 8-1 Each bulb produces a
cluster of yellow and white flowers on
short stems.
‡ 6in (15cm)

VERBASCUM COTSWOLD GROUP
'GAINSBOROUGH'
Perennial   page 446

VERBASCUM DUMULOSUM
Perennial   page 446

VERBASCUM 'HELEN JOHNSON'
Perennial   page 447

PLANTS FOR DAMP SHADE

A border that has damp soil and is in shade for much of the day is a useful place to grow woodland plants without having to plant trees. Without the drying effect of the trees, the soil will support a greater range of plants, and plants from more exotic places may well thrive, especially if the soil is acidic. It is also a good site for spring wildflowers, hellebores, lilies, and ferns.

ANEMONE NEMOROSA 'ROBINSONIANA'
Perennial   page **48**

ANEMONE RANUNCULOIDES
Perennial   page **48**

ATHYRIUM FILIX-FEMINA
Fern   page **63**

CARDIOCRINUM GIGANTEUM
Perennial   page **90**

DIGITALIS × *MERTONENSIS*
Perennial   page **150**

DODECATHEON MEADIA F. *ALBUM*
Perennial   page **151**

EPIMEDIUM YOUNGIANUM 'NIVEUM'
Perennial   page **157**

GALANTHUS ELWESII
Bulb   page **187**

GALANTHUS 'S. ARNOTT'
Bulb   page **189**

GENTIANA ASCLEPIADEA
Perennial   page **193**

HACQUETIA EPIPACTIS
Perennial, Z 5-7 H 7-5 Small ruffs of leaves surround clusters of yellow flowers.
↕ 2in (5cm) ↔ 6–12in (15–30cm)

HEPATICA TRANSSILVANICA
Perennial, Z 5-8 H 8-5 Flowers in pastels.
↕ 6in (15cm) ↔ 8in (20cm)

HYDRANGEA ASPERA VILLOSA GROUP
Shrub   page **227**

IRIS GRAMINEA
Perennial   page **241**

MAHONIA JAPONICA
Shrub   page **284**

ONOCLEA SENSIBILIS
Fern   page **304**

POLYGONATUM × *HYBRIDUM*
Perennial   page **346**

POLYSTICHUM ACULEATUM
Fern   page **347**

PRIMULA SIEBOLDII
Perennial, Z 3-8 H 8-3 Shades of pink and white. ↕ 12in (30cm) ↔ 18in (45cm)

PULMONARIA 'LEWIS PALMER'
Perennial   page **360**

SARCOCOCCA CONFUSA
Evergreen shrub   page **400**

THALICTRUM FLAVUM SUBSP. *GLAUCIUM*
Perennial   page **429**

TIARELLA CORDIFOLIA
Perennial   page **434**

TOLMEIA 'TAFF'S GOLD'
Perennial   page **434**

TRILLIUM LUTEUM
Perennial   page **437**

TROLLIUS × *CULTORUM* 'ORANGE PRINCESS'
Perennial   page **438**

UVULARIA GRANDIFLORA
Perennial   page **444**

VIBURNUM × *CARLCEPHALUM*
Shrub   page **450**

PLANTS FOR DRY SHADE

The dry shade under trees is not a hospitable place for most plants. Those that survive best are spring-flowering bulbs that disappear underground in summer before the soil dries out.

Some evergreens and winter-flowering plants also survive. Even these require good soil preparation and careful watering and feeding for several seasons until they are well established.

ASPLENIUM SCOLOPENDRIUM
Fern   page **57**

AUCUBA JAPONICA 'ROZANNE'
Evergreen shrub, Z 6-10 H 12-6 Cultivar with green leaves; the flowers are self-fertile, resulting in many red berries.
‡↔ 3ft (1m)

BERGENIA CORDIFOLIA
Perennial, Z 3-8 H 8-1 The large, rounded, evergreen leaves make a good ground-cover; showy pink flowers in spring.
‡ 24in (60cm) ↔ 30in (75cm)

DRYOPTERIS FILIX-MAS
Fern   page **151**

EUONYMUS FORTUNEI 'EMERALD 'N' GOLD'
Evergreen shrub   page **171**

GALANTHUS NIVALIS 'FLORE PLENO'
Bulb   page **188**

GERANIUM MACRORRHIZUM 'INGWERSEN'S VARIETY'
Perennial   page **196**

HEDERA HELIX 'LITTLE DIAMOND'
Evergreen climber   page **210**

HEDERA HIBERNICA 'SULPHUREA'
Evergreen climber, Z 6-10 H 12-5 An ivy with gold-edged leaves; good groundcover.
‡ 10ft (3m)

HELLEBORUS FOETIDUS 'WESTER FLISK'
Perennial, Z 6-9 H 9-6 Deep red stems, dark green, finely divided leaves, and red-edged green flowers.
‡ 24in (60cm) ↔ 3ft (1m)

IRIS FOETIDISSIMA
Perennial, Z 7-9 H 9-7 Evergreen leaves; purple and brown flowers; orange seeds.
‡ 12–36in (30–90cm)

IRIS FOETIDISSIMA 'VARIEGATA'
Perennial, Z 7-9 H 9-7 Evergreen leaves striped with white and gray-green; few flowers.
‡ 12–24in (30–60cm)

KERRIA JAPONICA 'GOLDEN GUINEA'
Shrub   page **249**

LAMIUM GALEOBDOLON 'HERMANN'S PRIDE'
Perennial, Z 4-8 H 8-1 Compact; leaves marked silver and pale yellow flowers.
‡ 18in (45cm) ↔ 3ft (1m)

RHODODENDRON 'CECILE'
Shrub   page **368**

RUBUS TRICOLOR
Evergreen shrub, Z 7-9 H 9-7 The creeping stems are covered with decorative red bristles, and the leaves are deep green.
‡ 24in (60cm) ↔ 6ft (2m)

RUSCUS ACULEATUS
Perennial, Z 7-9 H 9-7 No leaves, but the flattened, green, spiny stems are evergreen, and red berries are sometimes produced.
‡ 30in (75cm) ↔ 3ft (1m)

RUSCUS HYPOGLOSSUM
Perennial, Z 7-9 H 9-7 Arching stems are glossy and evergreen, without spines.
‡ 18in (45cm) ↔ 3ft (1m)

VINCA MINOR 'ATROPURPUREA'
Perennial   page **454**

PLANTS FOR EXPOSED SITUATIONS

Gardens exposed to strong winds, especially cold ones, make gardening difficult. Choose compact varieties that require less staking, and avoid large-leaved plants that may be damaged.

Late-flowering cultivars will not be caught by spring frosts. Protect plants with burlap when planting and in winter to reduce damage, and plant hedges and screens as windbreaks.

ASTER ALPINUS
Perennial   page **57**

BERBERIS THUNBERGII
'GOLDEN RING'
Shrub, Z 5-8 H 8-3 A spiny shrub with purple leaves edged with a thin gold band.
‡ 5ft (1.5m) ↔ 6ft (2m)

CALLUNA VULGARIS 'KINLOCHRUEL'
Evergreen shrub   page **82**

CHAENOMELES × SUPERBA
'PINK LADY'
Shrub   page **98**

DEUTZIA × HYBRIDA 'MONT ROSE'
Shrub   page **144**

DIANTHUS GRATIANOPOLITANUS
Perennial, Z 4-9 H 9-1 Low-growing mats of gray foliage and solitary pink flowers.
‡ 6in (15cm) ↔ 16in (40cm)

ERICA CARNEA 'VIVELLI'
Evergreen shrub   page **159**

ERICA × WATSONII 'DAWN'
Evergreen shrub   page **161**

HYPERICUM OLYMPICUM
Shrub, Z 6-8 H 8-6 Compact deciduous shrub with gray leaves and yellow flowers.
‡ 10in (25cm) ↔ 12in (30cm)

PHILADELPHUS 'VIRGINAL'
Shrub, Z 5-8 H 8-5 Scented, double white flowers are carried in clusters.
‡ 10ft (3m) ↔ 8ft (2.5m)

POTENTILLA FRUTICOSA
'ABBOTSWOOD'
Shrub   page **348**

SALIX GRACILISTYLA
'MELANOSTACHYS'
Shrub, Z 5-8 H 8-5 An upright shrub with gray leaves; black catkins with red anthers in early spring.
‡ 10ft (3m) ↔ 12ft (4m)

SALIX RETICULATA
Shrub, Z 2-6 H 6-1 A low-growing shrub with glossy leaves and erect, yellow and pink catkins in spring.
‡ 3in (8cm) ↔ 12in (30cm)

SAMBUCUS NIGRA 'GUINCHO
PURPLE'
Shrub   page **398**

SPIRAEA JAPONICA 'SHIROBANA'
Shrub, Z 4-9 H 9-1 Mounds of foliage are dotted with both pink and white flowers throughout summer.
‡ 24in (60cm) ↔ 36in (90cm)

SPIRAEA NIPPONICA 'SNOWMOUND'
Shrub   page **420**

TAMARIX TETRANDRA
Shrub   page **426**

VIBURNUM OPULUS 'ROSEUM'
Shrub, Z 4-8 H 8-1 Erect, fast-growing shrub with globular heads of white flowers in late spring.
‡ ↔ 12ft (4m)

PLANTS FOR COASTAL GARDENS

Coastal gardens are windy (see facing page) and, nearer the shore, plants may also need to cope with winds laden with salt. However, these gardens are usually milder than those even a little inland. Silver-leaved plants often thrive, and if the winds can be lessened, a wide range of plants should do well. Hydrangeas in particular are often the pride of coastal gardeners.

AGAPANTHUS CAULESCENS
Perennial   page **39**

ARBUTUS UNEDO
Evergreen tree   page **52**

BERBERIS DARWINII
Evergreen shrub   page **68**

BUDDLEJA GLOBOSA
Shrub   page **78**

CHOISYA TERNATA
Evergreen shrub   page **103**

CRAMBE MARITIMA
Perennial, Z 6-9 H 9-6 Silver-blue leaves, and branching heads of white flowers.
‡↔ 24in (60cm)

DIANTHUS ALPINUS 'JOAN'S BLOOD'
Perennial   page **145**

ELAEAGNUS × EBBINGEI 'GILT EDGE'
Evergreen shrub   page **154**

ERICA × WATSONII 'P. D. WILLIAMS'
Shrub   page **161**

ESCALLONIA 'DONARD RADIANCE'
Evergreen shrub, Z 8-9 H 9-8 Pink flowers.
‡↔ 8ft (2.5m)

ESCALLONIA 'IVEYI'
Evergreen shrub   page **167**

× *FATSHEDERA LIZEI*
Shrub   page **177**

FUCHSIA 'MRS. POPPLE'
Shrub   page **184**

FUCHSIA 'TOM THUMB'
Shrub   page **184**

× *HALIMIOCISTUS WINTONENSIS* 'MERRIST WOOD CREAM'
Evergreen shrub   page **204**

HEBE 'ALICIA AMHERST'
Evergreen shrub, Z 9-10 H 12-9 Mid-green leaves and dark violet flowers.
‡↔ 4ft (1.2m)

HEBE CUPRESSOIDES 'BOUGHTON DOME'
Shrub   page **206**

HEBE × FRANCISCANA 'VARIEGATA'
Evergreen shrub   page **207**

HEBE 'LA SÉDUISANTE'
Evergreen shrub, Z 9-10 H 12-9 Leaves tinted with purple; purple-red flowers in late summer. ‡↔ 3ft (1m)

HYDRANGEA MACROPHYLLA 'ALTONA'
Shrub   page **228**

HYDRANGEA MACROPHYLLA 'GEOFFREY CHADBUND'
Shrub, Z 6-9 H 9-6 Lacecap with red flowers.
‡ 3ft (1m) ↔ 5ft (1.5m)

LEPTOSPERMUM RUPESTRE
Shrub   page **259**

LUPINUS ARBOREUS
Shrub   page **276**

MATTHIOLA CINDERELLA SERIES
Biennial   page **289**

OLEARIA MACRODONTA
Evergreen shrub   page **303**

SENECIO CINERARIA 'SILVER DUST'
Biennial   page **411**

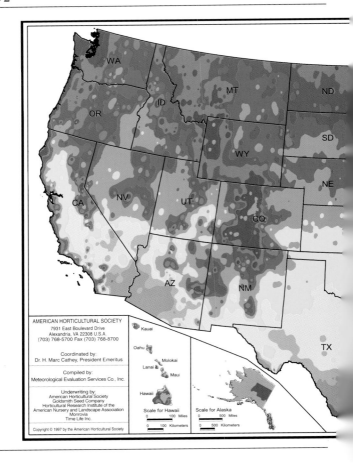

AMERICAN HORTICULTURAL SOCIETY
7931 East Boulevard Drive
Alexandria, VA 22308 U.S.A.
(703) 768-5700 Fax (703) 768-8700

Coordinated by:
Dr. H. Marc Cathey, President Emeritus

Compiled by:
Meteorological Evaluation Services Co., Inc.

Underwriting by:
American Horticultural Society
Goldsmith Seed Company
Horticultural Research Institute of the
American Nursery and Landscape Association
Monrovia
Time Life Inc.

Copyright © 1997 by the American Horticultural Society

Scale for Hawaii
0   100 Miles
0   100 Kilometers

Scale for Alaska
0   500 Miles
0   500 Kilometers

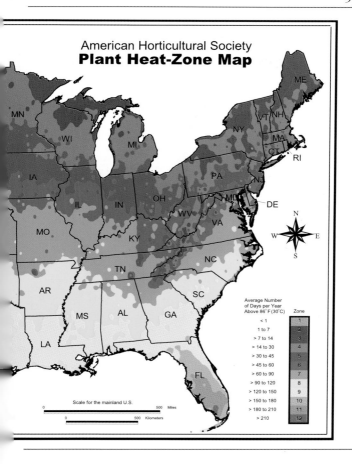

American Horticultural Society
Plant Heat-Zone Map

Average Number of Days per Year Above 86°F (30°C)	Zone
< 1	1
1 to 7	2
> 7 to 14	3
> 14 to 30	4
> 30 to 45	5
> 45 to 60	6
> 60 to 90	7
> 90 to 120	8
> 120 to 150	9
> 150 to 180	10
> 180 to 210	11
> 210	12

Scale for the mainland U.S.

0   500 Miles

0   500 Kilometers

Hardiness Zones

This map, produced by the United States Department of Agriculture, is based on average annual minimum temperatures. A hardiness zone range is given for every plant in this book, except tender plants and annuals.

Although useful as an indicator of a plant's dependability in a given area, a hardiness zone range is not the only indicator of the possible success of a plant. Many factors, including heat tolerance, soil type and fertility, soil moisture and drainage, humidity, and exposure to sun and wind determine a plant's success or failure.

See p. 8 for a more detailed discussion on hardiness, including the AHS heat zones.

°F	Zones	°C
Below -50°	1	Below -46°
-50° to -40°	2	-46° to -40°
-40° to -30°	3	-40° to -34°
-30° to -20°	4	-34° to -29°
-20° to -10°	5	-29° to -23°
-10° to 0°	6	-23° to -18°
0° to 10°	7	-18° to -12°
10° to 20°	8	-12° to -7°
20° to 30°	9	-7° to -1°
30° to 40°	10	-1° to 4°
Above 40°	11	Above 4°

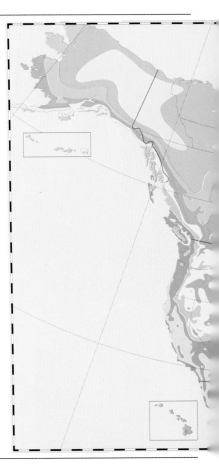

INDEX

A

ACKNOWLEDGEMENTS

The publisher would like to thank the following for their kind permission to reproduce the photographs:

l=left, r=right, t=top, c=center, a=above, b=below.

A–Z Botanical 216tl, Anthony Cooper 262tl, Geoff Kidd 184br, 196br, Malcolm Richards 454tl; Gillian Beckett 31tr; Neil Campbell-Sharp 58tl, 122tl, 281tr, 286tr; Garden Picture Library Brian Carter 39br, 122bl, 270tl, 356tl, 398bl, 411br, Densey Clyne 243tr, John Glover 6, 44bl, 128tl, 189br, 288tl, 292tl, 347br, 428tl, 433tr, Sunniva Harte 58bl, Neil Holmes 78bl, Lamontagne 101br, 153br, Jerry Pavia 226tl, Howard Rice 32tl, 63br, 313br, David Russel 426tl, 427tr, JS Sira 340tl; Derek Gould 126br; Diana Grenfell 223cl; Photos Horticultural 43br, 432bl, 447c; Andrew Lawson 26,

177tr, 287br; Clive Nichols 95br, 165br, 225tr, 232bl, 243br, 275tr, 388tl; RHS Garden, Wisley 12; Eric Sawford 76tr; Harry Smith Collection 39tr, 41tr, 51tr, 54bl, 55tr, 79tr, 92bl, 99l, 100bl, 106tl, 212tl, 252tl, 255bl, 256tl, 260bl, 269br, 284tl, 327tr, 399tr, 438bl.

Additional thanks to:
Text contributors and editorial assistance Geoff Stebbings, Candida Frith-Macdonald, Andrew Mikolajski, Sarah Wilde, Tanis Smith, James Nugent, Susanne Mitchell, Karen Wilson, and Barbara Haynes.
Design assistance Wendy Bartlet
Additional picture research Charlotte Oster
Index Ella Skene
Special thanks to Dr. H. Marc Cathey for providing the AHS Plant Heat Zones and to Helen Kindig and Betty Pearce for the cutflower list on pp. 528-29.